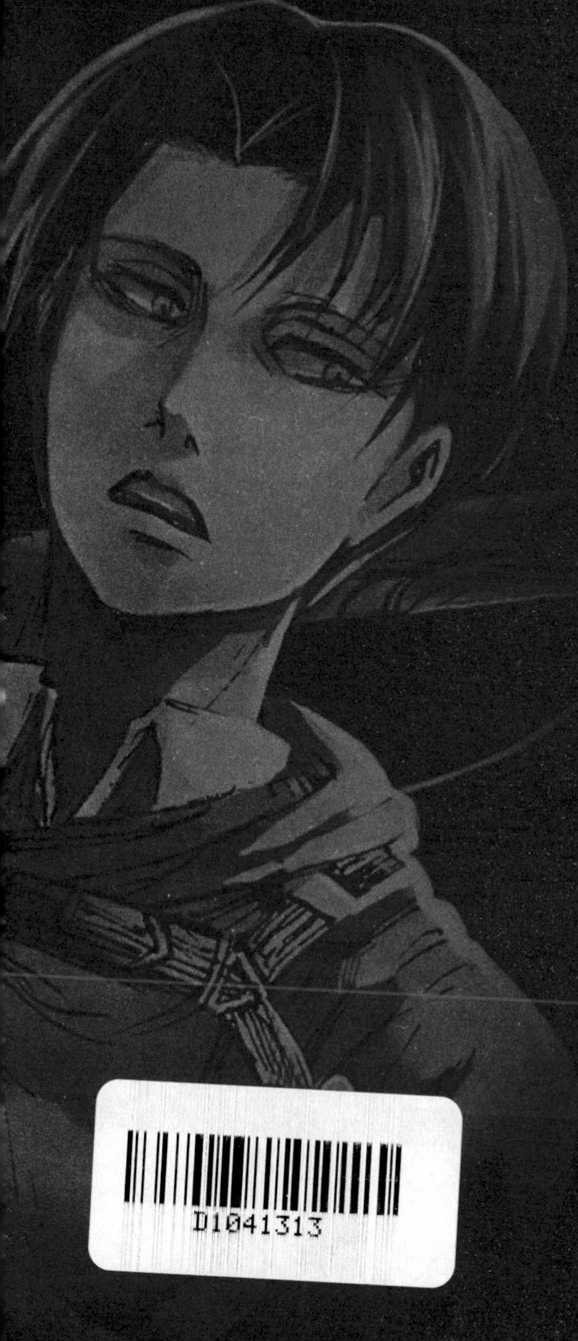

ATTACK ON TITAN 13

HAJIME ISAYAMA

"Attack on Titan" Character Introductions

104th Corps

...duated at
...op of her
...ning corps,
...a is a
...y talented
...er. Her
...nts were
...ered
...e her
when she
...a child,
...ren saved
...fe. Since
...she has
...it her
...ion to
...ct him.

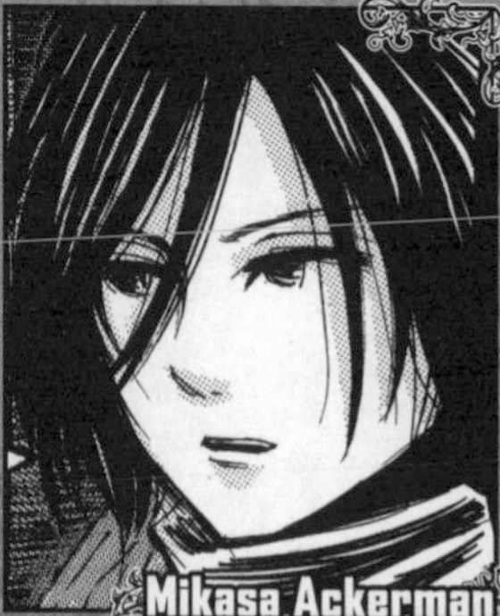

Mikasa Ackerman

Eren joined
the Survey
Corps out of
his longing
for the
outside
world and
his hatred of
the Titans.
He has the
power to
turn himself
into a Titan,
but its
origins are
unknown.

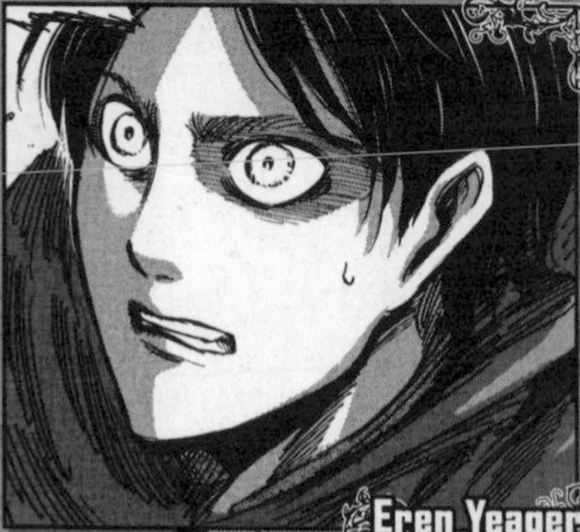

Eren Yeager

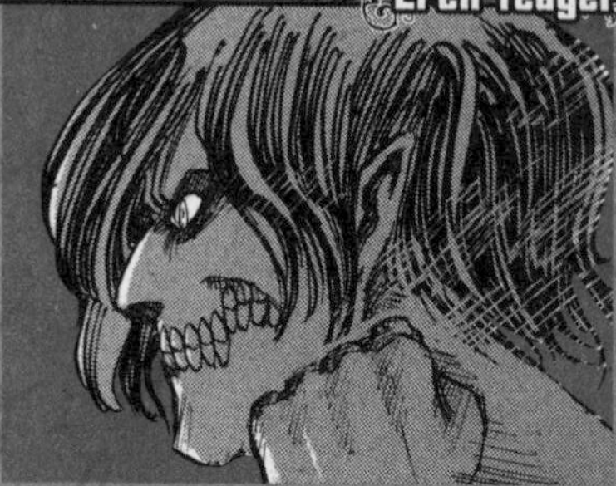

...and Mikasa's
...hood friend.
...gh Armin isn't
...tic in the least,
...ossesses both
...p observational
...ers and keen
...ht, and he
...bits an
...aordinary ability
...evelop
...egies.

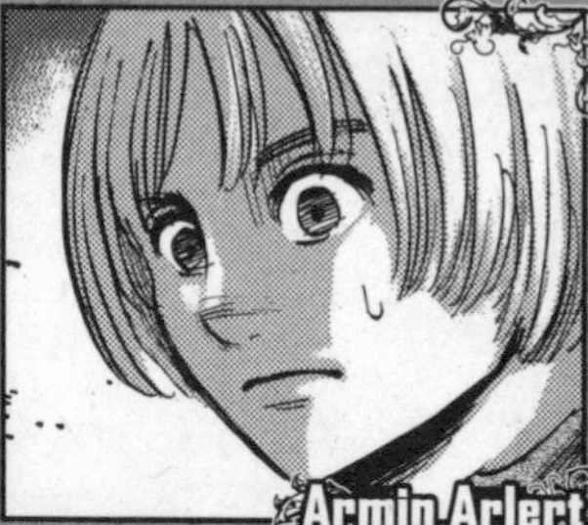

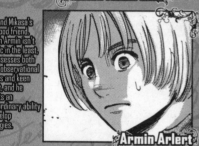

Armin Arlert

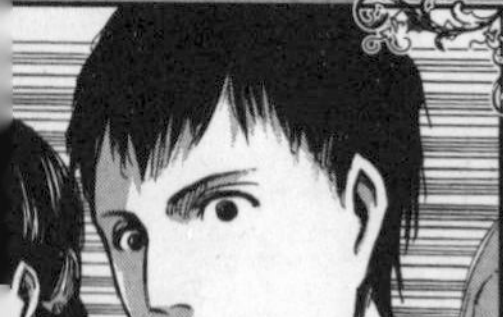

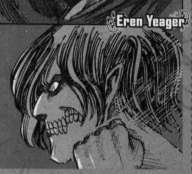

Bertolt Hoover

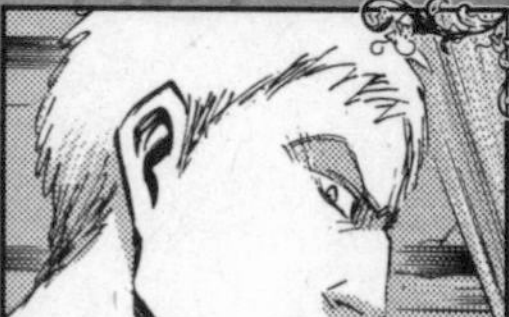

Reiner Braun

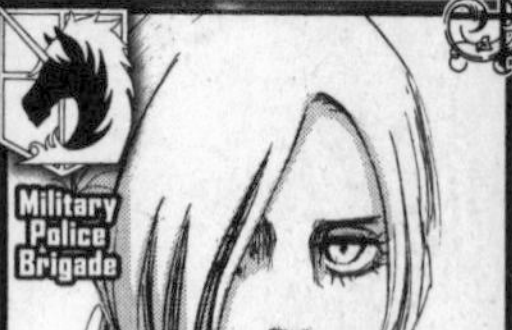
Military Police Brigade

Annie Leonhart

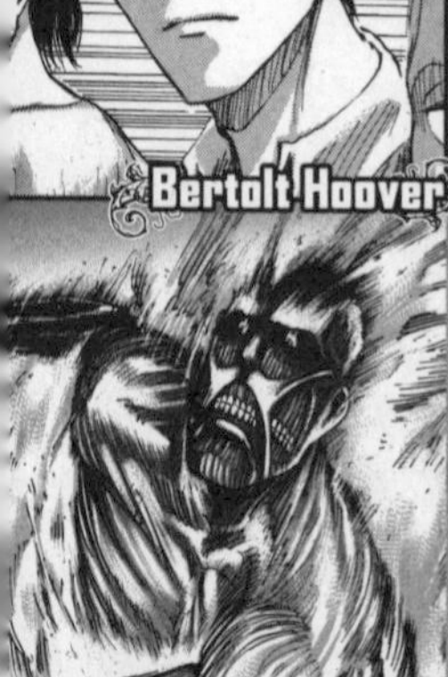

The Colossus Titan

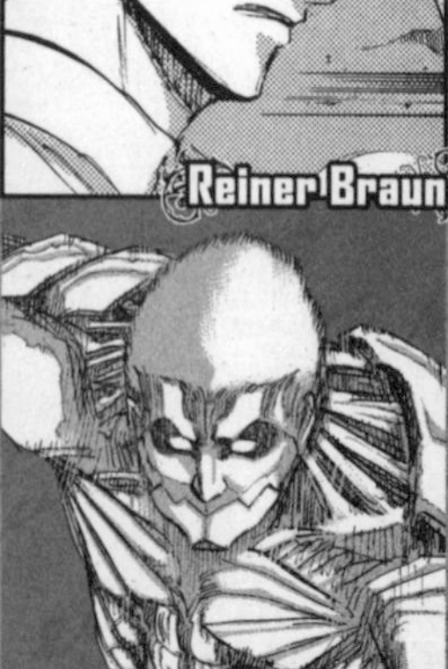

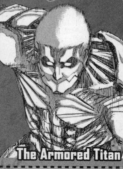

The Armored Titan

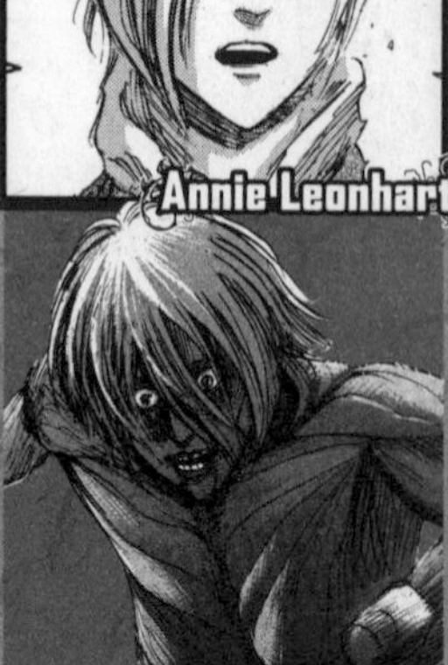

The Female Titan

The Garrison

Defenders of cities who work to reinforce the walls.

Survey Corps

Soldiers who are prepared to sacrifice themselves as they brave the Titan territory outside the walls.

Commander

Dot Pixis

Officer

Hannes

Squad Captain

Levi

13th Commander of the Survey Corps

Erwin Sm

Squad Leader

Hange Zoë

Jean Kirs

Ymir

Krista Lenz

Connie Sprin

Marco Bott

Sasha Bl

ATTACK on TITAN

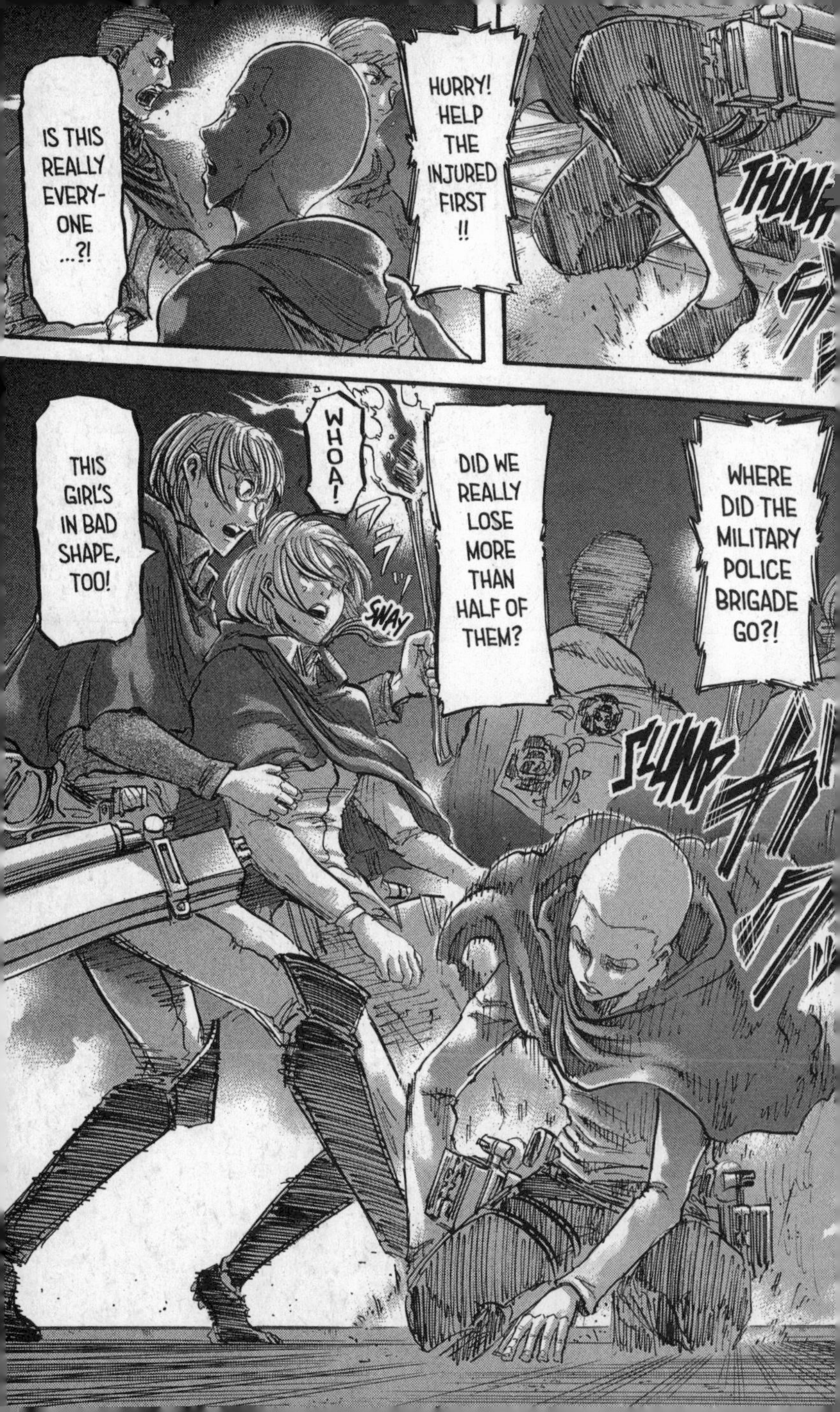
THUNK
HURRY! HELP THE INJURED FIRST!!
IS THIS REALLY EVERY-ONE ...?!
WHERE DID THE MILITARY POLICE BRIGADE GO?!
SLUMP
DID WE REALLY LOSE MORE THAN HALF OF THEM?
WHOA!
SWAY
THIS GIRL'S IN BAD SHAPE, TOO!

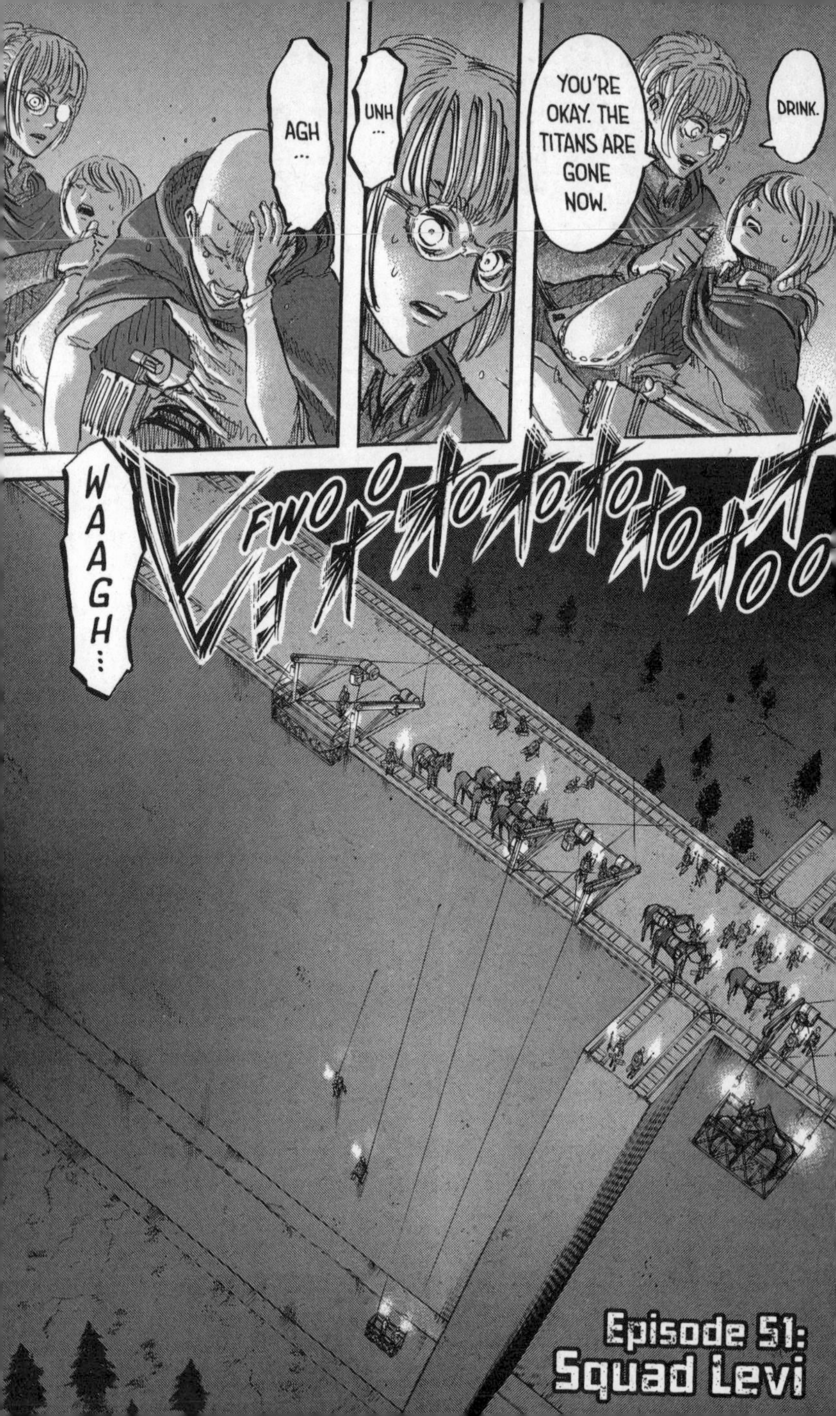
DRINK.
YOU'RE OKAY. THE TITANS ARE GONE NOW.
UNH ...
AGH ...
FWO
WAAAGH...
Episode 51:
Squad Levi

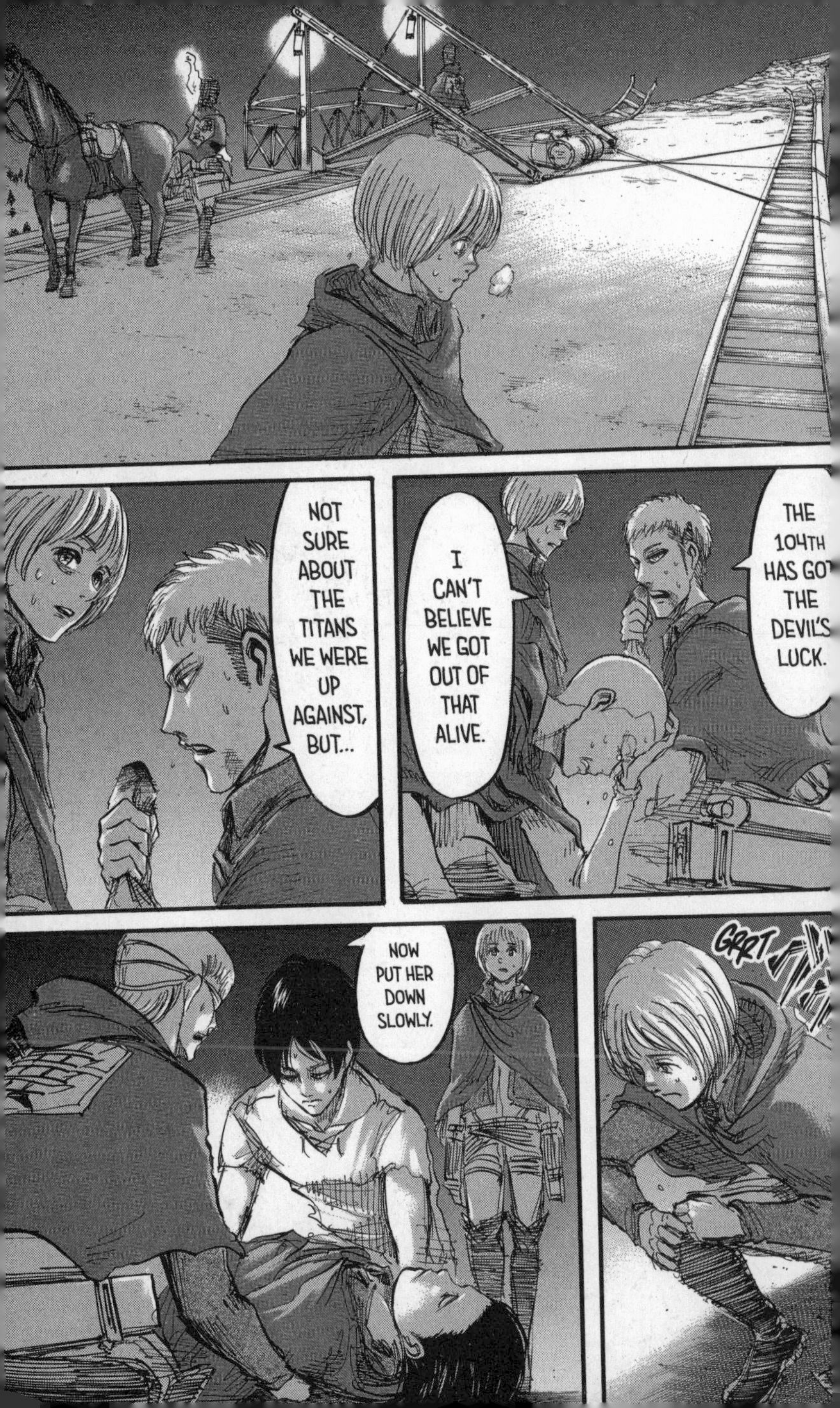
THE 104TH HAS GOT THE DEVIL'S LUCK.
I CAN'T BELIEVE WE GOT OUT OF THAT ALIVE.
NOT SURE ABOUT THE TITANS WE WERE UP AGAINST, BUT...
GRRT
NOW PUT HER DOWN SLOWLY.

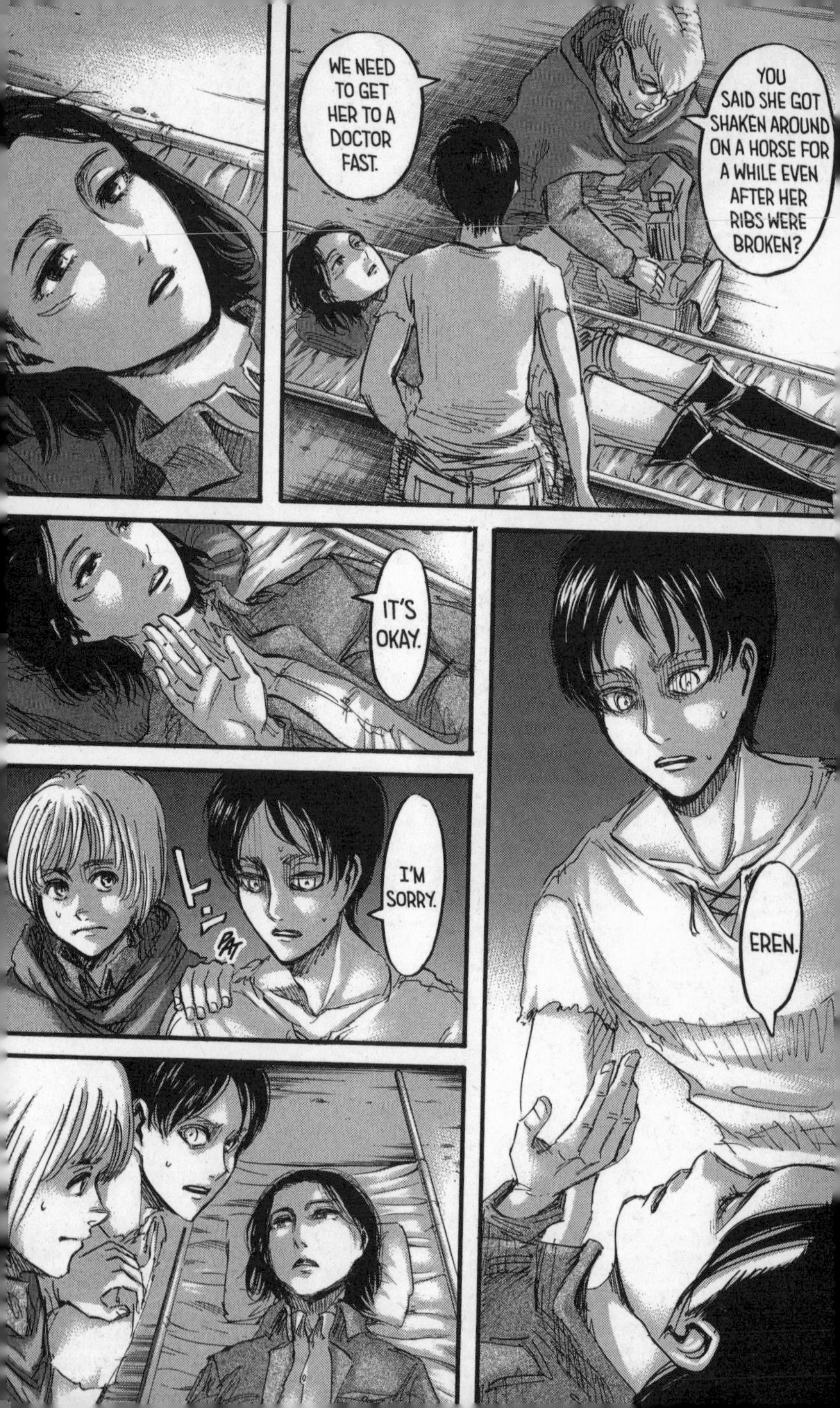
YOU SAID SHE GOT SHAKEN AROUND ON A HORSE FOR A WHILE EVEN AFTER HER RIBS WERE BROKEN?
WE NEED TO GET HER TO A DOCTOR FAST.
EREN.
IT'S OKAY.
PAT
I'M SORRY.

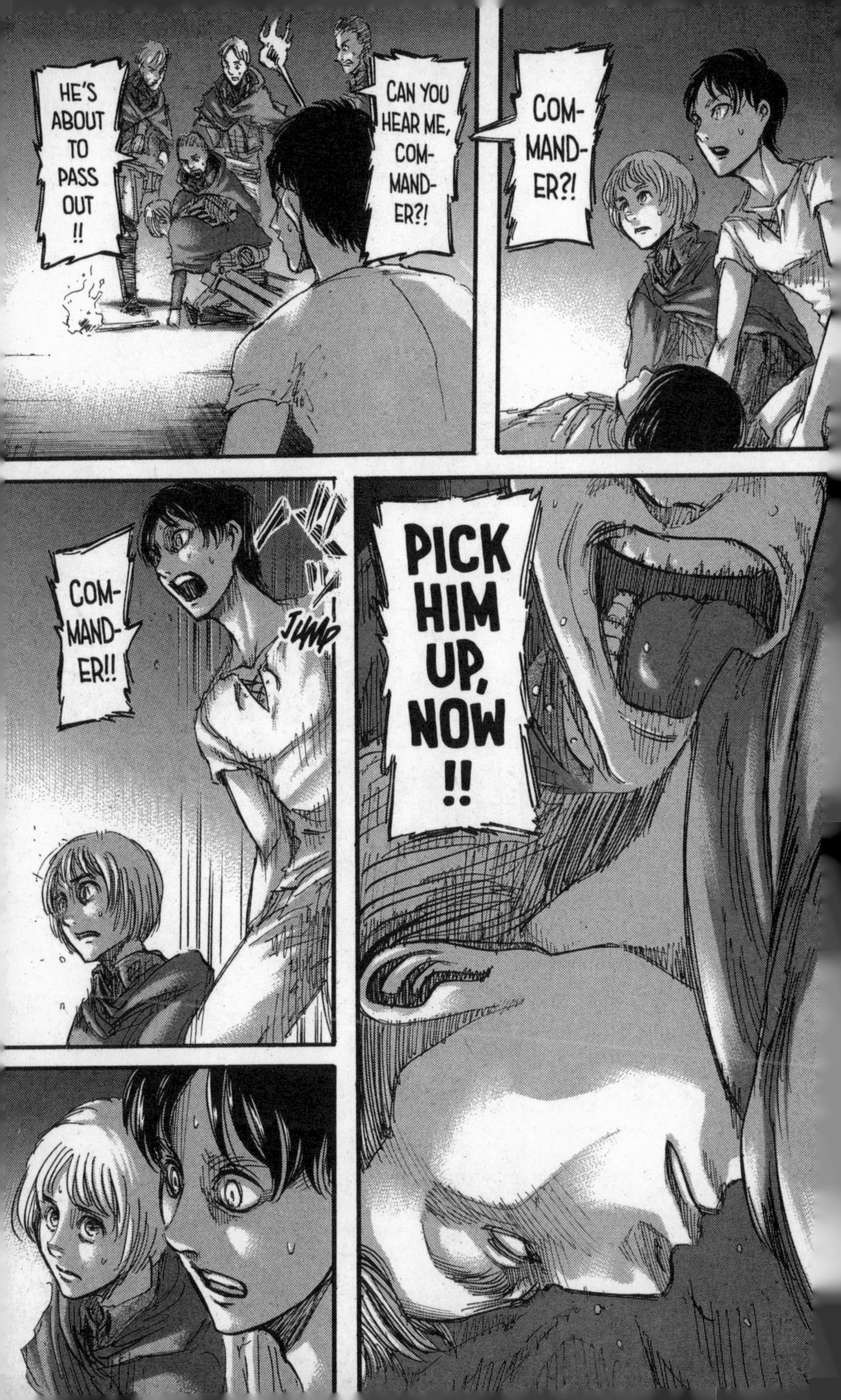
COMMANDER?!
CAN YOU HEAR ME, COMMANDER?!
HE'S ABOUT TO PASS OUT!!
PICK HIM UP, NOW!!
COMMANDER!!
JUMP

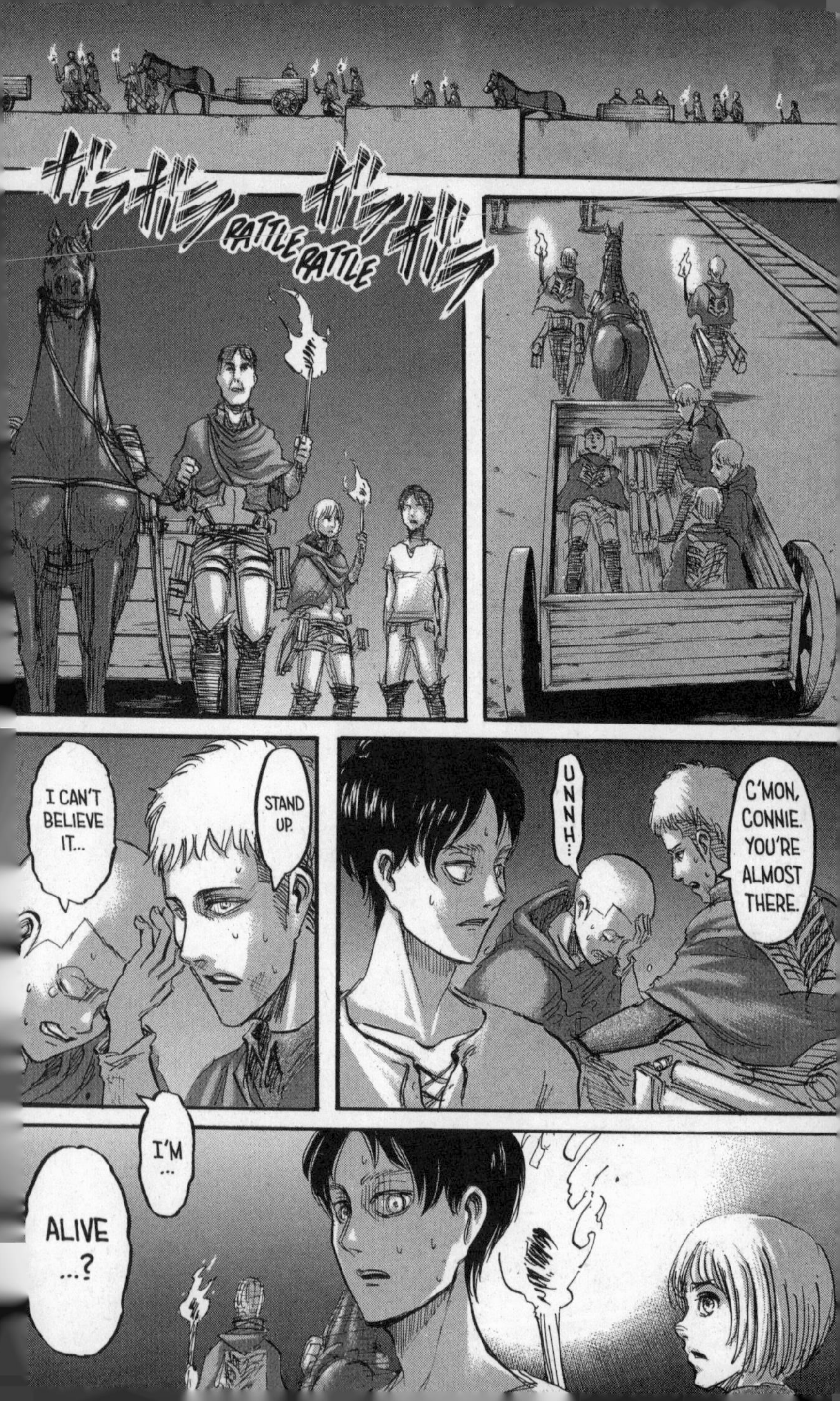

ガラガラ ガラガラ
RATTLE RATTLE
C'MON, CONNIE. YOU'RE ALMOST THERE.
UNNH...
STAND UP.
I CAN'T BELIEVE IT...
I'M ...
ALIVE ...?

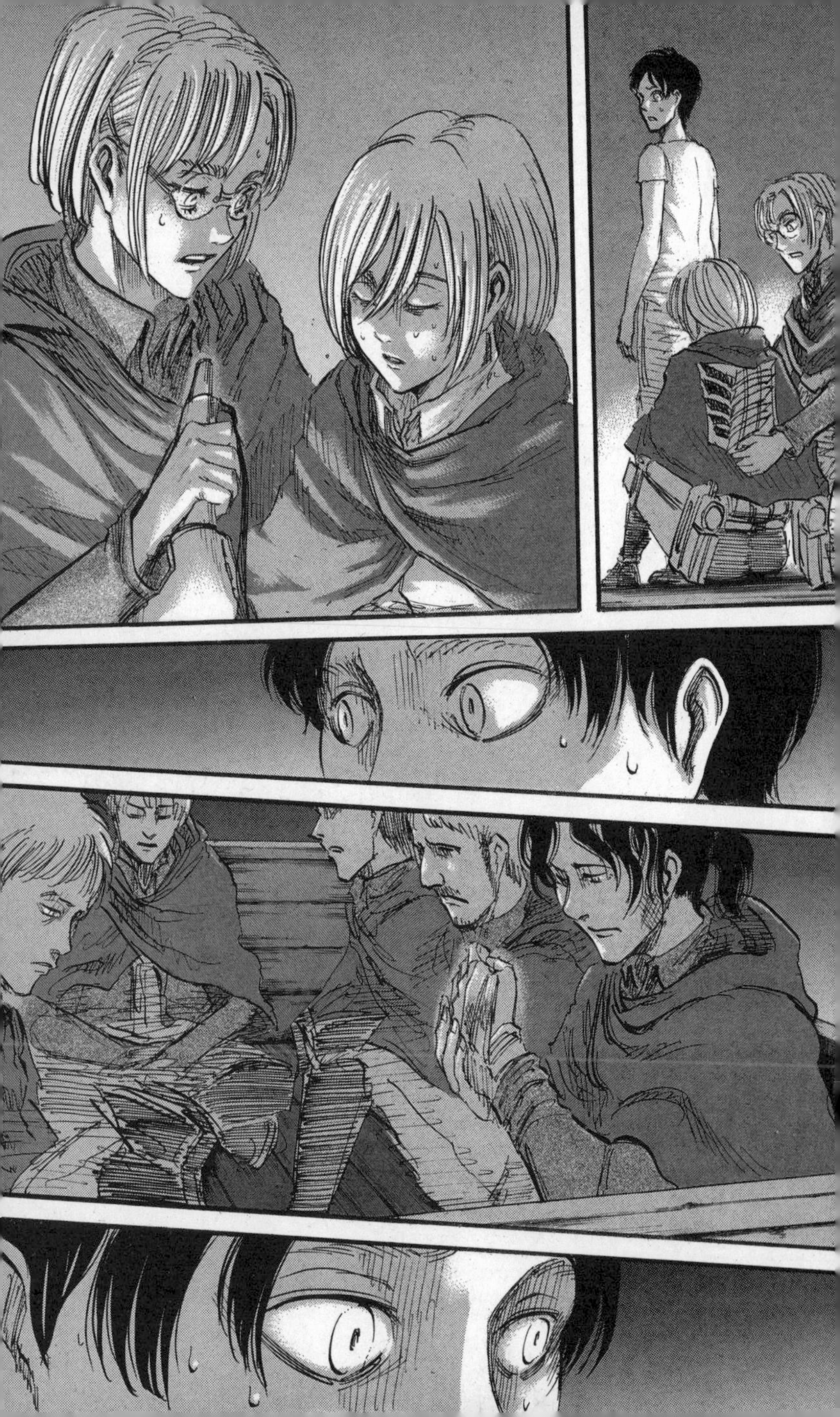

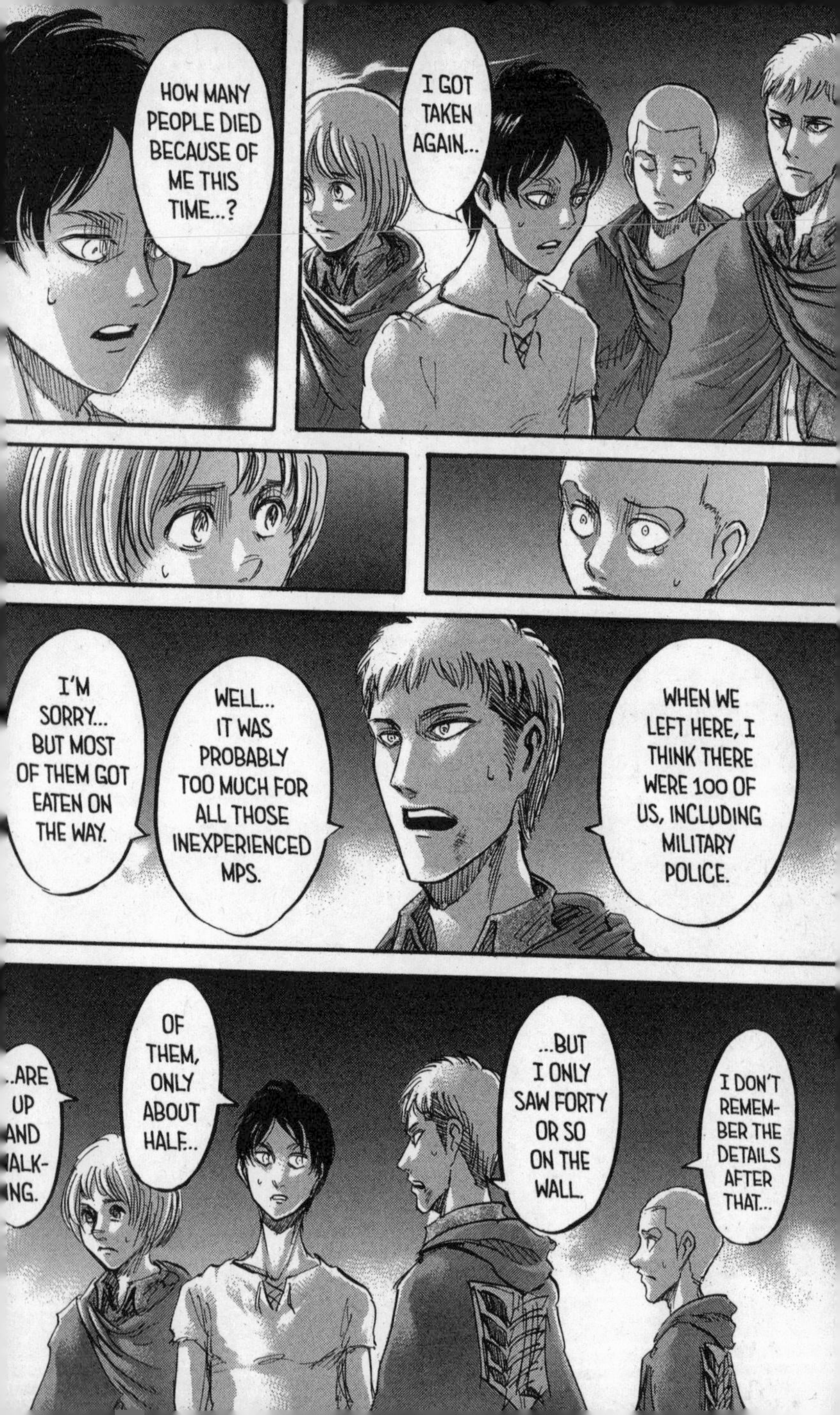
I GOT TAKEN AGAIN...
HOW MANY PEOPLE DIED BECAUSE OF ME THIS TIME...?
WHEN WE LEFT HERE, I THINK THERE WERE 100 OF US, INCLUDING MILITARY POLICE.
WELL... IT WAS PROBABLY TOO MUCH FOR ALL THOSE INEXPERIENCED MPS.
I'M SORRY... BUT MOST OF THEM GOT EATEN ON THE WAY.
I DON'T REMEM- BER THE DETAILS AFTER THAT...
...BUT I ONLY SAW FORTY OR SO ON THE WALL.
OF THEM, ONLY ABOUT HALF..
..ARE UP AND ALK- NG.

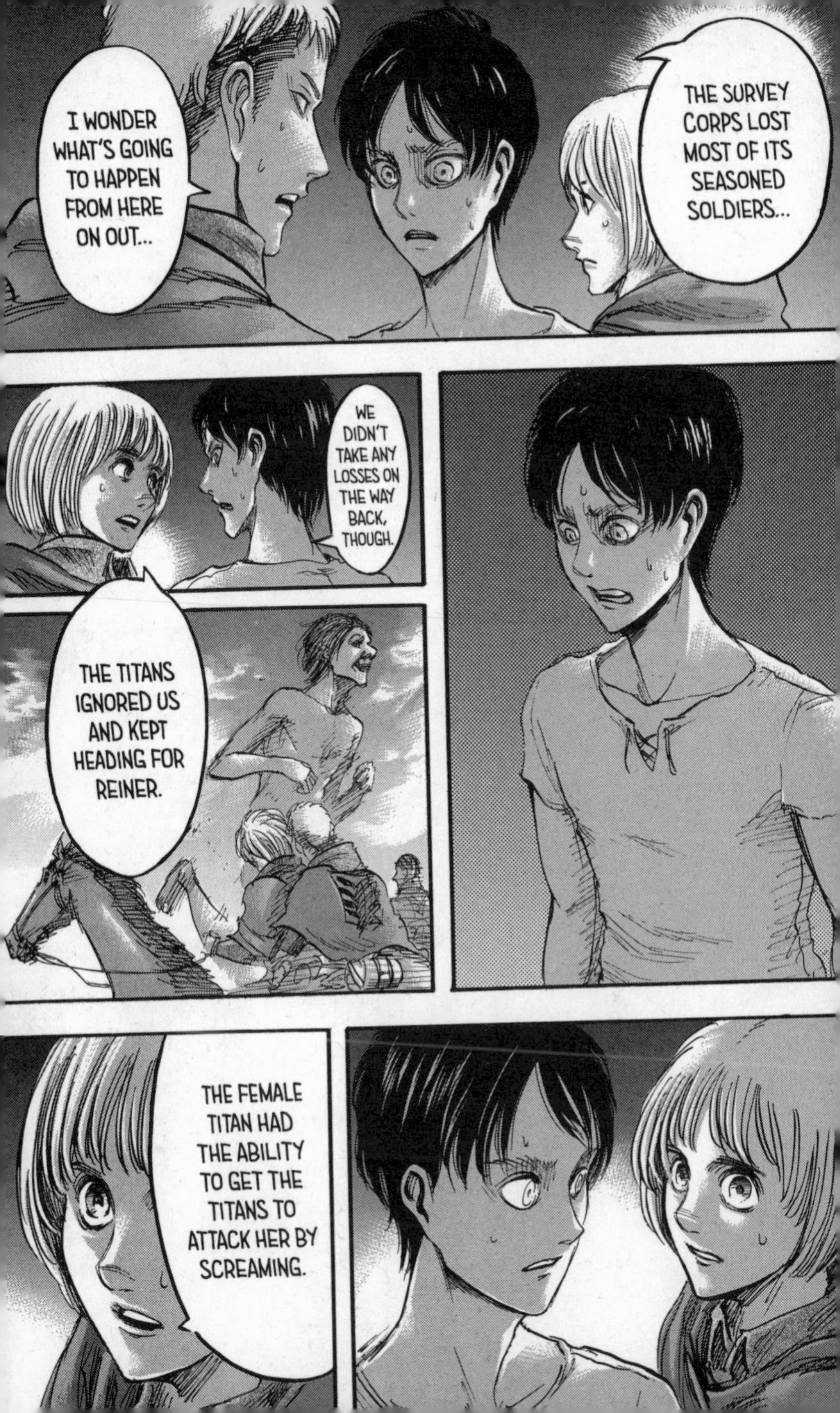
THE SURVEY CORPS LOST MOST OF ITS SEASONED SOLDIERS...
I WONDER WHAT'S GOING TO HAPPEN FROM HERE ON OUT...
WE DIDN'T TAKE ANY LOSSES ON THE WAY BACK, THOUGH.
THE TITANS IGNORED US AND KEPT HEADING FOR REINER.
THE FEMALE TITAN HAD THE ABILITY TO GET THE TITANS TO ATTACK HER BY SCREAMING.

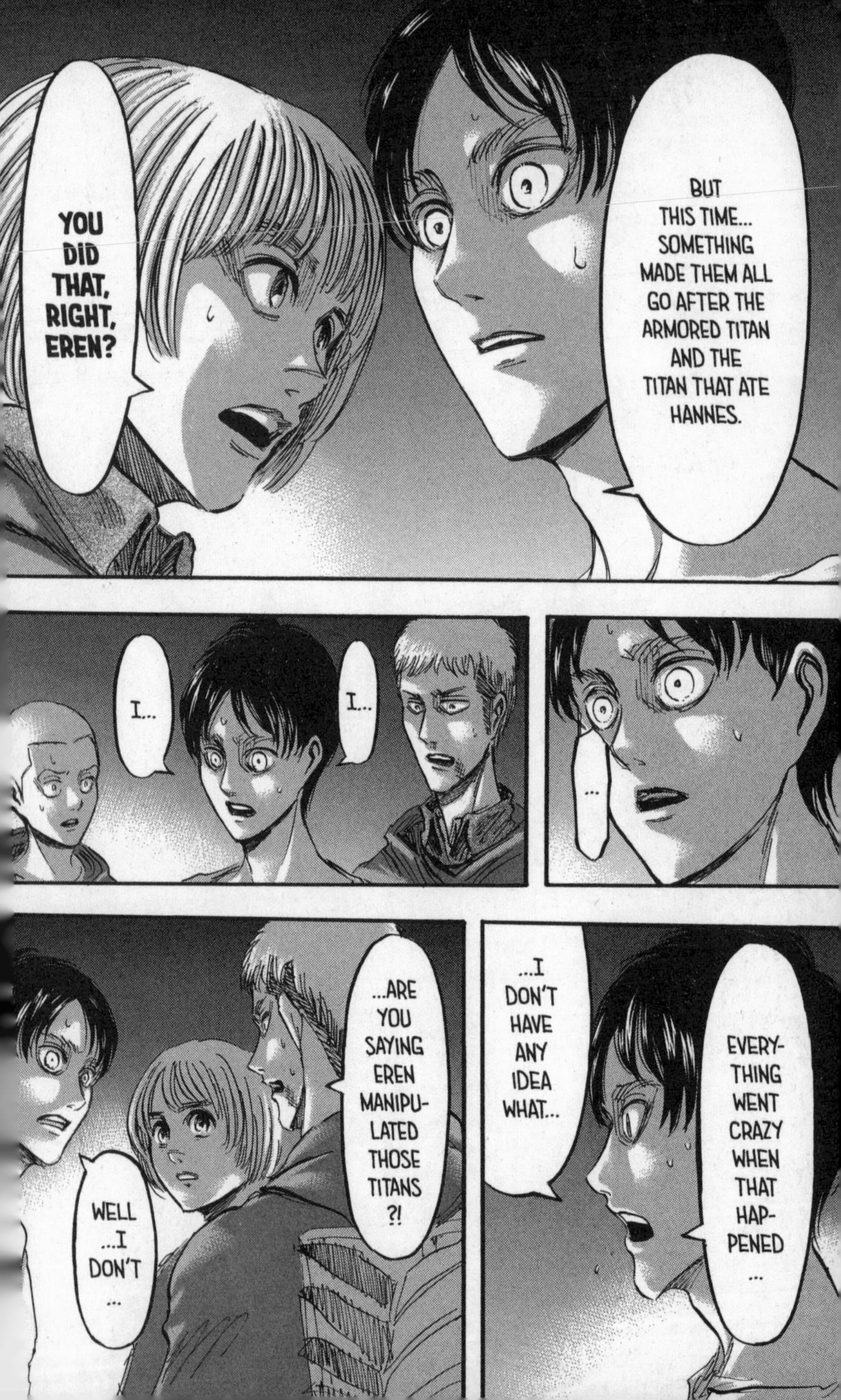
BUT THIS TIME... SOMETHING MADE THEM ALL GO AFTER THE ARMORED TITAN AND THE TITAN THAT ATE HANNES.
YOU DID THAT, RIGHT, EREN?
...
I...
I...
EVERY-THING WENT CRAZY WHEN THAT HAP-PENED ...
...I DON'T HAVE ANY IDEA WHAT...
...ARE YOU SAYING EREN MANIPU-LATED THOSE TITANS ?!
WELL ...I DON'T ...

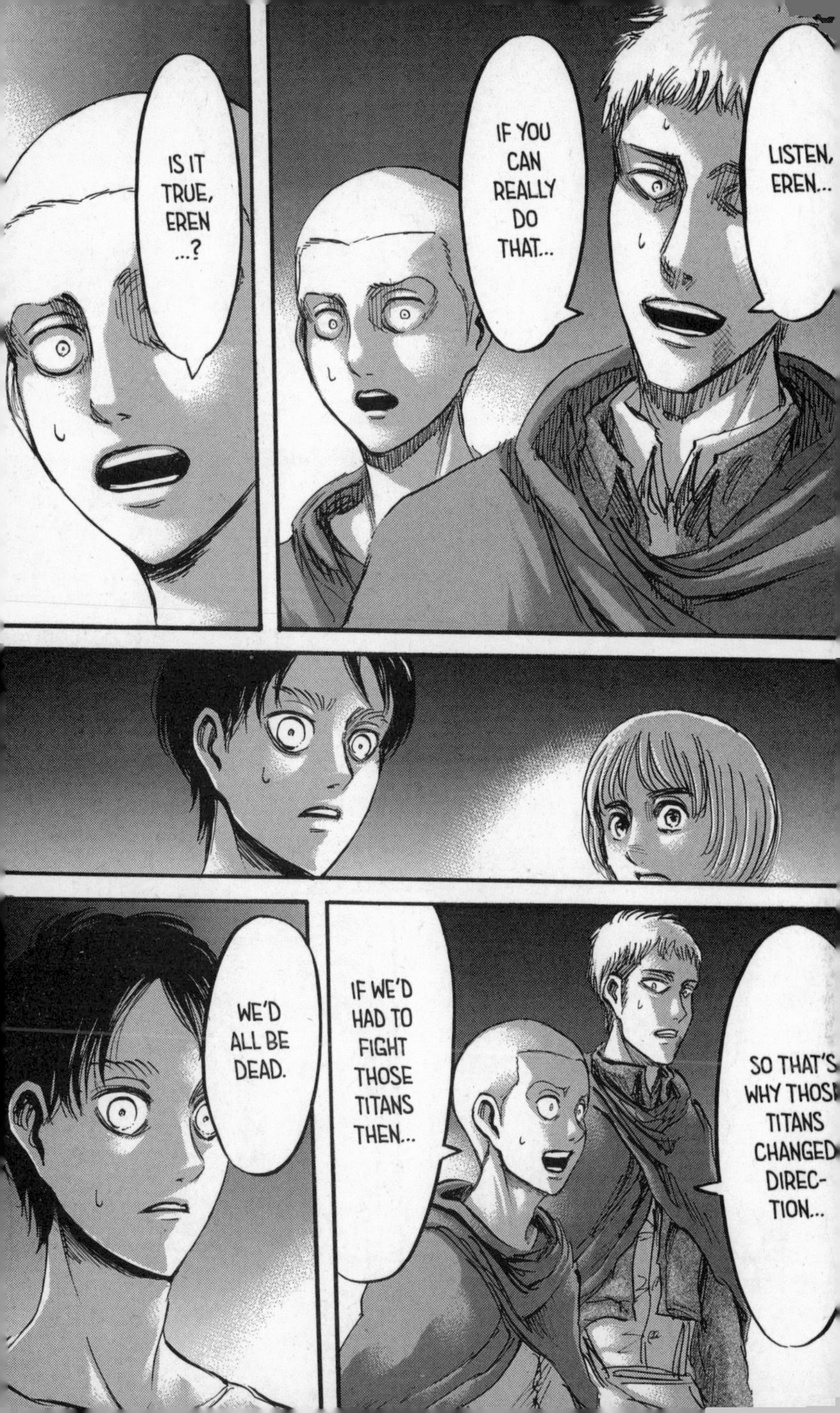

LISTEN, EREN...
IF YOU CAN REALLY DO THAT...
IS IT TRUE, EREN ...?
SO THAT'S WHY THOS TITANS CHANGED DIREC- TION...
IF WE'D HAD TO FIGHT THOSE TITANS THEN...
WE'D ALL BE DEAD.

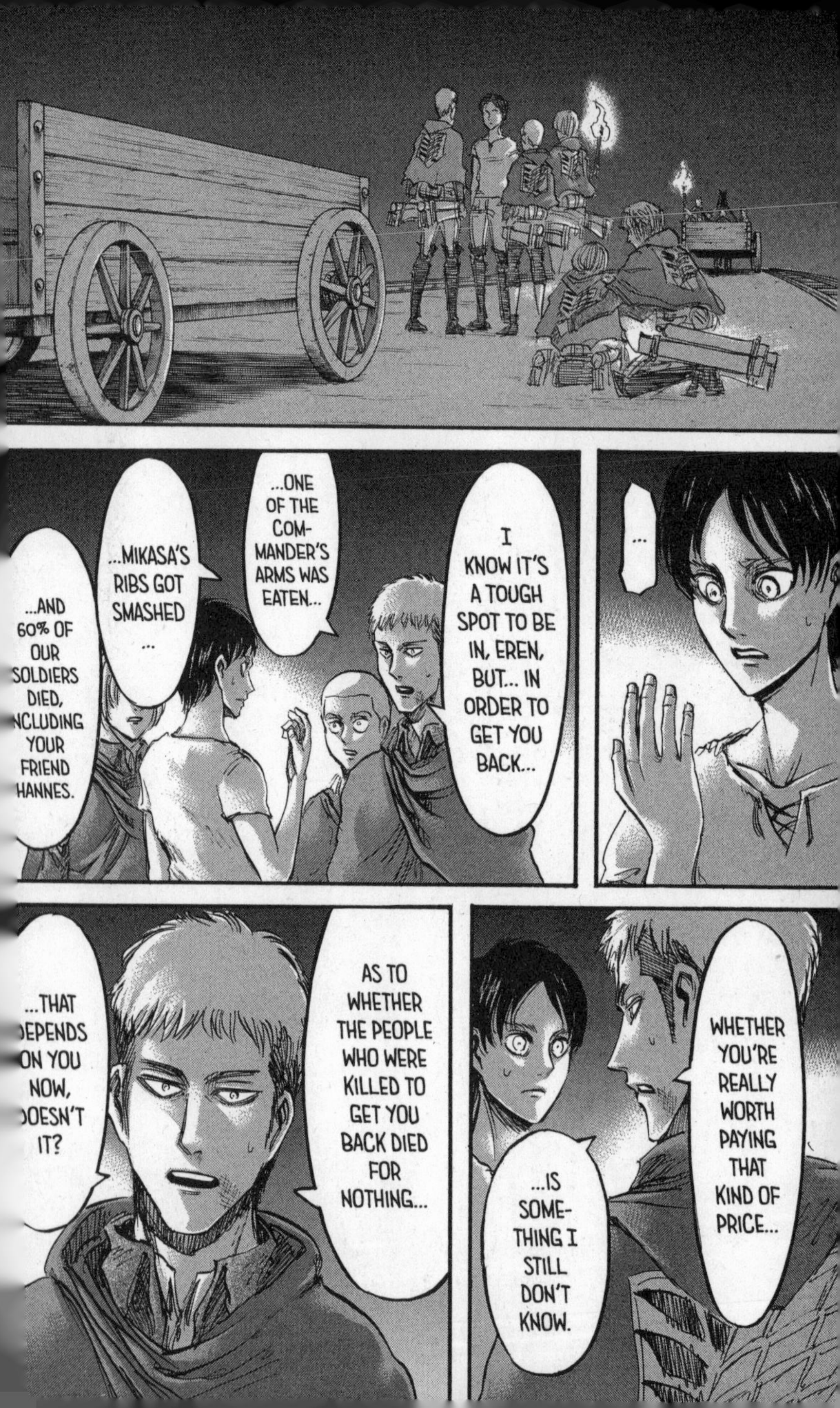
...
I KNOW IT'S A TOUGH SPOT TO BE IN, EREN, BUT... IN ORDER TO GET YOU BACK...
...ONE OF THE COMMANDER'S ARMS WAS EATEN...
...MIKASA'S RIBS GOT SMASHED ...
...AND 60% OF OUR SOLDIERS DIED, INCLUDING YOUR FRIEND HANNES.
WHETHER YOU'RE REALLY WORTH PAYING THAT KIND OF PRICE...
...IS SOMETHING I STILL DON'T KNOW.
AS TO WHETHER THE PEOPLE WHO WERE KILLED TO GET YOU BACK DIED FOR NOTHING...
...THAT DEPENDS ON YOU NOW, DOESN'T IT?

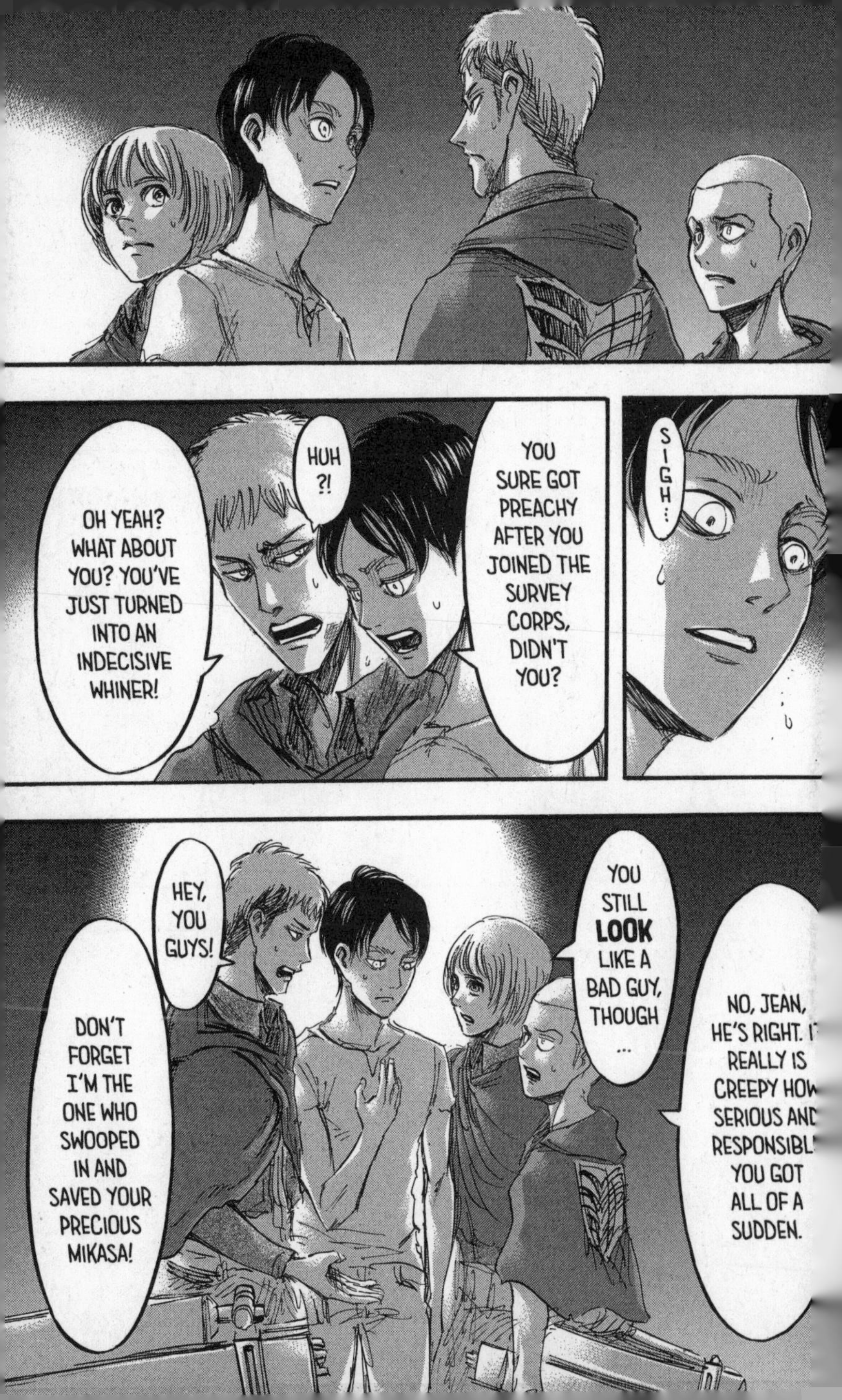
SIGH...
YOU SURE GOT PREACHY AFTER YOU JOINED THE SURVEY CORPS, DIDN'T YOU?
HUH ?!
OH YEAH? WHAT ABOUT YOU? YOU'VE JUST TURNED INTO AN INDECISIVE WHINER!
NO, JEAN, HE'S RIGHT. IT REALLY IS CREEPY HOW SERIOUS AND RESPONSIBLE YOU GOT ALL OF A SUDDEN.
YOU STILL **LOOK** LIKE A BAD GUY, THOUGH ...
HEY, YOU GUYS!
DON'T FORGET I'M THE ONE WHO SWOOPED IN AND SAVED YOUR PRECIOUS MIKASA!

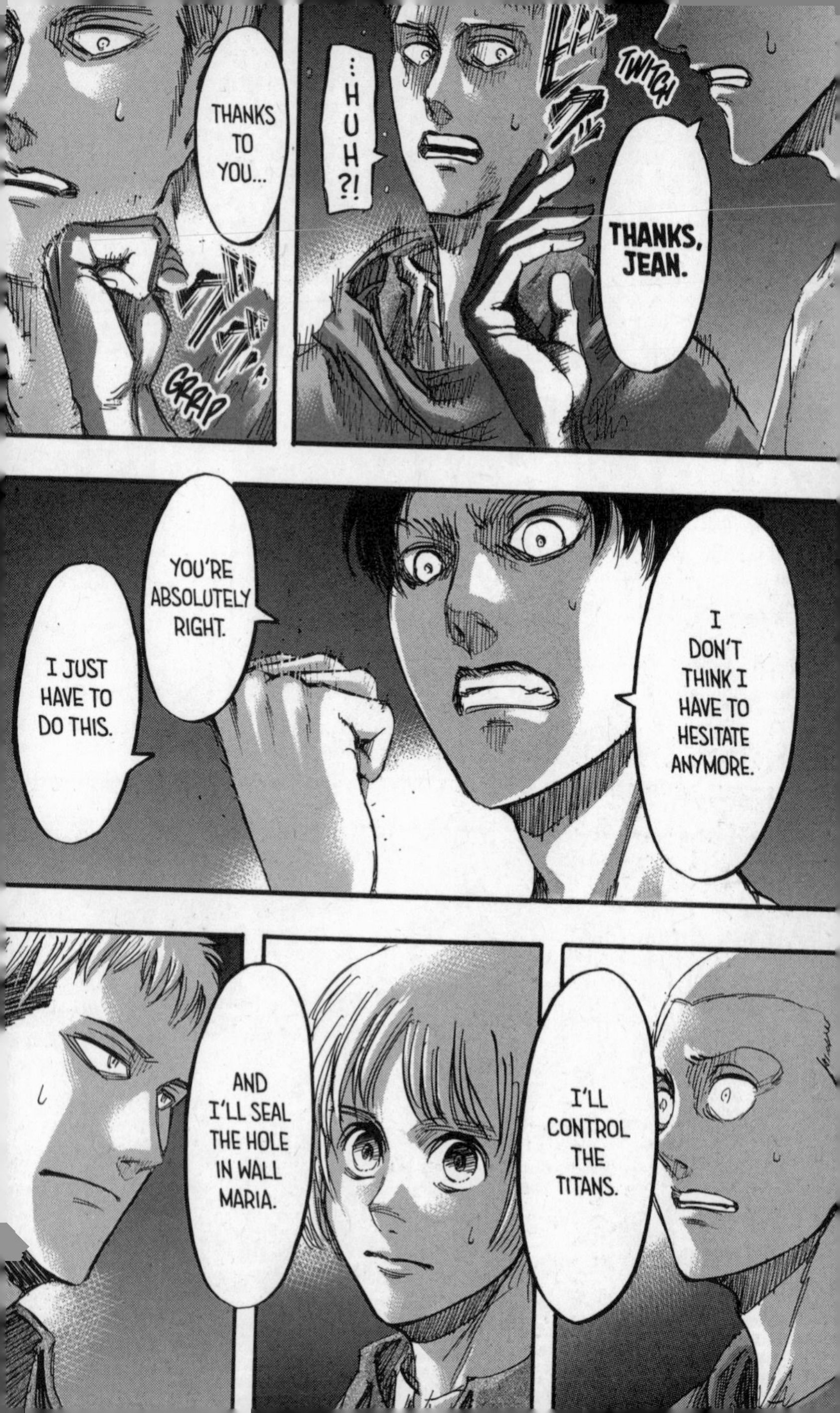
TWITCH
THANKS, JEAN.
...HUH?!
THANKS TO YOU...
GRAB
I DON'T THINK I HAVE TO HESITATE ANYMORE.
YOU'RE ABSOLUTELY RIGHT.
I JUST HAVE TO DO THIS.
I'LL CONTROL THE TITANS.
AND I'LL SEAL THE HOLE IN WALL MARIA.

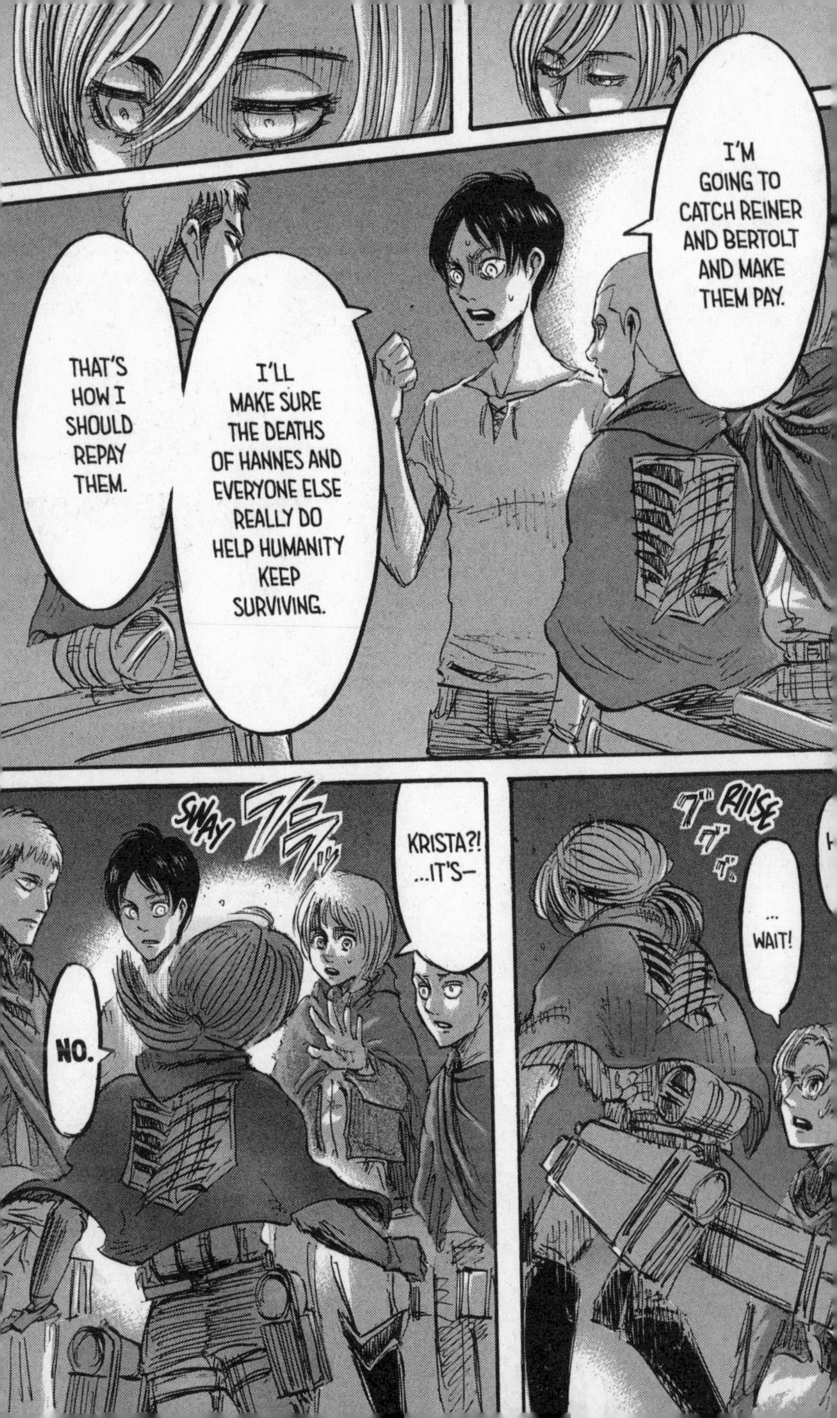
I'M GOING TO CATCH REINER AND BERTOLT AND MAKE THEM PAY.
I'LL MAKE SURE THE DEATHS OF HANNES AND EVERYONE ELSE REALLY DO HELP HUMANITY KEEP SURVIVING.
THAT'S HOW I SHOULD REPAY THEM.
RIIISE
... WAIT!
KRISTA?! ...IT'S—
SWAY
NO.

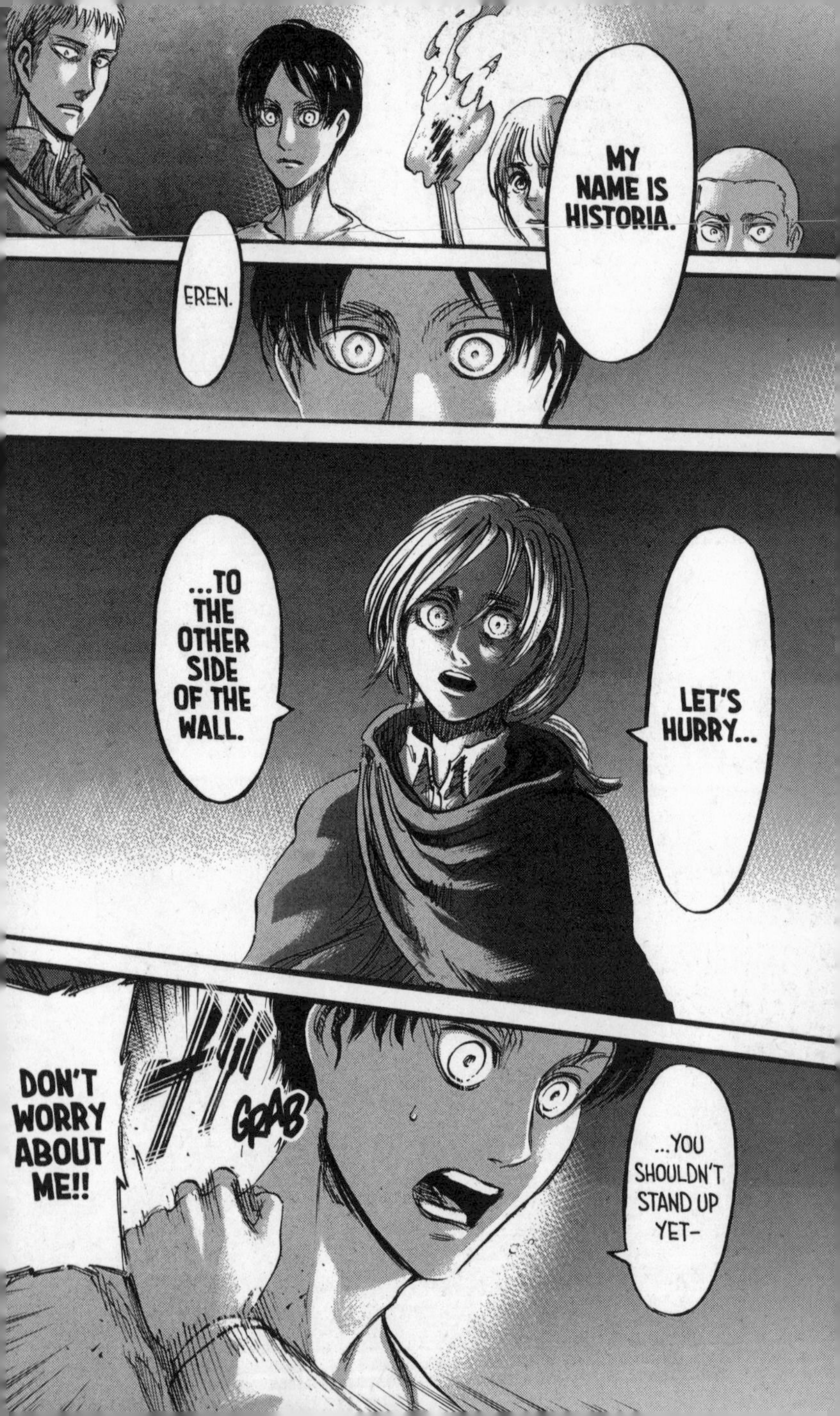
MY NAME IS HISTORIA.
EREN.
LET'S HURRY...
...TO THE OTHER SIDE OF THE WALL.
...YOU SHOULDN'T STAND UP YET-
GRAB
DON'T WORRY ABOUT ME!!

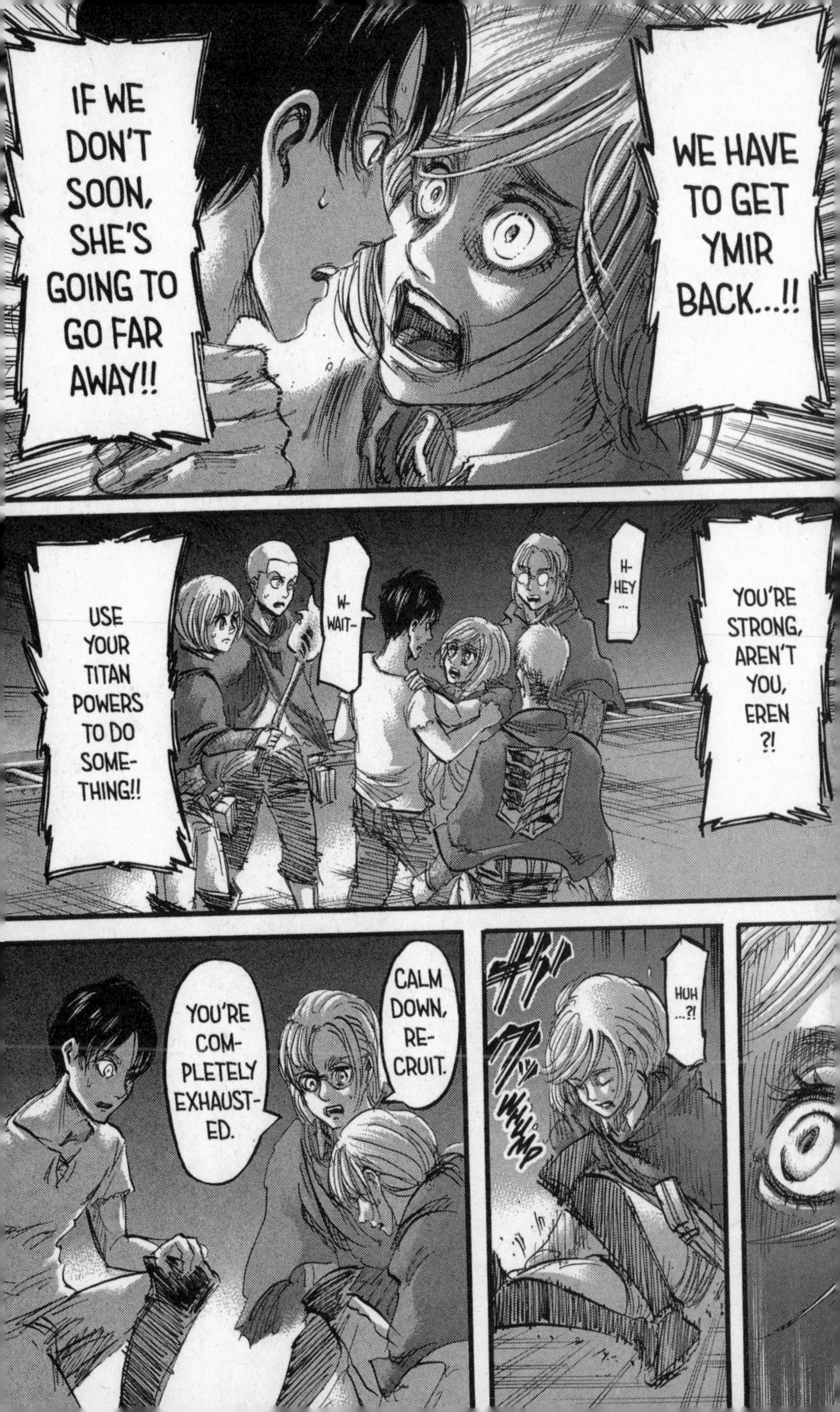

WE HAVE TO GET YMIR BACK...!!
IF WE DON'T SOON, SHE'S GOING TO GO FAR AWAY!!
YOU'RE STRONG, AREN'T YOU, EREN?!
H-HEY...
W-WAIT-
USE YOUR TITAN POWERS TO DO SOME-THING!!
HUH...?!
CALM DOWN, RE-CRUIT.
YOU'RE COM-PLETELY EXHAUST-ED.

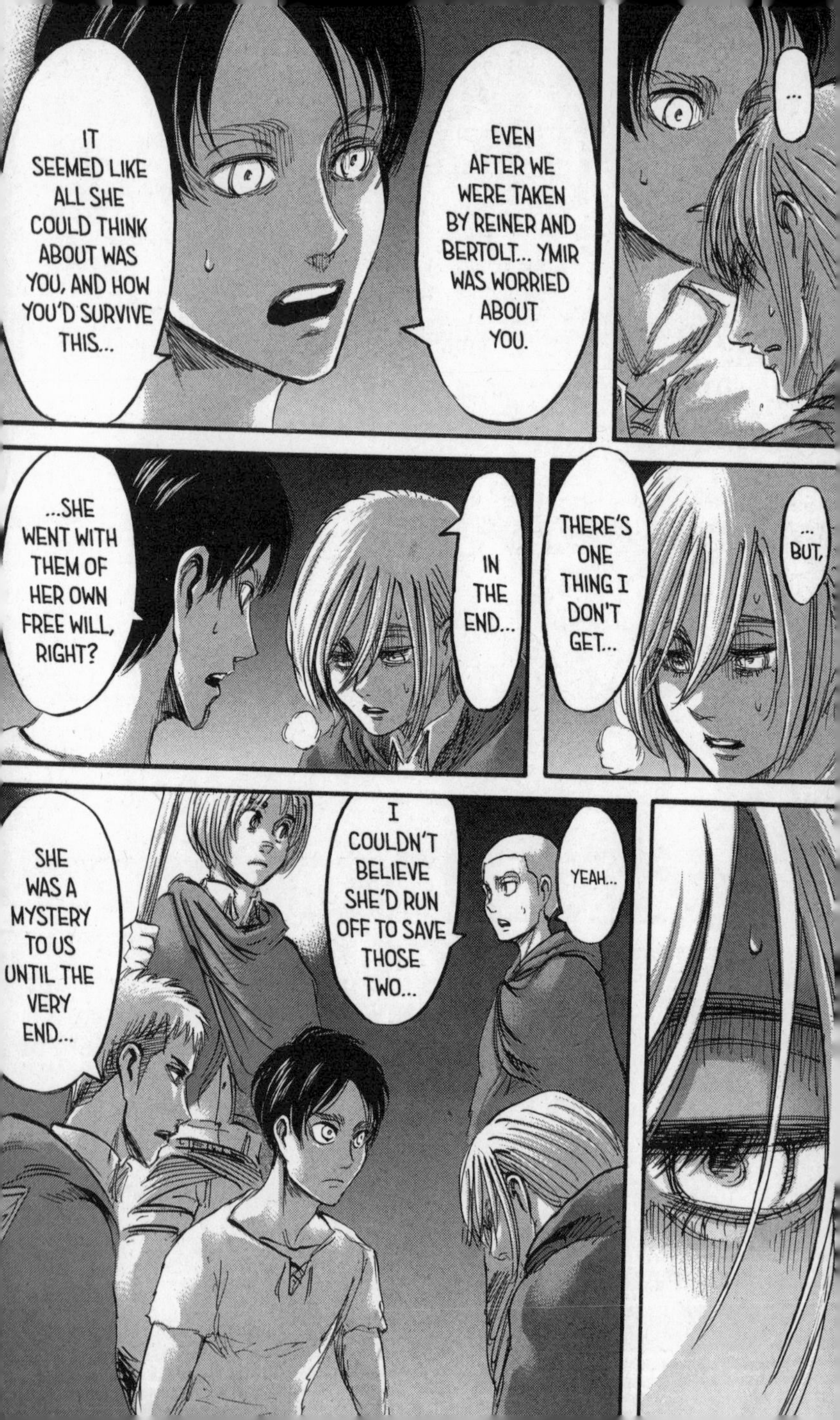
...
EVEN AFTER WE WERE TAKEN BY REINER AND BERTOLT... YMIR WAS WORRIED ABOUT YOU.
IT SEEMED LIKE ALL SHE COULD THINK ABOUT WAS YOU, AND HOW YOU'D SURVIVE THIS...
... BUT,
THERE'S ONE THING I DON'T GET...
IN THE END...
...SHE WENT WITH THEM OF HER OWN FREE WILL, RIGHT?
YEAH...
I COULDN'T BELIEVE SHE'D RUN OFF TO SAVE THOSE TWO...
SHE WAS A MYSTERY TO US UNTIL THE VERY END...

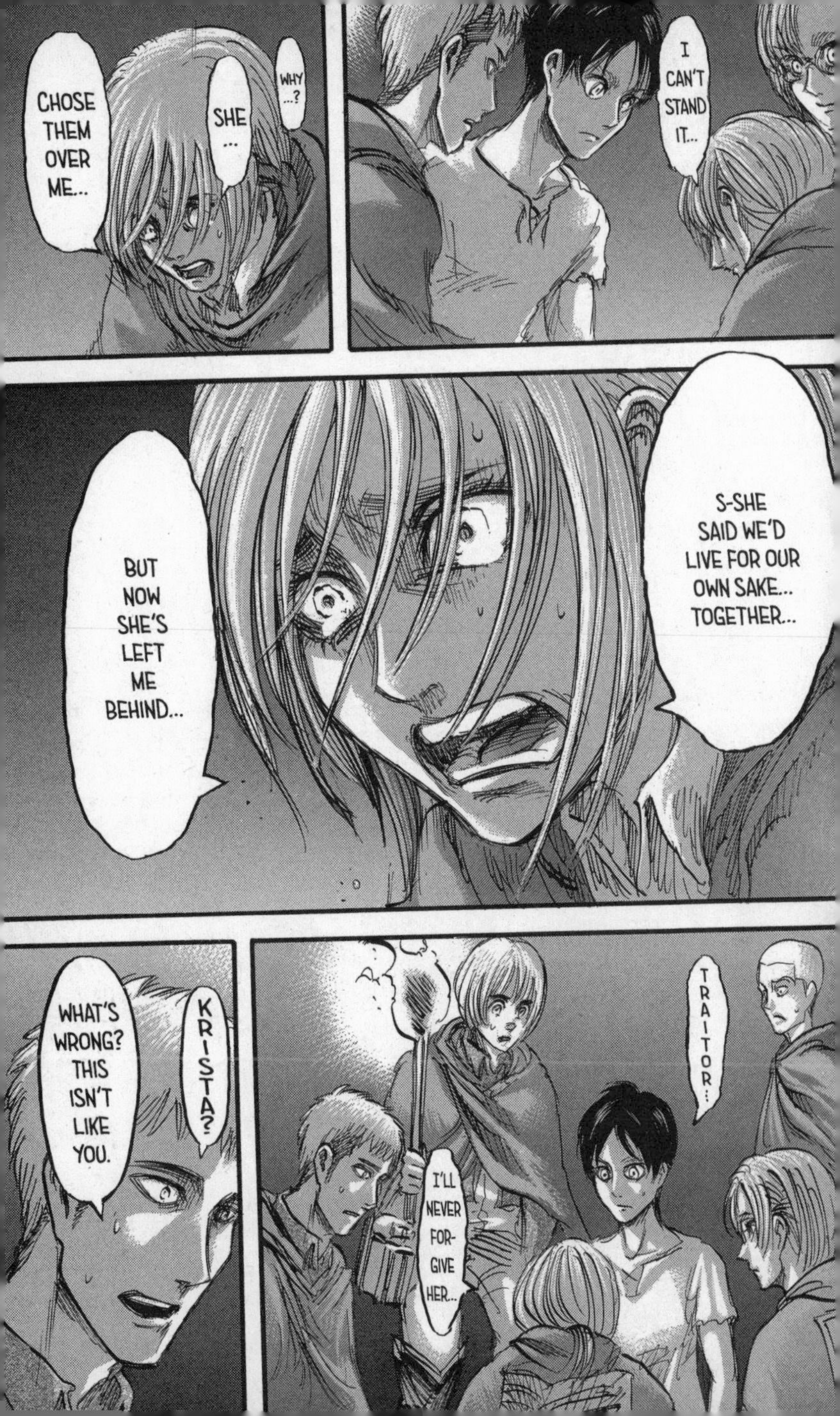
I CAN'T STAND IT...
WHY ...?
SHE ...
CHOSE THEM OVER ME...
S-SHE SAID WE'D LIVE FOR OUR OWN SAKE... TOGETHER...
BUT NOW SHE'S LEFT ME BEHIND...
TRAITOR...
I'LL NEVER FOR-GIVE HER...
KRISTA?
WHAT'S WRONG? THIS ISN'T LIKE YOU.

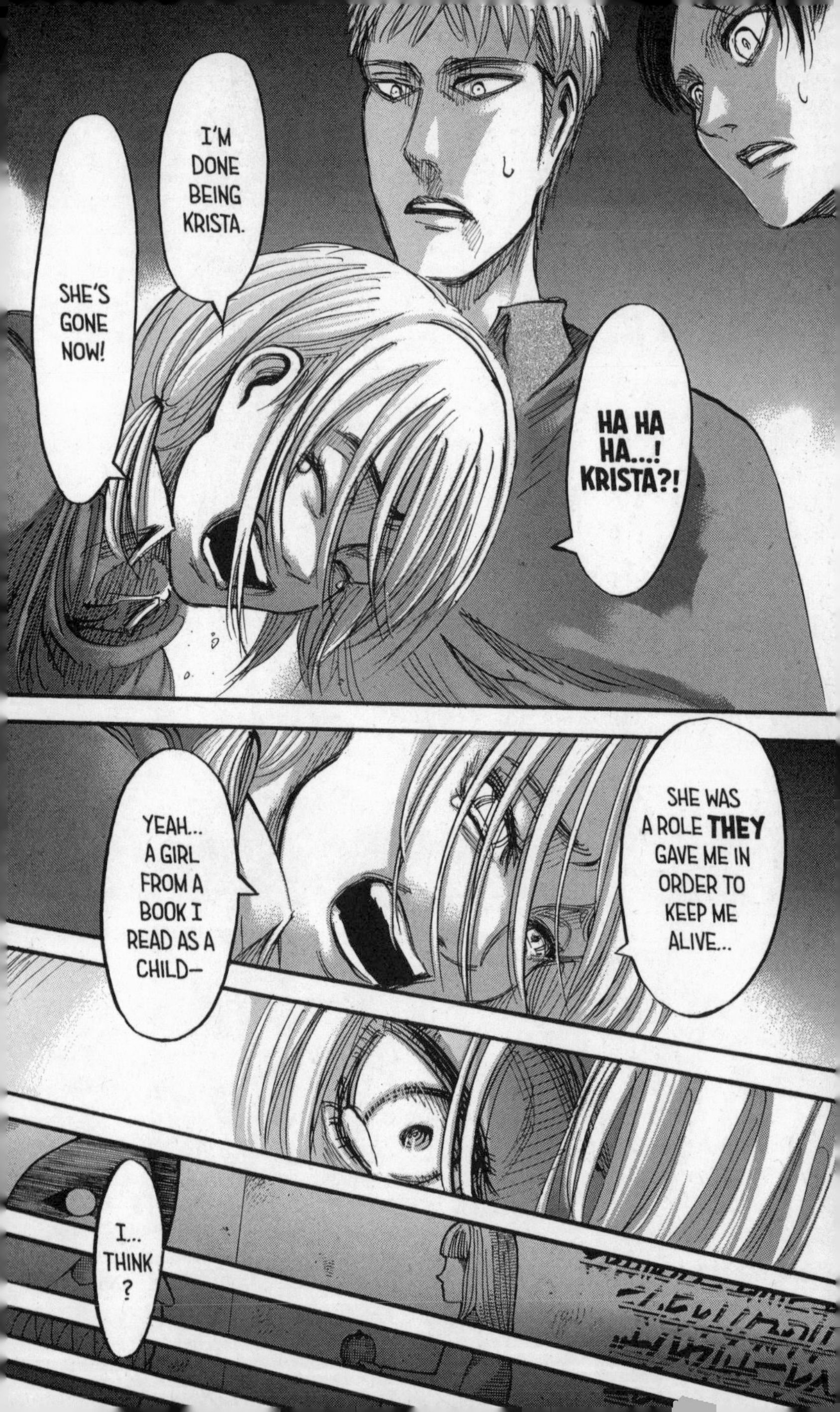
HA HA HA...! KRISTA?!
I'M DONE BEING KRISTA.
SHE'S GONE NOW!
SHE WAS A ROLE THEY GAVE ME IN ORDER TO KEEP ME ALIVE...
YEAH... A GIRL FROM A BOOK I READ AS A CHILD—
I... THINK ?

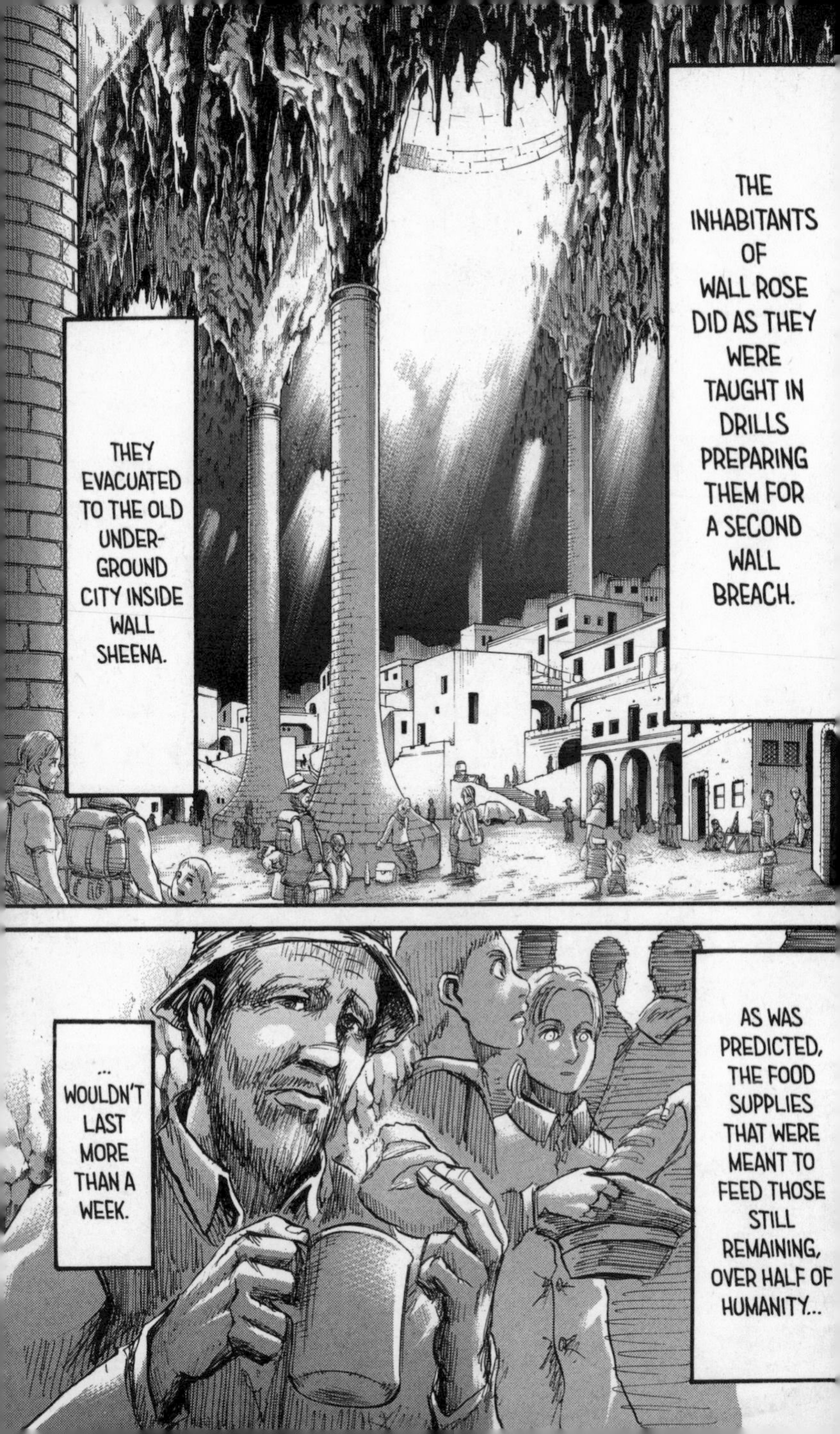
THE INHABITANTS OF WALL ROSE DID AS THEY WERE TAUGHT IN DRILLS PREPARING THEM FOR A SECOND WALL BREACH.
THEY EVACUATED TO THE OLD UNDER-GROUND CITY INSIDE WALL SHEENA.
AS WAS PREDICTED, THE FOOD SUPPLIES THAT WERE MEANT TO FEED THOSE STILL REMAINING, OVER HALF OF HUMANITY...
...WOULDN'T LAST MORE THAN A WEEK.

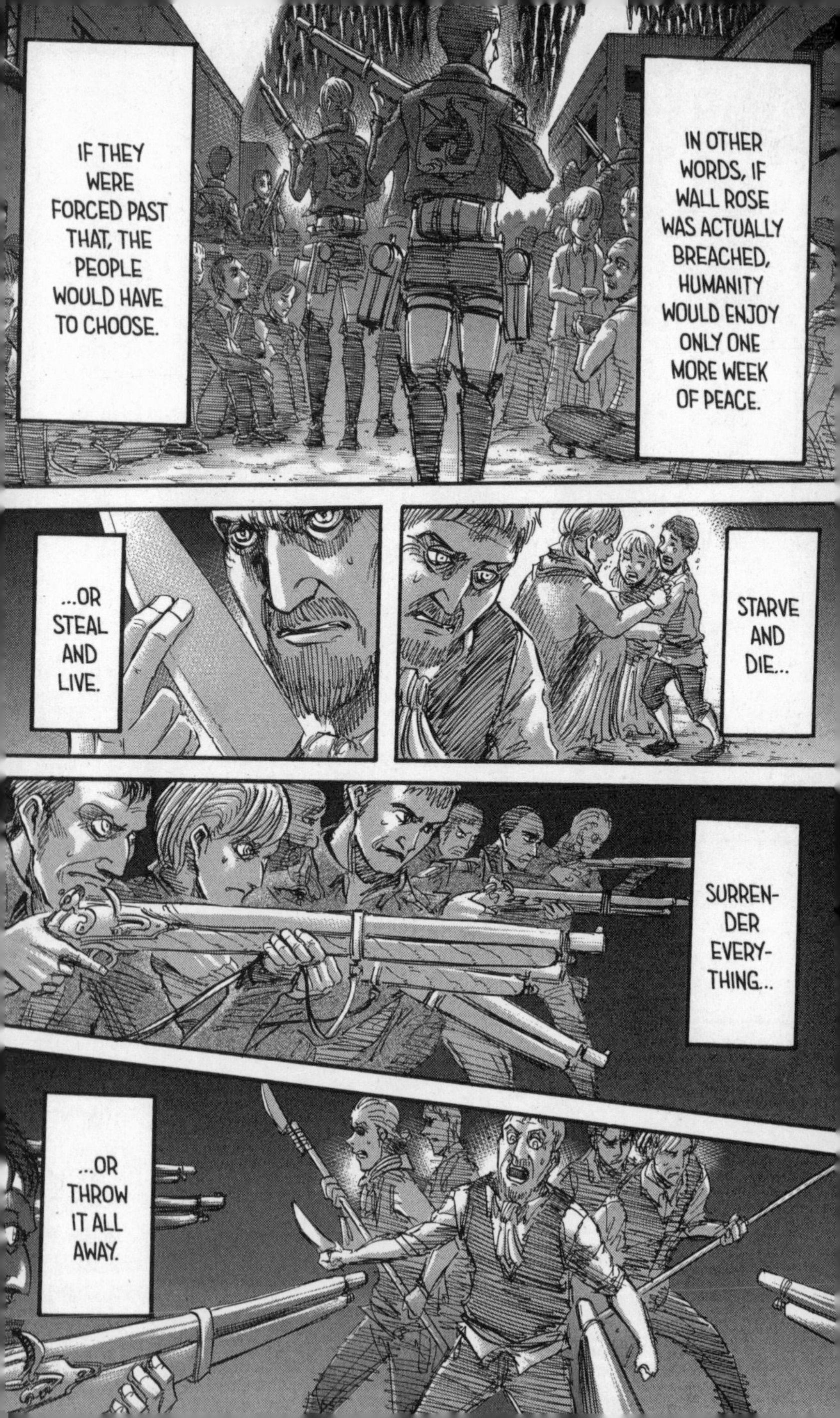
IN OTHER WORDS, IF WALL ROSE WAS ACTUALLY BREACHED, HUMANITY WOULD ENJOY ONLY ONE MORE WEEK OF PEACE.
IF THEY WERE FORCED PAST THAT, THE PEOPLE WOULD HAVE TO CHOOSE.
STARVE AND DIE...
...OR STEAL AND LIVE.
SURREN-DER EVERY-THING...
...OR THROW IT ALL AWAY.

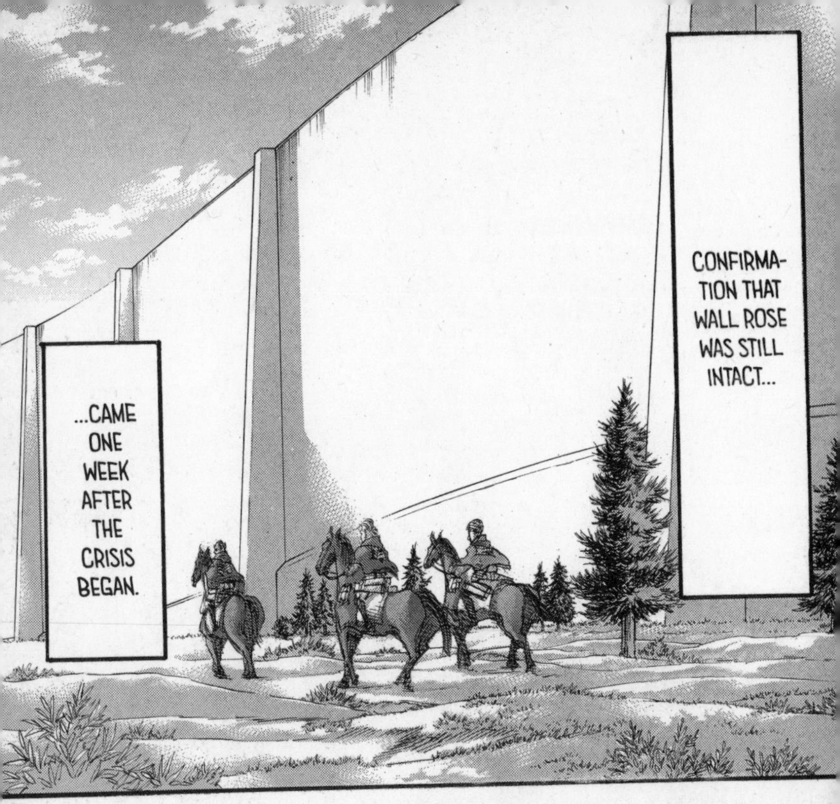
CONFIRMATION THAT WALL ROSE WAS STILL INTACT...
...CAME ONE WEEK AFTER THE CRISIS BEGAN.

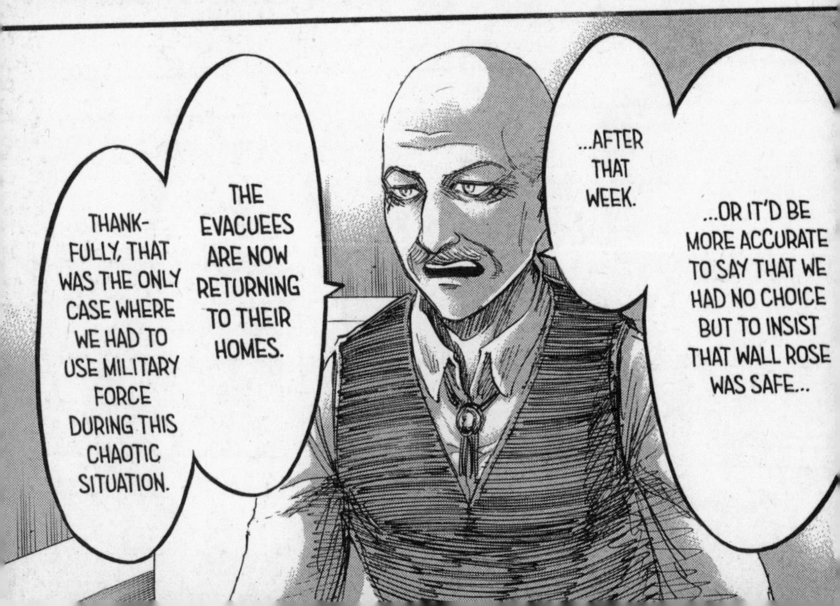
...OR IT'D BE MORE ACCURATE TO SAY THAT WE HAD NO CHOICE BUT TO INSIST THAT WALL ROSE WAS SAFE...
...AFTER THAT WEEK.
THE EVACUEES ARE NOW RETURNING TO THEIR HOMES.
THANKFULLY, THAT WAS THE ONLY CASE WHERE WE HAD TO USE MILITARY FORCE DURING THIS CHAOTIC SITUATION.

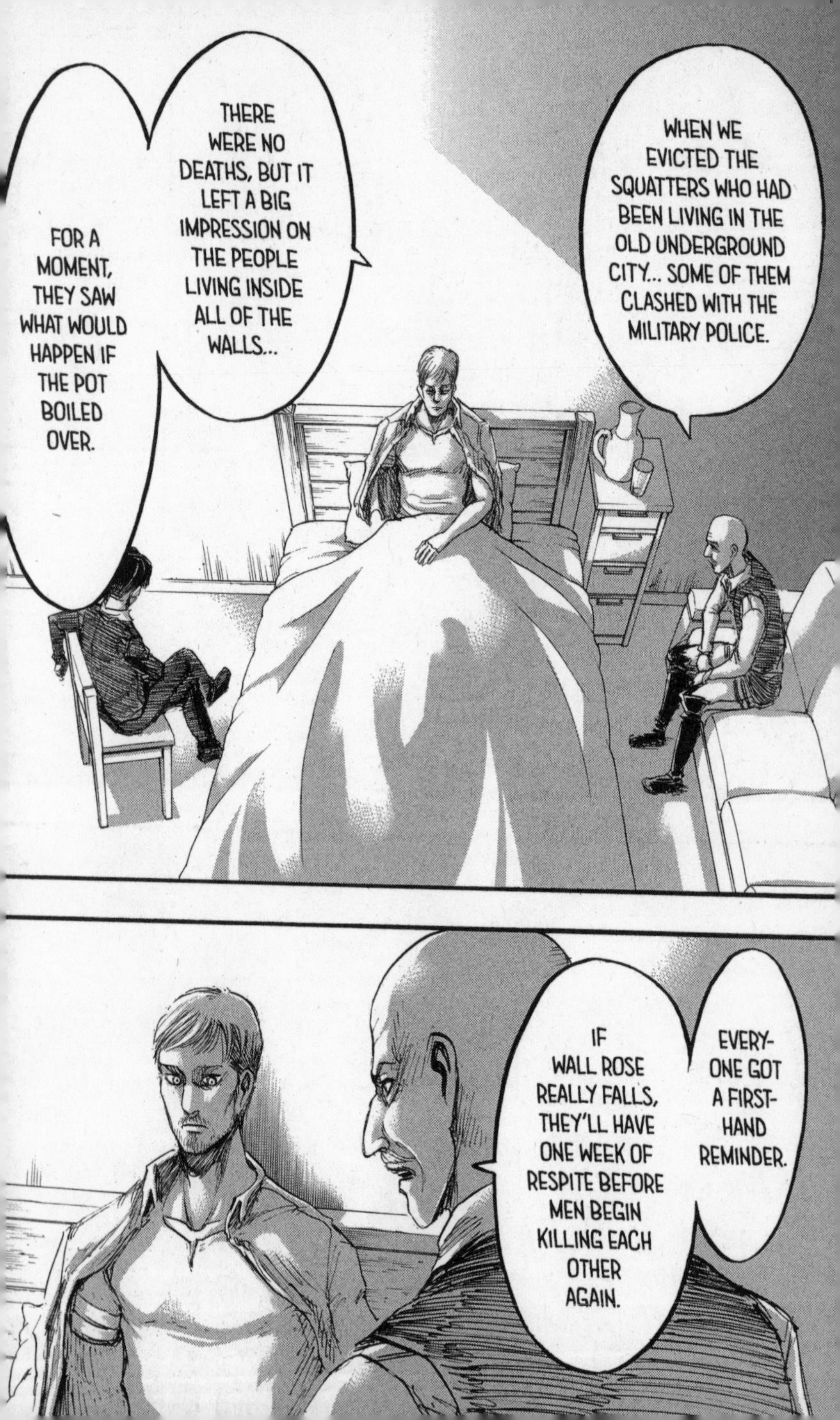
WHEN WE EVICTED THE SQUATTERS WHO HAD BEEN LIVING IN THE OLD UNDERGROUND CITY... SOME OF THEM CLASHED WITH THE MILITARY POLICE.
THERE WERE NO DEATHS, BUT IT LEFT A BIG IMPRESSION ON THE PEOPLE LIVING INSIDE ALL OF THE WALLS...
FOR A MOMENT, THEY SAW WHAT WOULD HAPPEN IF THE POT BOILED OVER.
EVERY-ONE GOT A FIRST-HAND REMINDER.
IF WALL ROSE REALLY FALLS, THEY'LL HAVE ONE WEEK OF RESPITE BEFORE MEN BEGIN KILLING EACH OTHER AGAIN.

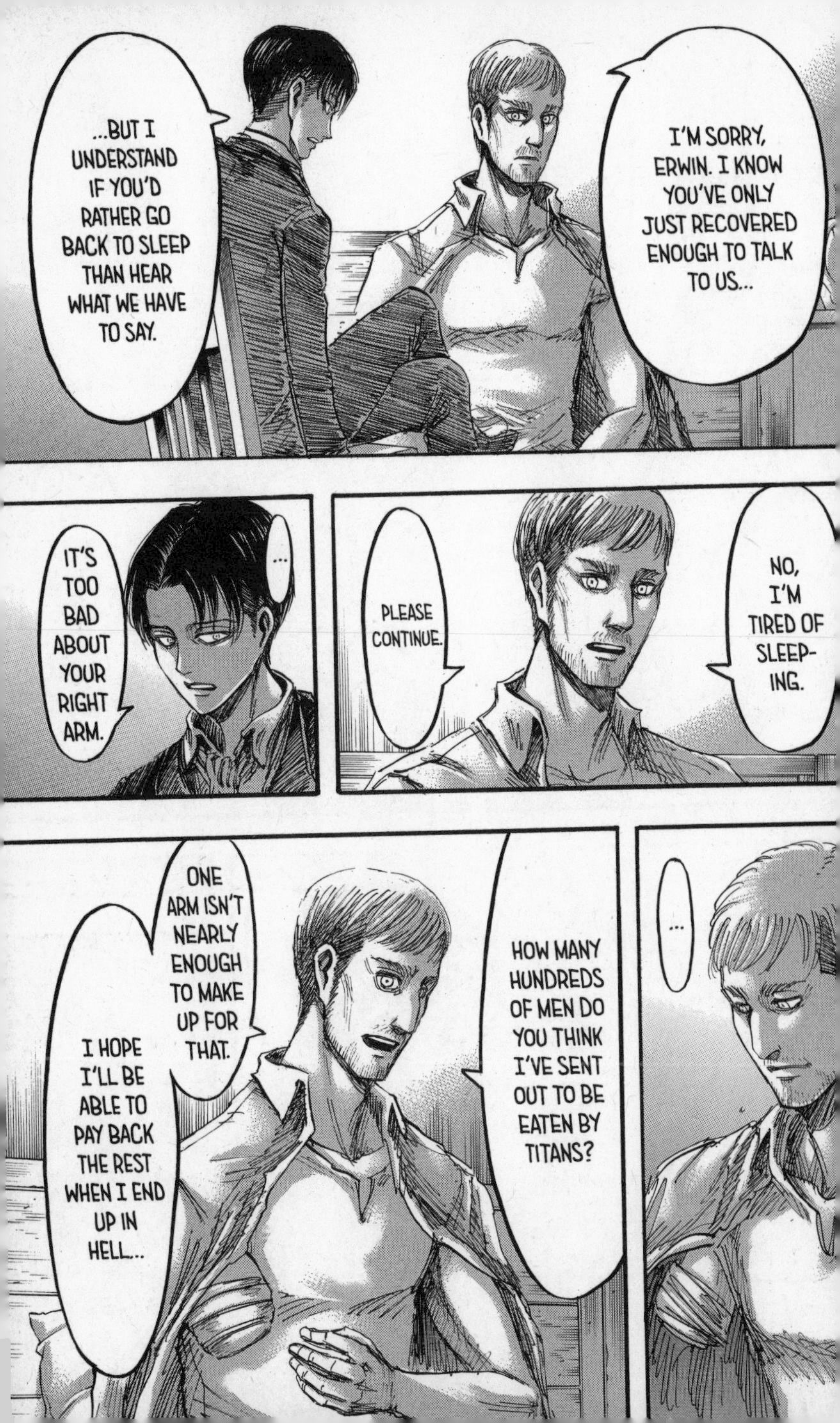
I'M SORRY, ERWIN. I KNOW YOU'VE ONLY JUST RECOVERED ENOUGH TO TALK TO US...
...BUT I UNDERSTAND IF YOU'D RATHER GO BACK TO SLEEP THAN HEAR WHAT WE HAVE TO SAY.
NO, I'M TIRED OF SLEEP-ING.
PLEASE CONTINUE.
...
IT'S TOO BAD ABOUT YOUR RIGHT ARM.
...
HOW MANY HUNDREDS OF MEN DO YOU THINK I'VE SENT OUT TO BE EATEN BY TITANS?
ONE ARM ISN'T NEARLY ENOUGH TO MAKE UP FOR THAT.
I HOPE I'LL BE ABLE TO PAY BACK THE REST WHEN I END UP IN HELL...

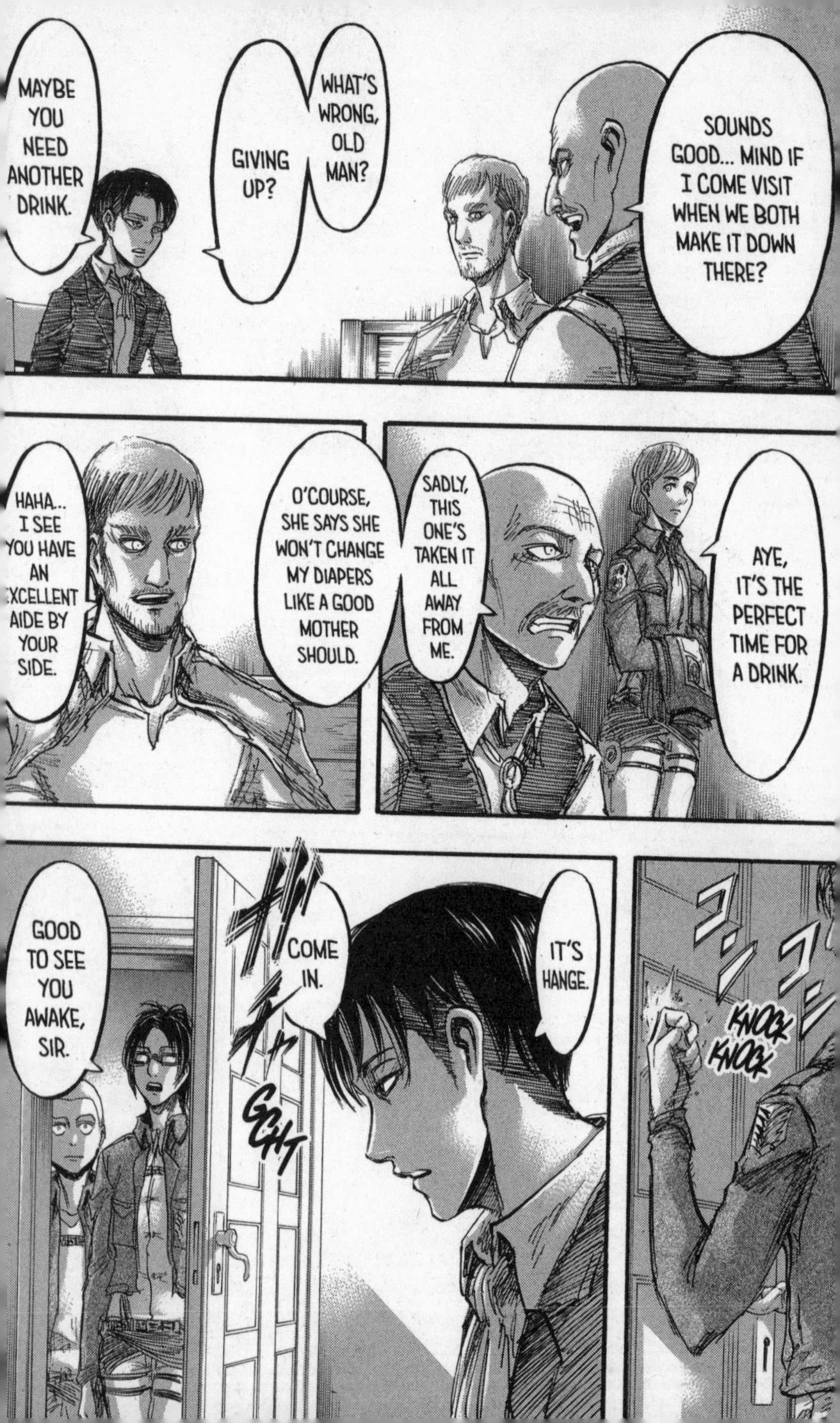

SOUNDS GOOD... MIND IF I COME VISIT WHEN WE BOTH MAKE IT DOWN THERE?
WHAT'S WRONG, OLD MAN?
GIVING UP?
MAYBE YOU NEED ANOTHER DRINK.
AYE, IT'S THE PERFECT TIME FOR A DRINK.
SADLY, THIS ONE'S TAKEN IT ALL AWAY FROM ME.
O'COURSE, SHE SAYS SHE WON'T CHANGE MY DIAPERS LIKE A GOOD MOTHER SHOULD.
HAHA... I SEE YOU HAVE AN EXCELLENT AIDE BY YOUR SIDE.
KNOCK KNOCK
IT'S HANGE.
COME IN.
GCHT
GOOD TO SEE YOU AWAKE, SIR.

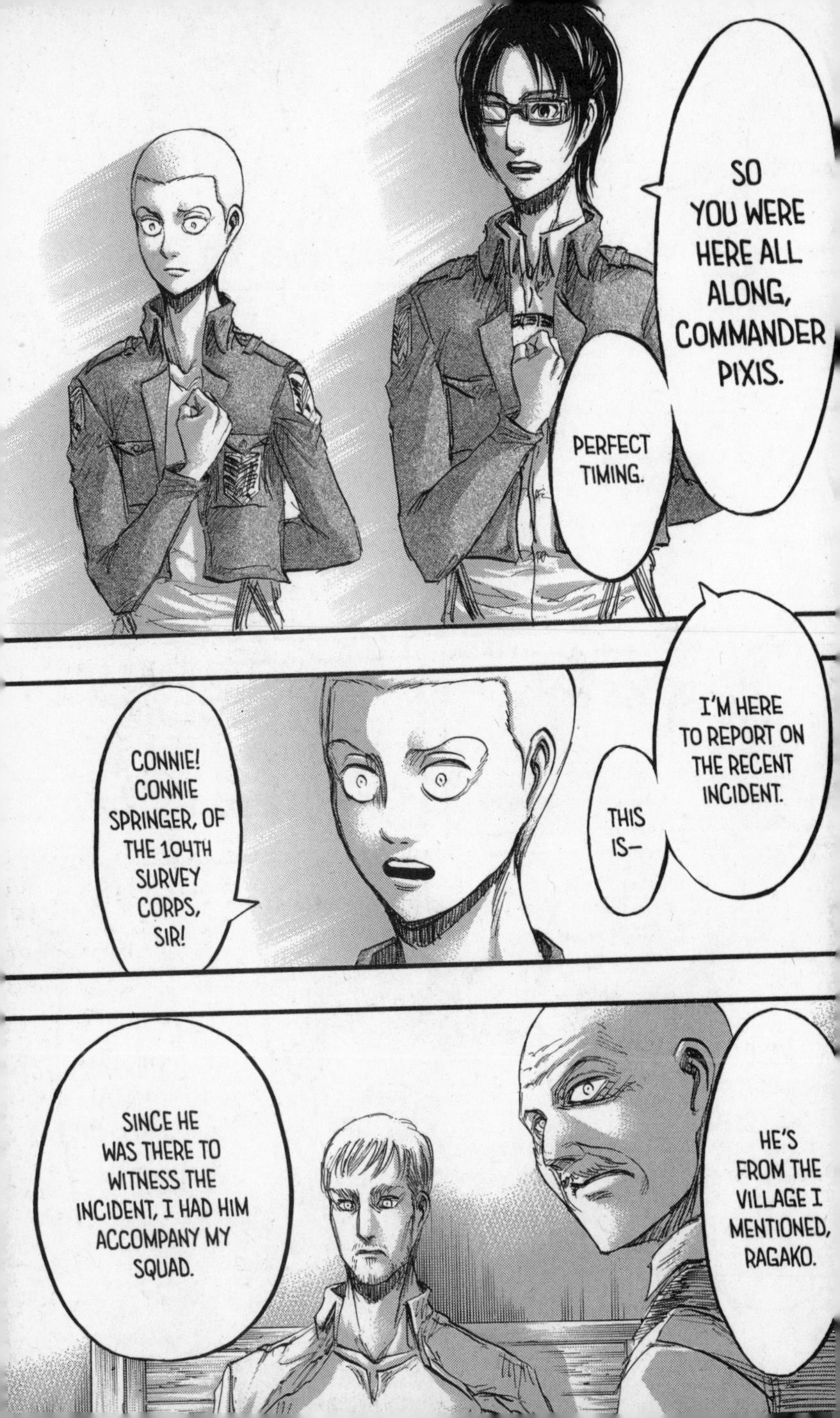
SO YOU WERE HERE ALL ALONG, COMMANDER PIXIS.
PERFECT TIMING.
I'M HERE TO REPORT ON THE RECENT INCIDENT.
THIS IS—
CONNIE! CONNIE SPRINGER, OF THE 104TH SURVEY CORPS, SIR!
HE'S FROM THE VILLAGE I MENTIONED, RAGAKO.
SINCE HE WAS THERE TO WITNESS THE INCIDENT, I HAD HIM ACCOMPANY MY SQUAD.

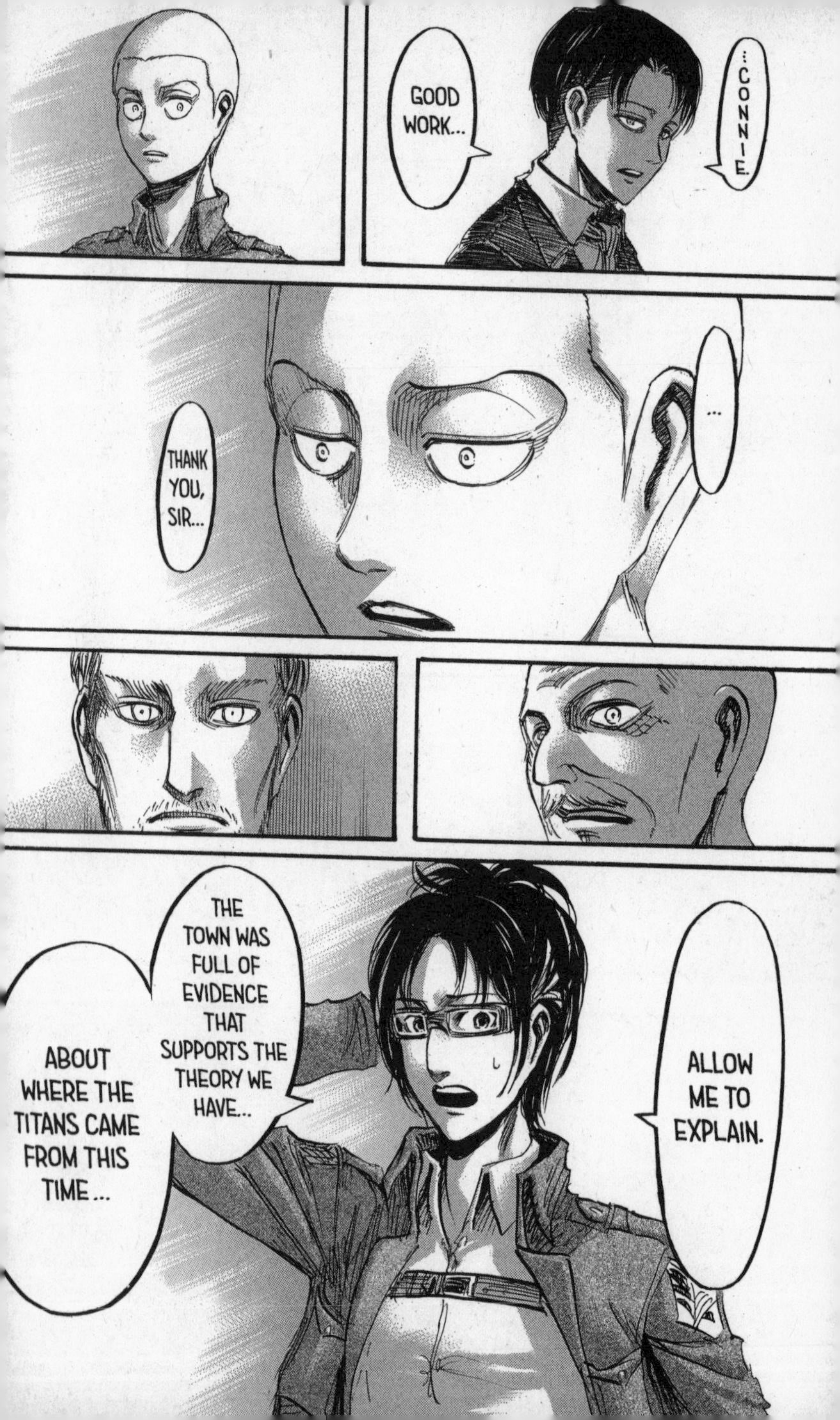
...CONNIE.
GOOD WORK...
...
THANK YOU, SIR...
ALLOW ME TO EXPLAIN.
THE TOWN WAS FULL OF EVIDENCE THAT SUPPORTS THE THEORY WE HAVE...
ABOUT WHERE THE TITANS CAME FROM THIS TIME...

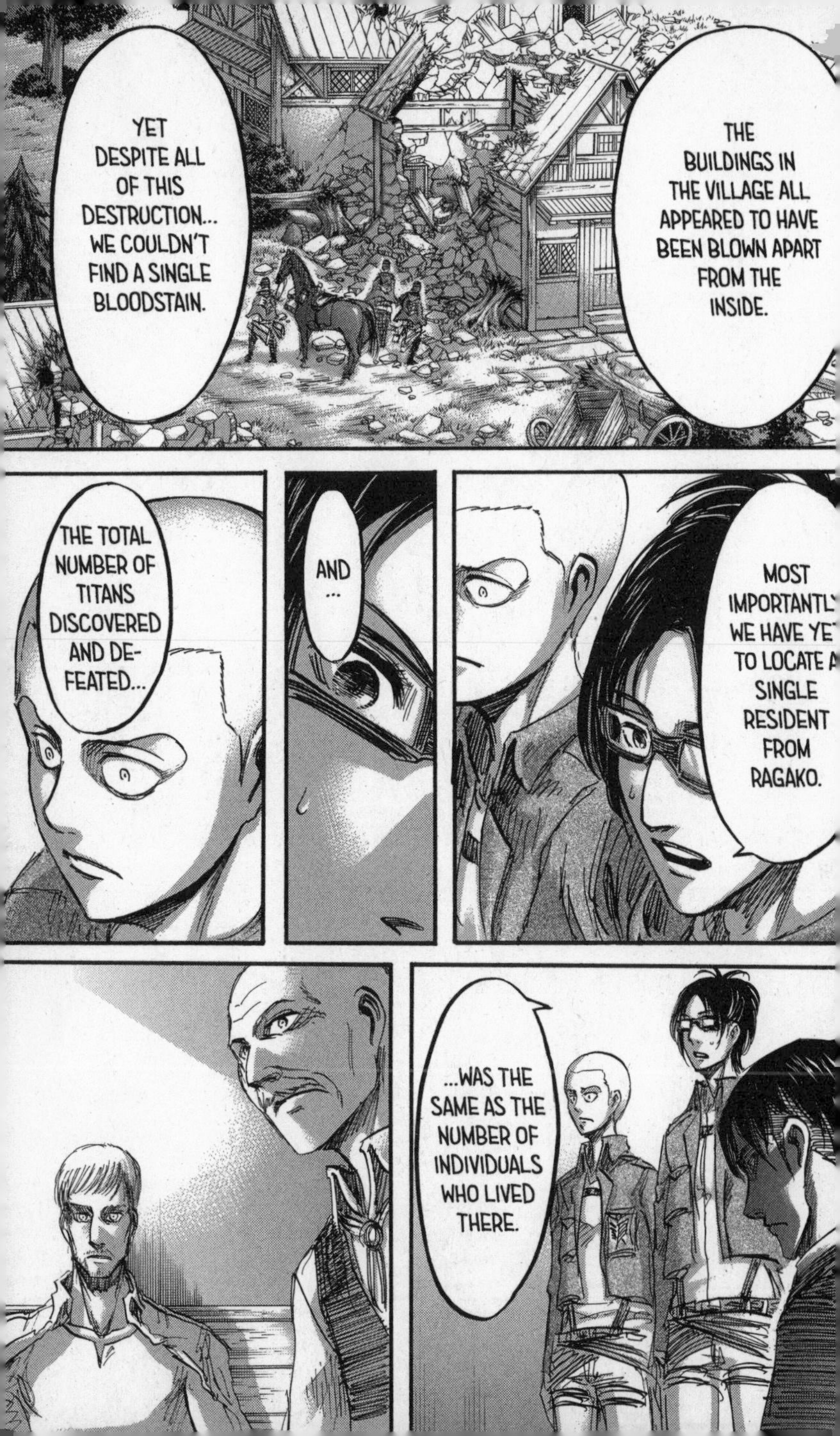
THE BUILDINGS IN THE VILLAGE ALL APPEARED TO HAVE BEEN BLOWN APART FROM THE INSIDE.
YET DESPITE ALL OF THIS DESTRUCTION... WE COULDN'T FIND A SINGLE BLOODSTAIN.
MOST IMPORTANTLY WE HAVE YET TO LOCATE A SINGLE RESIDENT FROM RAGAKO.
AND ...
THE TOTAL NUMBER OF TITANS DISCOVERED AND DE-FEATED...
...WAS THE SAME AS THE NUMBER OF INDIVIDUALS WHO LIVED THERE.

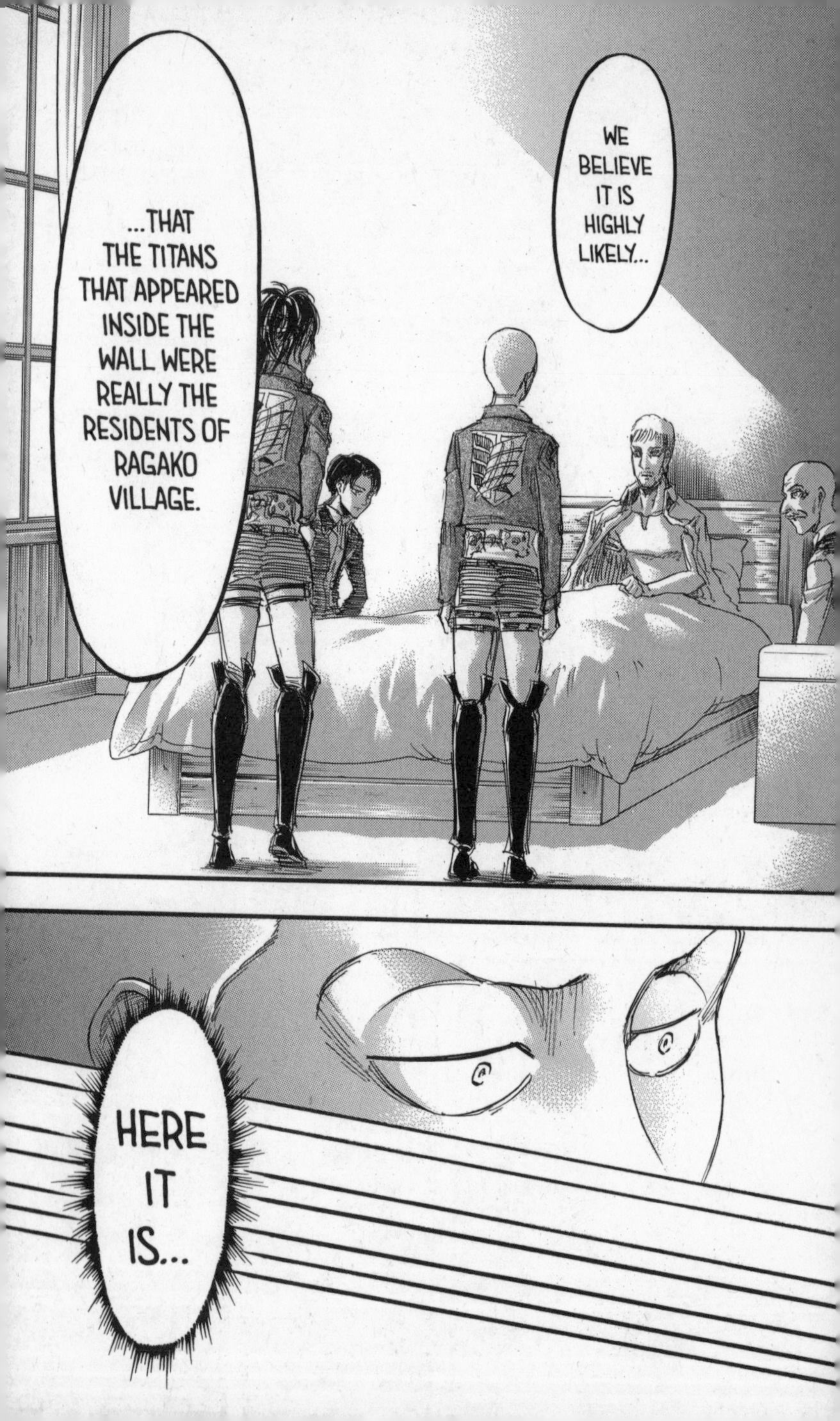
WE BELIEVE IT IS HIGHLY LIKELY...
...THAT THE TITANS THAT APPEARED INSIDE THE WALL WERE REALLY THE RESIDENTS OF RAGAKO VILLAGE.
HERE IT IS...

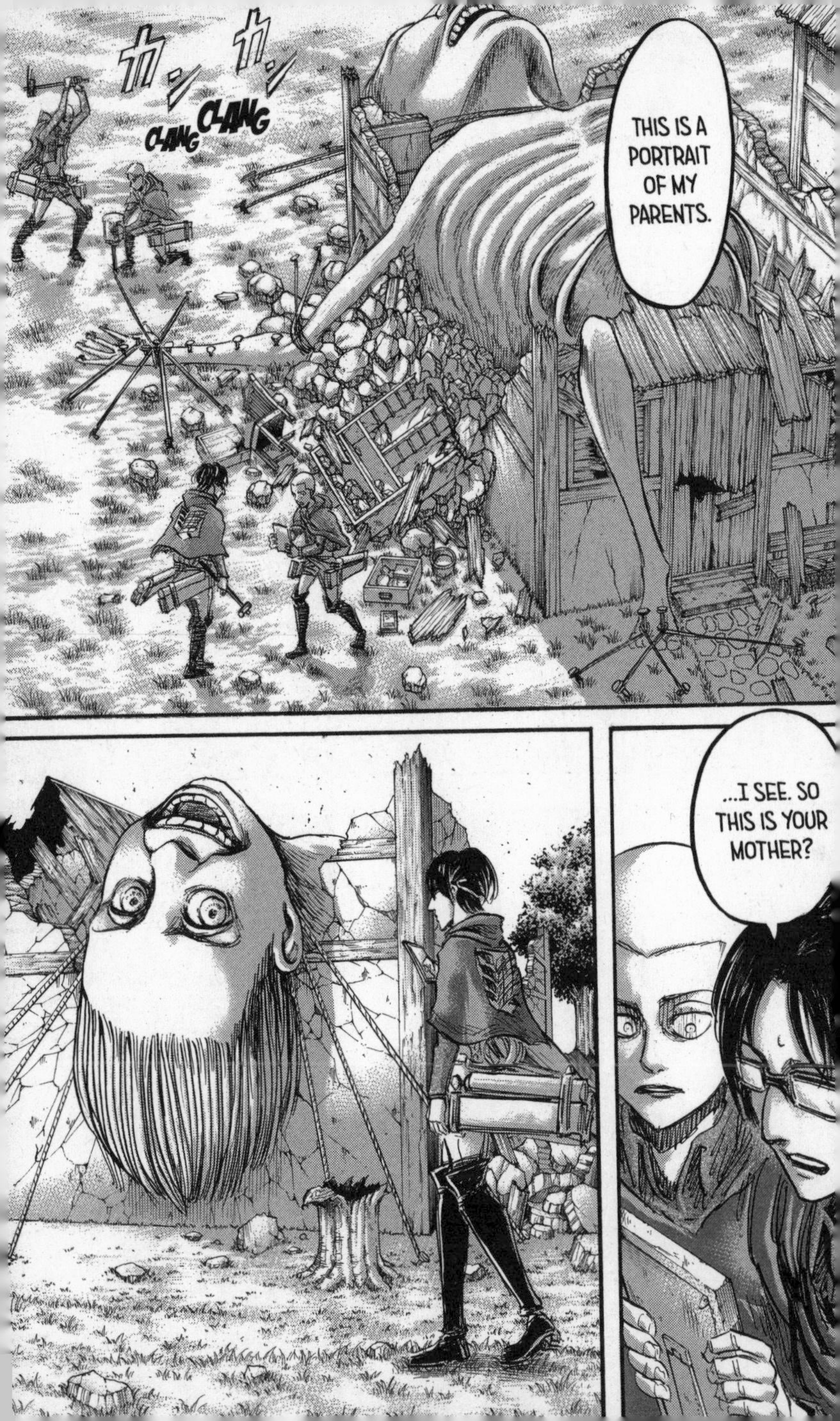
カン カン
CLANG CLANG
THIS IS A PORTRAIT OF MY PARENTS.
...I SEE. SO THIS IS YOUR MOTHER?

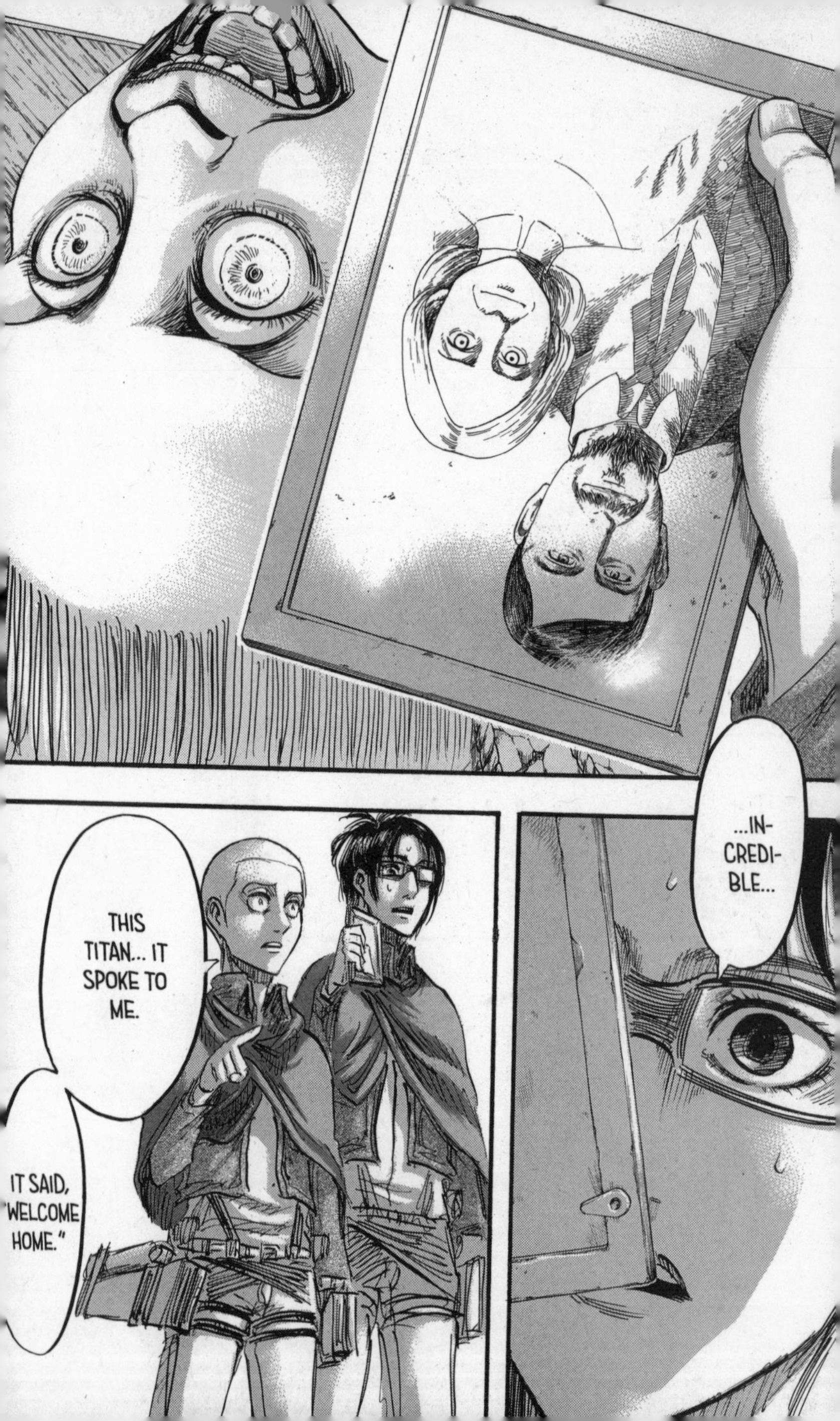
...IN-CREDI-BLE...
THIS TITAN... IT SPOKE TO ME.
IT SAID, "WELCOME HOME."

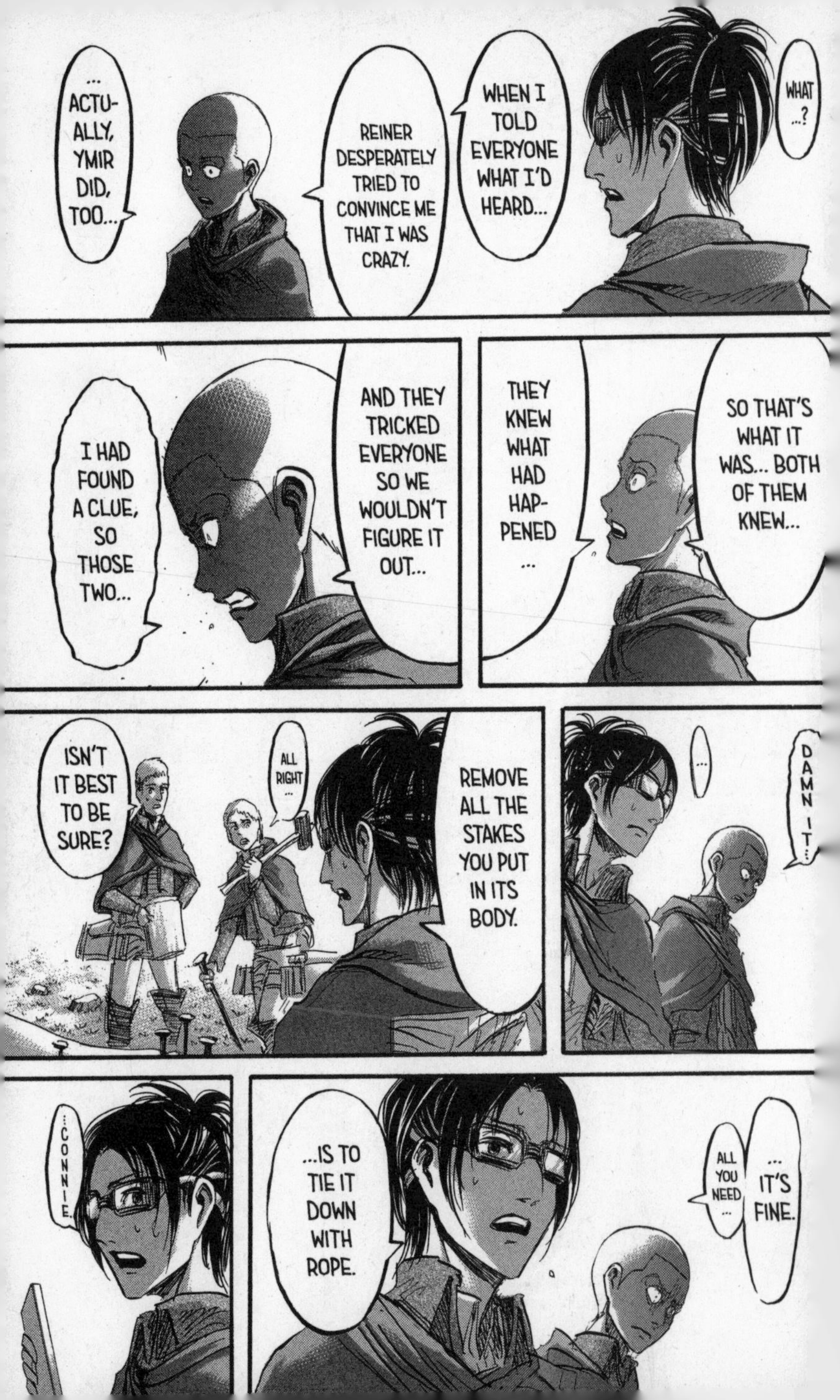
WHAT ...?
WHEN I TOLD EVERYONE WHAT I'D HEARD...
REINER DESPERATELY TRIED TO CONVINCE ME THAT I WAS CRAZY.
... ACTUALLY, YMIR DID, TOO...
SO THAT'S WHAT IT WAS... BOTH OF THEM KNEW...
THEY KNEW WHAT HAD HAPPENED ...
AND THEY TRICKED EVERYONE SO WE WOULDN'T FIGURE IT OUT...
I HAD FOUND A CLUE, SO THOSE TWO...
DAMN IT...
...
REMOVE ALL THE STAKES YOU PUT IN ITS BODY.
ALL RIGHT ...
ISN'T IT BEST TO BE SURE?
... IT'S FINE.
ALL YOU NEED ...
...IS TO TIE IT DOWN WITH ROPE.
...CONNIE.

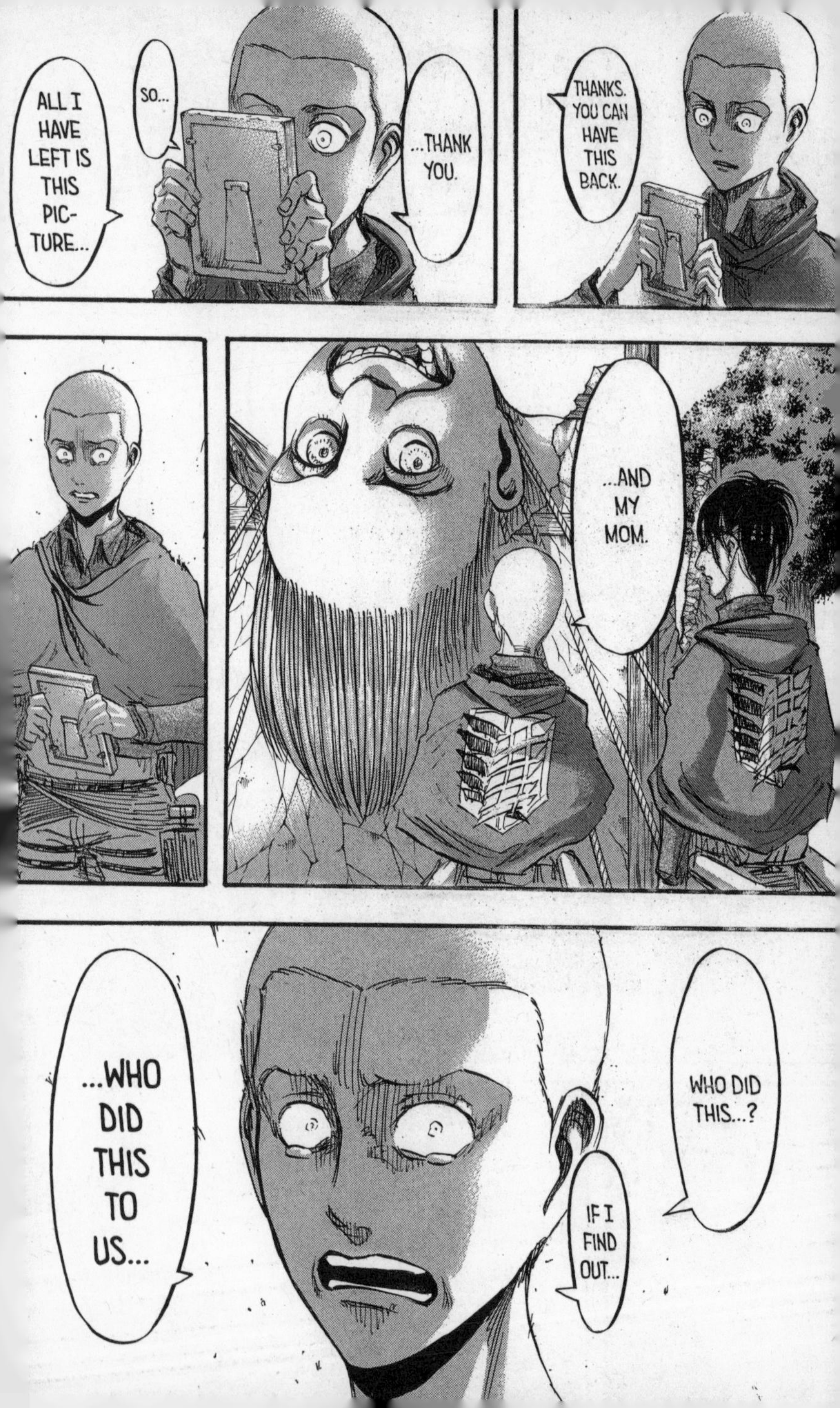
THANKS. YOU CAN HAVE THIS BACK.
...THANK YOU.
SO...
ALL I HAVE LEFT IS THIS PIC-TURE...
...AND MY MOM.
WHO DID THIS...?
IF I FIND OUT...
...WHO DID THIS TO US...

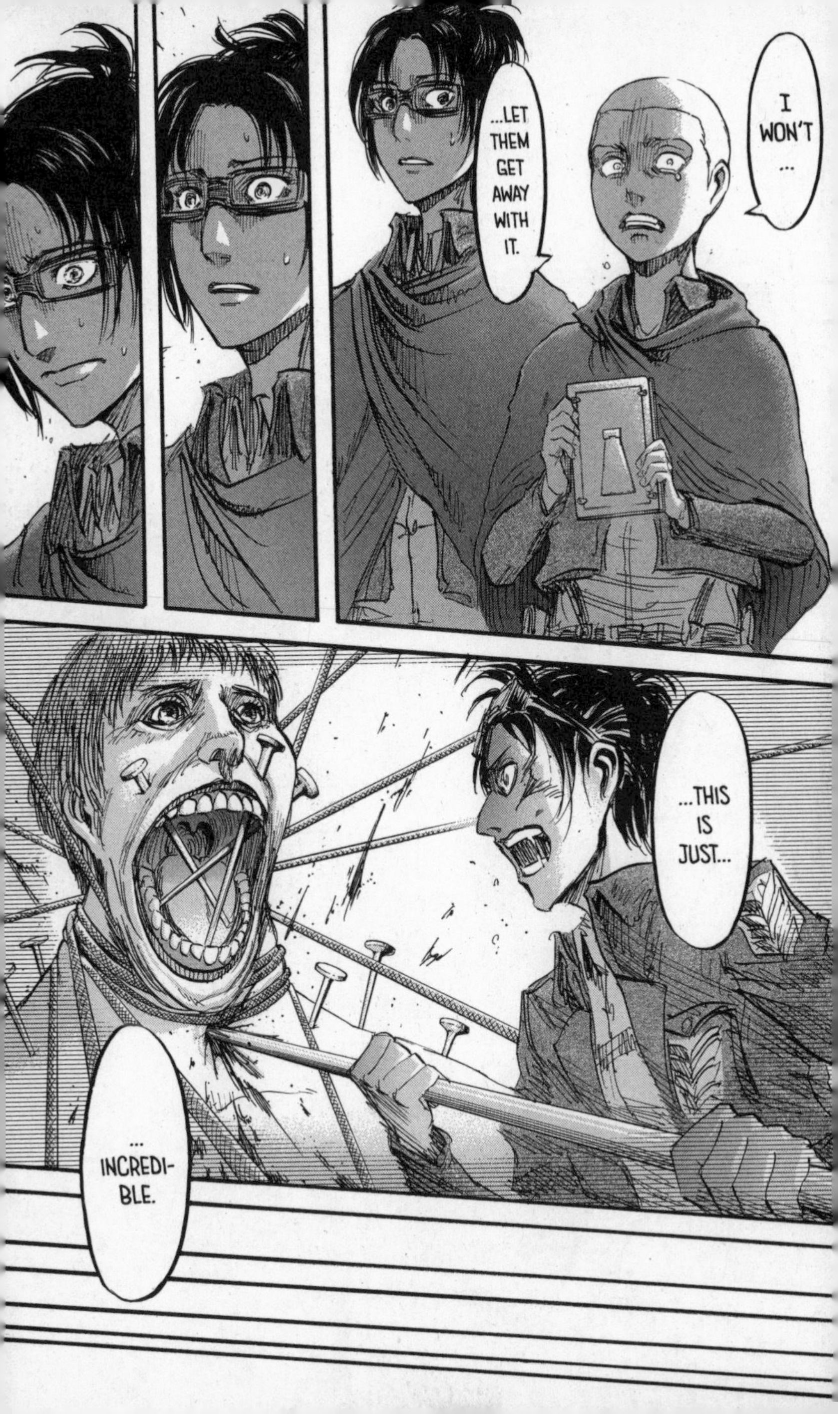
I WON'T ...
...LET THEM GET AWAY WITH IT.
...THIS IS JUST...
... INCREDI-BLE.

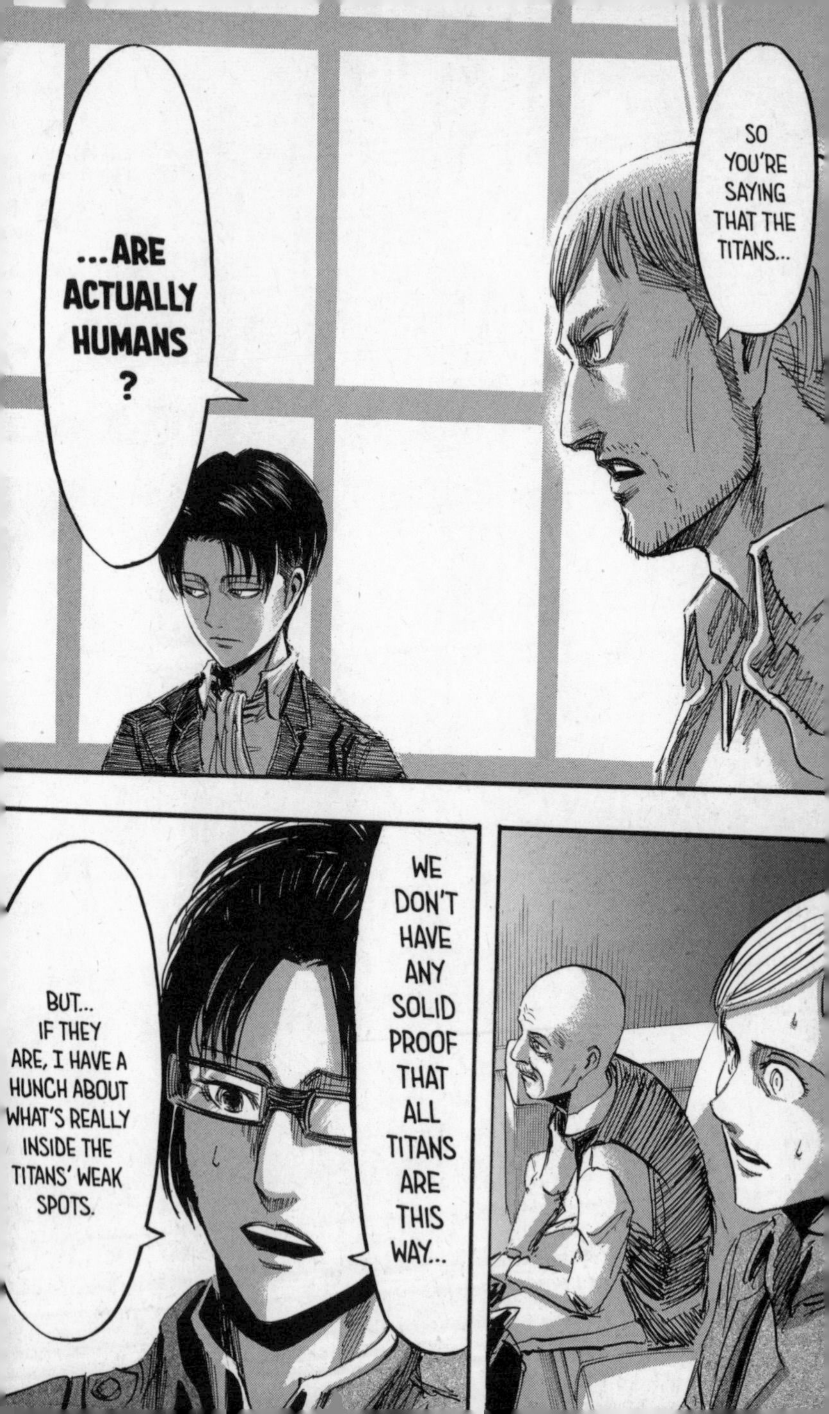
SO YOU'RE SAYING THAT THE TITANS...
...ARE ACTUALLY HUMANS?
WE DON'T HAVE ANY SOLID PROOF THAT ALL TITANS ARE THIS WAY...
BUT... IF THEY ARE, I HAVE A HUNCH ABOUT WHAT'S REALLY INSIDE THE TITANS' WEAK SPOTS.

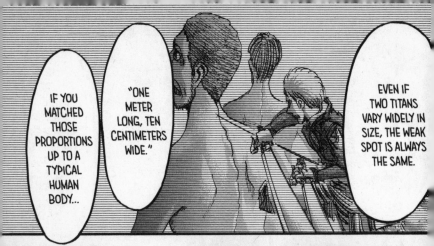

EVEN IF TWO TITANS VARY WIDELY IN SIZE, THE WEAK SPOT IS ALWAYS THE SAME.
"ONE METER LONG, TEN CENTIMETERS WIDE."
IF YOU MATCHED THOSE PROPORTIONS UP TO A TYPICAL HUMAN BODY...
...YOU'D GET THE SPINAL COLUMN, LEADING OUT OF THE BRAIN.
A TITAN CAN'T REGENERATE AND CEASES TO FUNCTION IF YOU CUT THIS AREA...
...PROBABLY BECAUSE THESE ORGANS ARE INDEPENDENT FROM THE REST OF THE TITAN'S BODY.

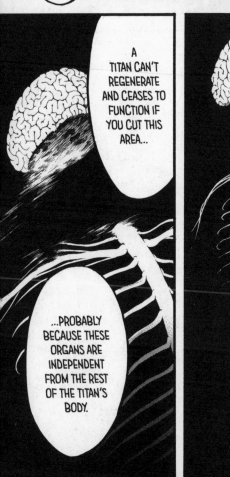

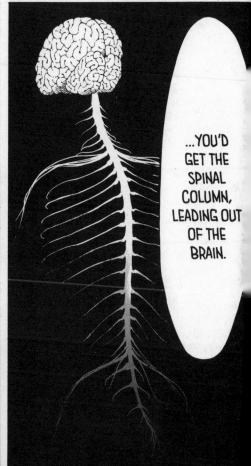

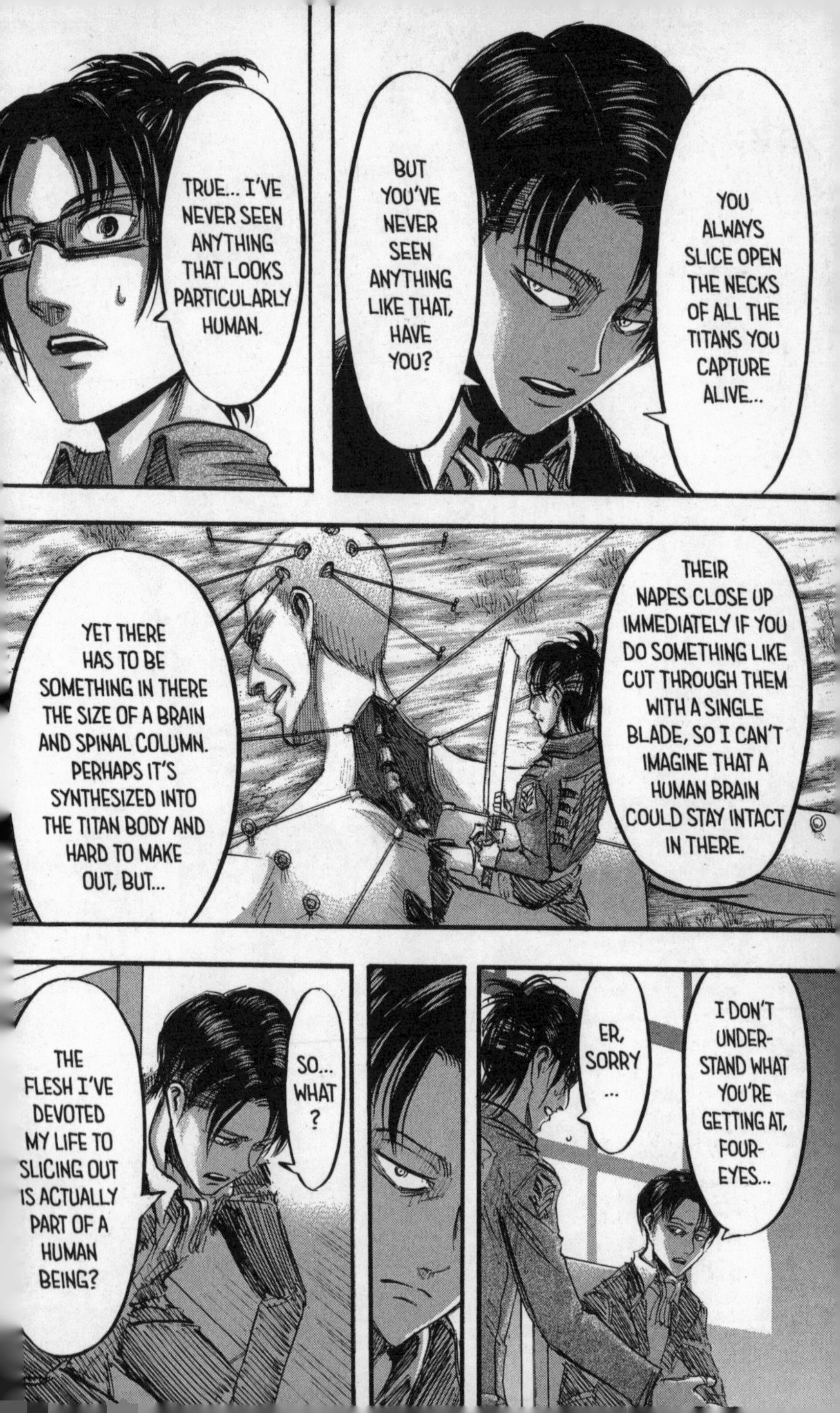
YOU ALWAYS SLICE OPEN THE NECKS OF ALL THE TITANS YOU CAPTURE ALIVE...
BUT YOU'VE NEVER SEEN ANYTHING LIKE THAT, HAVE YOU?
TRUE... I'VE NEVER SEEN ANYTHING THAT LOOKS PARTICULARLY HUMAN.
THEIR NAPES CLOSE UP IMMEDIATELY IF YOU DO SOMETHING LIKE CUT THROUGH THEM WITH A SINGLE BLADE, SO I CAN'T IMAGINE THAT A HUMAN BRAIN COULD STAY INTACT IN THERE.
YET THERE HAS TO BE SOMETHING IN THERE THE SIZE OF A BRAIN AND SPINAL COLUMN. PERHAPS IT'S SYNTHESIZED INTO THE TITAN BODY AND HARD TO MAKE OUT, BUT...
I DON'T UNDER-STAND WHAT YOU'RE GETTING AT, FOUR-EYES...
ER, SORRY...
SO... WHAT?
THE FLESH I'VE DEVOTED MY LIFE TO SLICING OUT IS ACTUALLY PART OF A HUMAN BEING?

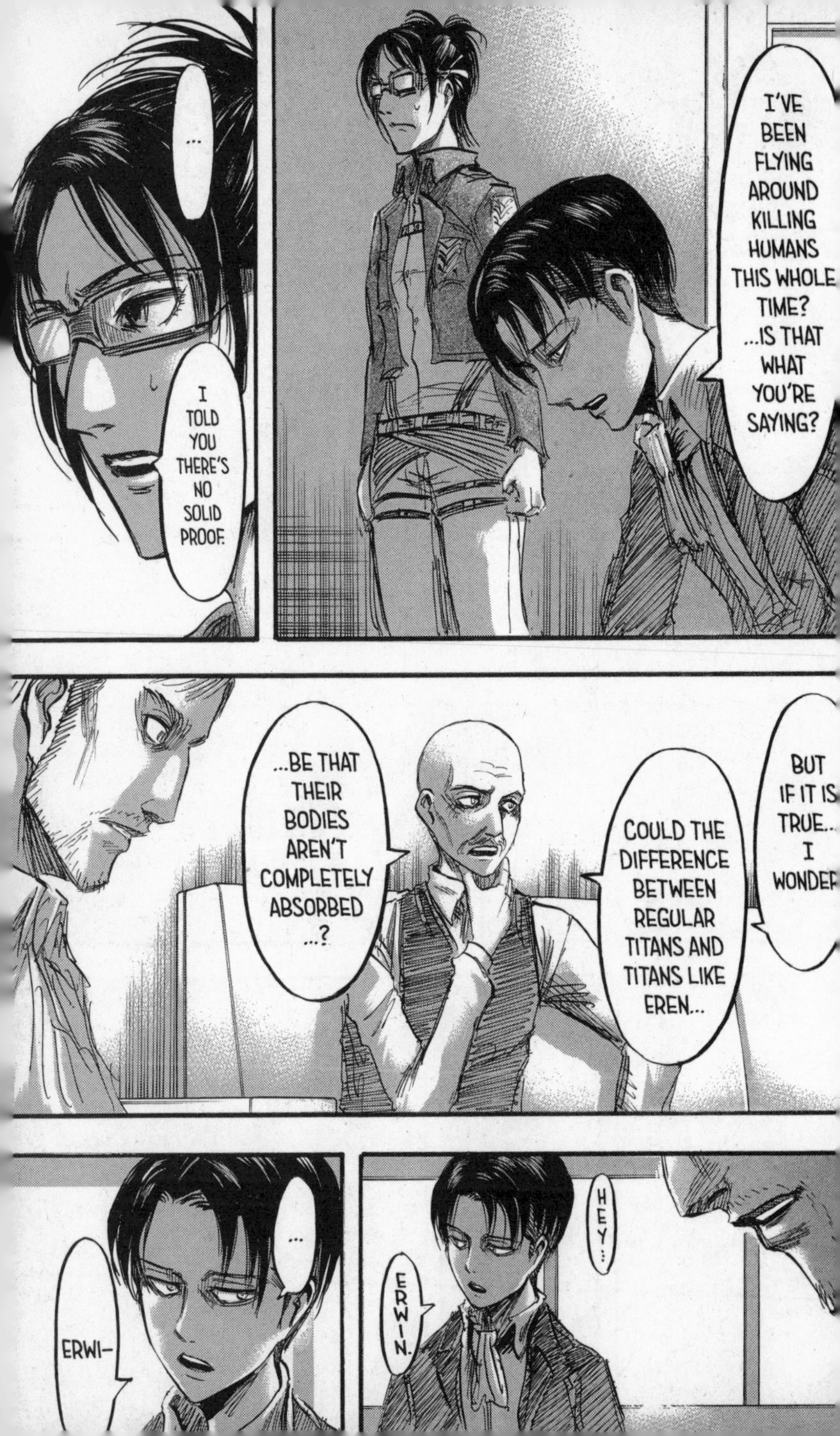
I'VE BEEN FLYING AROUND KILLING HUMANS THIS WHOLE TIME? ...IS THAT WHAT YOU'RE SAYING?
...
I TOLD YOU THERE'S NO SOLID PROOF.
BUT IF IT IS TRUE... I WONDER
COULD THE DIFFERENCE BETWEEN REGULAR TITANS AND TITANS LIKE EREN...
...BE THAT THEIR BODIES AREN'T COMPLETELY ABSORBED ...?
HEY...
ERWIN.
...
ERWI-

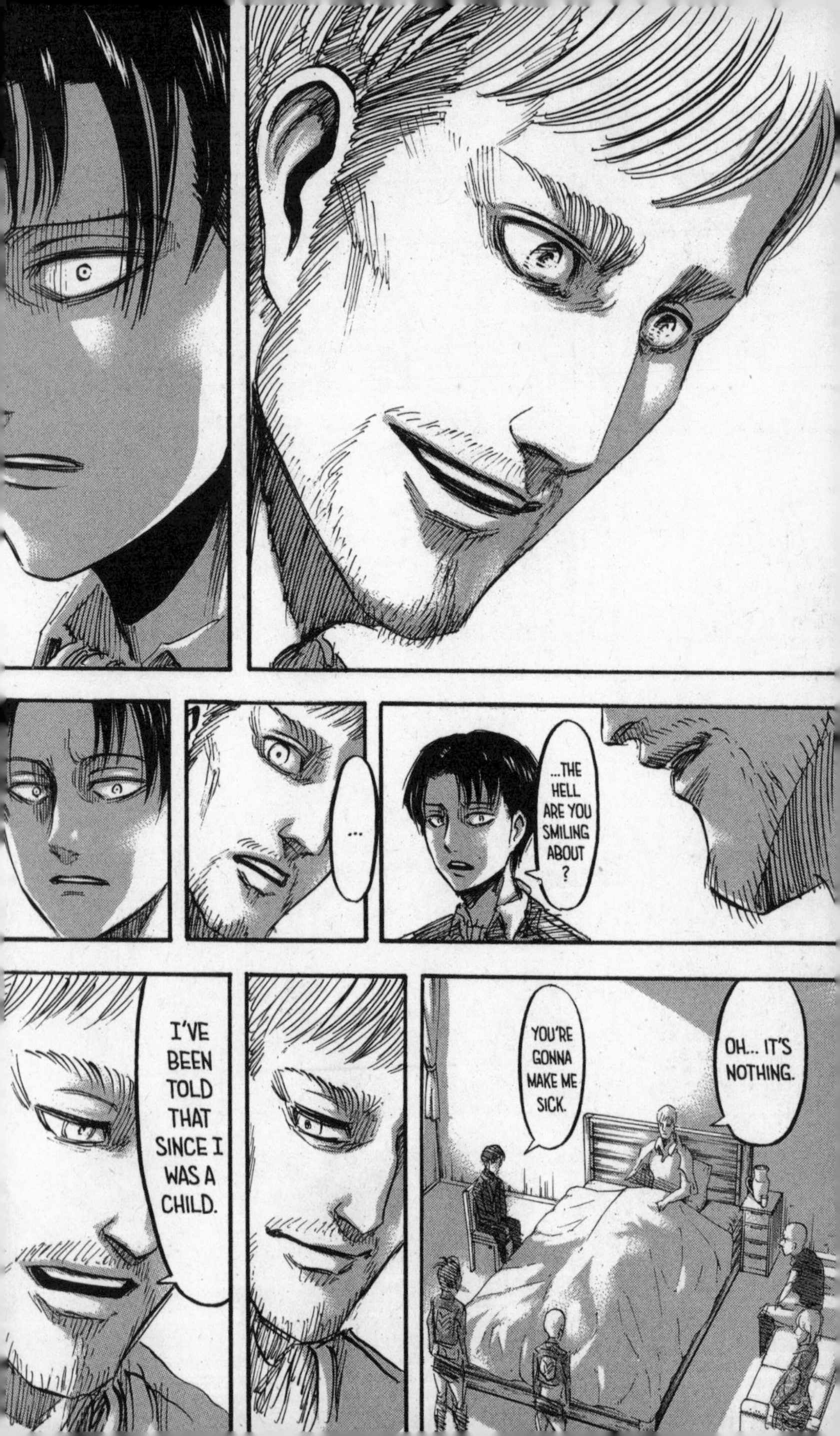
...THE HELL ARE YOU SMILING ABOUT ?
...
OH... IT'S NOTHING.
YOU'RE GONNA MAKE ME SICK.
I'VE BEEN TOLD THAT SINCE I WAS A CHILD.

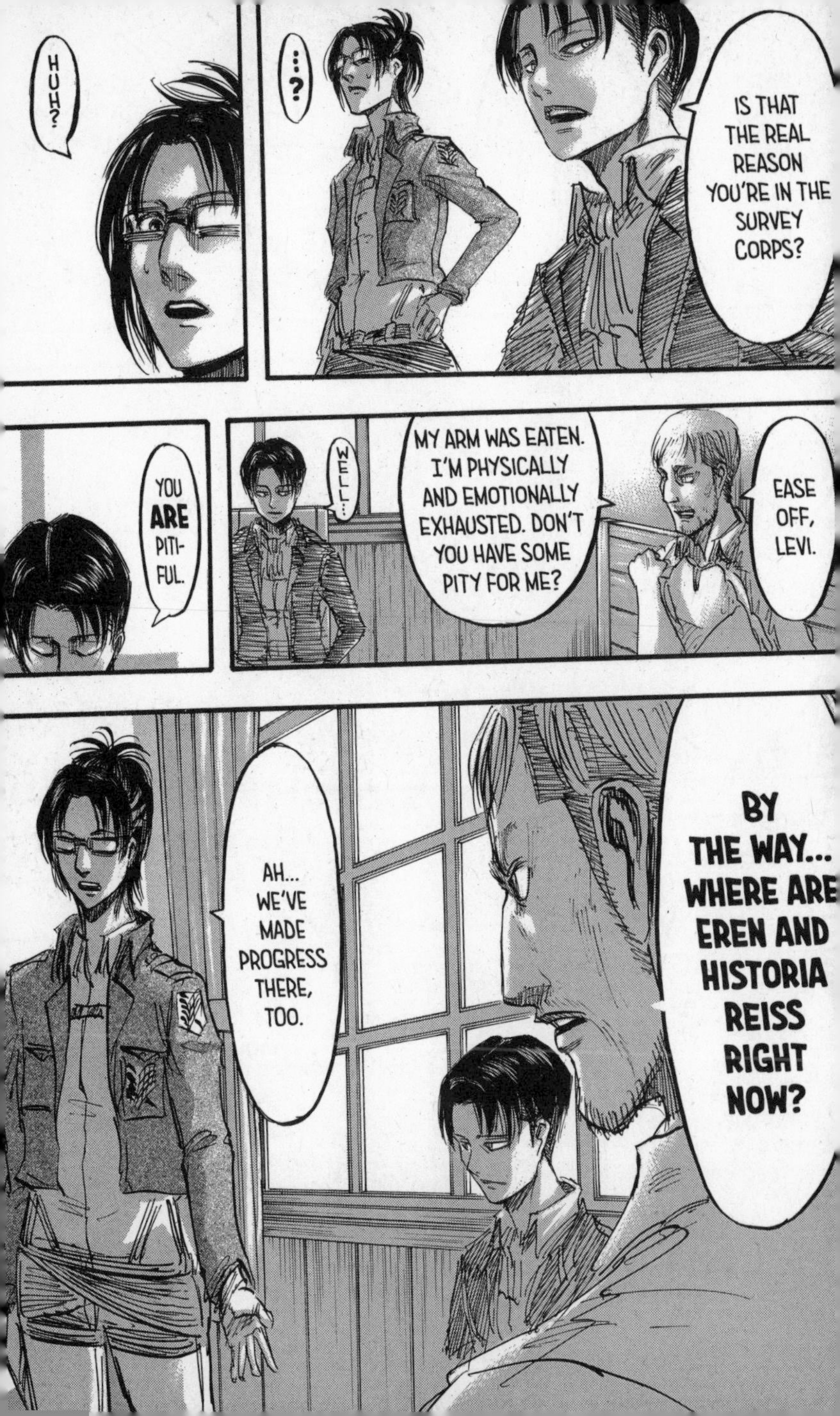
IS THAT THE REAL REASON YOU'RE IN THE SURVEY CORPS?
...?
HUH?
EASE OFF, LEVI.
MY ARM WAS EATEN. I'M PHYSICALLY AND EMOTIONALLY EXHAUSTED. DON'T YOU HAVE SOME PITY FOR ME?
WELL...
YOU **ARE** PITIFUL.
BY THE WAY... WHERE ARE EREN AND HISTORIA REISS RIGHT NOW?
AH... WE'VE MADE PROGRESS THERE, TOO.

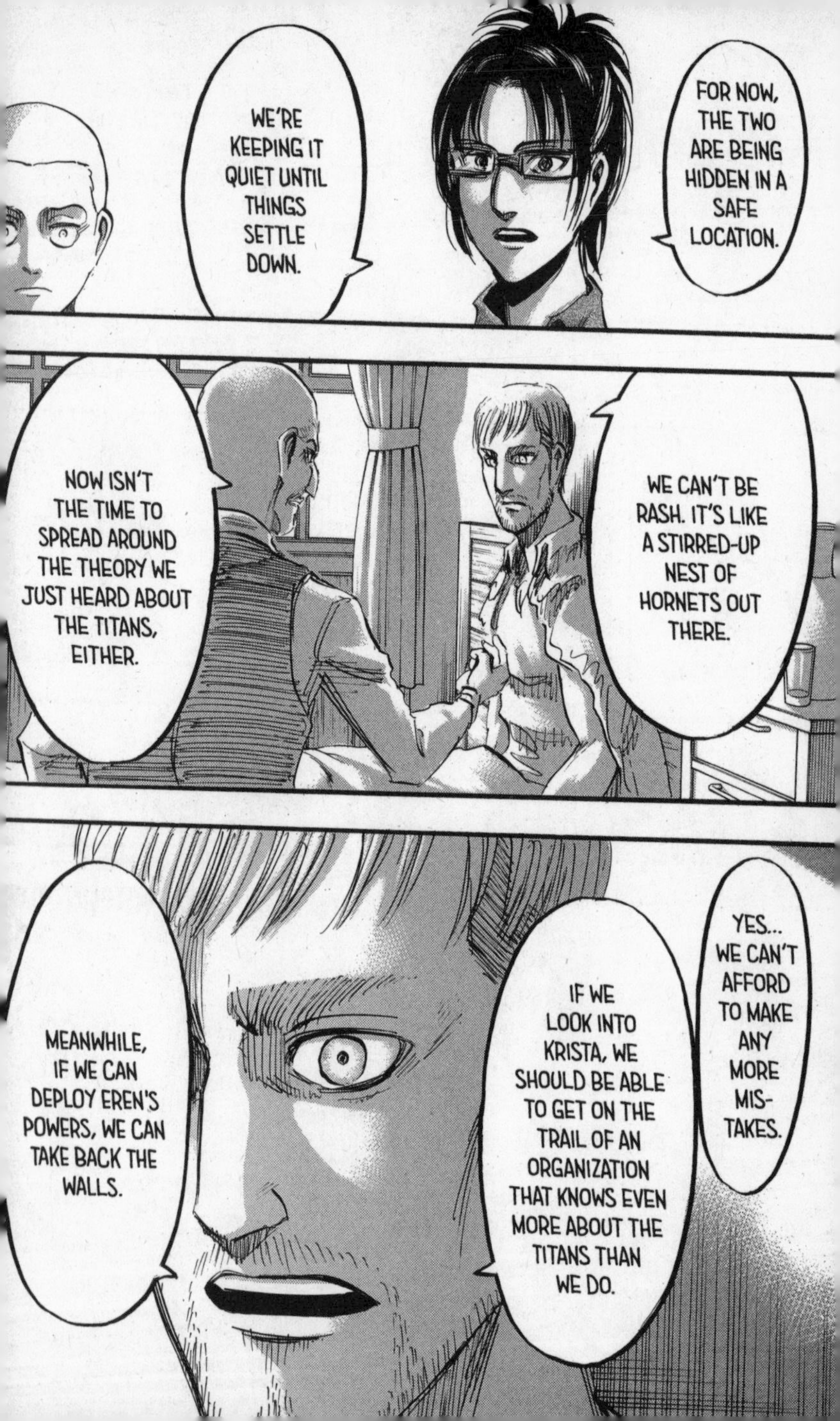
FOR NOW, THE TWO ARE BEING HIDDEN IN A SAFE LOCATION.
WE'RE KEEPING IT QUIET UNTIL THINGS SETTLE DOWN.
WE CAN'T BE RASH. IT'S LIKE A STIRRED-UP NEST OF HORNETS OUT THERE.
NOW ISN'T THE TIME TO SPREAD AROUND THE THEORY WE JUST HEARD ABOUT THE TITANS, EITHER.
YES... WE CAN'T AFFORD TO MAKE ANY MORE MIS-TAKES.
IF WE LOOK INTO KRISTA, WE SHOULD BE ABLE TO GET ON THE TRAIL OF AN ORGANIZATION THAT KNOWS EVEN MORE ABOUT THE TITANS THAN WE DO.
MEANWHILE, IF WE CAN DEPLOY EREN'S POWERS, WE CAN TAKE BACK THE WALLS.

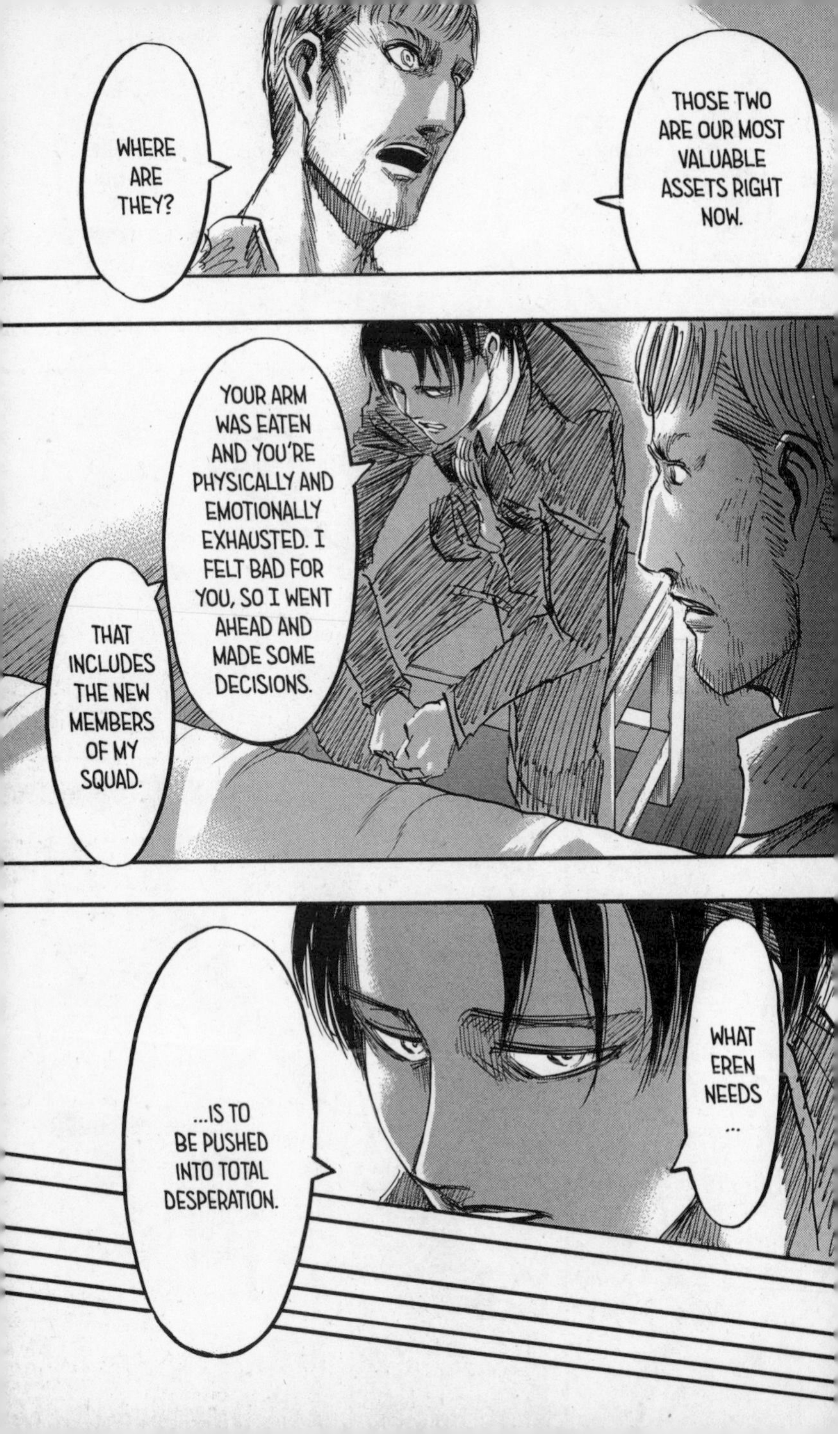
THOSE TWO ARE OUR MOST VALUABLE ASSETS RIGHT NOW.
WHERE ARE THEY?
YOUR ARM WAS EATEN AND YOU'RE PHYSICALLY AND EMOTIONALLY EXHAUSTED. I FELT BAD FOR YOU, SO I WENT AHEAD AND MADE SOME DECISIONS.
THAT INCLUDES THE NEW MEMBERS OF MY SQUAD.
WHAT EREN NEEDS ...
...IS TO BE PUSHED INTO TOTAL DESPERATION.

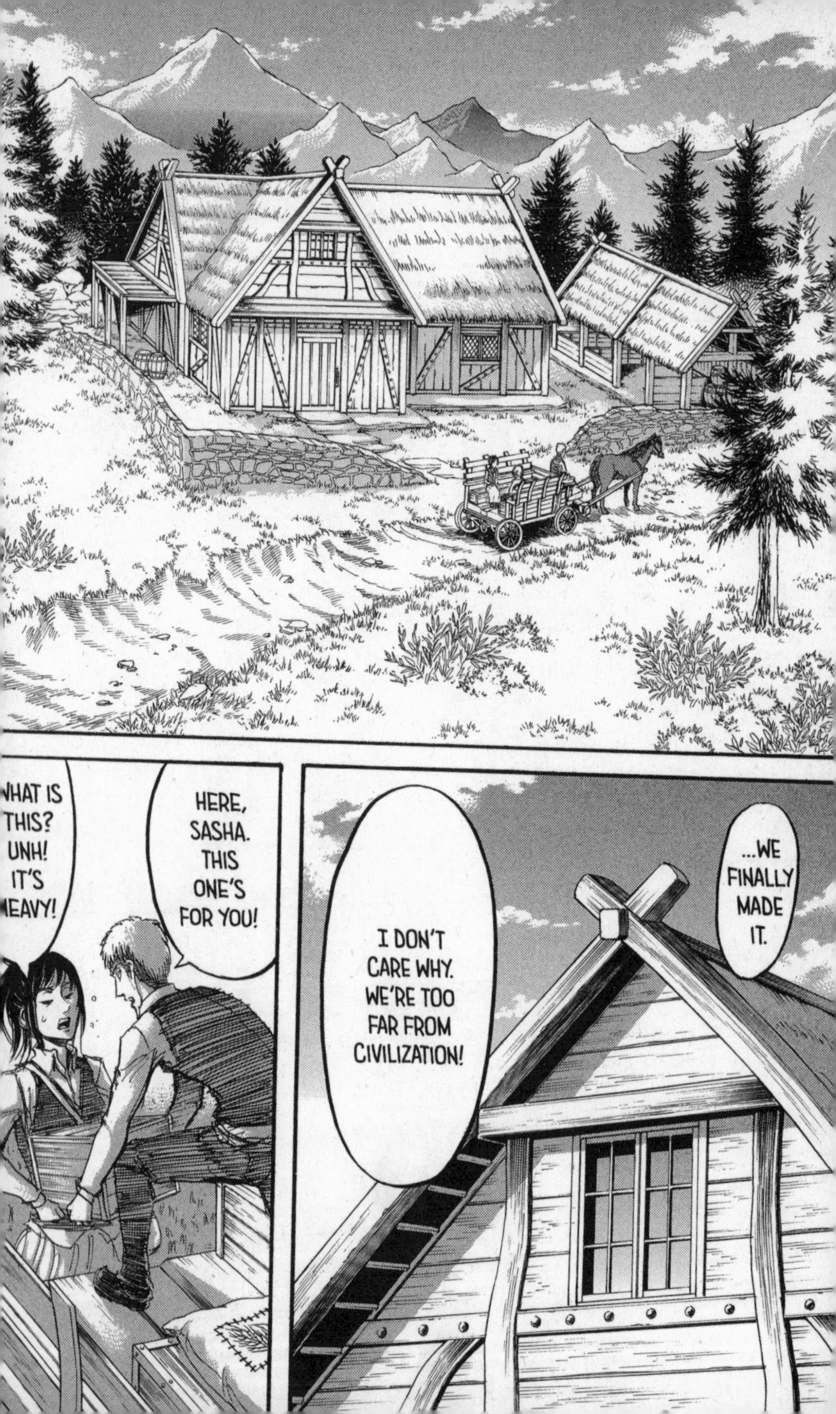
...WE FINALLY MADE IT.
I DON'T CARE WHY. WE'RE TOO FAR FROM CIVILIZATION!
HERE, SASHA. THIS ONE'S FOR YOU!
WHAT IS THIS? UNH! IT'S HEAVY!

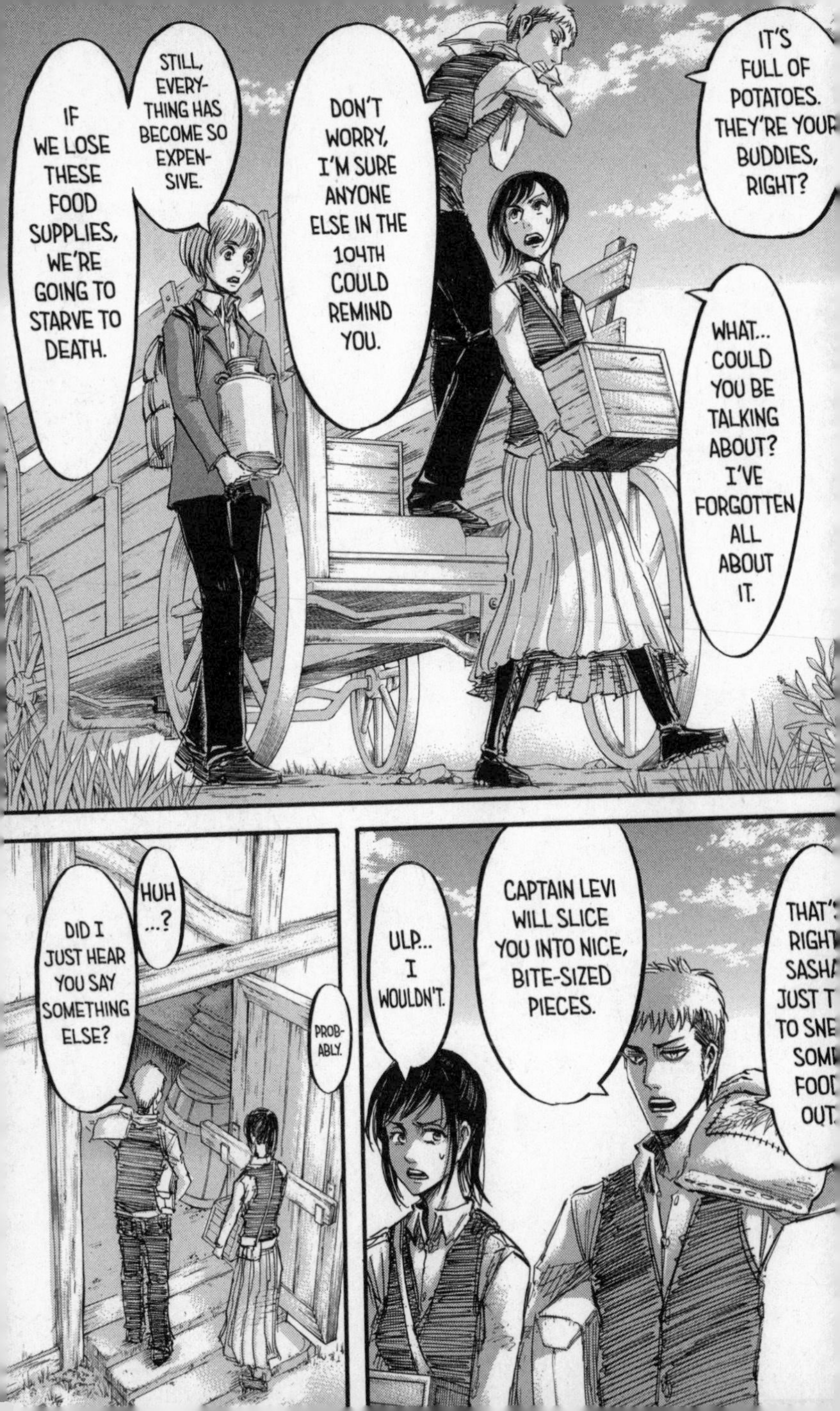
IT'S FULL OF POTATOES. THEY'RE YOUR BUDDIES, RIGHT?
WHAT... COULD YOU BE TALKING ABOUT? I'VE FORGOTTEN ALL ABOUT IT.
DON'T WORRY, I'M SURE ANYONE ELSE IN THE 104TH COULD REMIND YOU.
STILL, EVERYTHING HAS BECOME SO EXPENSIVE.
IF WE LOSE THESE FOOD SUPPLIES, WE'RE GOING TO STARVE TO DEATH.
THAT' RIGHT SASH JUST T TO SNE SOM FOOD OUT.
CAPTAIN LEVI WILL SLICE YOU INTO NICE, BITE-SIZED PIECES.
ULP... I WOULDN'T.
HUH ...?
DID I JUST HEAR YOU SAY SOMETHING ELSE?
PROBABLY.

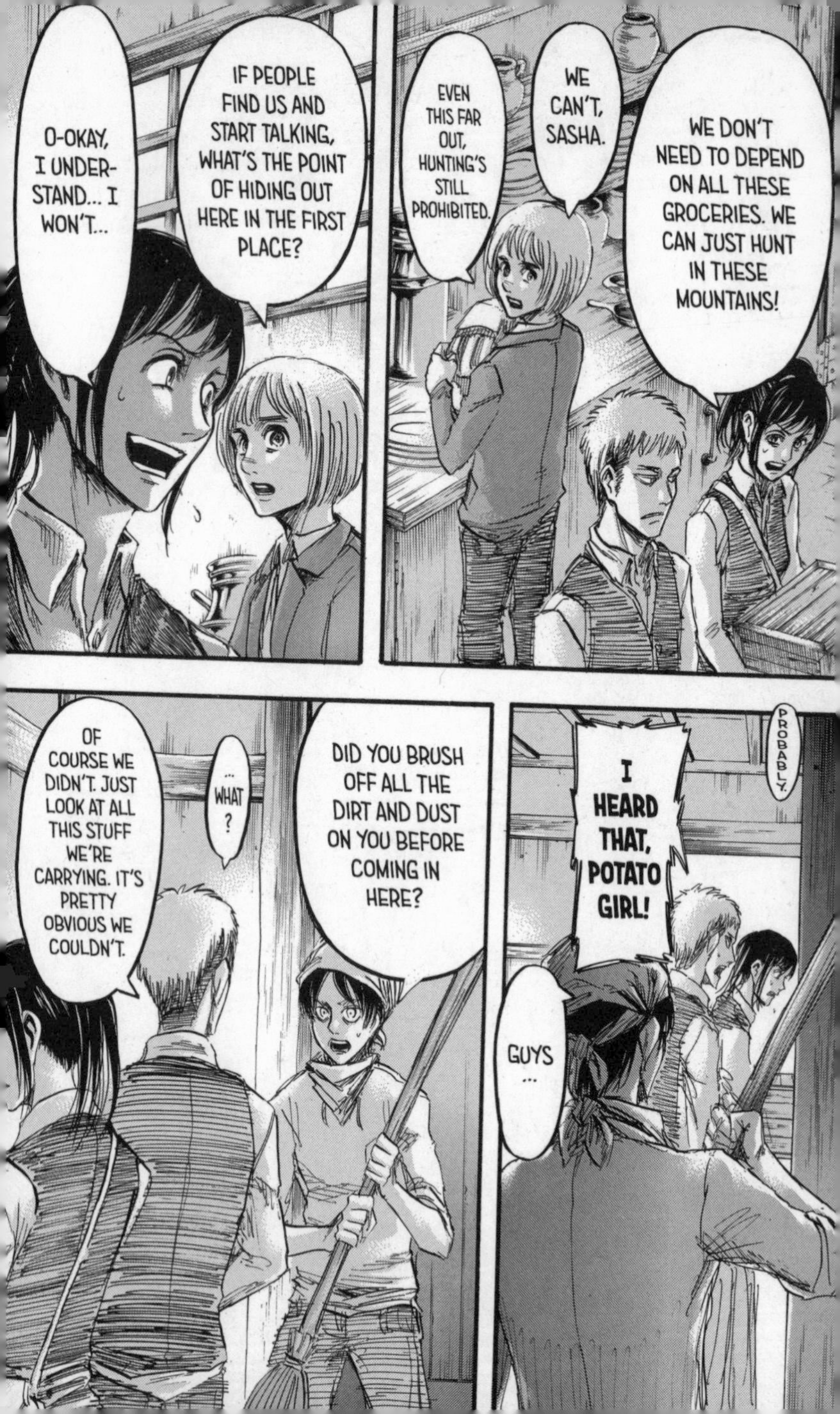
WE DON'T NEED TO DEPEND ON ALL THESE GROCERIES. WE CAN JUST HUNT IN THESE MOUNTAINS!
WE CAN'T, SASHA.
EVEN THIS FAR OUT, HUNTING'S STILL PROHIBITED.
IF PEOPLE FIND US AND START TALKING, WHAT'S THE POINT OF HIDING OUT HERE IN THE FIRST PLACE?
O-OKAY, I UNDER-STAND... I WON'T...
PROBABLY.
I HEARD THAT, POTATO GIRL!
GUYS ...
DID YOU BRUSH OFF ALL THE DIRT AND DUST ON YOU BEFORE COMING IN HERE?
... WHAT ?
OF COURSE WE DIDN'T. JUST LOOK AT ALL THIS STUFF WE'RE CARRYING. IT'S PRETTY OBVIOUS WE COULDN'T.

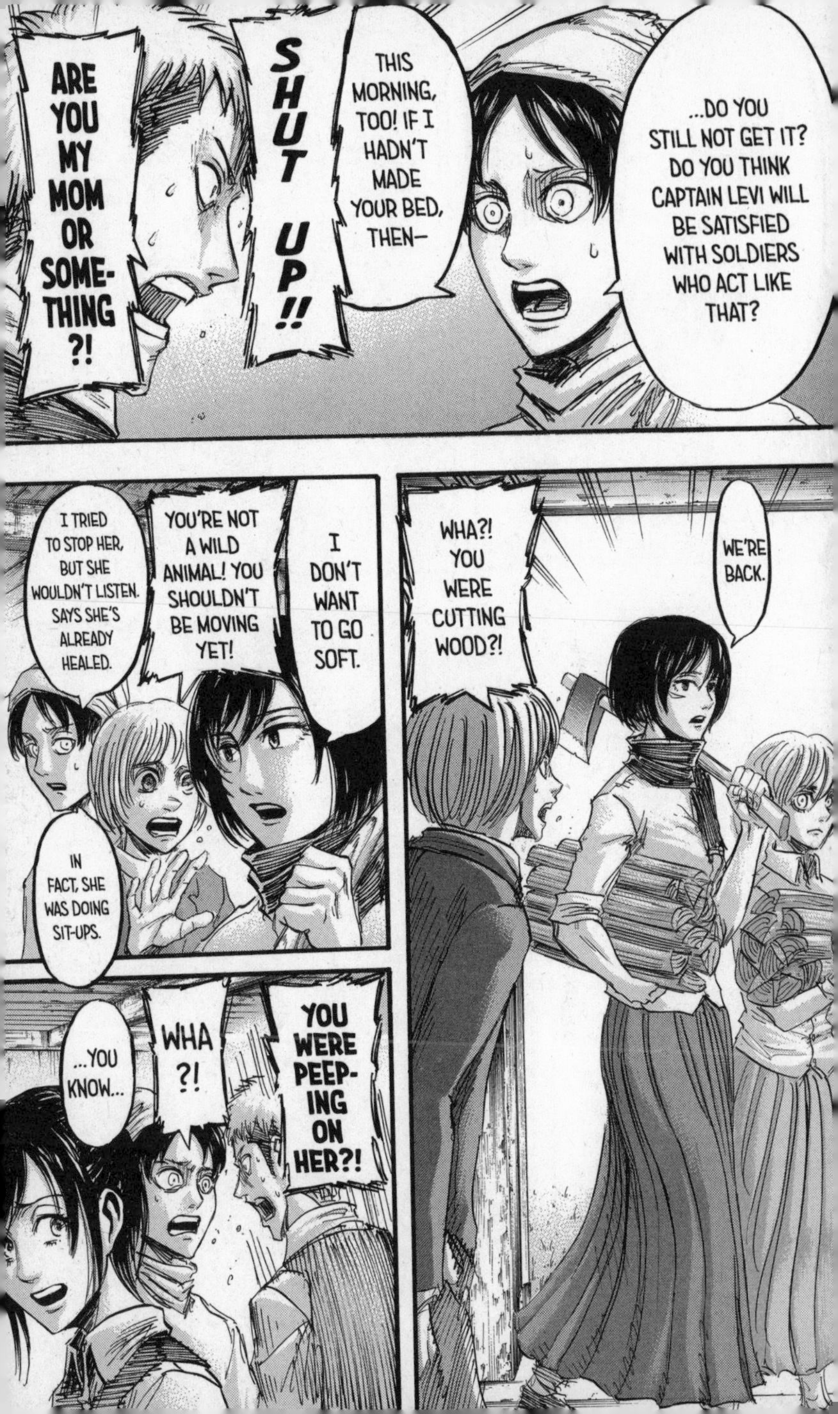
...DO YOU STILL NOT GET IT? DO YOU THINK CAPTAIN LEVI WILL BE SATISFIED WITH SOLDIERS WHO ACT LIKE THAT?
THIS MORNING, TOO! IF I HADN'T MADE YOUR BED, THEN—
SHUT UP!!
ARE YOU MY MOM OR SOME-THING?!
WE'RE BACK.
WHA?! YOU WERE CUTTING WOOD?!
I DON'T WANT TO GO SOFT.
YOU'RE NOT A WILD ANIMAL! YOU SHOULDN'T BE MOVING YET!
I TRIED TO STOP HER, BUT SHE WOULDN'T LISTEN. SAYS SHE'S ALREADY HEALED.
IN FACT, SHE WAS DOING SIT-UPS.
YOU WERE PEEP-ING ON HER?!
WHA?!
...YOU KNOW...

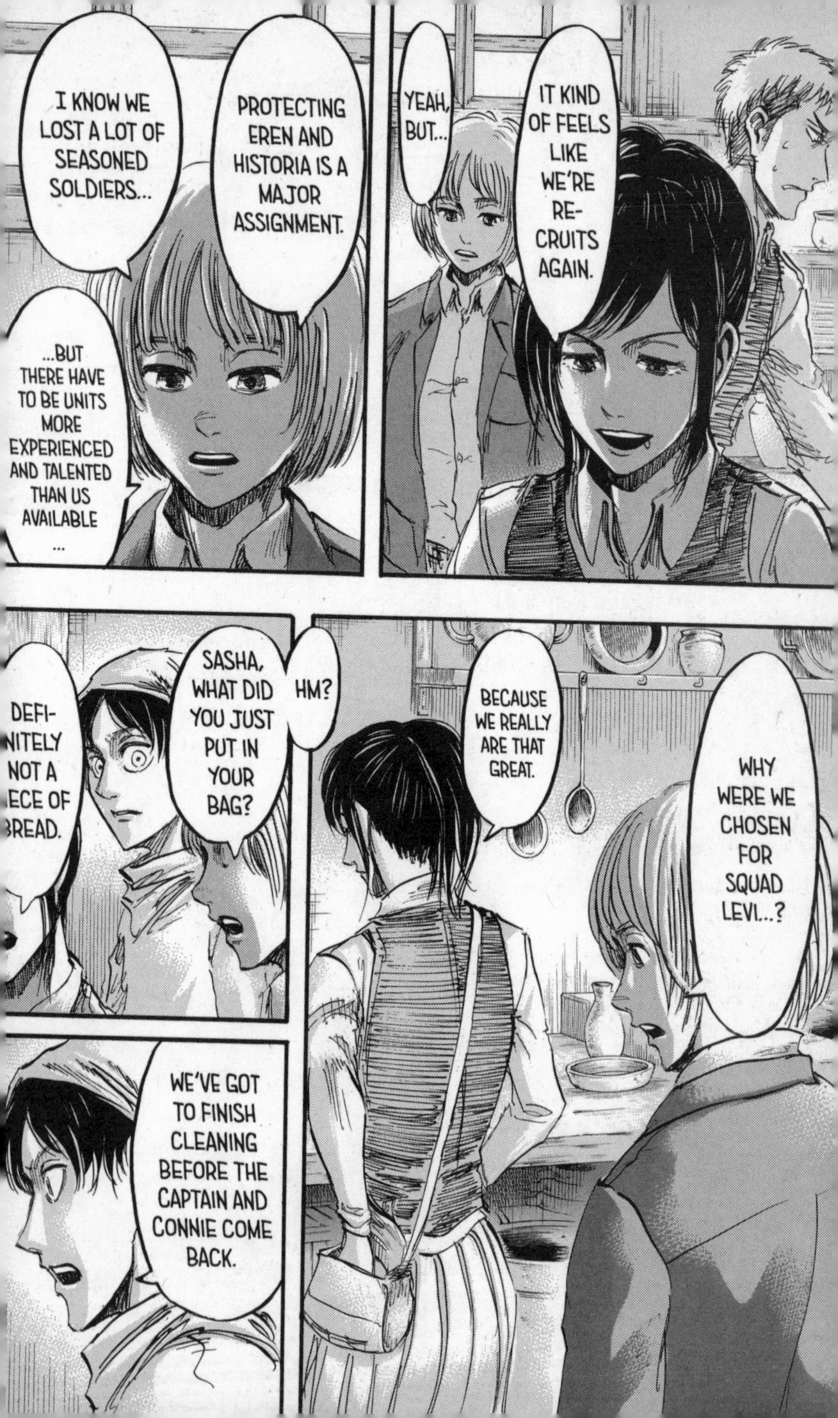
IT KIND OF FEELS LIKE WE'RE RE-CRUITS AGAIN.
YEAH, BUT...
PROTECTING EREN AND HISTORIA IS A MAJOR ASSIGNMENT.
I KNOW WE LOST A LOT OF SEASONED SOLDIERS...
...BUT THERE HAVE TO BE UNITS MORE EXPERIENCED AND TALENTED THAN US AVAILABLE ...
WHY WERE WE CHOSEN FOR SQUAD LEVI...?
BECAUSE WE REALLY ARE THAT GREAT.
HM?
SASHA, WHAT DID YOU JUST PUT IN YOUR BAG?
DEFI-NITELY NOT A ECE OF BREAD.
WE'VE GOT TO FINISH CLEANING BEFORE THE CAPTAIN AND CONNIE COME BACK.

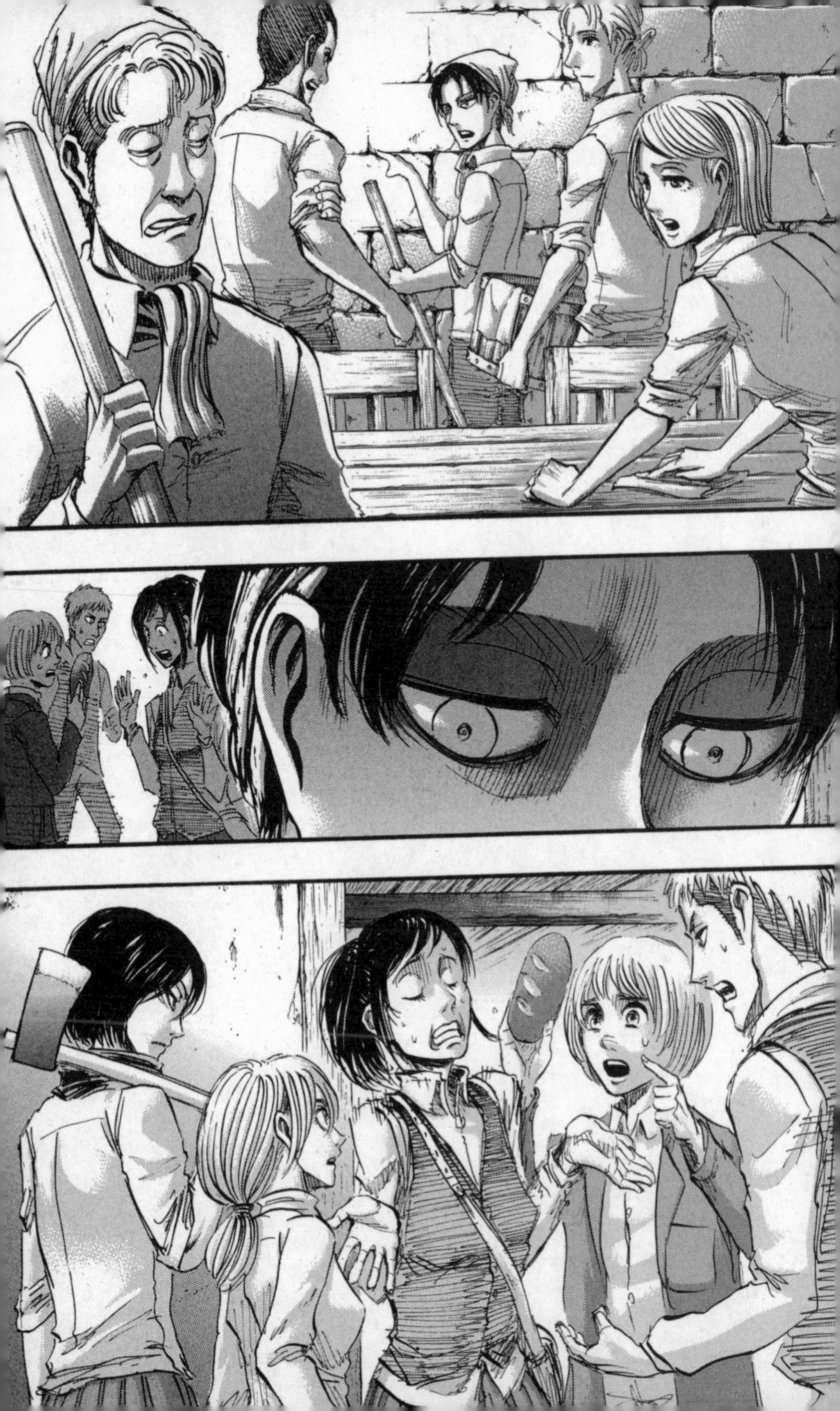

ATTACK on TITAN

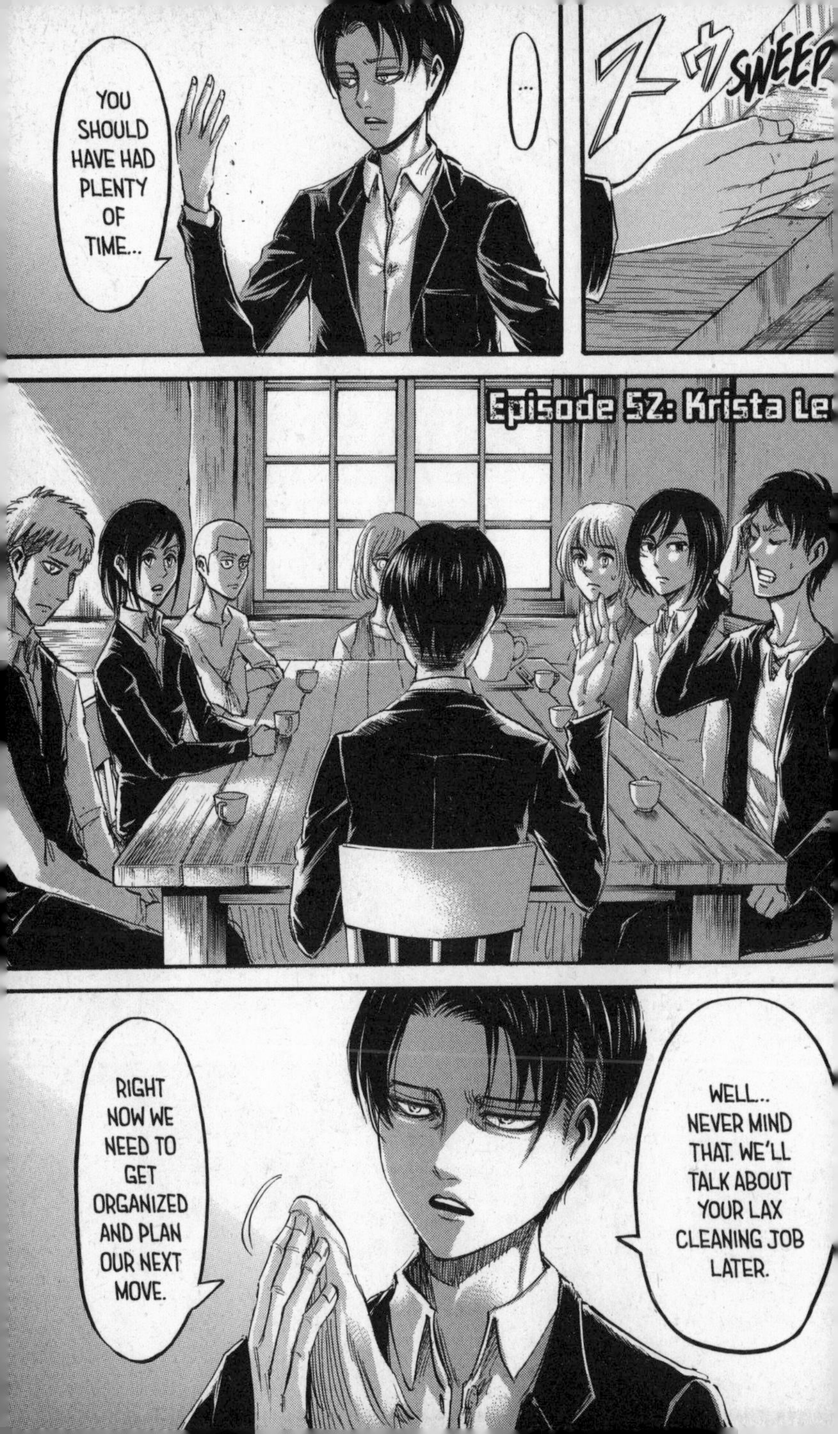
SWEEP
...
YOU SHOULD HAVE HAD PLENTY OF TIME...
Episode 52: Krista Le
WELL.. NEVER MIND THAT. WE'LL TALK ABOUT YOUR LAX CLEANING JOB LATER.
RIGHT NOW WE NEED TO GET ORGANIZED AND PLAN OUR NEXT MOVE.

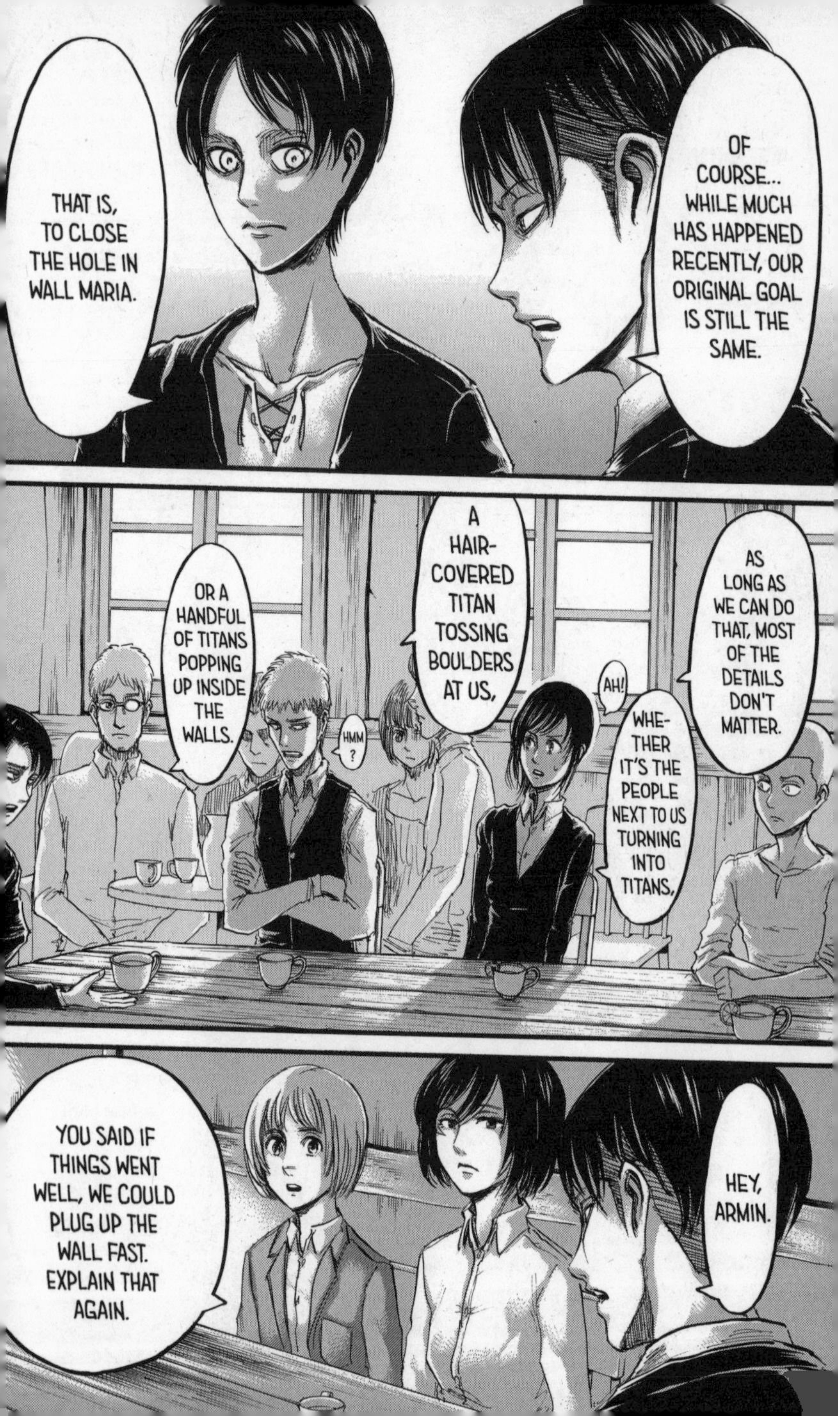
OF COURSE... WHILE MUCH HAS HAPPENED RECENTLY, OUR ORIGINAL GOAL IS STILL THE SAME.
THAT IS, TO CLOSE THE HOLE IN WALL MARIA.
AS LONG AS WE CAN DO THAT, MOST OF THE DETAILS DON'T MATTER.
AH!
WHE-THER IT'S THE PEOPLE NEXT TO US TURNING INTO TITANS,
A HAIR-COVERED TITAN TOSSING BOULDERS AT US,
HMM?
OR A HANDFUL OF TITANS POPPING UP INSIDE THE WALLS.
HEY, ARMIN.
YOU SAID IF THINGS WENT WELL, WE COULD PLUG UP THE WALL FAST. EXPLAIN THAT AGAIN.

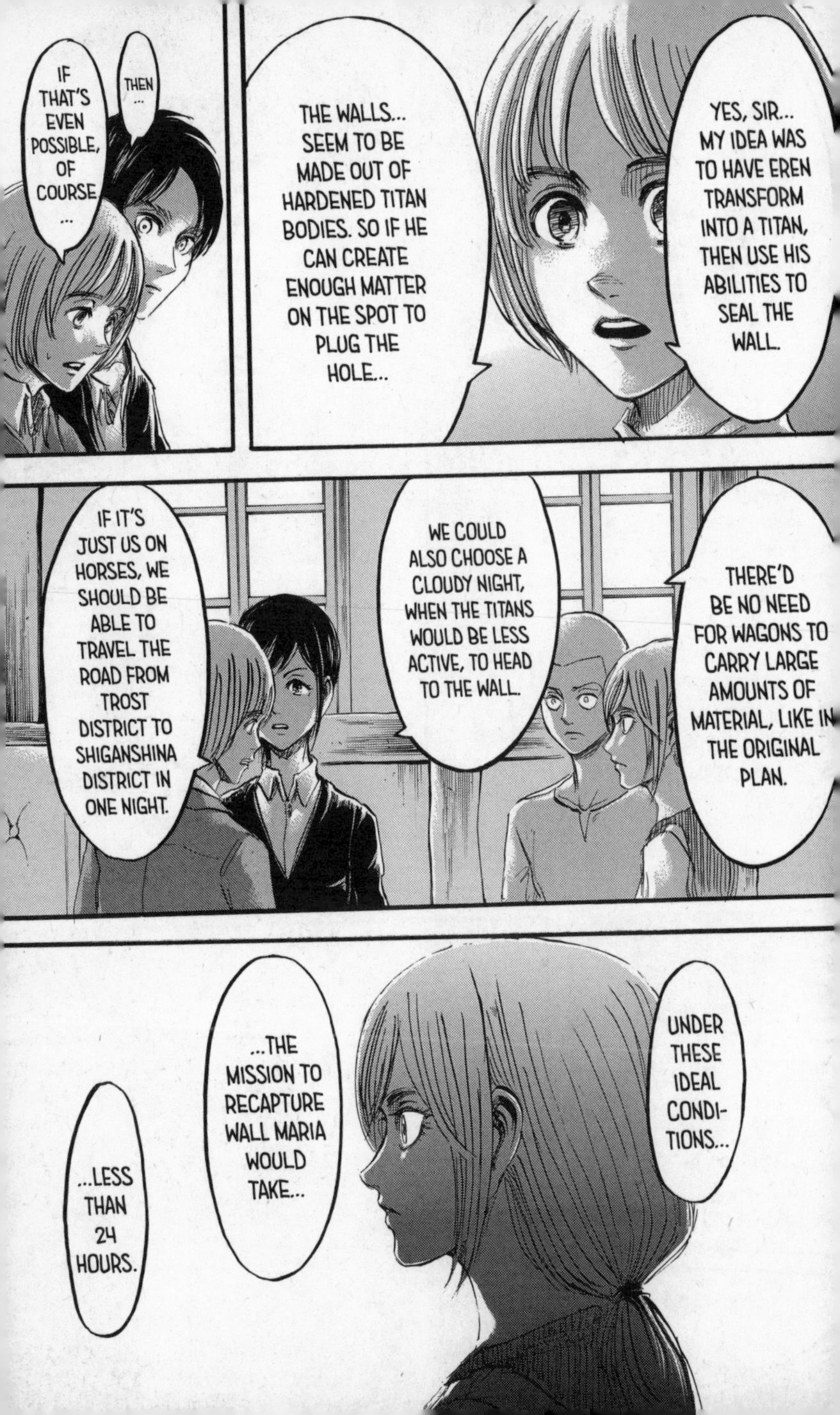
YES, SIR... MY IDEA WAS TO HAVE EREN TRANSFORM INTO A TITAN, THEN USE HIS ABILITIES TO SEAL THE WALL.
THE WALLS... SEEM TO BE MADE OUT OF HARDENED TITAN BODIES. SO IF HE CAN CREATE ENOUGH MATTER ON THE SPOT TO PLUG THE HOLE...
THEN ...
IF THAT'S EVEN POSSIBLE, OF COURSE ...
THERE'D BE NO NEED FOR WAGONS TO CARRY LARGE AMOUNTS OF MATERIAL, LIKE IN THE ORIGINAL PLAN.
WE COULD ALSO CHOOSE A CLOUDY NIGHT, WHEN THE TITANS WOULD BE LESS ACTIVE, TO HEAD TO THE WALL.
IF IT'S JUST US ON HORSES, WE SHOULD BE ABLE TO TRAVEL THE ROAD FROM TROST DISTRICT TO SHIGANSHINA DISTRICT IN ONE NIGHT.
UNDER THESE IDEAL CONDI-TIONS...
...THE MISSION TO RECAPTURE WALL MARIA WOULD TAKE...
...LESS THAN 24 HOURS.

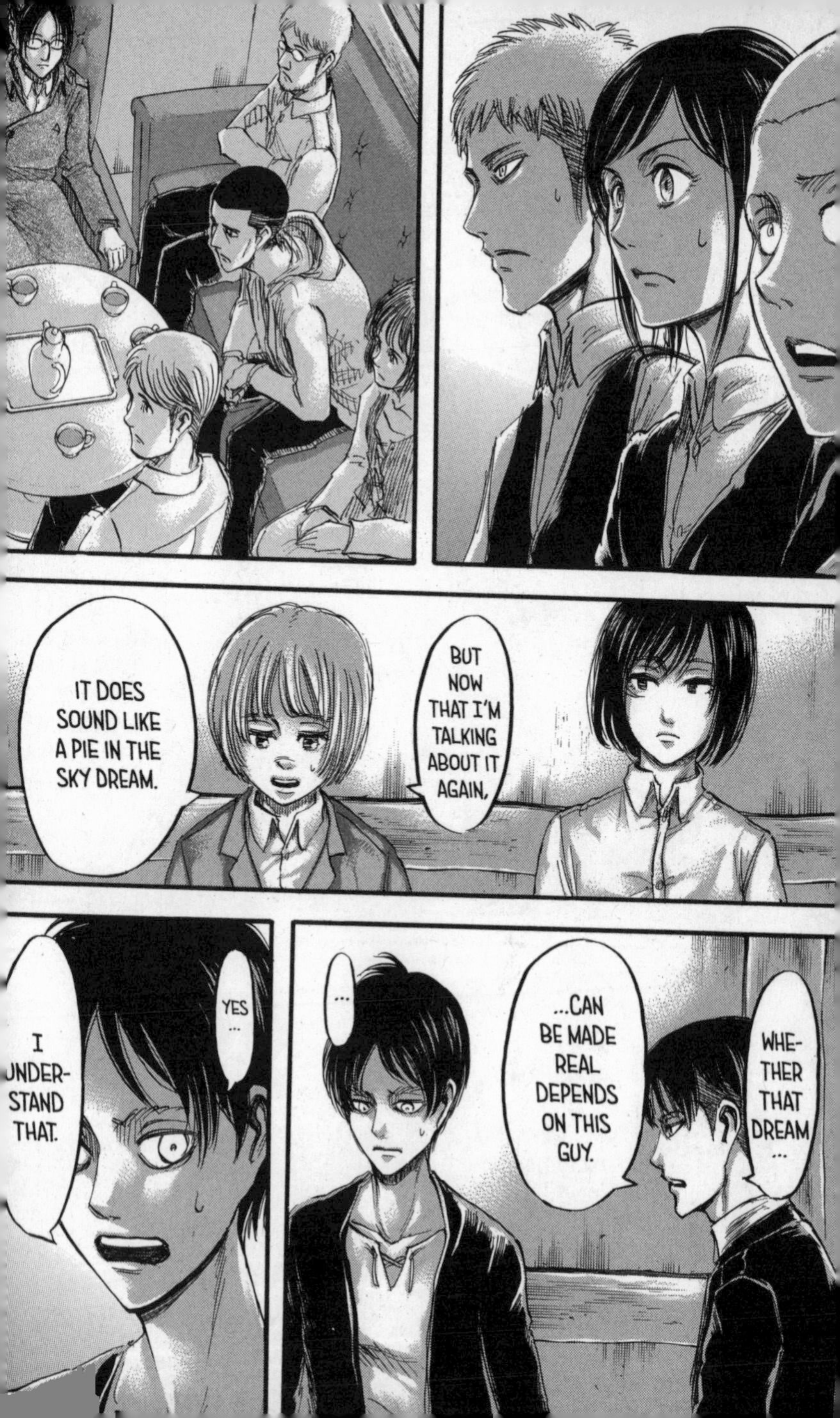
BUT NOW THAT I'M TALKING ABOUT IT AGAIN,
IT DOES SOUND LIKE A PIE IN THE SKY DREAM.
WHE-THER THAT DREAM...
...CAN BE MADE REAL DEPENDS ON THIS GUY.
...
YES...
I UNDER-STAND THAT.

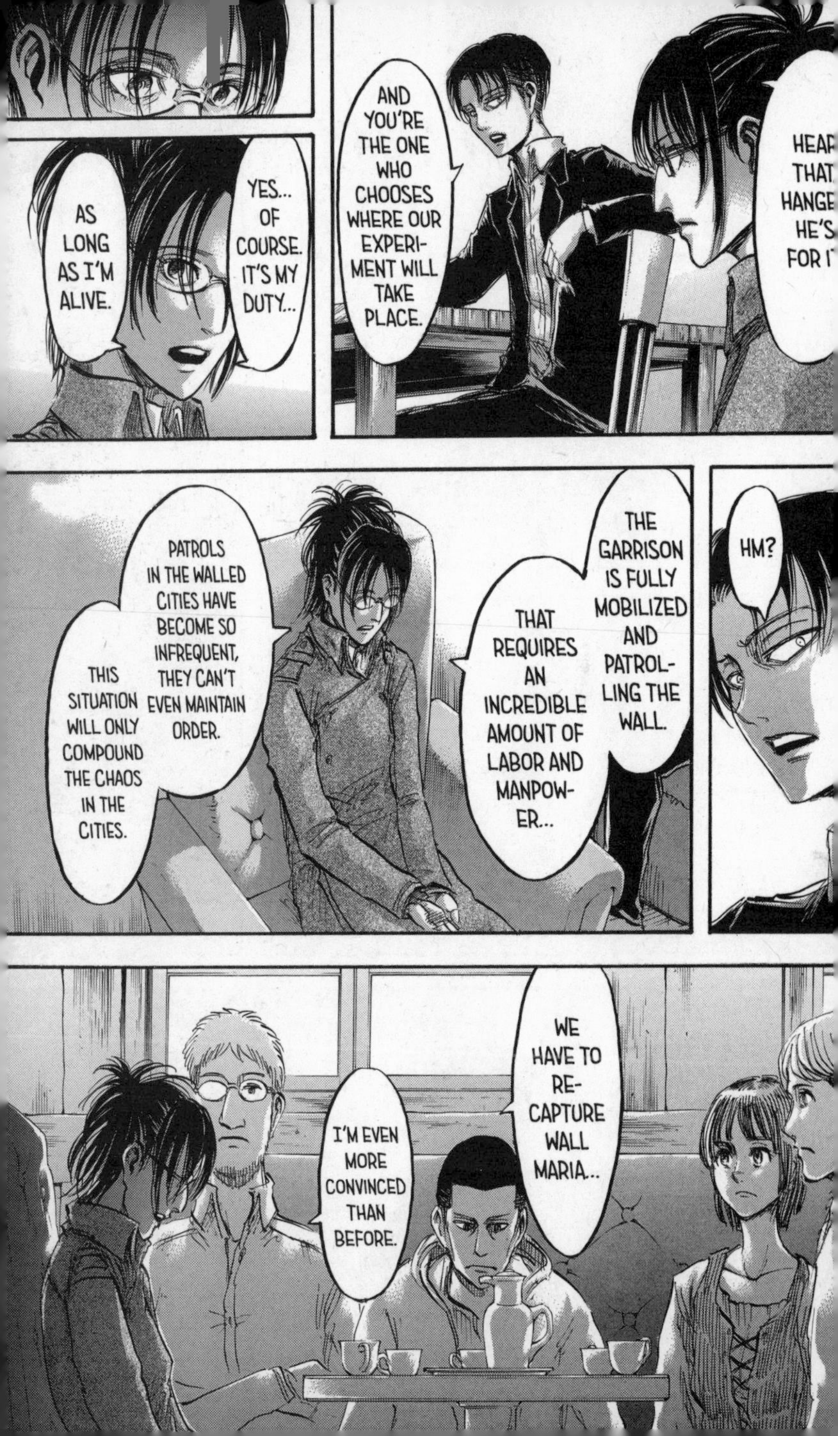
HEAR THAT HANGE HE'S FOR I
AND YOU'RE THE ONE WHO CHOOSES WHERE OUR EXPERI- MENT WILL TAKE PLACE.
YES... OF COURSE. IT'S MY DUTY...
AS LONG AS I'M ALIVE.
HM?
THE GARRISON IS FULLY MOBILIZED AND PATROL- LING THE WALL.
THAT REQUIRES AN INCREDIBLE AMOUNT OF LABOR AND MANPOW- ER...
PATROLS IN THE WALLED CITIES HAVE BECOME SO INFREQUENT, THEY CAN'T EVEN MAINTAIN ORDER.
THIS SITUATION WILL ONLY COMPOUND THE CHAOS IN THE CITIES.
WE HAVE TO RE- CAPTURE WALL MARIA...
I'M EVEN MORE CONVINCED THAN BEFORE.

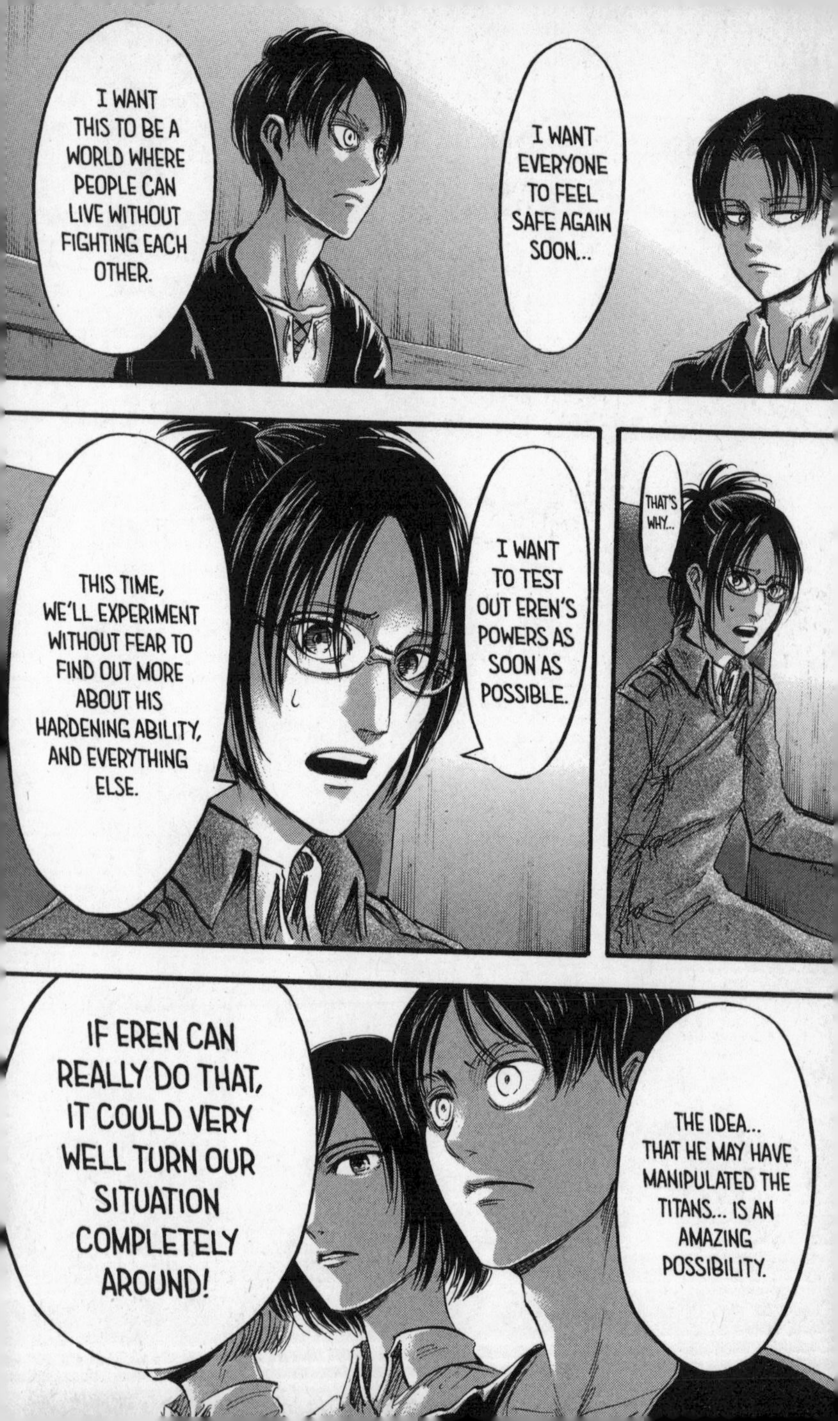
I WANT EVERYONE TO FEEL SAFE AGAIN SOON...
I WANT THIS TO BE A WORLD WHERE PEOPLE CAN LIVE WITHOUT FIGHTING EACH OTHER.
THAT'S WHY...
I WANT TO TEST OUT EREN'S POWERS AS SOON AS POSSIBLE.
THIS TIME, WE'LL EXPERIMENT WITHOUT FEAR TO FIND OUT MORE ABOUT HIS HARDENING ABILITY, AND EVERYTHING ELSE.
THE IDEA... THAT HE MAY HAVE MANIPULATED THE TITANS... IS AN AMAZING POSSIBILITY.
IF EREN CAN REALLY DO THAT, IT COULD VERY WELL TURN OUR SITUATION COMPLETELY AROUND!

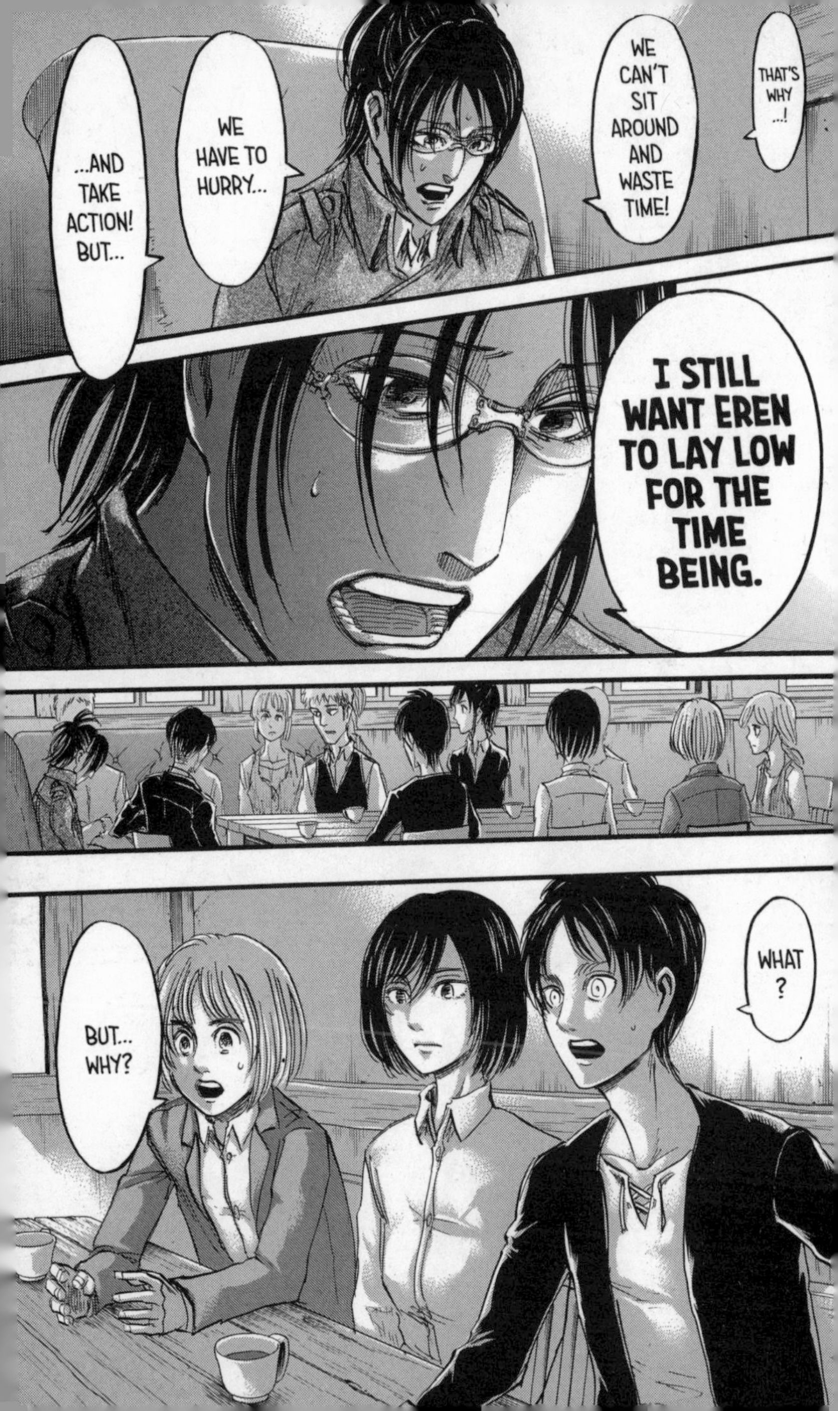
THAT'S WHY ...!
WE CAN'T SIT AROUND AND WASTE TIME!
WE HAVE TO HURRY...
...AND TAKE ACTION! BUT...
I STILL WANT EREN TO LAY LOW FOR THE TIME BEING.
WHAT?
BUT... WHY?

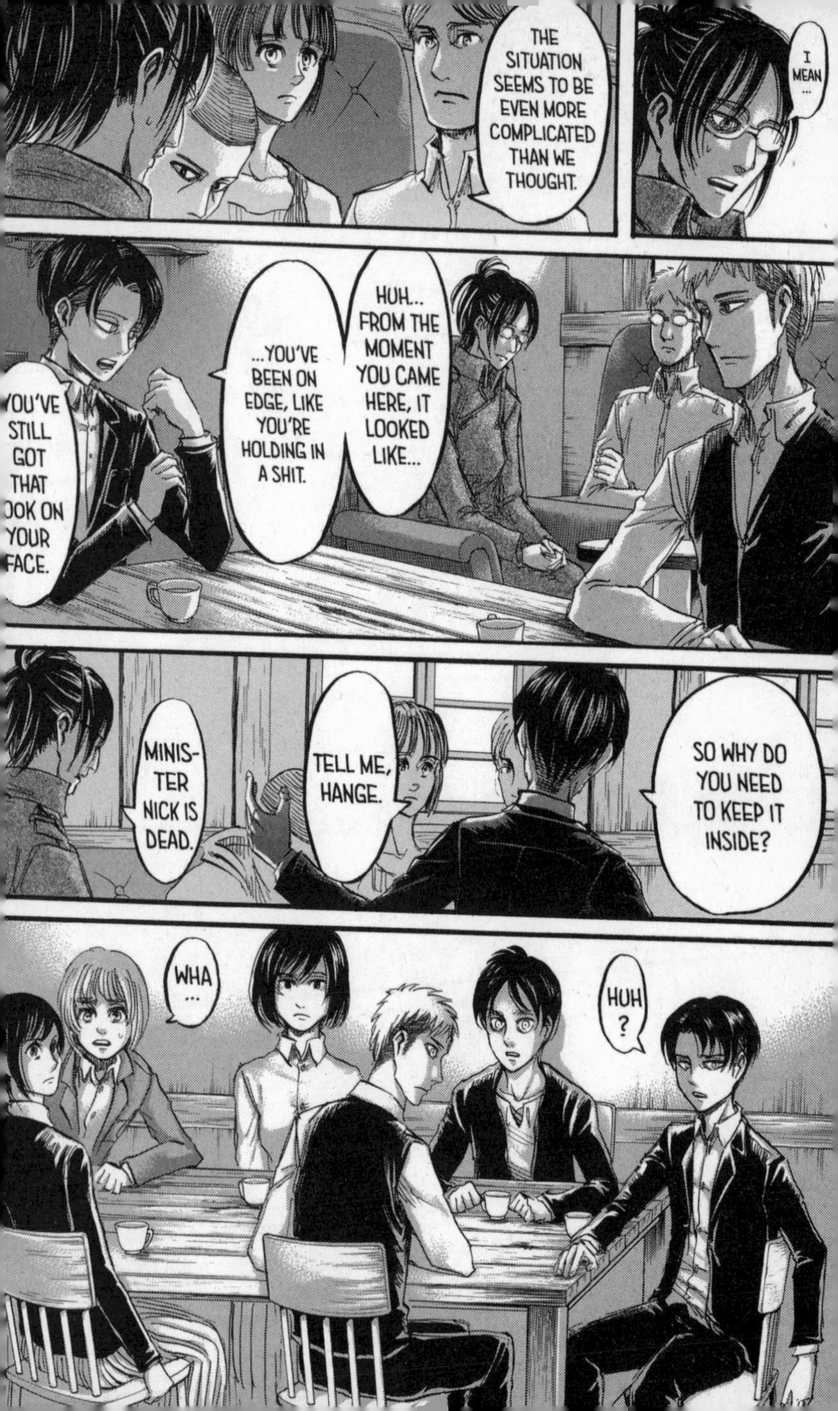
I MEAN...
THE SITUATION SEEMS TO BE EVEN MORE COMPLICATED THAN WE THOUGHT.
HUH... FROM THE MOMENT YOU CAME HERE, IT LOOKED LIKE...
...YOU'VE BEEN ON EDGE, LIKE YOU'RE HOLDING IN A SHIT.
YOU'VE STILL GOT THAT LOOK ON YOUR FACE.
SO WHY DO YOU NEED TO KEEP IT INSIDE?
TELL ME, HANGE.
MINIS-TER NICK IS DEAD.
HUH?
WHA...

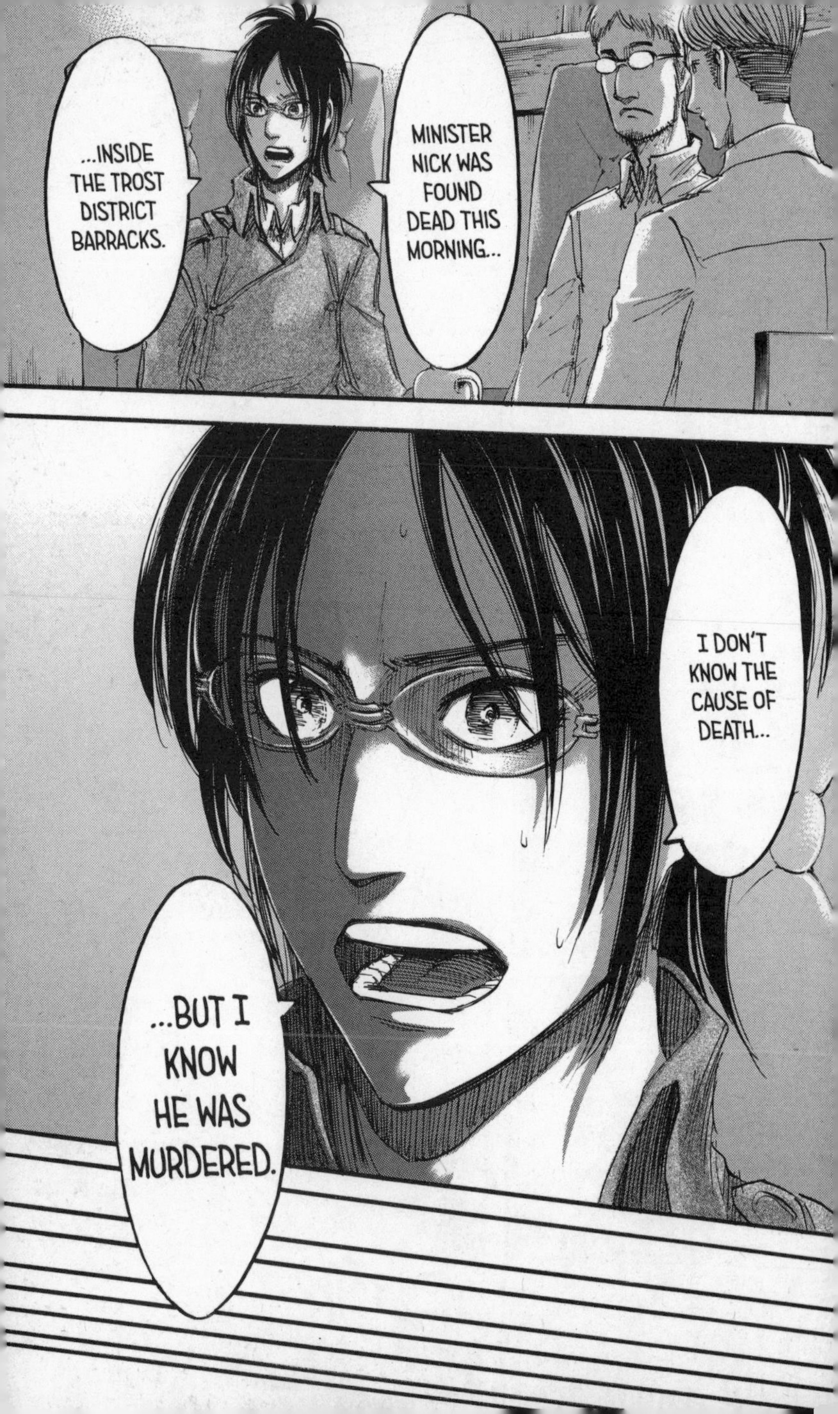
MINISTER NICK WAS FOUND DEAD THIS MORNING...
...INSIDE THE TROST DISTRICT BARRACKS.
I DON'T KNOW THE CAUSE OF DEATH...
...BUT I KNOW HE WAS MURDERED.

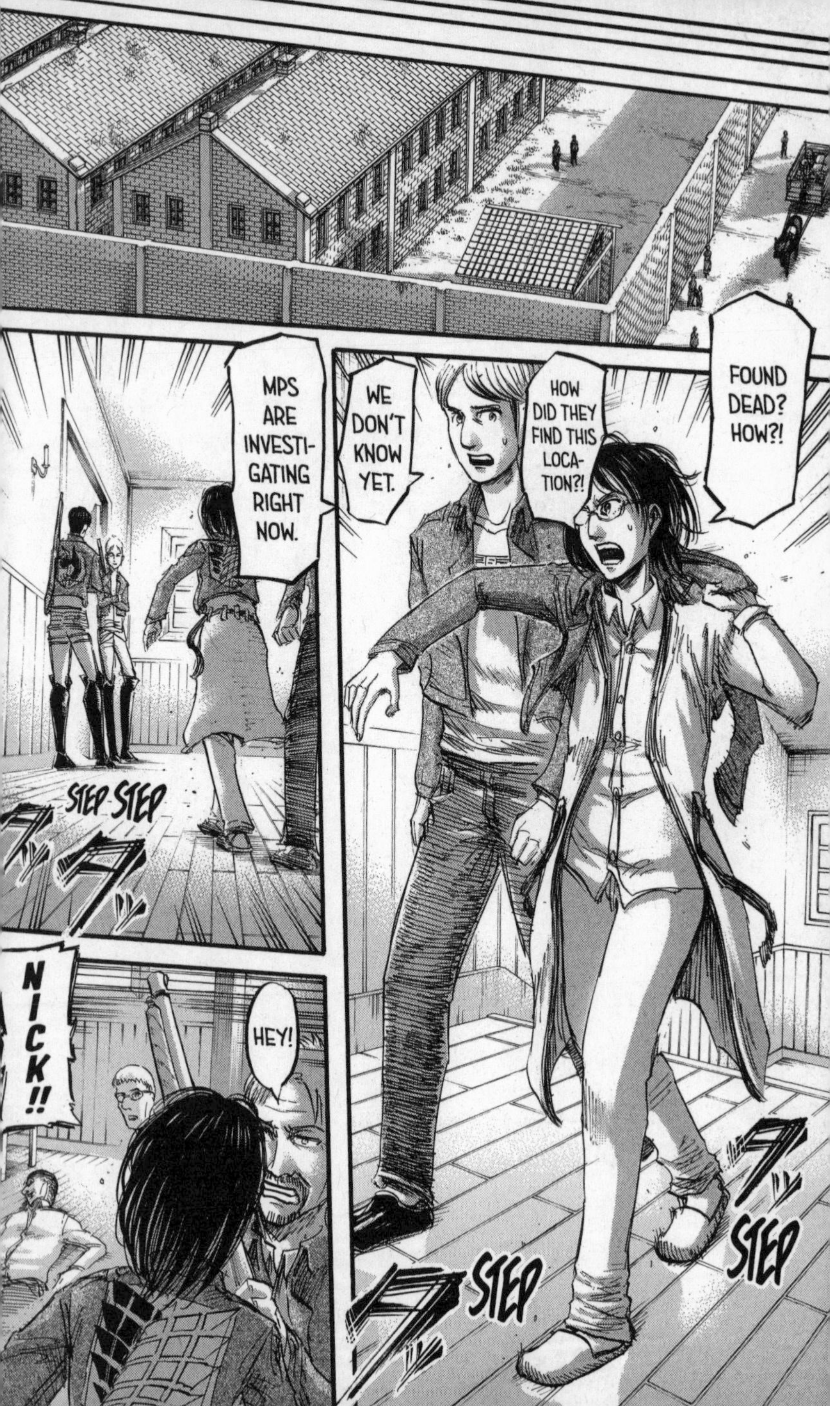
FOUND DEAD? HOW?!
HOW DID THEY FIND THIS LOCA-TION?!
WE DON'T KNOW YET.
STEP
STEP
MPS ARE INVESTI-GATING RIGHT NOW.
STEP-STEP
NICK!!
HEY!

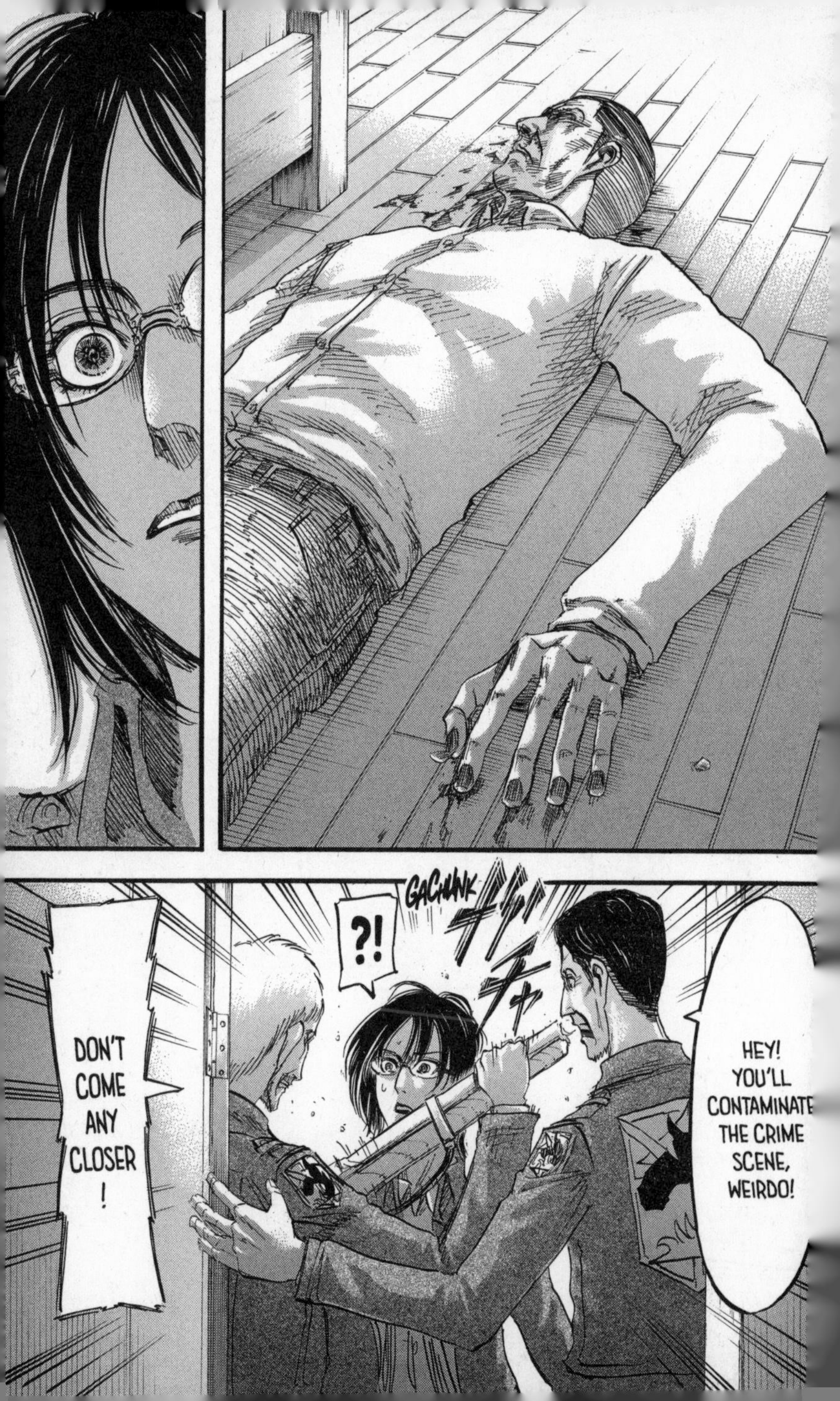
HEY! YOU'LL CONTAMINATE THE CRIME SCENE, WEIRDO!
GACHUNK
?!
DON'T COME ANY CLOSER!

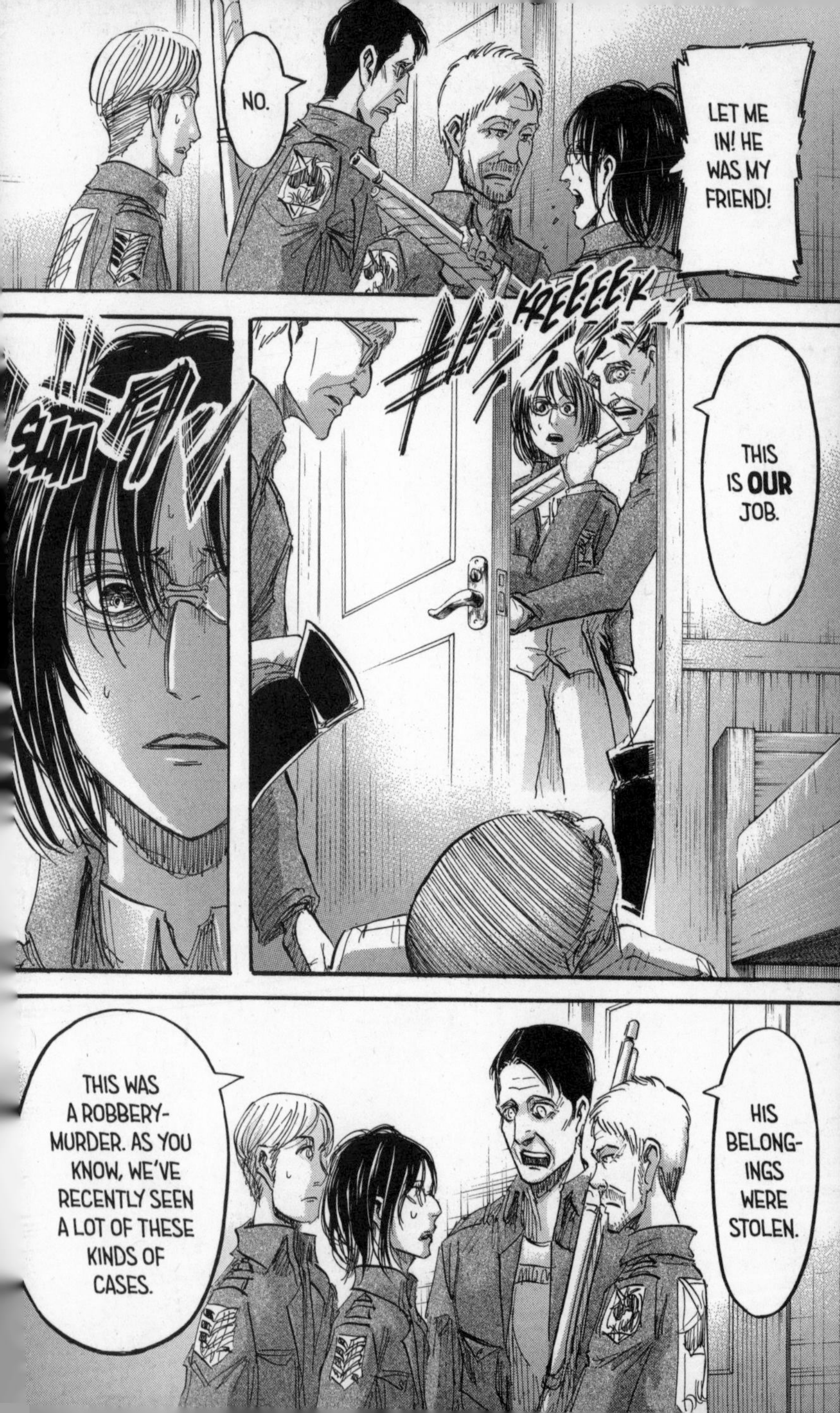

LET ME IN! HE WAS MY FRIEND!
NO.
KREEEEK
THIS IS OUR JOB.
SLAM
HIS BELONG-INGS WERE STOLEN.
THIS WAS A ROBBERY-MURDER. AS YOU KNOW, WE'VE RECENTLY SEEN A LOT OF THESE KINDS OF CASES.

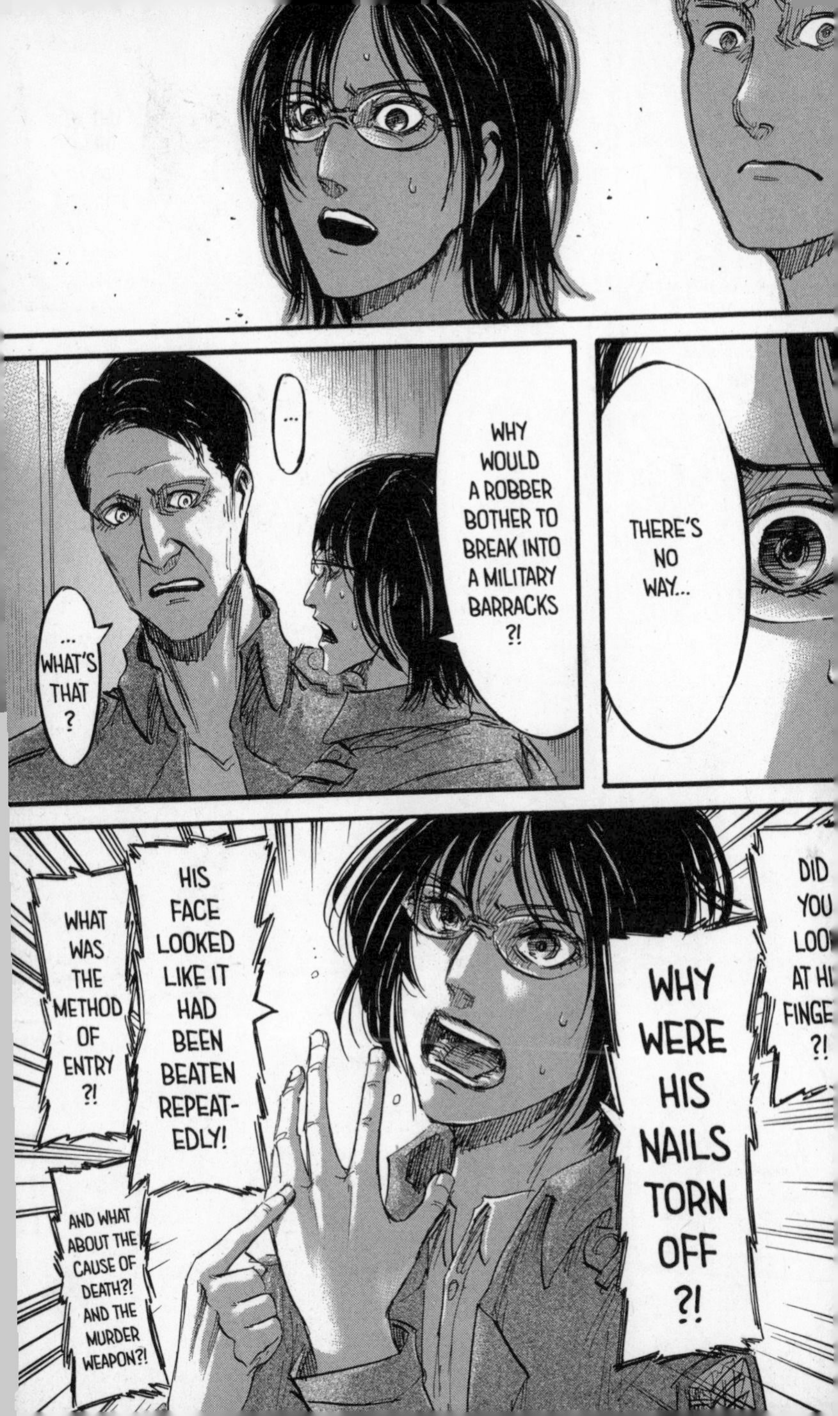
THERE'S NO WAY...
WHY WOULD A ROBBER BOTHER TO BREAK INTO A MILITARY BARRACKS?!
...
...WHAT'S THAT?
DID YOU LOO AT HI FINGE ?!
WHY WERE HIS NAILS TORN OFF?!
HIS FACE LOOKED LIKE IT HAD BEEN BEATEN REPEAT-EDLY!
WHAT WAS THE METHOD OF ENTRY?!
AND WHAT ABOUT THE CAUSE OF DEATH?! AND THE MURDER WEAPON?!

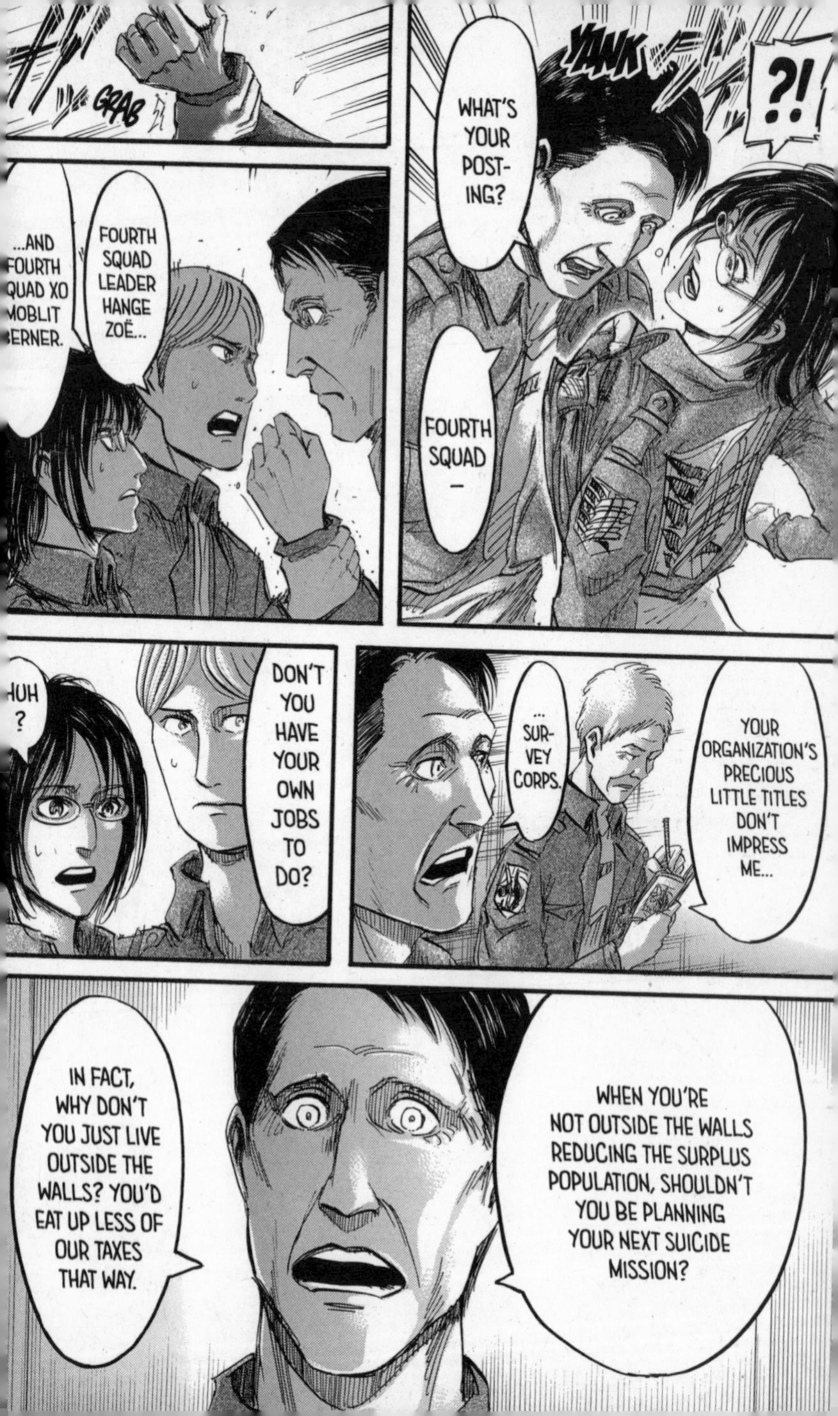
YANK
?!
WHAT'S YOUR POSTING?
FOURTH SQUAD—
GRAB
FOURTH SQUAD LEADER HANGE ZOË...
...AND FOURTH QUAD XO MOBLIT ERNER.
YOUR ORGANIZATION'S PRECIOUS LITTLE TITLES DON'T IMPRESS ME...
...SURVEY CORPS.
DON'T YOU HAVE YOUR OWN JOBS TO DO?
HUH?
WHEN YOU'RE NOT OUTSIDE THE WALLS REDUCING THE SURPLUS POPULATION, SHOULDN'T YOU BE PLANNING YOUR NEXT SUICIDE MISSION?
IN FACT, WHY DON'T YOU JUST LIVE OUTSIDE THE WALLS? YOU'D EAT UP LESS OF OUR TAXES THAT WAY.

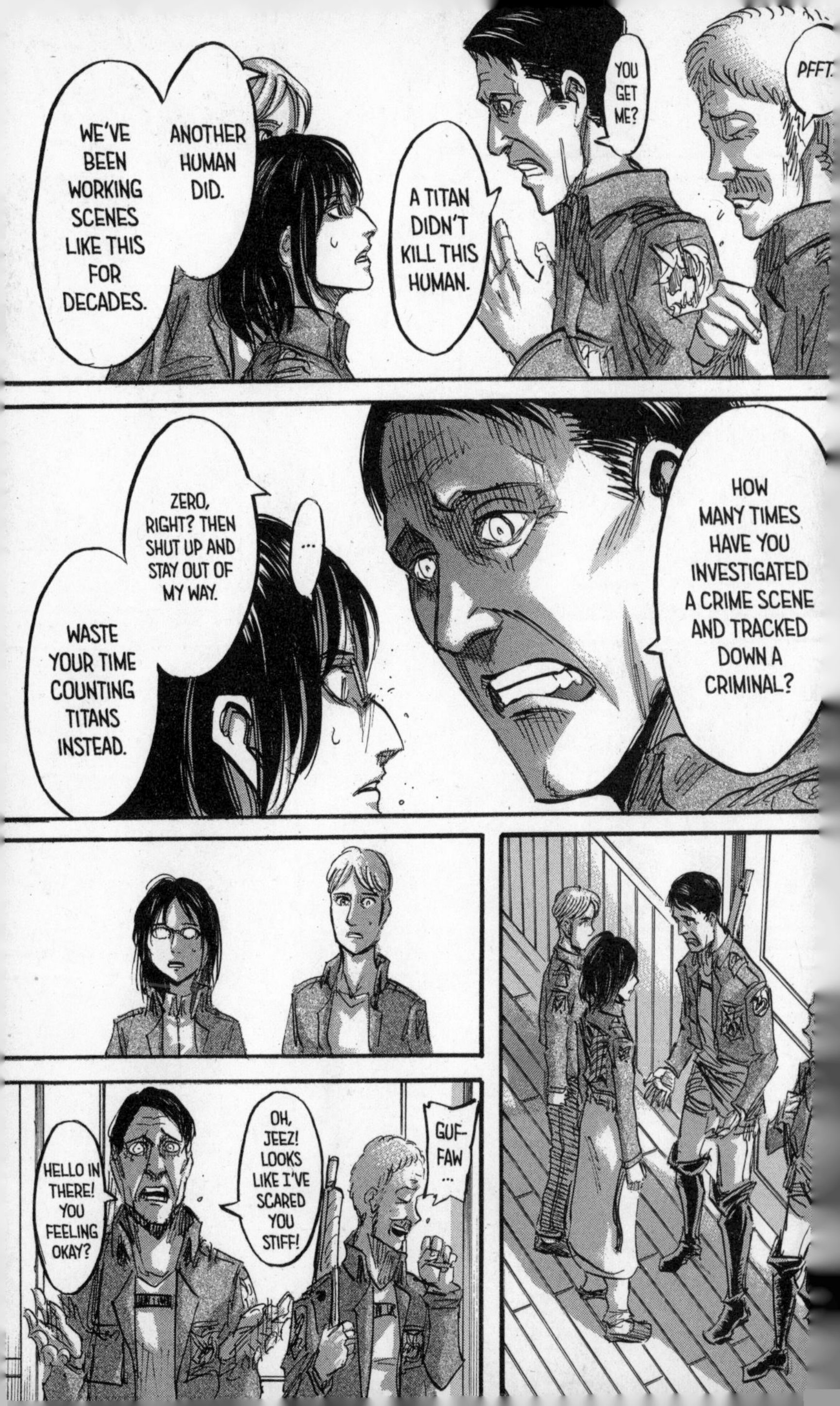
PFFT.
YOU GET ME?
A TITAN DIDN'T KILL THIS HUMAN.
ANOTHER HUMAN DID.
WE'VE BEEN WORKING SCENES LIKE THIS FOR DECADES.
HOW MANY TIMES HAVE YOU INVESTIGATED A CRIME SCENE AND TRACKED DOWN A CRIMINAL?
...
ZERO, RIGHT? THEN SHUT UP AND STAY OUT OF MY WAY.
WASTE YOUR TIME COUNTING TITANS INSTEAD.
GUF-FAW...
OH, JEEZ! LOOKS LIKE I'VE SCARED YOU STIFF!
HELLO IN THERE! YOU FEELING OKAY?

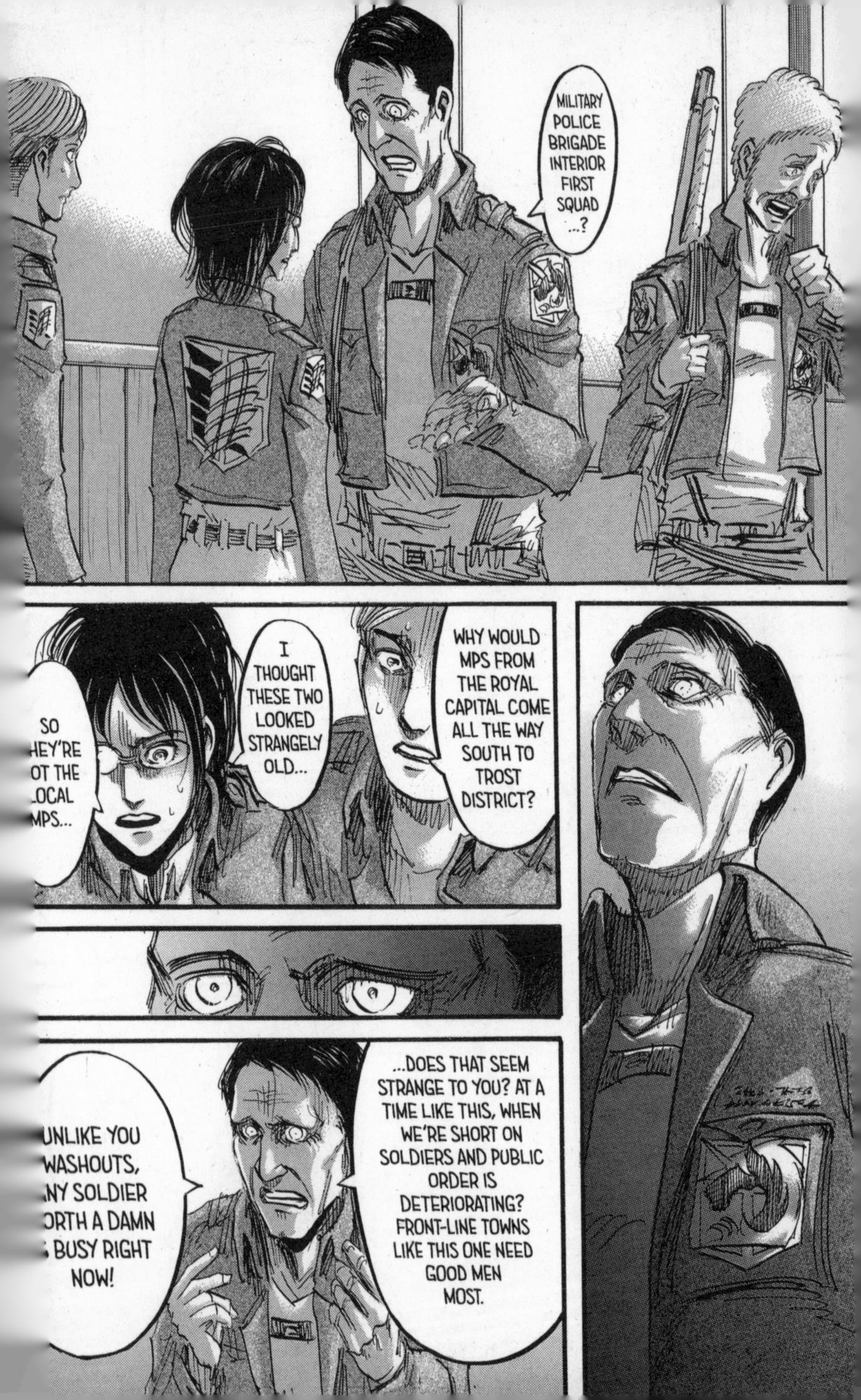
MILITARY POLICE BRIGADE INTERIOR FIRST SQUAD ...?
WHY WOULD MPS FROM THE ROYAL CAPITAL COME ALL THE WAY SOUTH TO TROST DISTRICT?
I THOUGHT THESE TWO LOOKED STRANGELY OLD...
SO HEY'RE OT THE OCAL MPS...
...DOES THAT SEEM STRANGE TO YOU? AT A TIME LIKE THIS, WHEN WE'RE SHORT ON SOLDIERS AND PUBLIC ORDER IS DETERIORATING? FRONT-LINE TOWNS LIKE THIS ONE NEED GOOD MEN MOST.
UNLIKE YOU WASHOUTS, NY SOLDIER ORTH A DAMN BUSY RIGHT NOW!

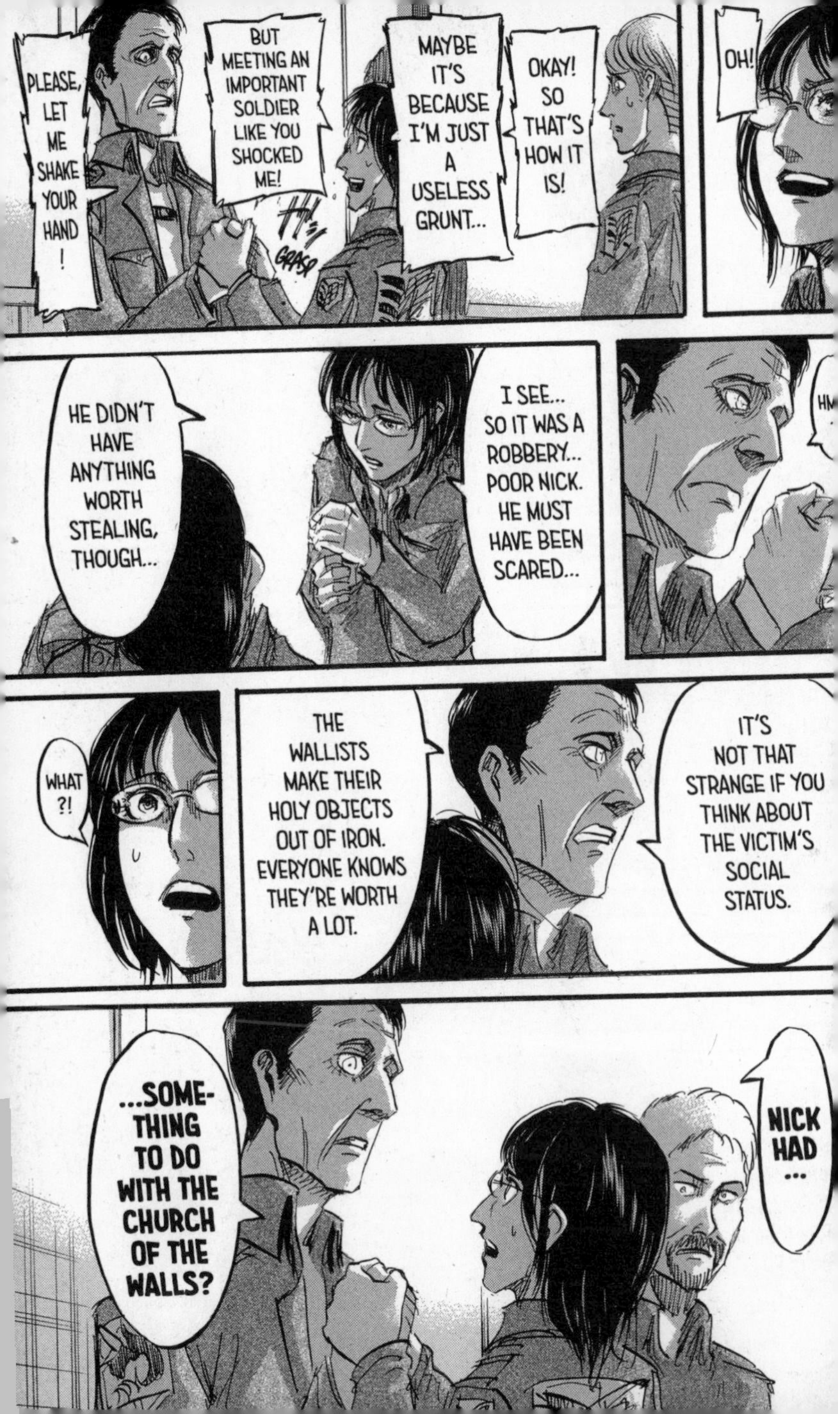
OH!
OKAY! SO THAT'S HOW IT IS!
MAYBE IT'S BECAUSE I'M JUST A USELESS GRUNT...
BUT MEETING AN IMPORTANT SOLDIER LIKE YOU SHOCKED ME!
PLEASE, LET ME SHAKE YOUR HAND!
GRASP
HM
I SEE... SO IT WAS A ROBBERY... POOR NICK. HE MUST HAVE BEEN SCARED...
HE DIDN'T HAVE ANYTHING WORTH STEALING, THOUGH...
IT'S NOT THAT STRANGE IF YOU THINK ABOUT THE VICTIM'S SOCIAL STATUS.
THE WALLISTS MAKE THEIR HOLY OBJECTS OUT OF IRON. EVERYONE KNOWS THEY'RE WORTH A LOT.
WHAT?!
NICK HAD...
...SOME-THING TO DO WITH THE CHURCH OF THE WALLS?

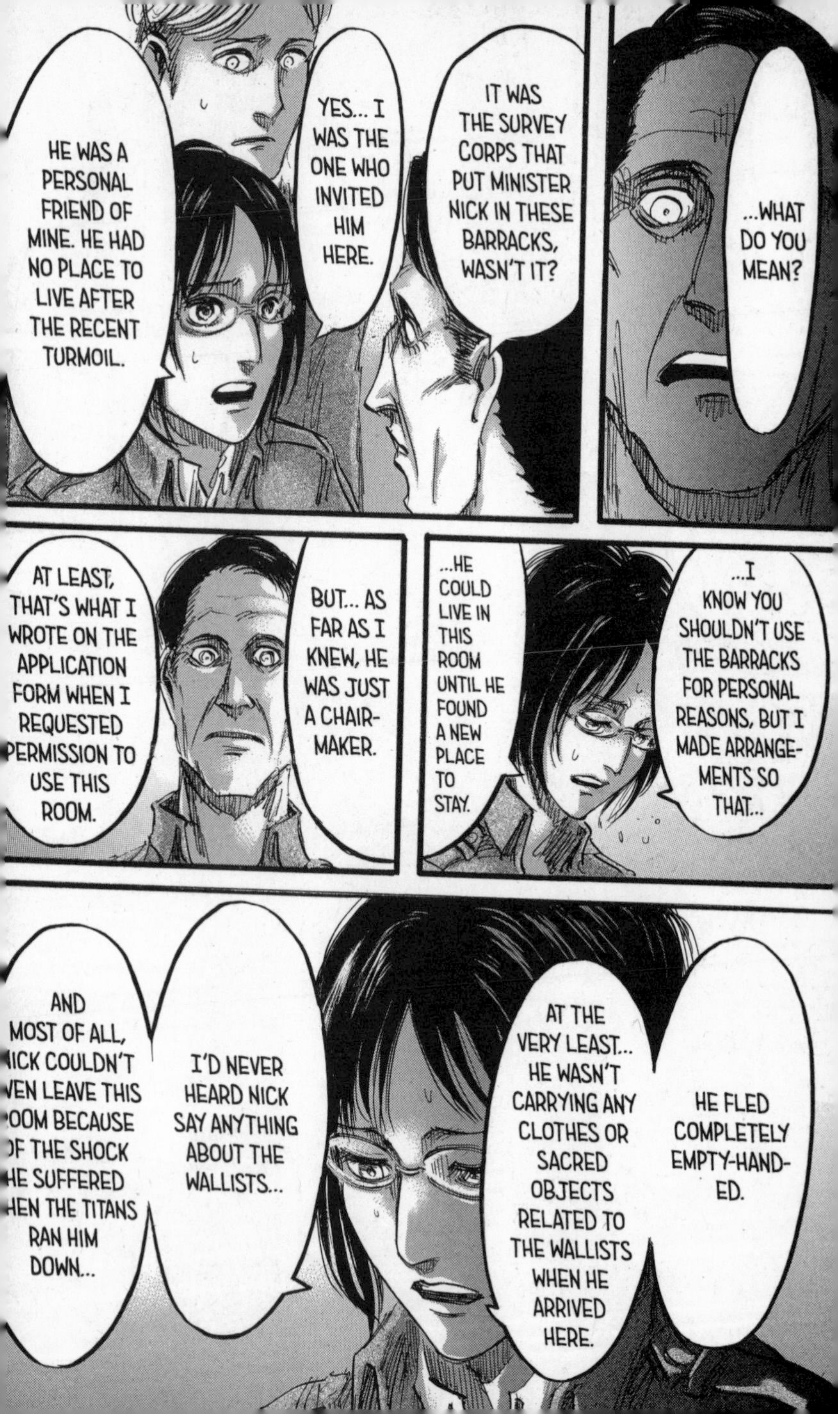
...WHAT DO YOU MEAN?
IT WAS THE SURVEY CORPS THAT PUT MINISTER NICK IN THESE BARRACKS, WASN'T IT?
YES... I WAS THE ONE WHO INVITED HIM HERE.
HE WAS A PERSONAL FRIEND OF MINE. HE HAD NO PLACE TO LIVE AFTER THE RECENT TURMOIL.
...I KNOW YOU SHOULDN'T USE THE BARRACKS FOR PERSONAL REASONS, BUT I MADE ARRANGE-MENTS SO THAT...
...HE COULD LIVE IN THIS ROOM UNTIL HE FOUND A NEW PLACE TO STAY.
BUT... AS FAR AS I KNEW, HE WAS JUST A CHAIR-MAKER.
AT LEAST, THAT'S WHAT I WROTE ON THE APPLICATION FORM WHEN I REQUESTED PERMISSION TO USE THIS ROOM.
HE FLED COMPLETELY EMPTY-HAND-ED.
AT THE VERY LEAST... HE WASN'T CARRYING ANY CLOTHES OR SACRED OBJECTS RELATED TO THE WALLISTS WHEN HE ARRIVED HERE.
I'D NEVER HEARD NICK SAY ANYTHING ABOUT THE WALLISTS...
AND MOST OF ALL, ICK COULDN'T VEN LEAVE THIS OOM BECAUSE F THE SHOCK HE SUFFERED HEN THE TITANS RAN HIM DOWN...

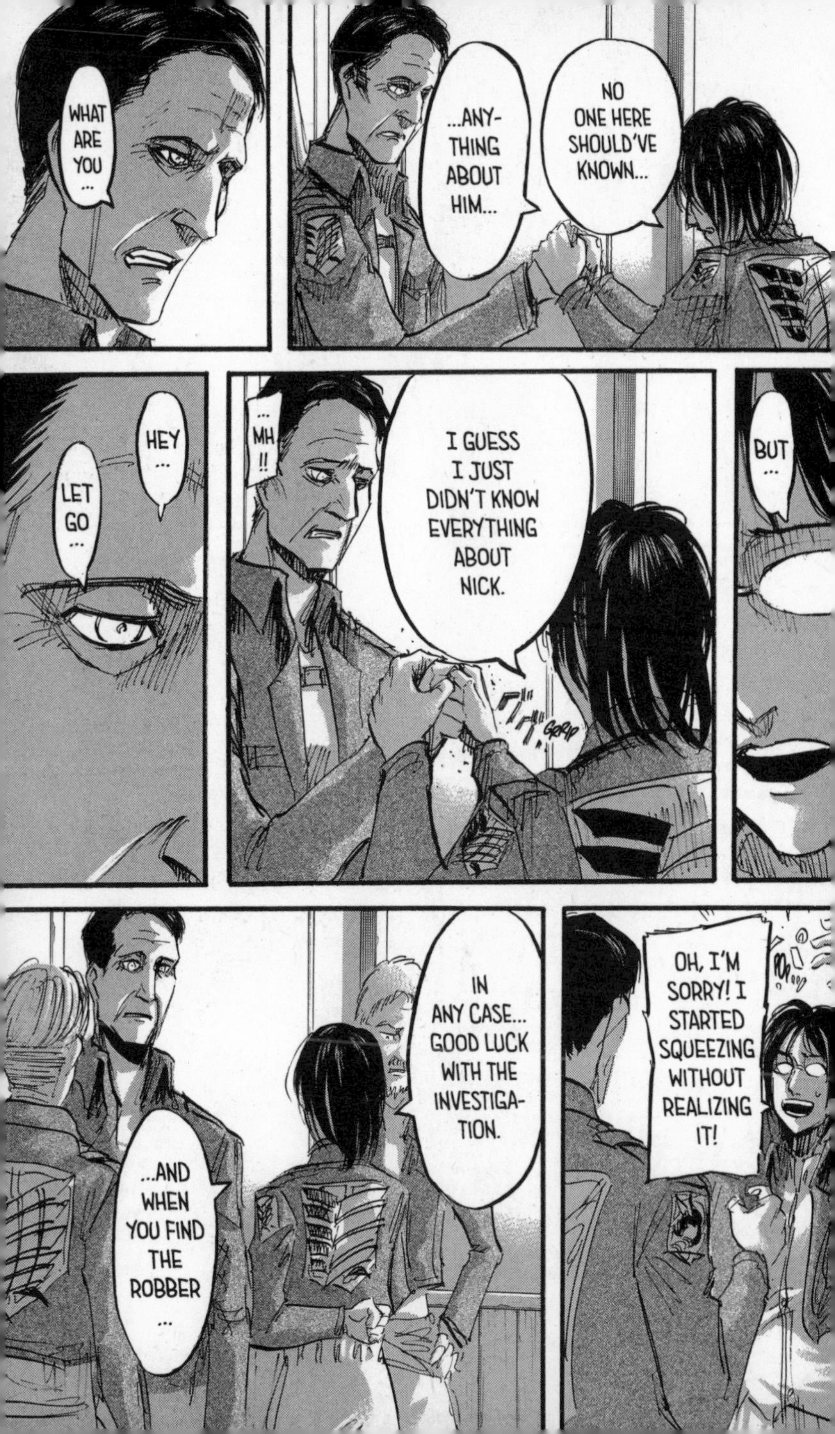
NO ONE HERE SHOULD'VE KNOWN...
...ANYTHING ABOUT HIM...
WHAT ARE YOU ...
BUT ...
I GUESS I JUST DIDN'T KNOW EVERYTHING ABOUT NICK.
... MH !!
GRRIP
HEY ...
LET GO ...
OH, I'M SORRY! I STARTED SQUEEZING WITHOUT REALIZING IT!
IN ANY CASE... GOOD LUCK WITH THE INVESTIGATION.
...AND WHEN YOU FIND THE ROBBER ...

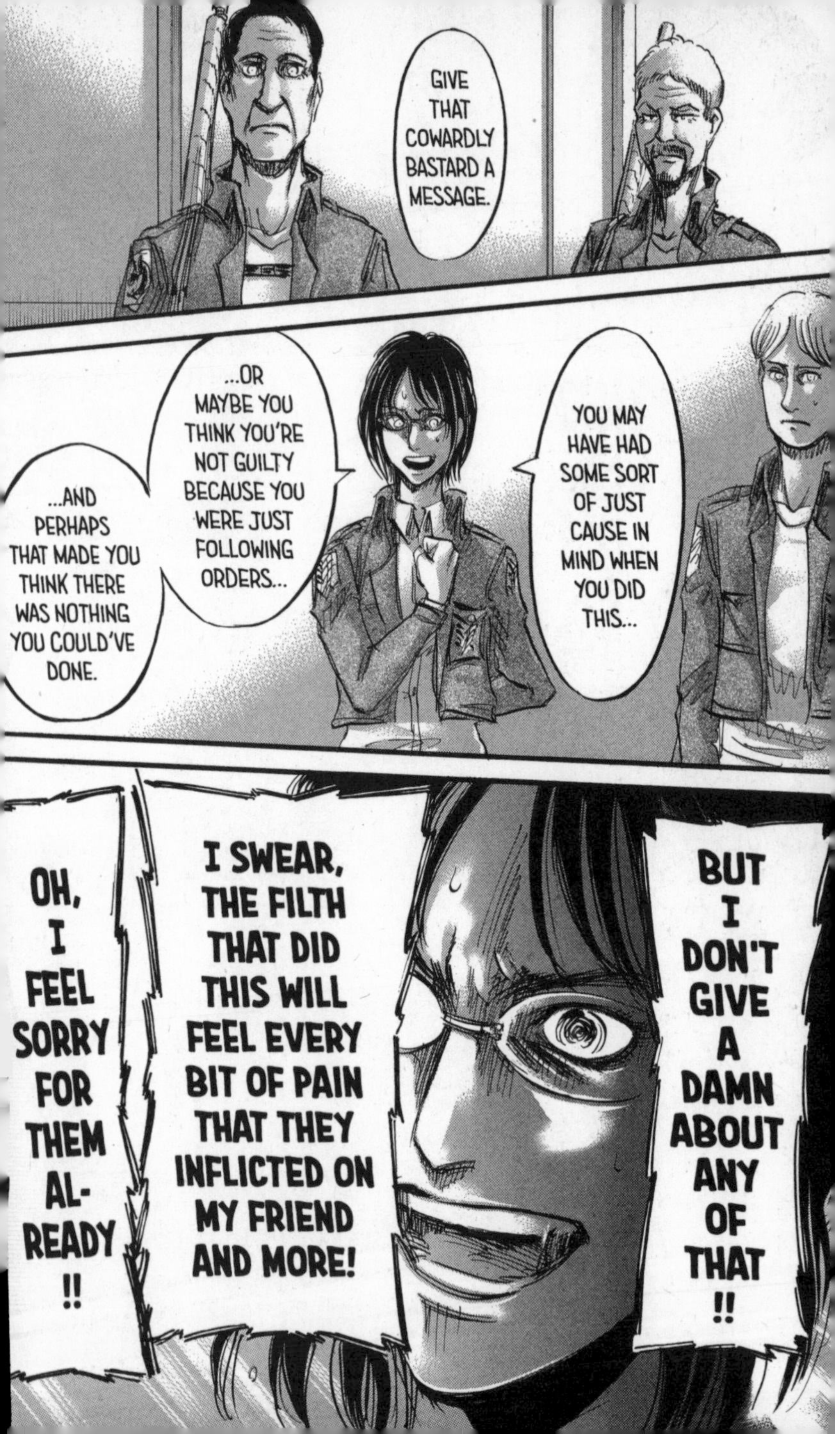
GIVE THAT COWARDLY BASTARD A MESSAGE.
YOU MAY HAVE HAD SOME SORT OF JUST CAUSE IN MIND WHEN YOU DID THIS...
...OR MAYBE YOU THINK YOU'RE NOT GUILTY BECAUSE YOU WERE JUST FOLLOWING ORDERS...
...AND PERHAPS THAT MADE YOU THINK THERE WAS NOTHING YOU COULD'VE DONE.
BUT I DON'T GIVE A DAMN ABOUT ANY OF THAT!!
I SWEAR, THE FILTH THAT DID THIS WILL FEEL EVERY BIT OF PAIN THAT THEY INFLICTED ON MY FRIEND AND MORE!
OH, I FEEL SORRY FOR THEM AL-READY!!

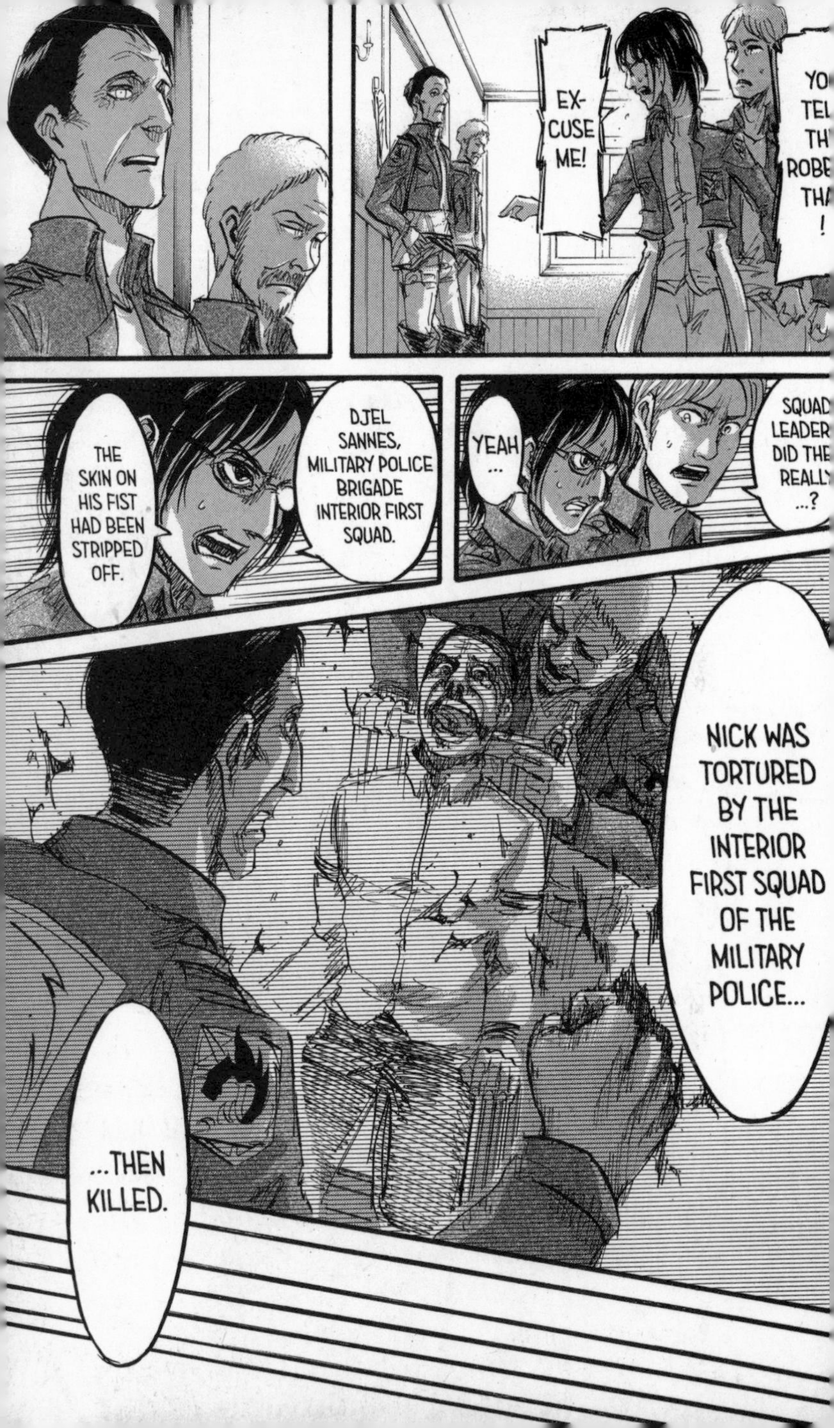

YO TEL TH ROBB THA !
EX-CUSE ME!
SQUAD LEADER DID THE REALLY ...?
YEAH ...
DJEL SANNES, MILITARY POLICE BRIGADE INTERIOR FIRST SQUAD.
THE SKIN ON HIS FIST HAD BEEN STRIPPED OFF.
NICK WAS TORTURED BY THE INTERIOR FIRST SQUAD OF THE MILITARY POLICE...
...THEN KILLED.

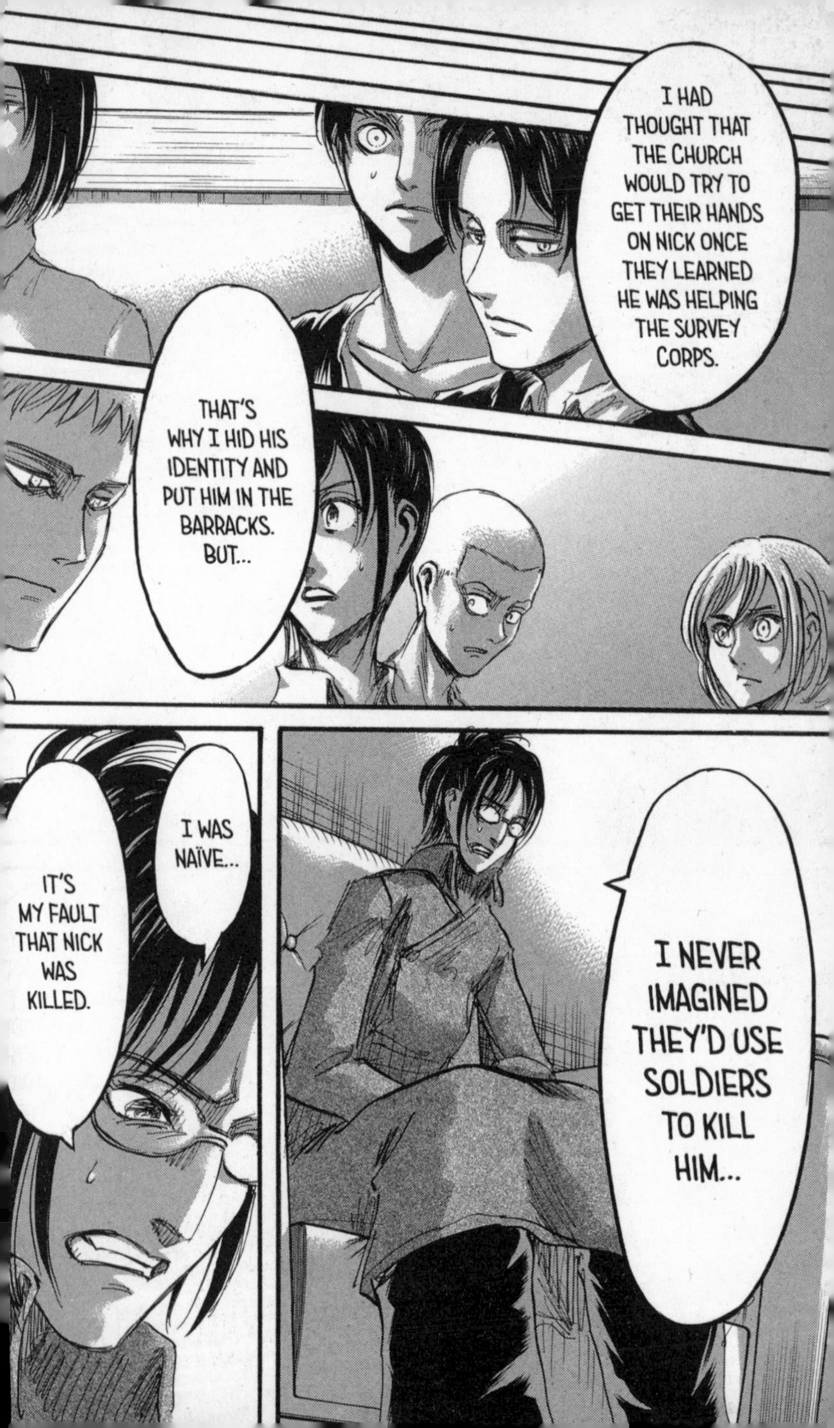
I HAD THOUGHT THAT THE CHURCH WOULD TRY TO GET THEIR HANDS ON NICK ONCE THEY LEARNED HE WAS HELPING THE SURVEY CORPS.
THAT'S WHY I HID HIS IDENTITY AND PUT HIM IN THE BARRACKS. BUT...
I NEVER IMAGINED THEY'D USE SOLDIERS TO KILL HIM...
I WAS NAÏVE...
IT'S MY FAULT THAT NICK WAS KILLED.

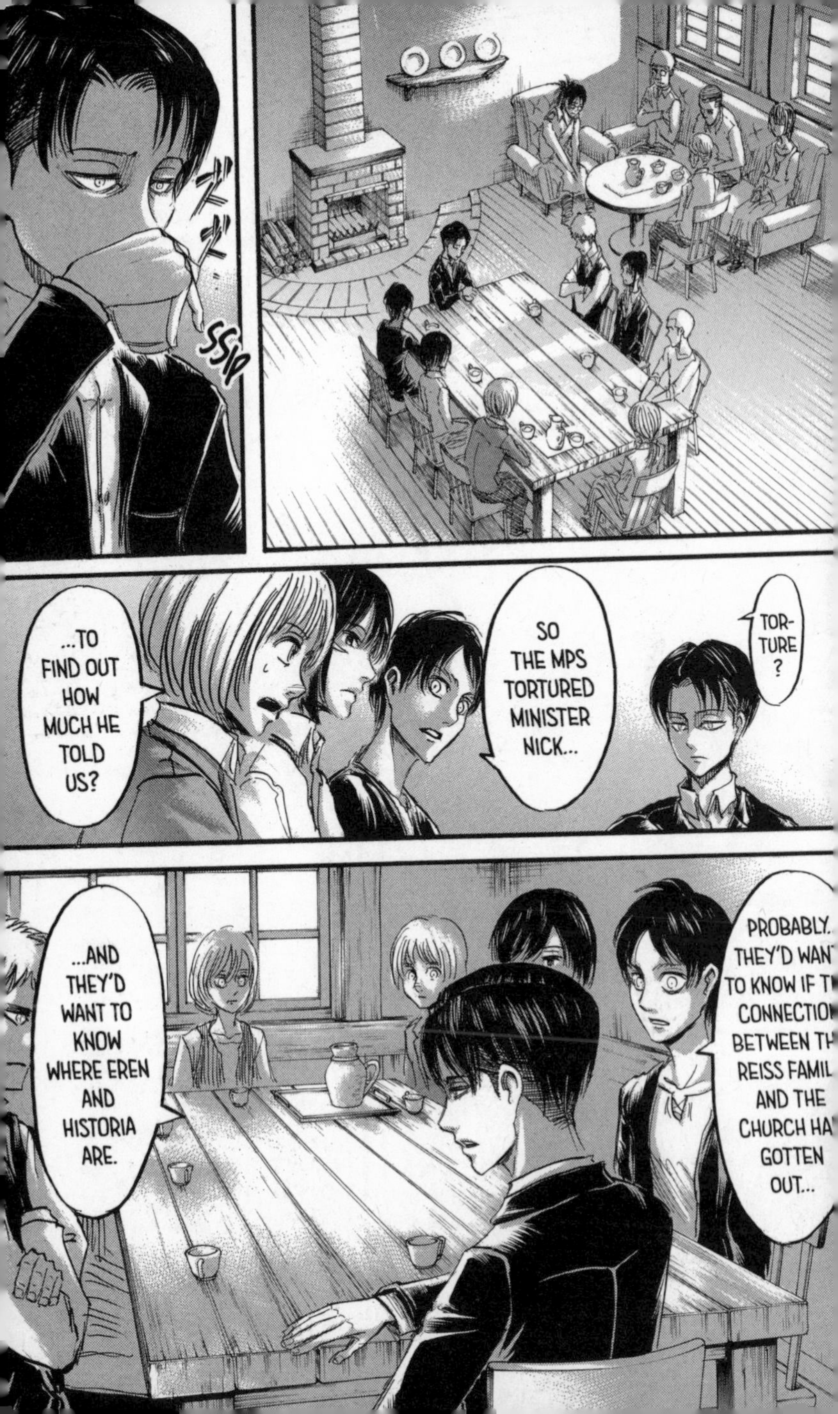
SSIP
TOR-TURE?
SO THE MPS TORTURED MINISTER NICK...
...TO FIND OUT HOW MUCH HE TOLD US?
PROBABLY. THEY'D WAN TO KNOW IF T CONNECTIO BETWEEN TH REISS FAMIL AND THE CHURCH HA GOTTEN OUT...
...AND THEY'D WANT TO KNOW WHERE EREN AND HISTORIA ARE.

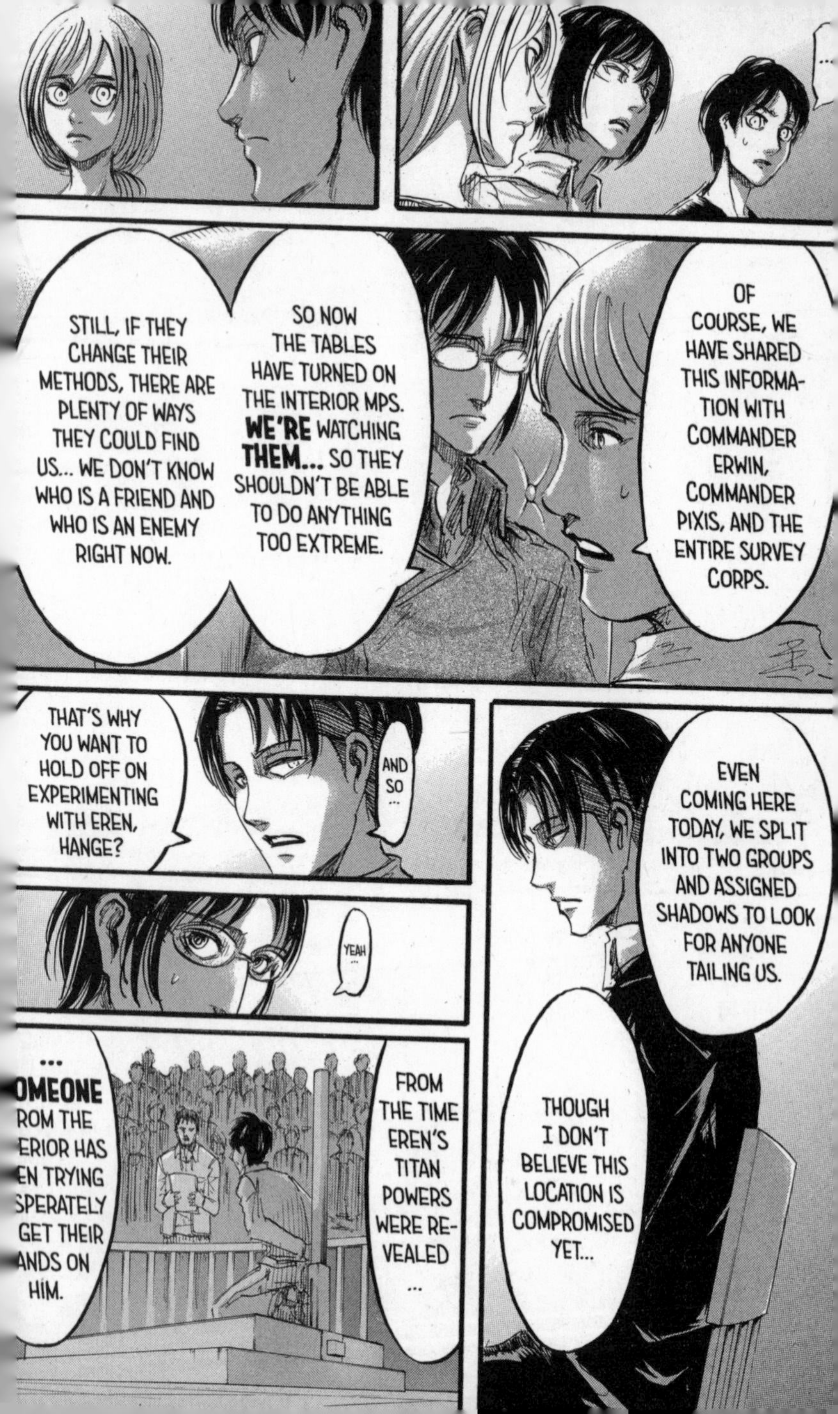
...
OF COURSE, WE HAVE SHARED THIS INFORMA-TION WITH COMMANDER ERWIN, COMMANDER PIXIS, AND THE ENTIRE SURVEY CORPS.
SO NOW THE TABLES HAVE TURNED ON THE INTERIOR MPS. **WE'RE** WATCHING **THEM...** SO THEY SHOULDN'T BE ABLE TO DO ANYTHING TOO EXTREME.
STILL, IF THEY CHANGE THEIR METHODS, THERE ARE PLENTY OF WAYS THEY COULD FIND US... WE DON'T KNOW WHO IS A FRIEND AND WHO IS AN ENEMY RIGHT NOW.
EVEN COMING HERE TODAY, WE SPLIT INTO TWO GROUPS AND ASSIGNED SHADOWS TO LOOK FOR ANYONE TAILING US.
THOUGH I DON'T BELIEVE THIS LOCATION IS COMPROMISED YET...
AND SO...
THAT'S WHY YOU WANT TO HOLD OFF ON EXPERIMENTING WITH EREN, HANGE?
YEAH...
FROM THE TIME EREN'S TITAN POWERS WERE RE-VEALED...
... **OMEONE** ROM THE ERIOR HAS EN TRYING SPERATELY GET THEIR ANDS ON HIM.

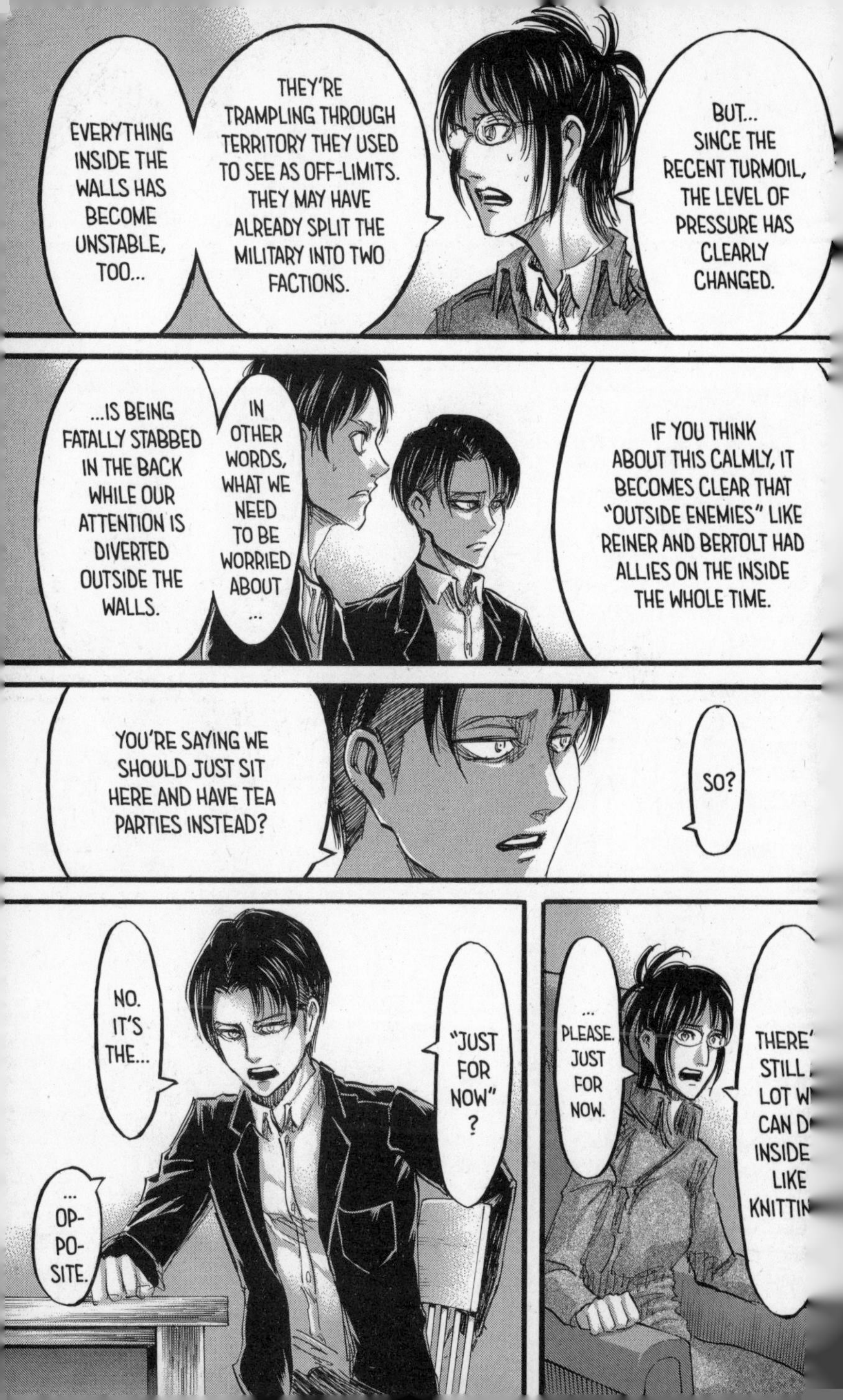
BUT... SINCE THE RECENT TURMOIL, THE LEVEL OF PRESSURE HAS CLEARLY CHANGED.
THEY'RE TRAMPLING THROUGH TERRITORY THEY USED TO SEE AS OFF-LIMITS. THEY MAY HAVE ALREADY SPLIT THE MILITARY INTO TWO FACTIONS.
EVERYTHING INSIDE THE WALLS HAS BECOME UNSTABLE, TOO...
IF YOU THINK ABOUT THIS CALMLY, IT BECOMES CLEAR THAT "OUTSIDE ENEMIES" LIKE REINER AND BERTOLT HAD ALLIES ON THE INSIDE THE WHOLE TIME.
IN OTHER WORDS, WHAT WE NEED TO BE WORRIED ABOUT ...
...IS BEING FATALLY STABBED IN THE BACK WHILE OUR ATTENTION IS DIVERTED OUTSIDE THE WALLS.
SO?
YOU'RE SAYING WE SHOULD JUST SIT HERE AND HAVE TEA PARTIES INSTEAD?
THERE' STILL LOT W CAN D INSIDE LIKE KNITTIN
... PLEASE. JUST FOR NOW.
"JUST FOR NOW" ?
NO. IT'S THE...
... OP-PO-SITE.

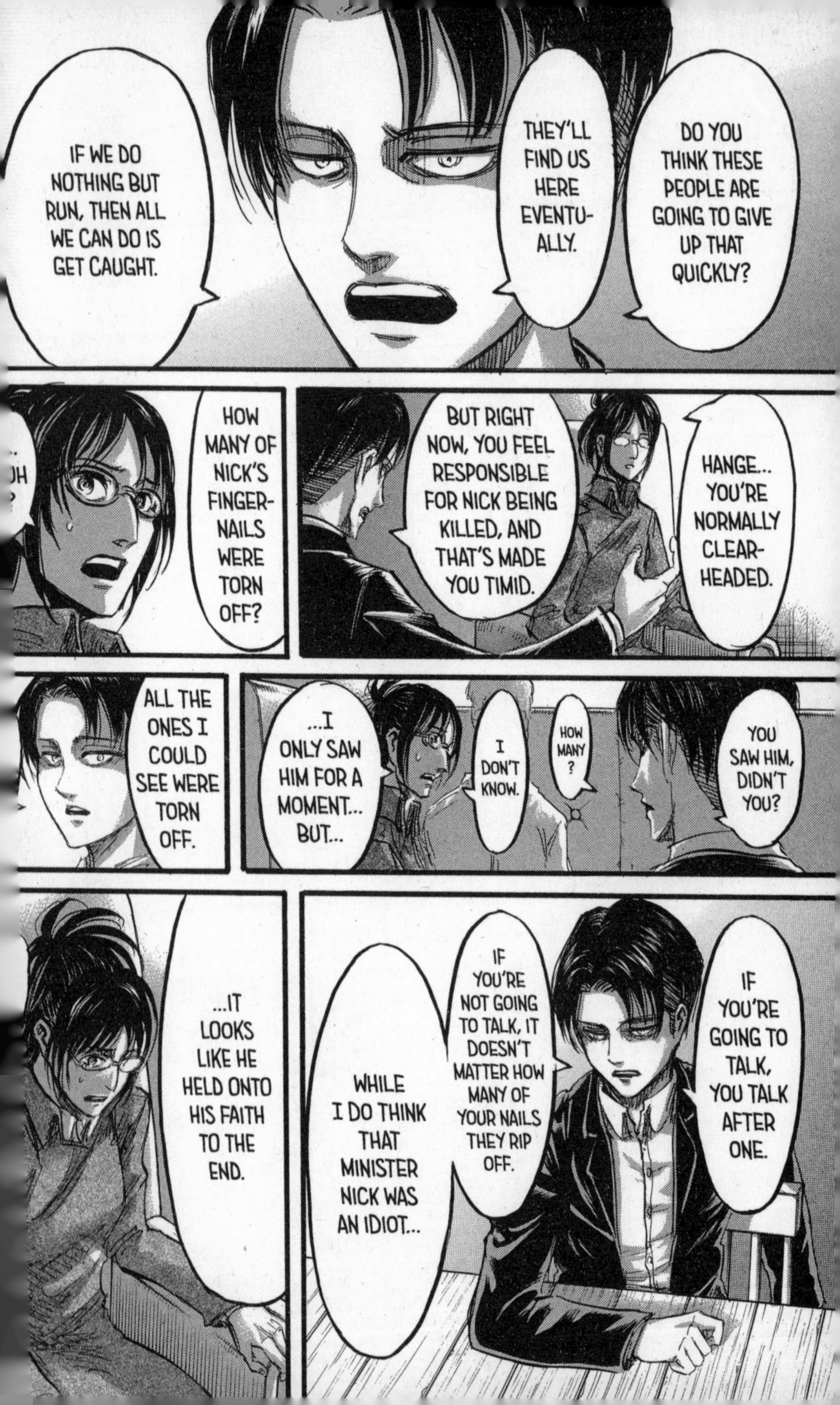
DO YOU THINK THESE PEOPLE ARE GOING TO GIVE UP THAT QUICKLY?
THEY'LL FIND US HERE EVENTU-ALLY.
IF WE DO NOTHING BUT RUN, THEN ALL WE CAN DO IS GET CAUGHT.
HANGE... YOU'RE NORMALLY CLEAR-HEADED.
BUT RIGHT NOW, YOU FEEL RESPONSIBLE FOR NICK BEING KILLED, AND THAT'S MADE YOU TIMID.
HOW MANY OF NICK'S FINGER-NAILS WERE TORN OFF?
YOU SAW HIM, DIDN'T YOU?
HOW MANY ?
I DON'T KNOW.
...I ONLY SAW HIM FOR A MOMENT... BUT...
ALL THE ONES I COULD SEE WERE TORN OFF.
IF YOU'RE GOING TO TALK, YOU TALK AFTER ONE.
IF YOU'RE NOT GOING TO TALK, IT DOESN'T MATTER HOW MANY OF YOUR NAILS THEY RIP OFF.
WHILE I DO THINK THAT MINISTER NICK WAS AN IDIOT...
...IT LOOKS LIKE HE HELD ONTO HIS FAITH TO THE END.

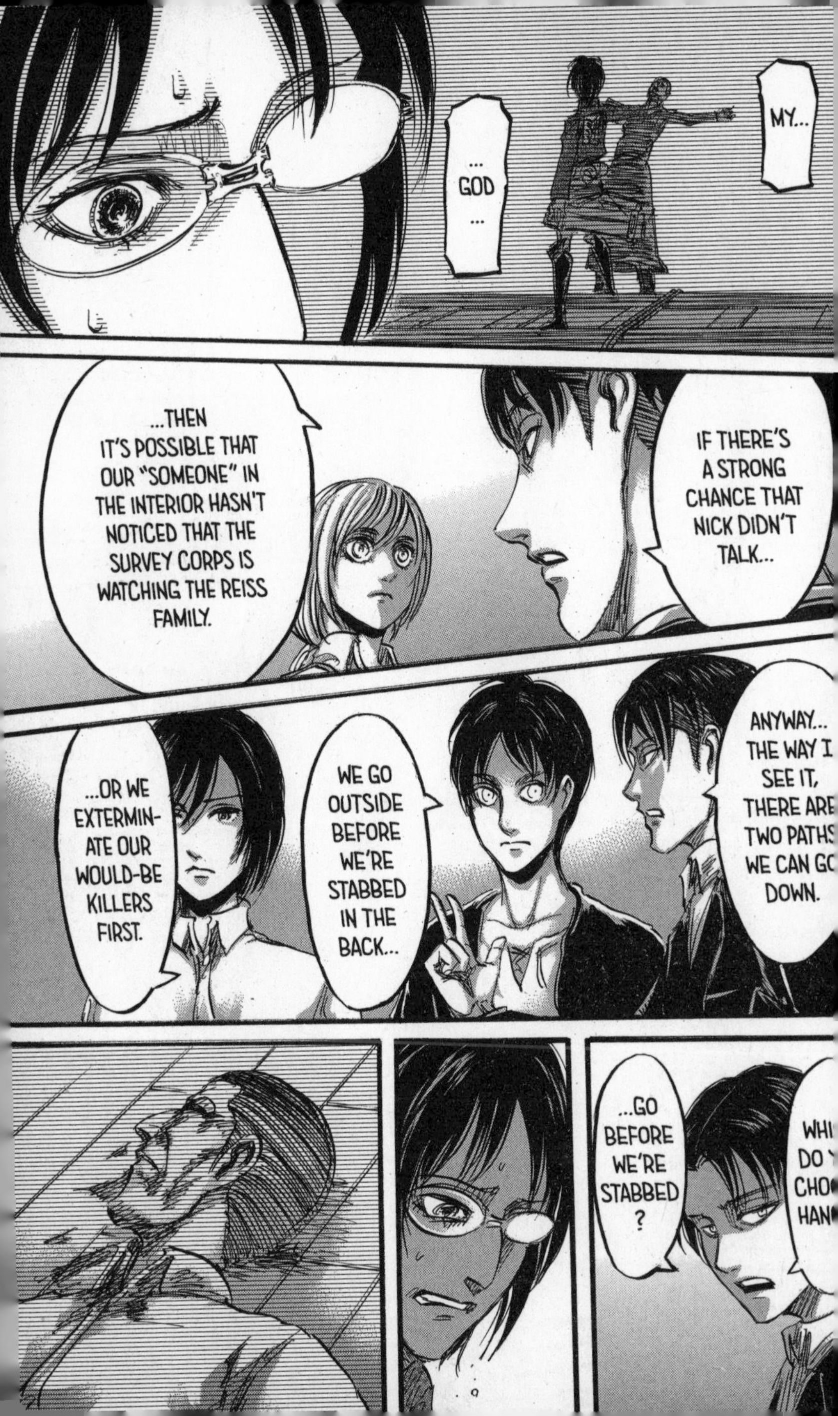
MY...
...GOD...
IF THERE'S A STRONG CHANCE THAT NICK DIDN'T TALK...
...THEN IT'S POSSIBLE THAT OUR "SOMEONE" IN THE INTERIOR HASN'T NOTICED THAT THE SURVEY CORPS IS WATCHING THE REISS FAMILY.
ANYWAY... THE WAY I SEE IT, THERE ARE TWO PATHS WE CAN GO DOWN.
WE GO OUTSIDE BEFORE WE'RE STABBED IN THE BACK...
...OR WE EXTERMIN-ATE OUR WOULD-BE KILLERS FIRST.
WHI DO CHO HAN
...GO BEFORE WE'RE STABBED ?

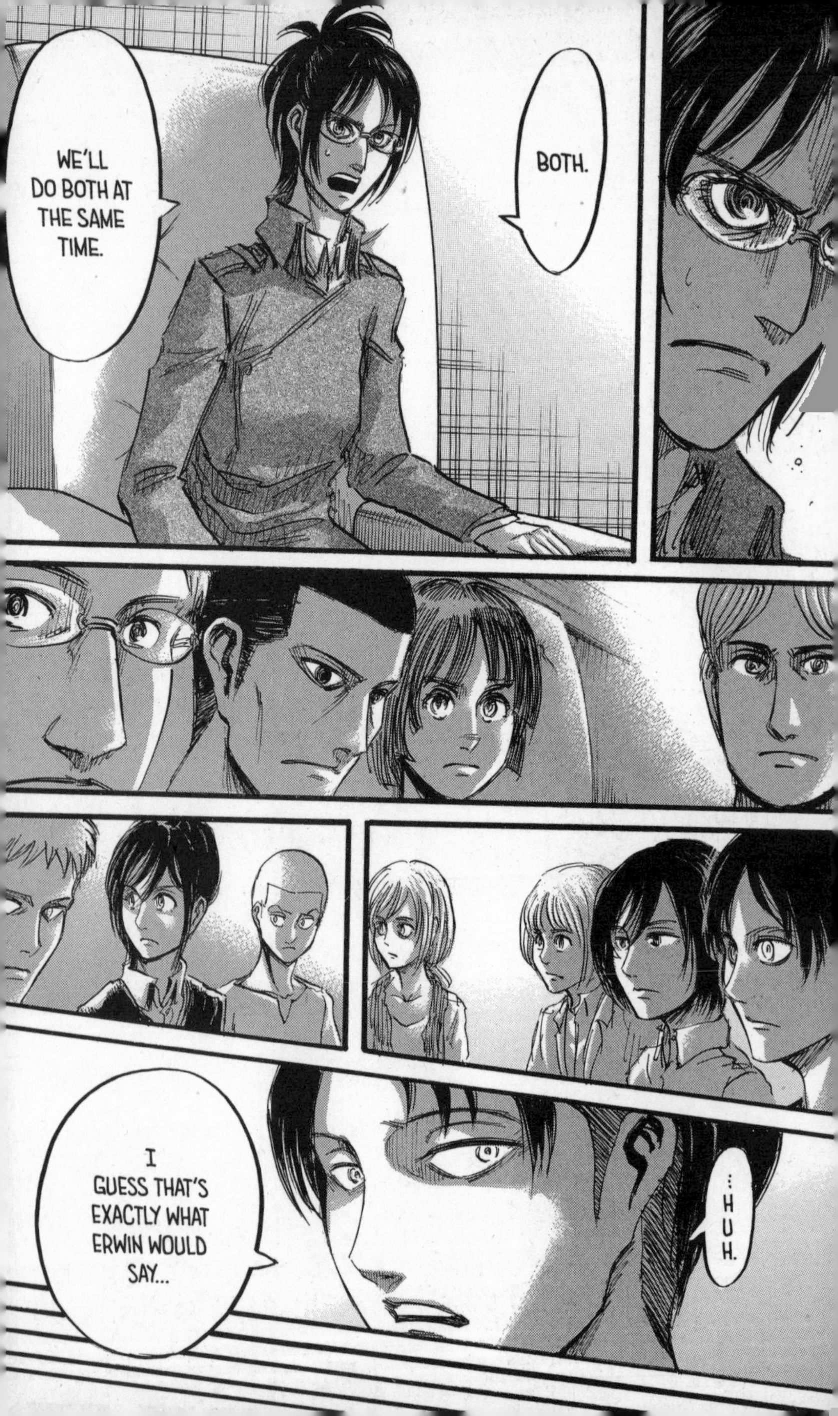
BOTH.
WE'LL DO BOTH AT THE SAME TIME.
...HUH.
I GUESS THAT'S EXACTLY WHAT ERWIN WOULD SAY...

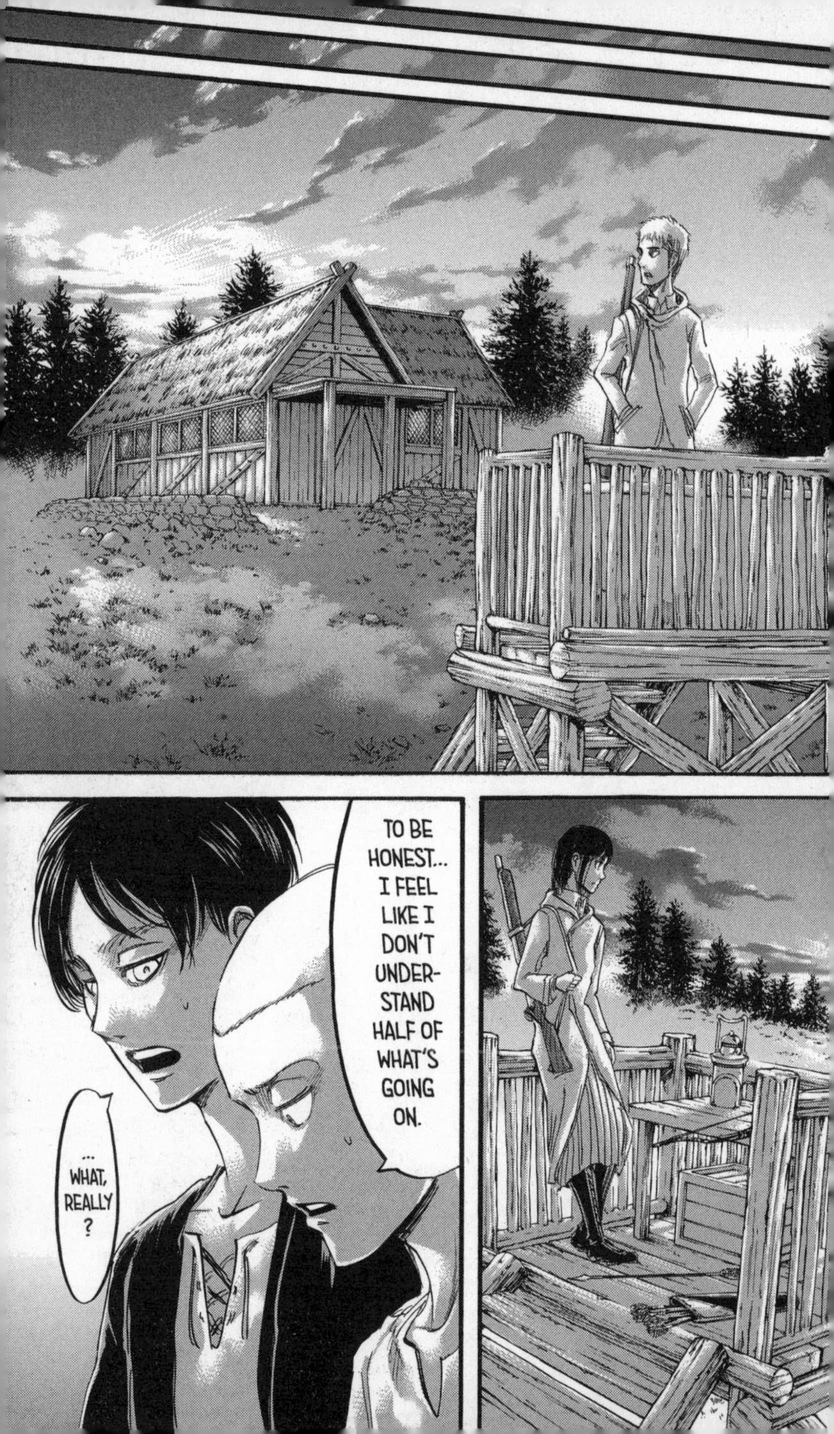
TO BE HONEST... I FEEL LIKE I DON'T UNDERSTAND HALF OF WHAT'S GOING ON.
... WHAT, REALLY?

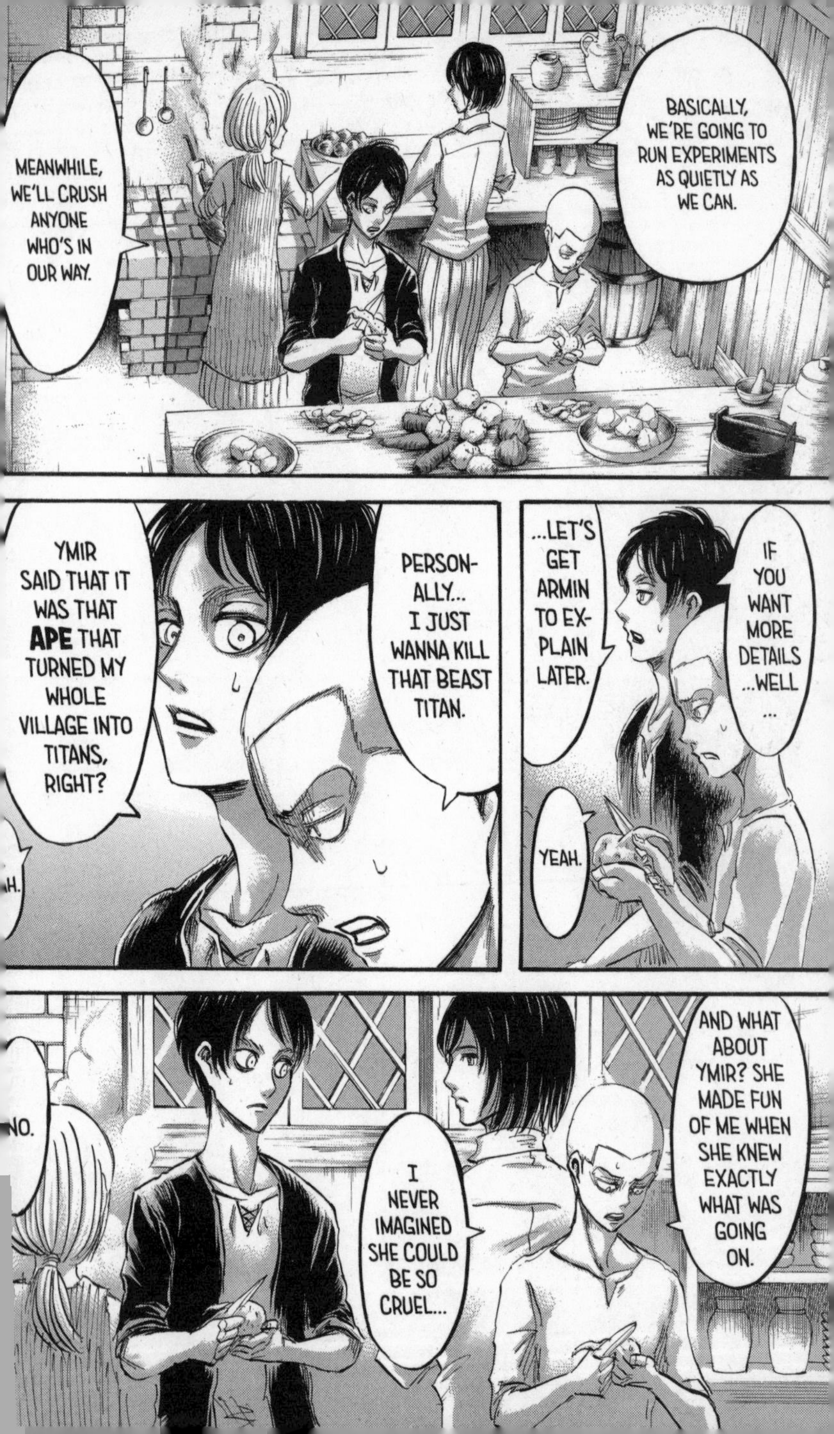
BASICALLY, WE'RE GOING TO RUN EXPERIMENTS AS QUIETLY AS WE CAN.
MEANWHILE, WE'LL CRUSH ANYONE WHO'S IN OUR WAY.
IF YOU WANT MORE DETAILS ...WELL ...
...LET'S GET ARMIN TO EX- PLAIN LATER.
YEAH.
PERSON- ALLY... I JUST WANNA KILL THAT BEAST TITAN.
YMIR SAID THAT IT WAS THAT **APE** THAT TURNED MY WHOLE VILLAGE INTO TITANS, RIGHT?
AND WHAT ABOUT YMIR? SHE MADE FUN OF ME WHEN SHE KNEW EXACTLY WHAT WAS GOING ON.
I NEVER IMAGINED SHE COULD BE SO CRUEL...
NO.

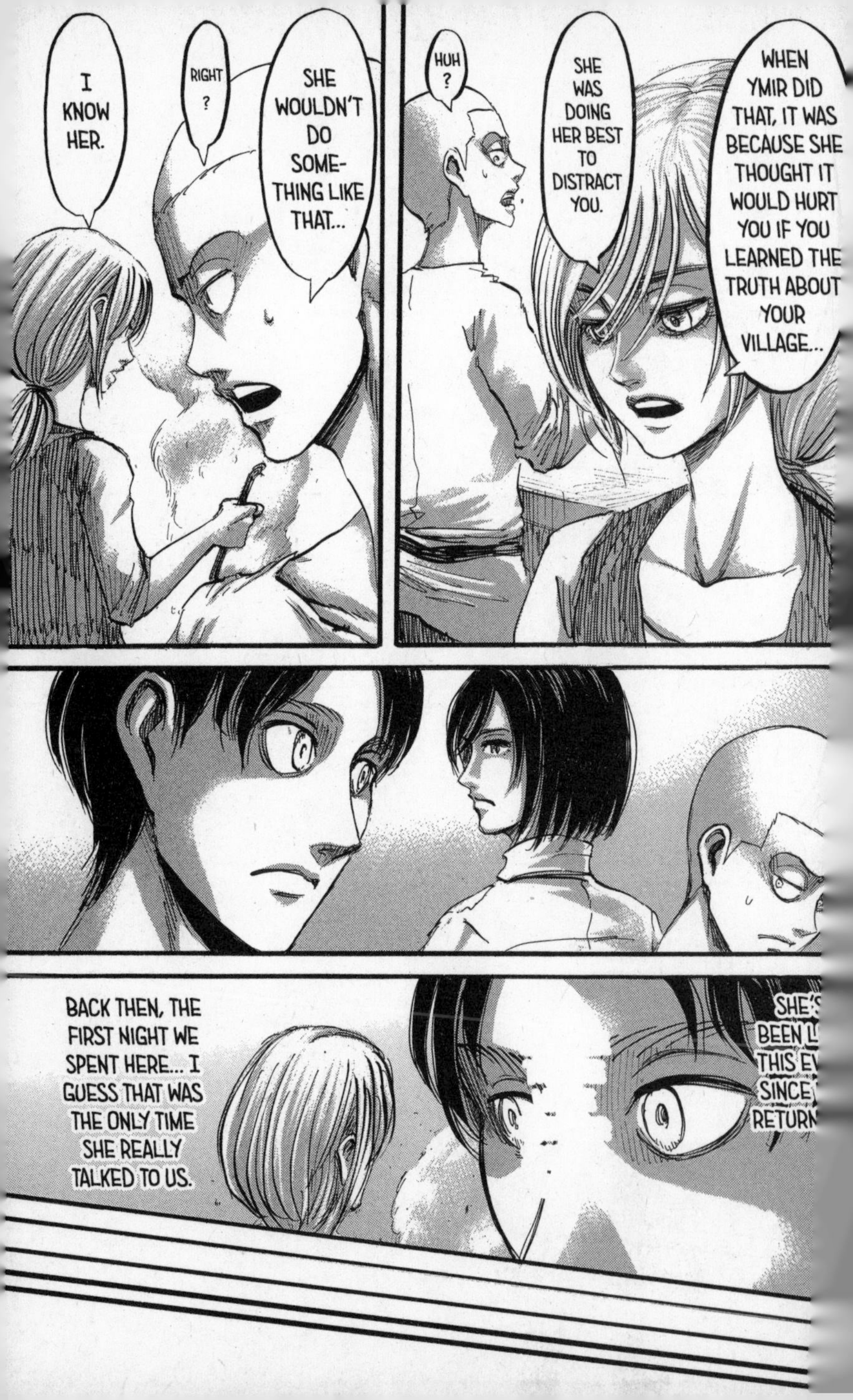
WHEN YMIR DID THAT, IT WAS BECAUSE SHE THOUGHT IT WOULD HURT YOU IF YOU LEARNED THE TRUTH ABOUT YOUR VILLAGE...
SHE WAS DOING HER BEST TO DISTRACT YOU.
HUH?
SHE WOULDN'T DO SOME-THING LIKE THAT...
RIGHT?
I KNOW HER.
SHE'S BEEN L THIS EV SINCE RETURN
BACK THEN, THE FIRST NIGHT WE SPENT HERE... I GUESS THAT WAS THE ONLY TIME SHE REALLY TALKED TO US.

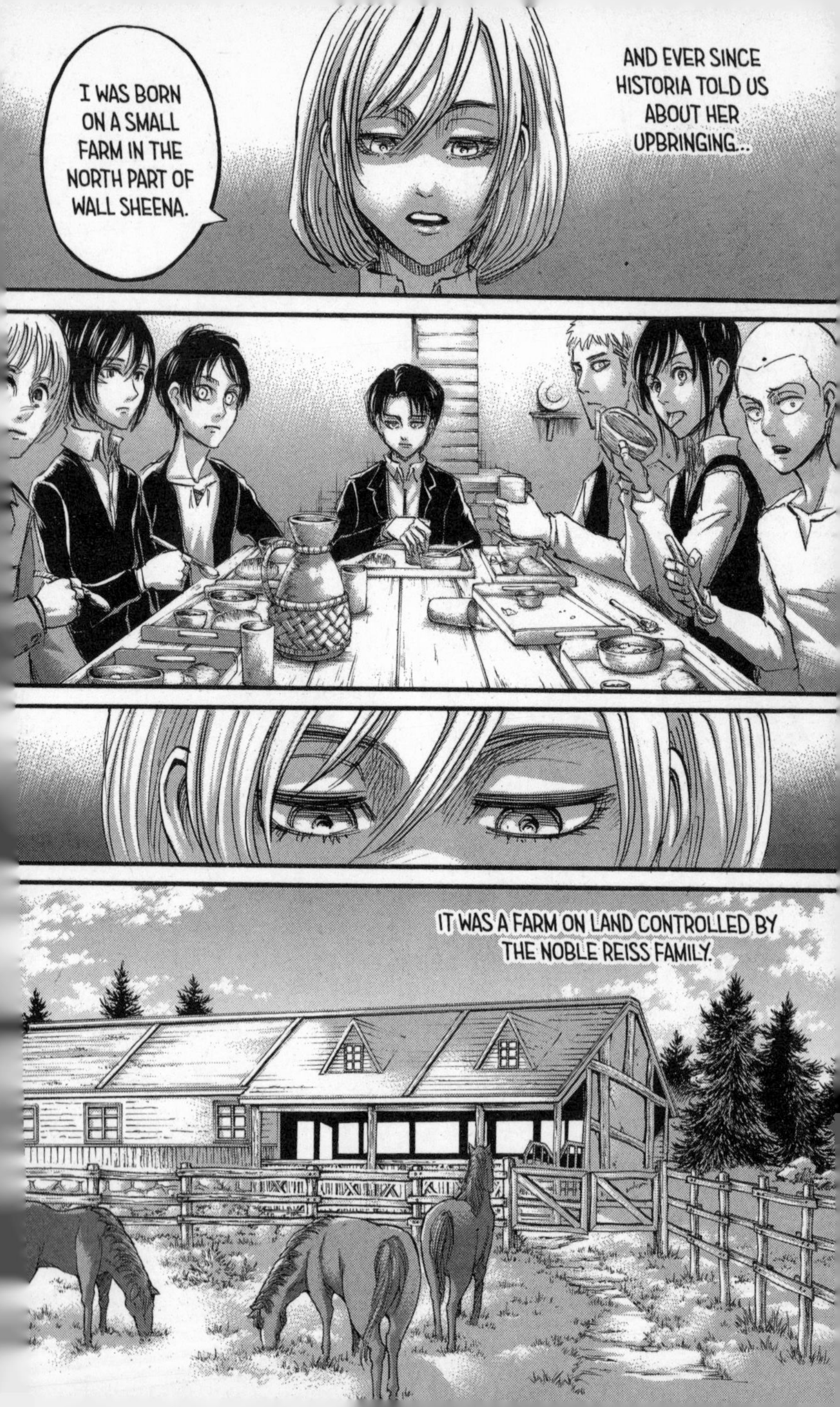
AND EVER SINCE HISTORIA TOLD US ABOUT HER UPBRINGING...
I WAS BORN ON A SMALL FARM IN THE NORTH PART OF WALL SHEENA.
IT WAS A FARM ON LAND CONTROLLED BY THE NOBLE REISS FAMILY.

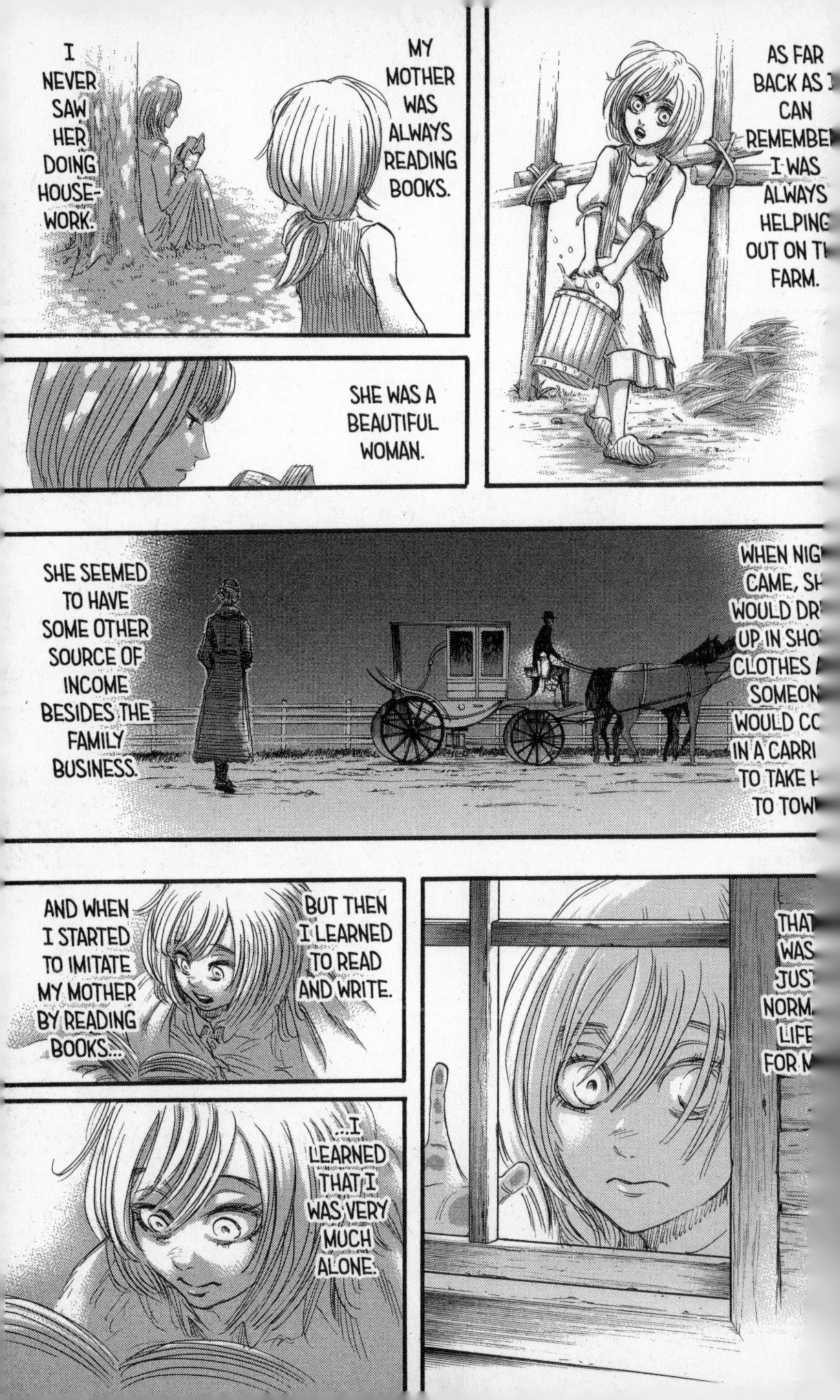

AS FAR BACK AS
CAN REMEMBE
I WAS ALWAYS HELPING OUT ON T
FARM.
MY MOTHER WAS ALWAYS READING BOOKS.
I NEVER SAW HER DOING HOUSE-WORK.
SHE WAS A BEAUTIFUL WOMAN.
WHEN NIG CAME, SH WOULD DR UP IN SHO CLOTHES A SOMEON WOULD CO IN A CARRI TO TAKE H TO TOW
SHE SEEMED TO HAVE SOME OTHER SOURCE OF INCOME BESIDES THE FAMILY BUSINESS.
THA WAS JUST NORM LIFE FOR M
BUT THEN I LEARNED TO READ AND WRITE.
AND WHEN I STARTED TO IMITATE MY MOTHER BY READING BOOKS...
...I LEARNED THAT I WAS VERY MUCH ALONE.

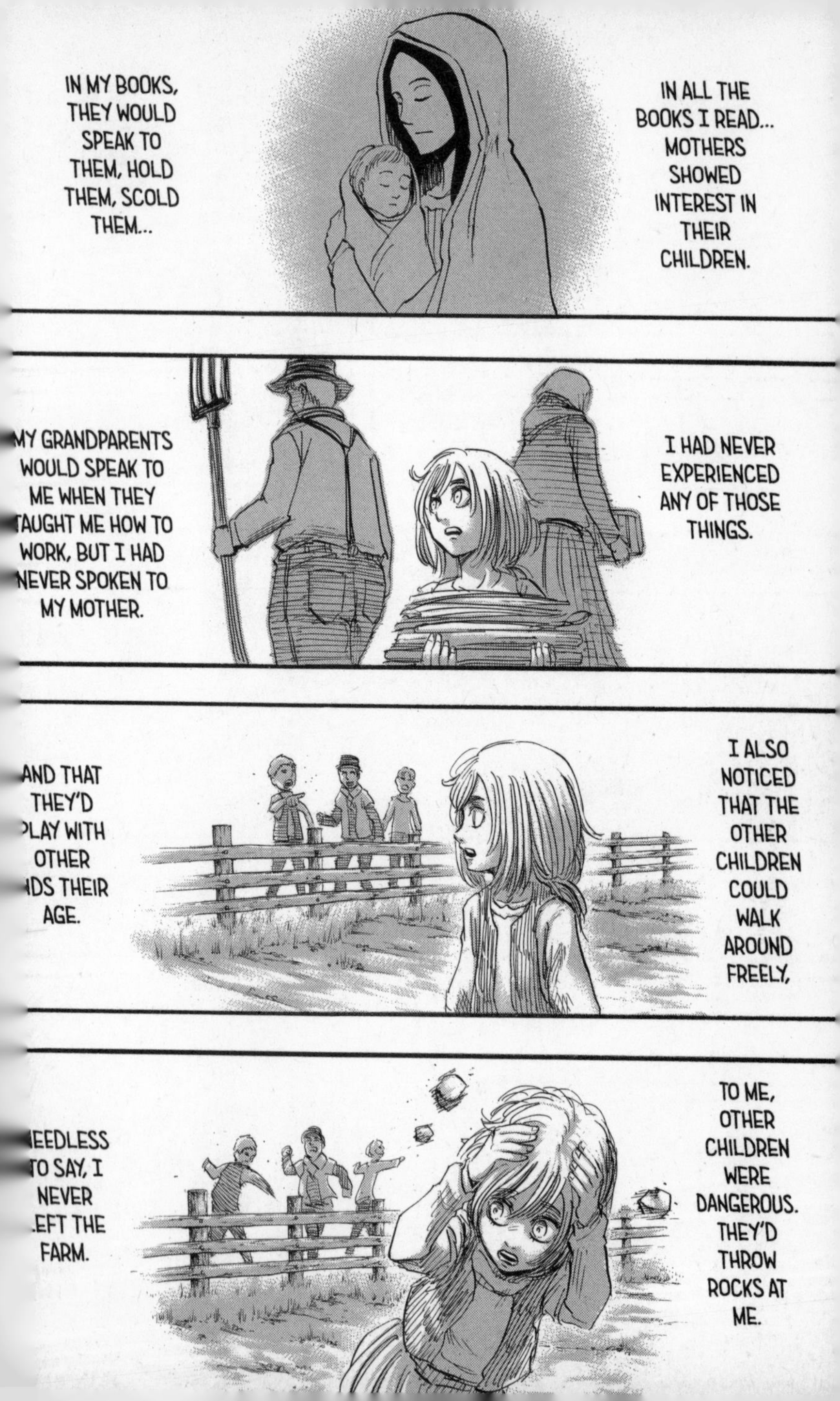
IN ALL THE BOOKS I READ... MOTHERS SHOWED INTEREST IN THEIR CHILDREN.
IN MY BOOKS, THEY WOULD SPEAK TO THEM, HOLD THEM, SCOLD THEM...
I HAD NEVER EXPERIENCED ANY OF THOSE THINGS.
MY GRANDPARENTS WOULD SPEAK TO ME WHEN THEY TAUGHT ME HOW TO WORK, BUT I HAD NEVER SPOKEN TO MY MOTHER.
I ALSO NOTICED THAT THE OTHER CHILDREN COULD WALK AROUND FREELY,
AND THAT THEY'D PLAY WITH OTHER KIDS THEIR AGE.
TO ME, OTHER CHILDREN WERE DANGEROUS. THEY'D THROW ROCKS AT ME.
NEEDLESS TO SAY, I NEVER LEFT THE FARM.

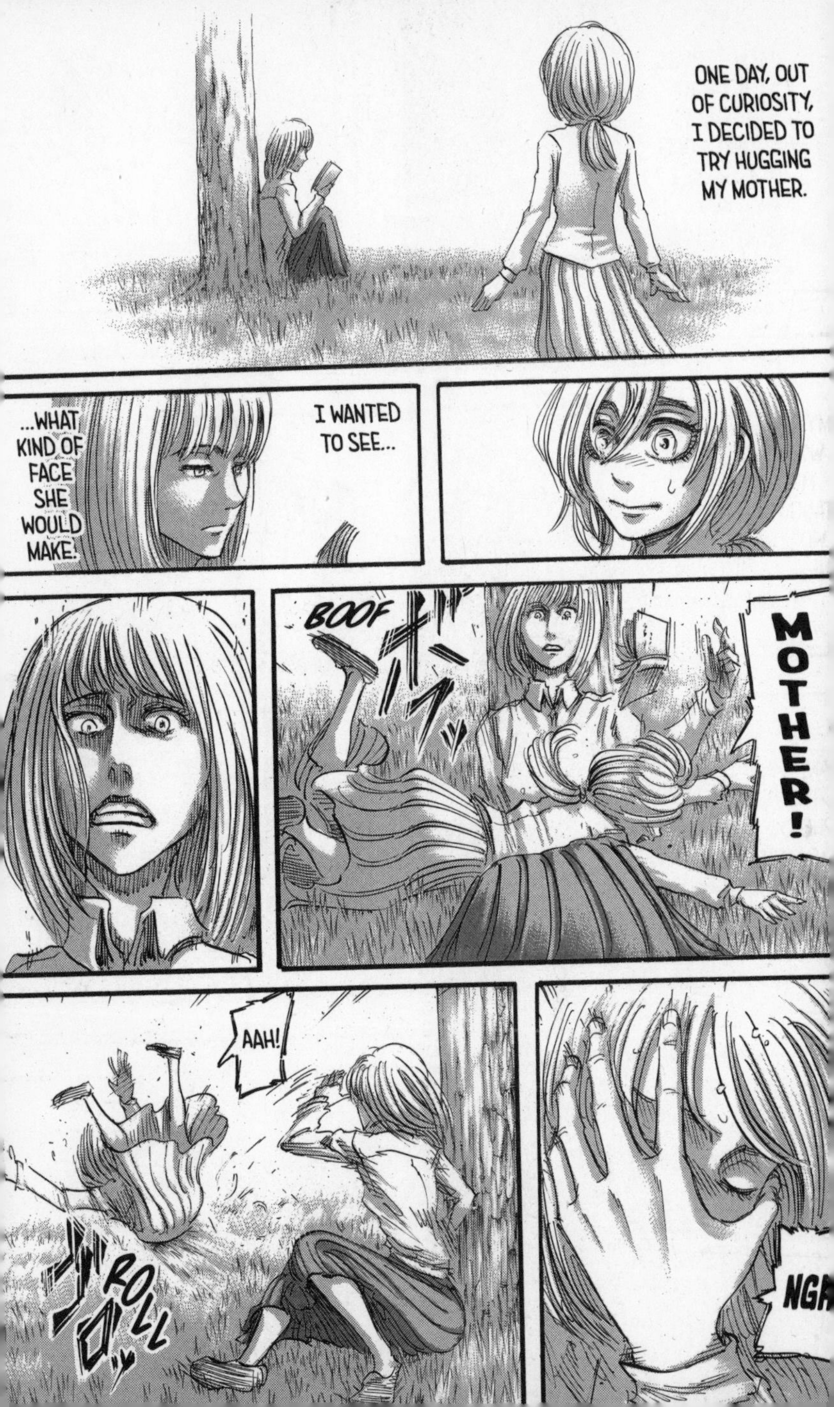
ONE DAY, OUT OF CURIOSITY, I DECIDED TO TRY HUGGING MY MOTHER.
I WANTED TO SEE...
...WHAT KIND OF FACE SHE WOULD MAKE.
MOTHER!
BOOF
NGA
AAH!
ROLL

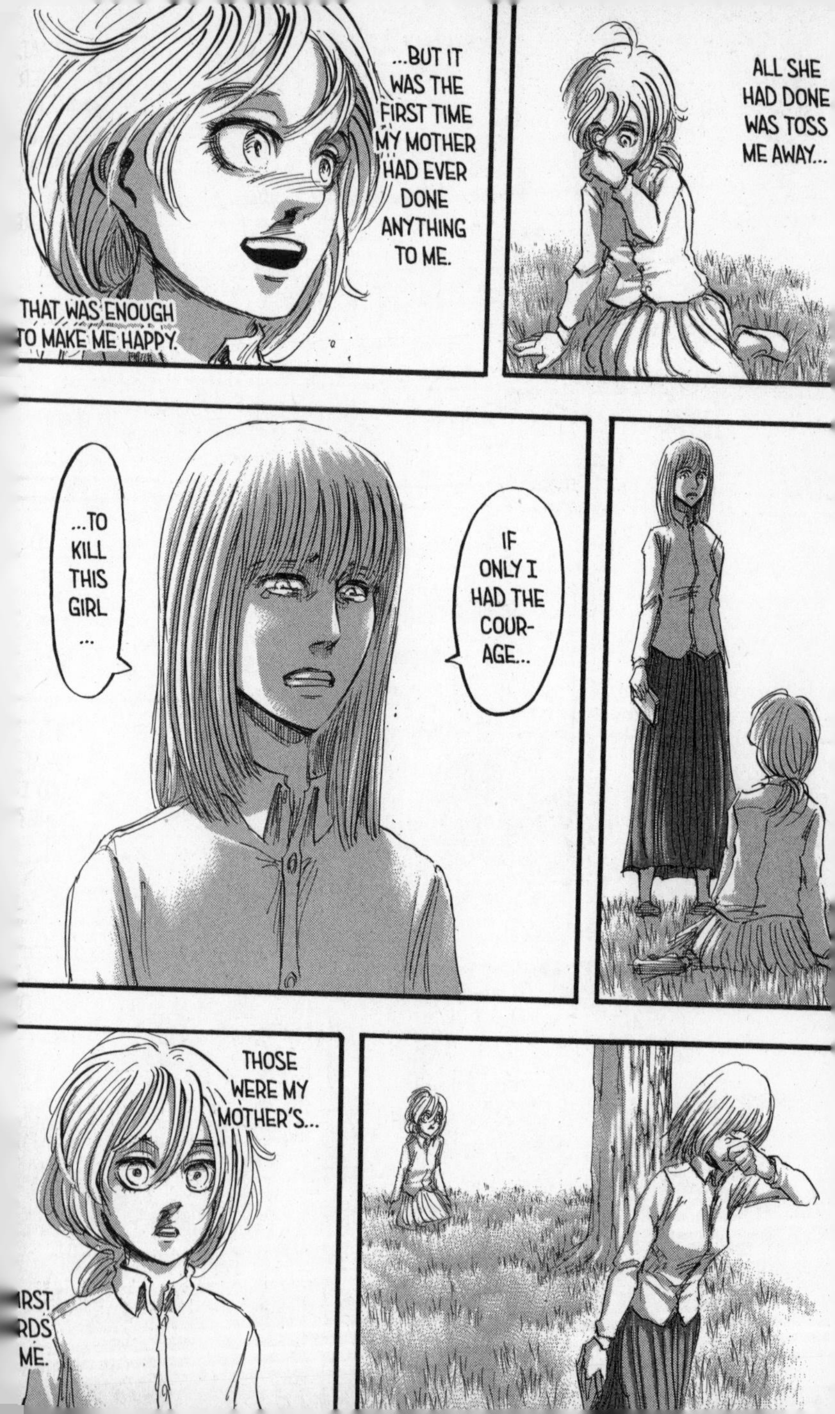
ALL SHE HAD DONE WAS TOSS ME AWAY...
...BUT IT WAS THE FIRST TIME MY MOTHER HAD EVER DONE ANYTHING TO ME.
THAT WAS ENOUGH TO MAKE ME HAPPY.
IF ONLY I HAD THE COURAGE...
...TO KILL THIS GIRL ...
THOSE WERE MY MOTHER'S...
IRST RDS ME.

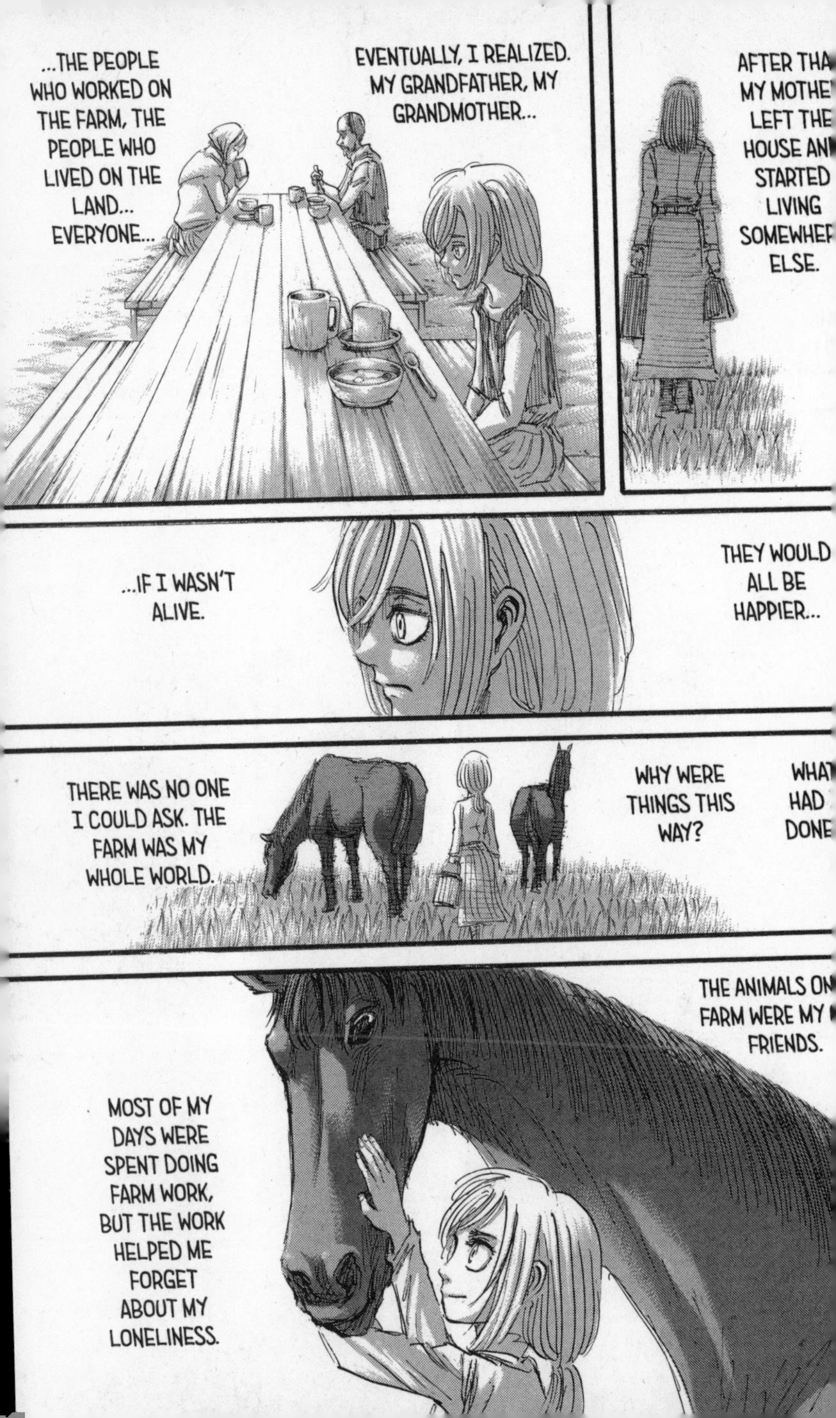
AFTER THA MY MOTHE LEFT THE HOUSE AN STARTED LIVING SOMEWHE ELSE.
EVENTUALLY, I REALIZED. MY GRANDFATHER, MY GRANDMOTHER...
...THE PEOPLE WHO WORKED ON THE FARM, THE PEOPLE WHO LIVED ON THE LAND... EVERYONE...
THEY WOULD ALL BE HAPPIER...
...IF I WASN'T ALIVE.
WHAT HAD DONE
WHY WERE THINGS THIS WAY?
THERE WAS NO ONE I COULD ASK. THE FARM WAS MY WHOLE WORLD.
THE ANIMALS ON FARM WERE MY FRIENDS.
MOST OF MY DAYS WERE SPENT DOING FARM WORK, BUT THE WORK HELPED ME FORGET ABOUT MY LONELINESS.

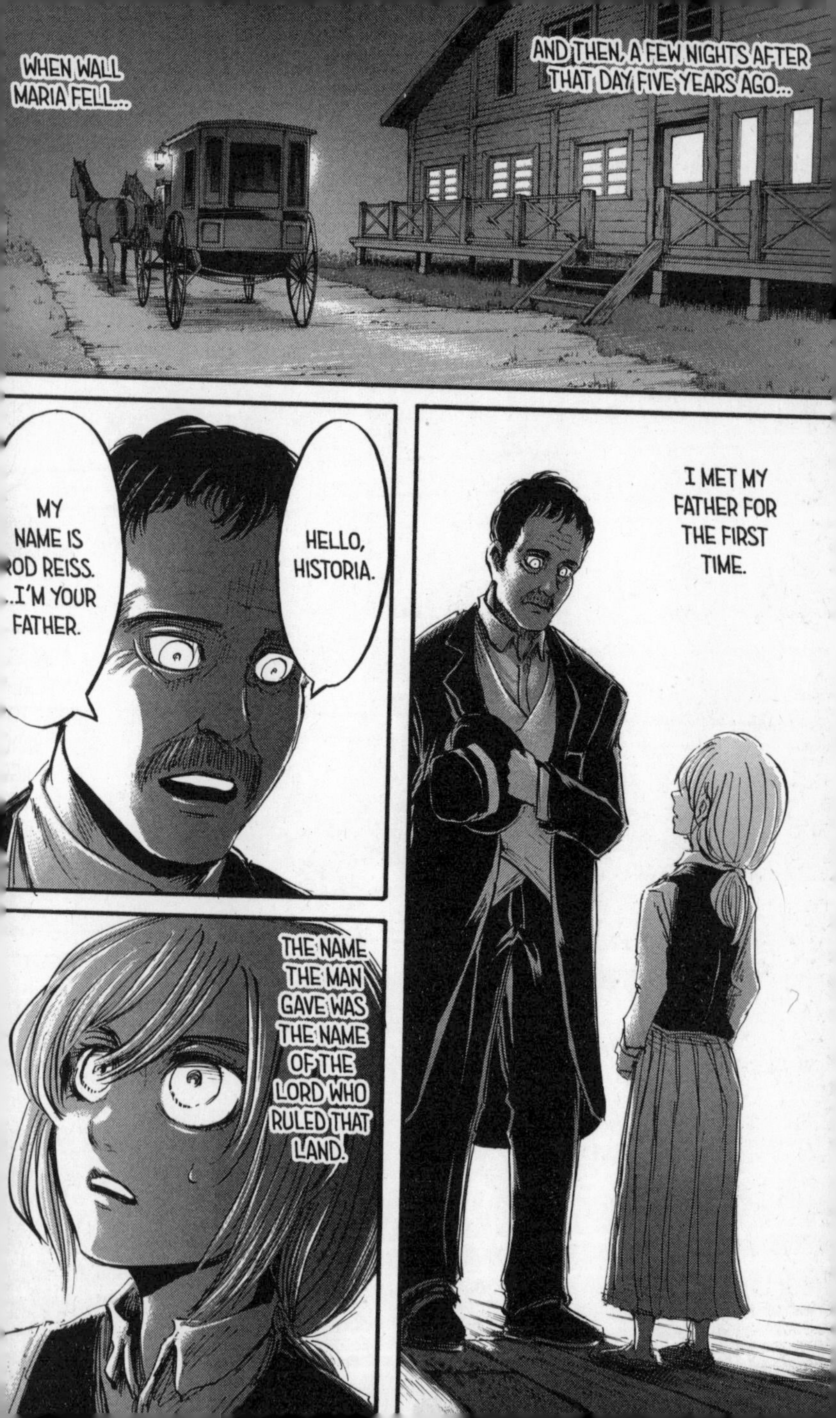
AND THEN, A FEW NIGHTS AFTER THAT DAY FIVE YEARS AGO...
WHEN WALL MARIA FELL...
I MET MY FATHER FOR THE FIRST TIME.
HELLO, HISTORIA.
MY NAME IS ROD REISS. ...I'M YOUR FATHER.
THE NAME THE MAN GAVE WAS THE NAME OF THE LORD WHO RULED THAT LAND.

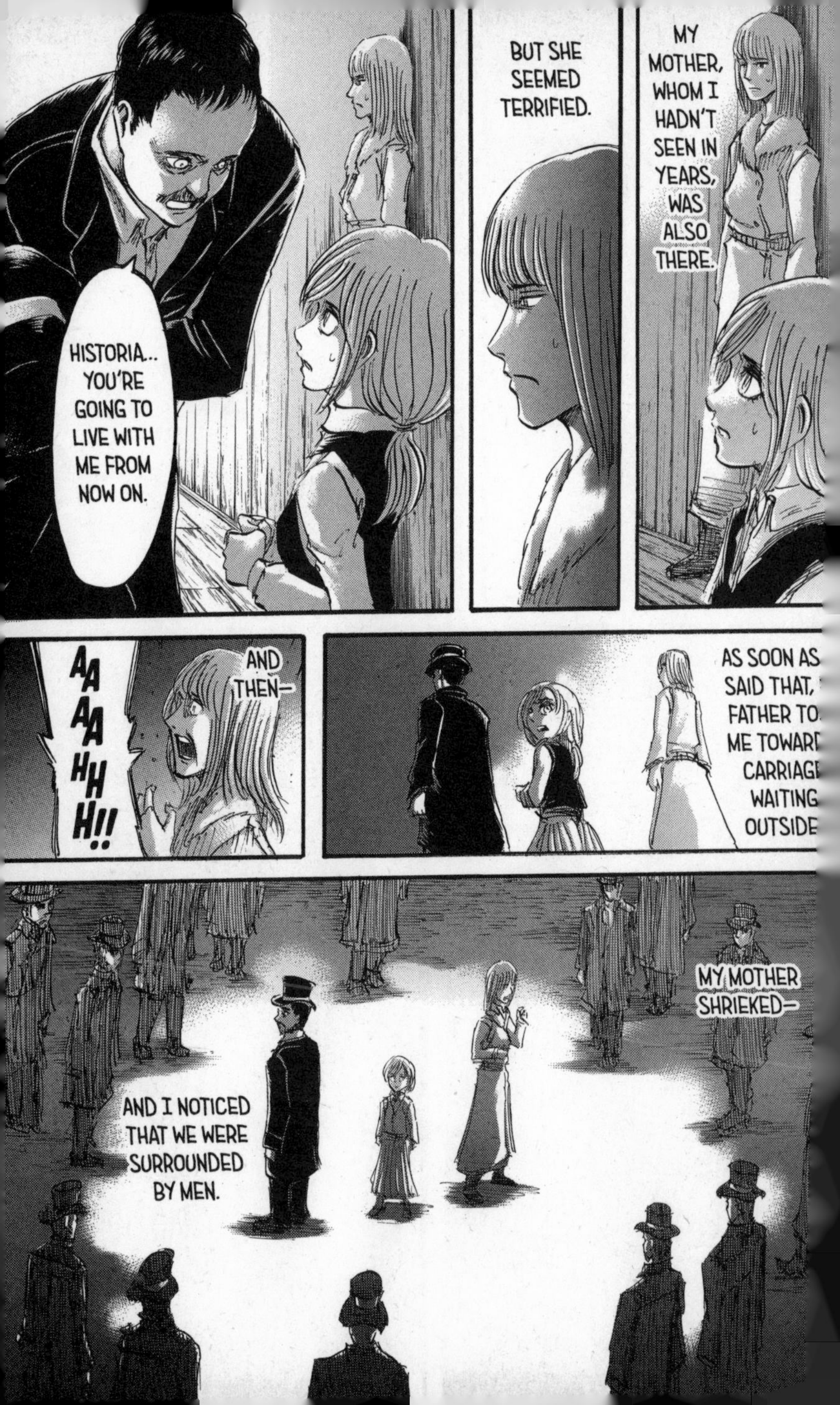
MY MOTHER, WHOM I HADN'T SEEN IN YEARS, WAS ALSO THERE.
BUT SHE SEEMED TERRIFIED.
HISTORIA... YOU'RE GOING TO LIVE WITH ME FROM NOW ON.
AS SOON AS SAID THAT, FATHER TO ME TOWAR CARRIAG WAITING OUTSIDE
AND THEN—
AAAHHH!!
MY MOTHER SHRIEKED—
AND I NOTICED THAT WE WERE SURROUNDED BY MEN.

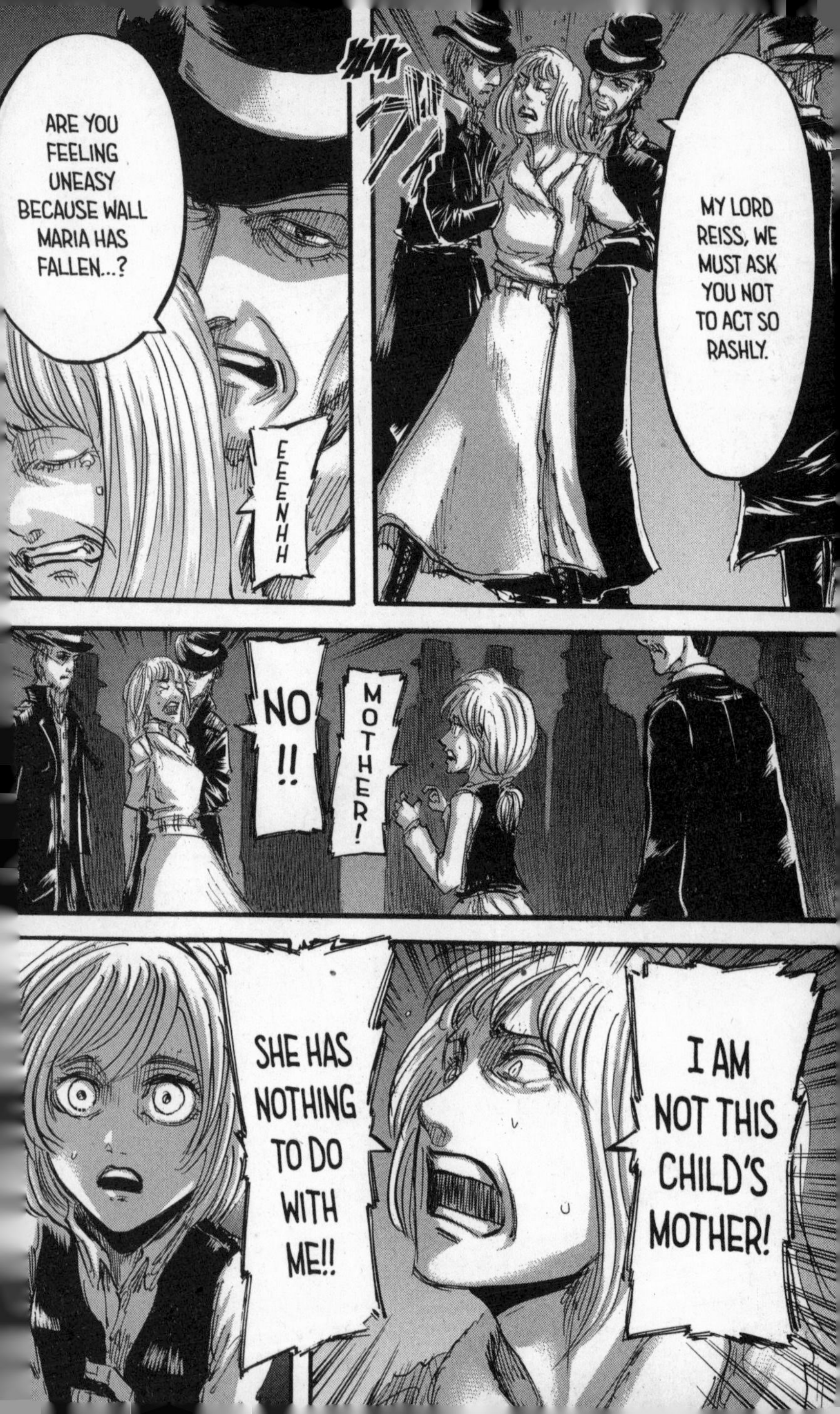
MY LORD REISS, WE MUST ASK YOU NOT TO ACT SO RASHLY.
ARE YOU FEELING UNEASY BECAUSE WALL MARIA HAS FALLEN...?
EEEENHH
MOTHER!
NO!!
I AM NOT THIS CHILD'S MOTHER!
SHE HAS NOTHING TO DO WITH ME!!

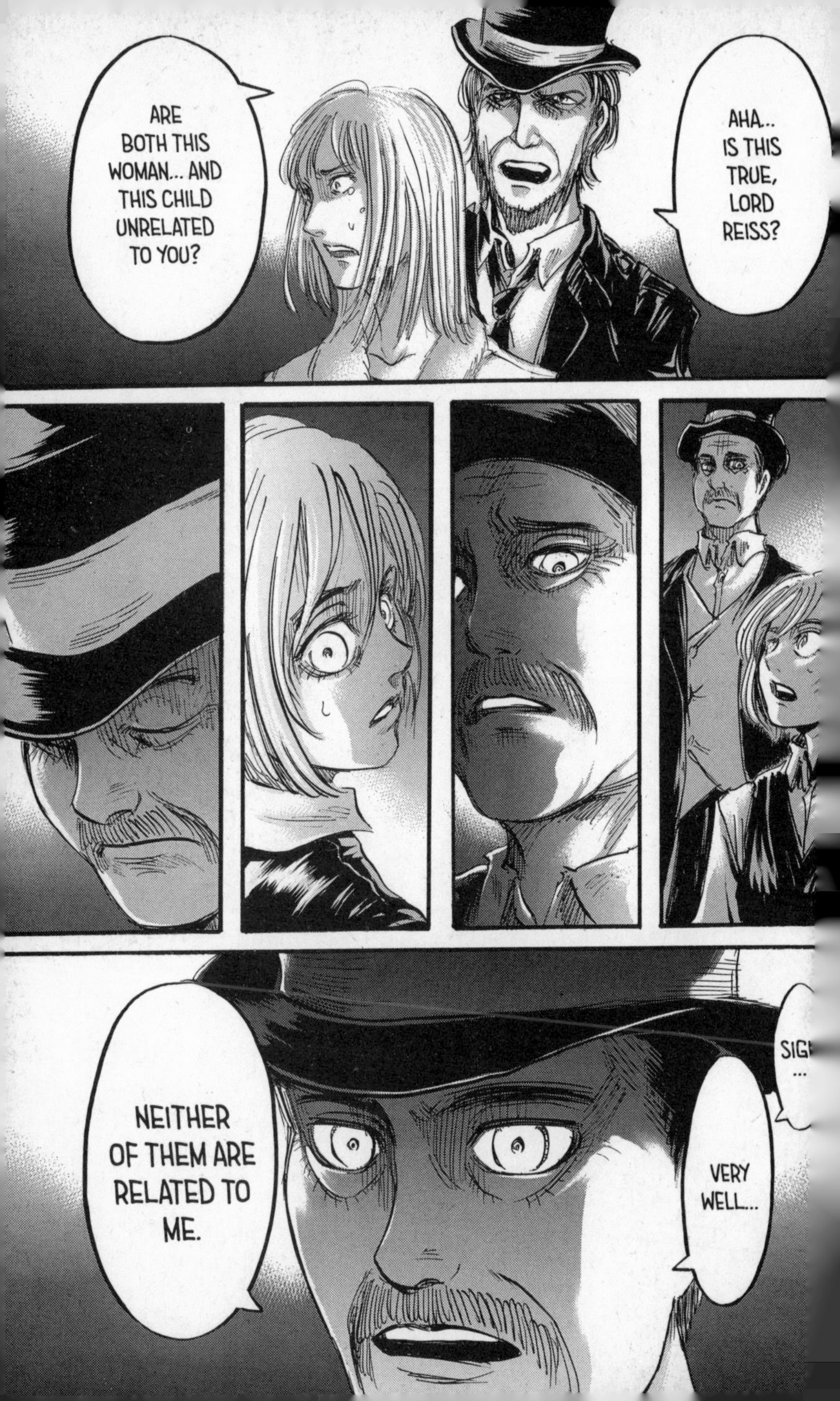
AHA... IS THIS TRUE, LORD REISS?
ARE BOTH THIS WOMAN... AND THIS CHILD UNRELATED TO YOU?
SIG ...
VERY WELL...
NEITHER OF THEM ARE RELATED TO ME.

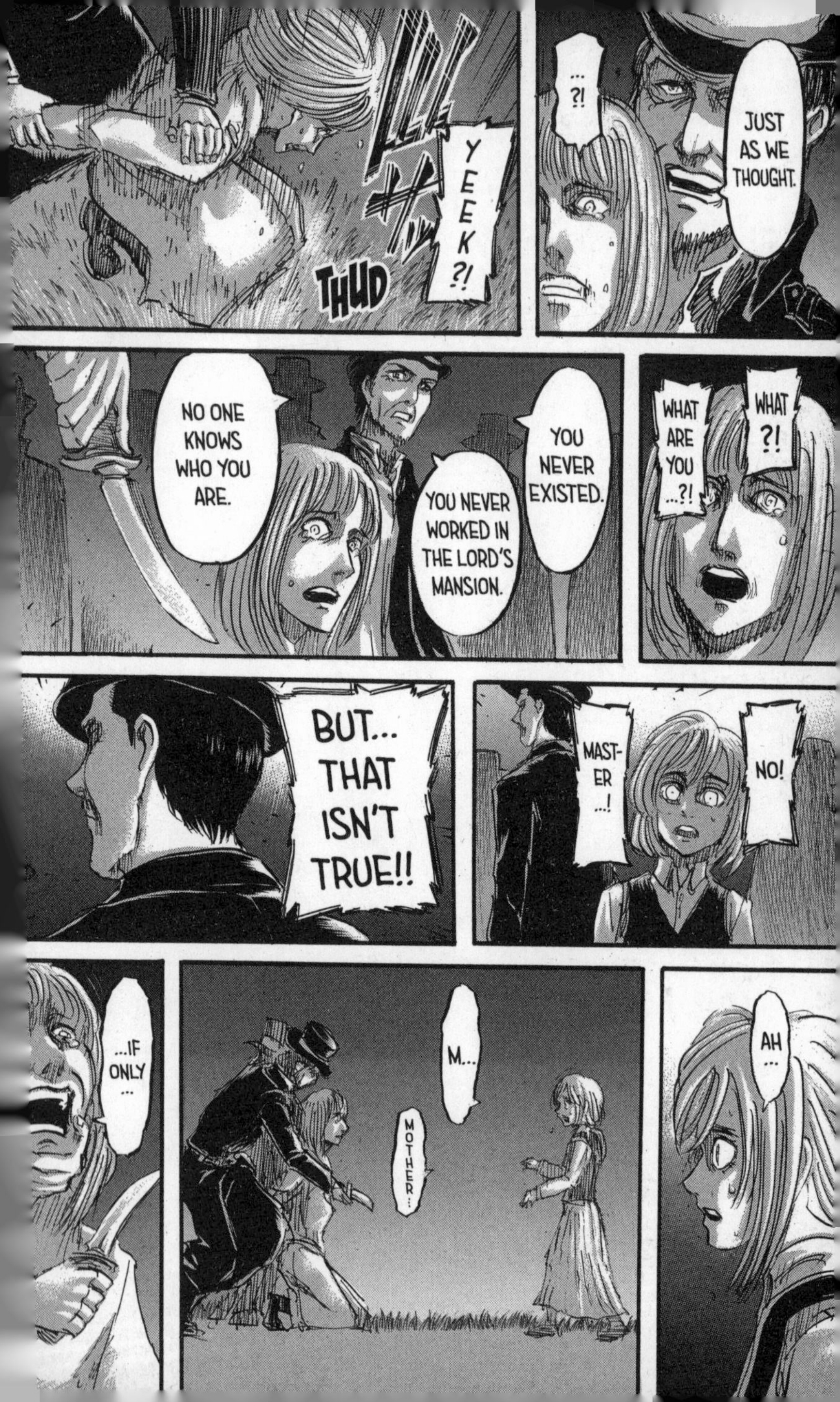
JUST AS WE THOUGHT.
...?!
YEEK?!
THUD
WHAT ?!
WHAT ARE YOU ...?!
YOU NEVER EXISTED.
YOU NEVER WORKED IN THE LORD'S MANSION.
NO ONE KNOWS WHO YOU ARE.
NO!
MAST-ER ...!
BUT... THAT ISN'T TRUE!!
AH ...
M...
MOTHER...
...IF ONLY ...

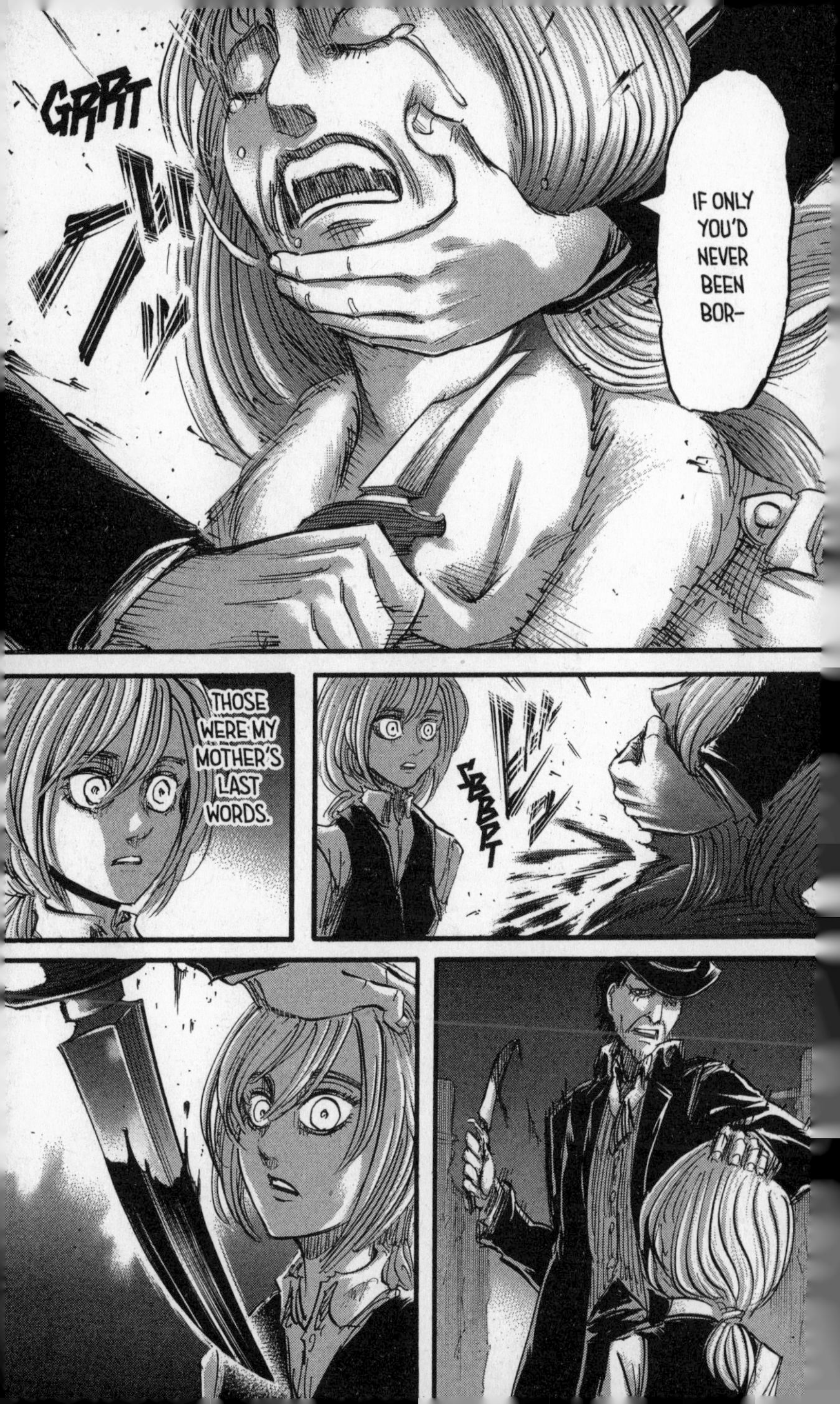
IF ONLY YOU'D NEVER BEEN BOR-
GRRT
CRRRT
THOSE WERE MY MOTHER'S LAST WORDS.

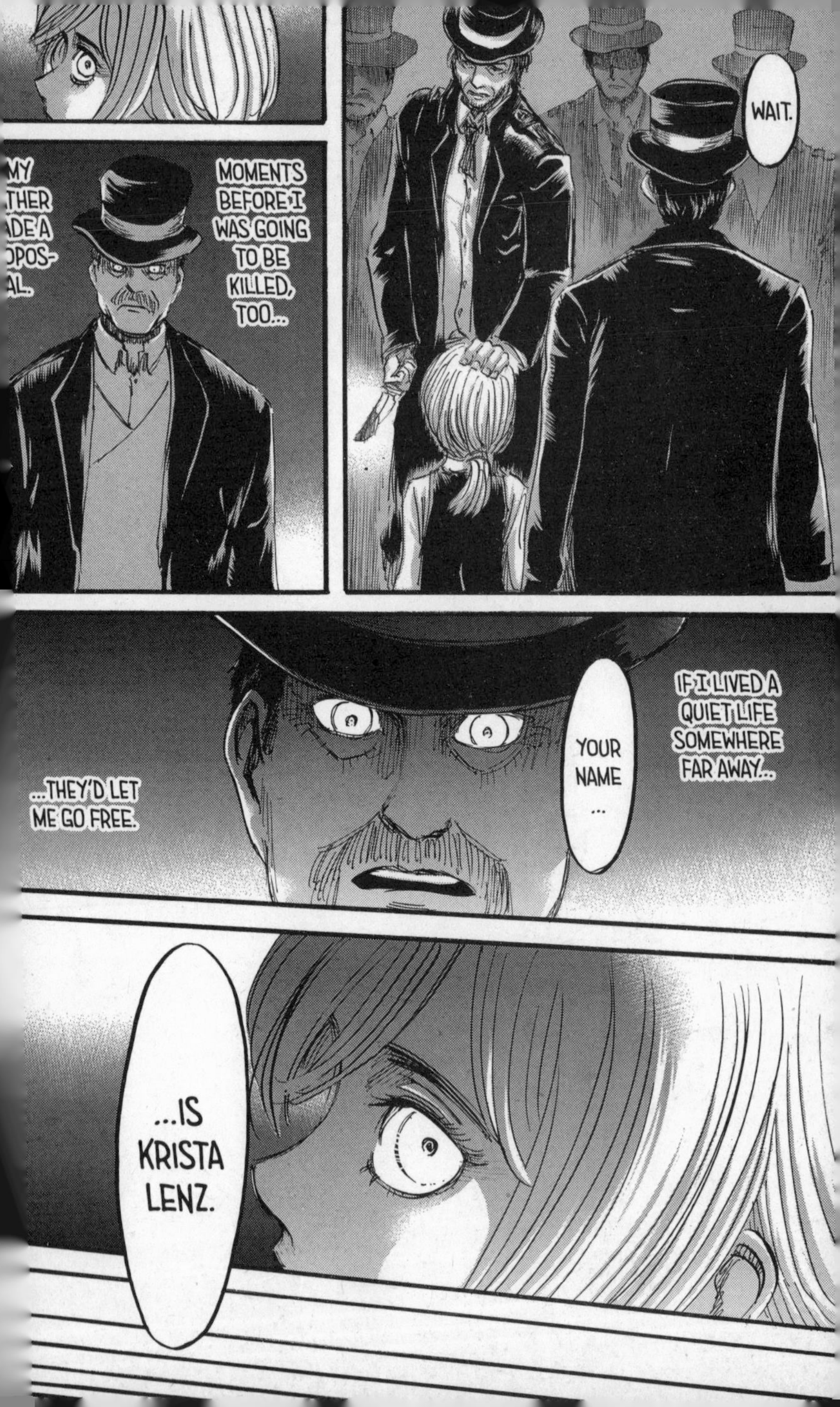

WAIT.
MOMENTS BEFORE I WAS GOING TO BE KILLED, TOO...
MY
THER
ADE A
OPOS-
AL.
IF I LIVED A QUIET LIFE SOMEWHERE FAR AWAY...
YOUR NAME ...
...THEY'D LET ME GO FREE.
...IS KRISTA LENZ.

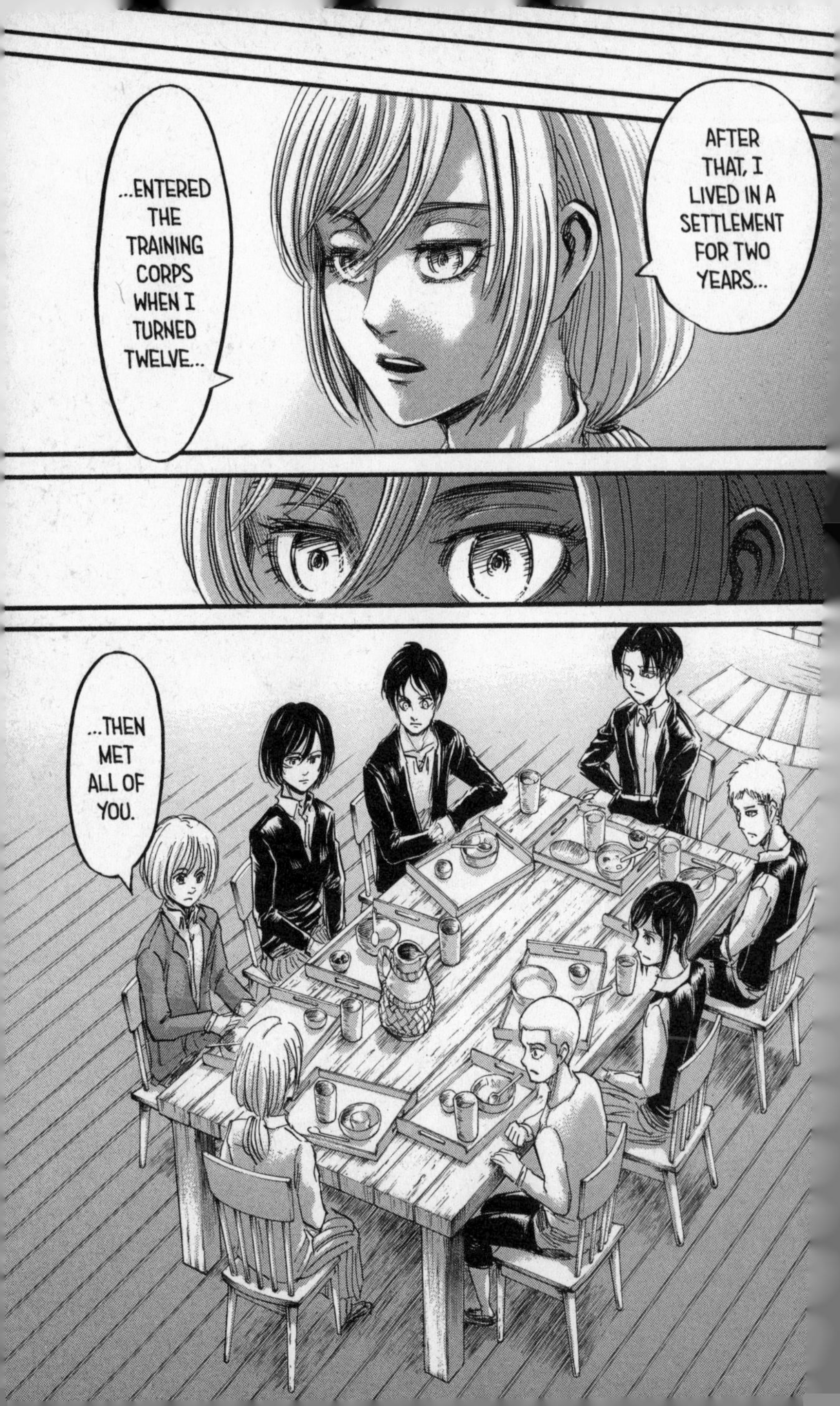
AFTER THAT, I LIVED IN A SETTLEMENT FOR TWO YEARS...
...ENTERED THE TRAINING CORPS WHEN I TURNED TWELVE...
...THEN MET ALL OF YOU.

ATTACK on TITAN

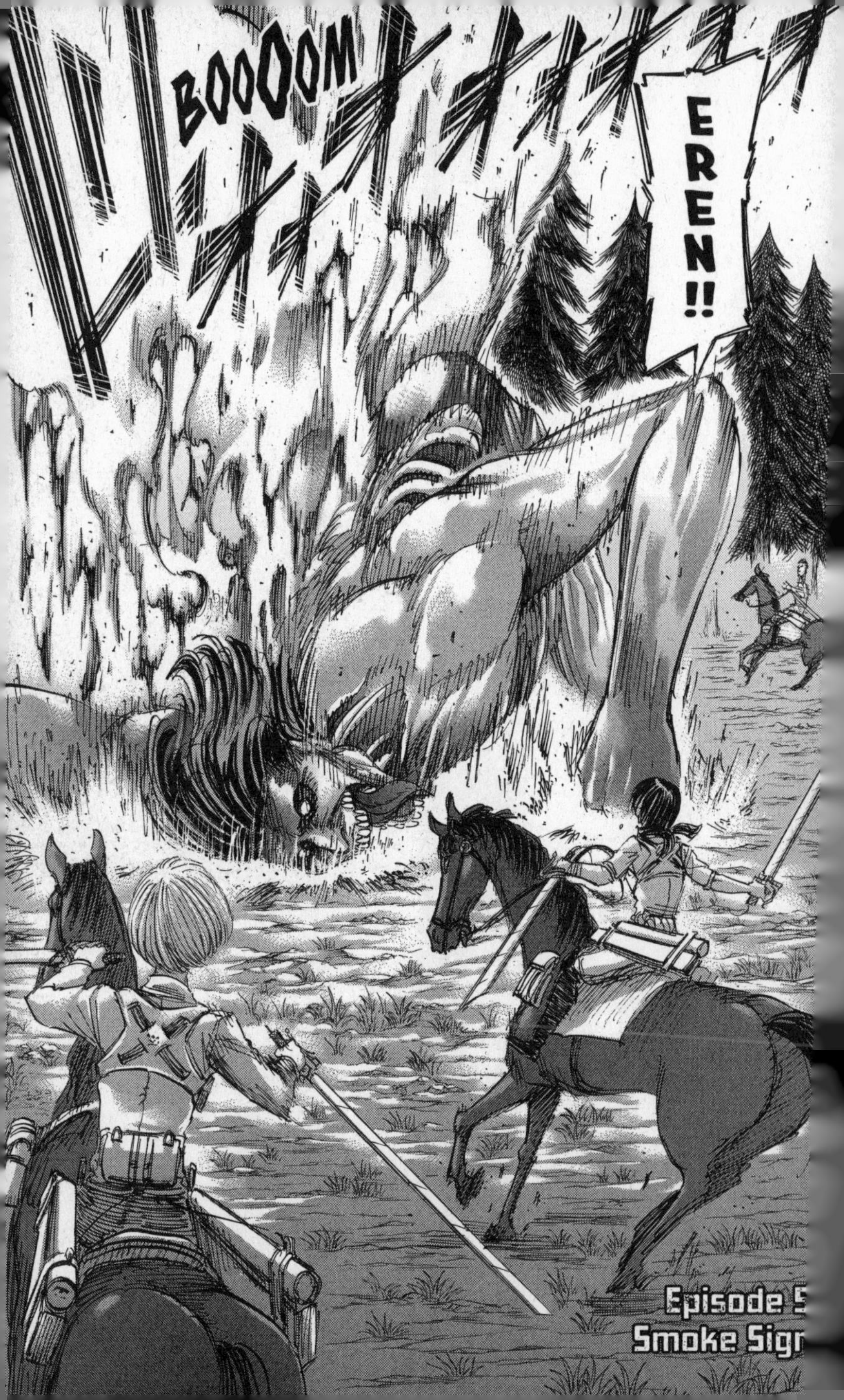
EREN!!
BOOOOM
Episode
Smoke Sig

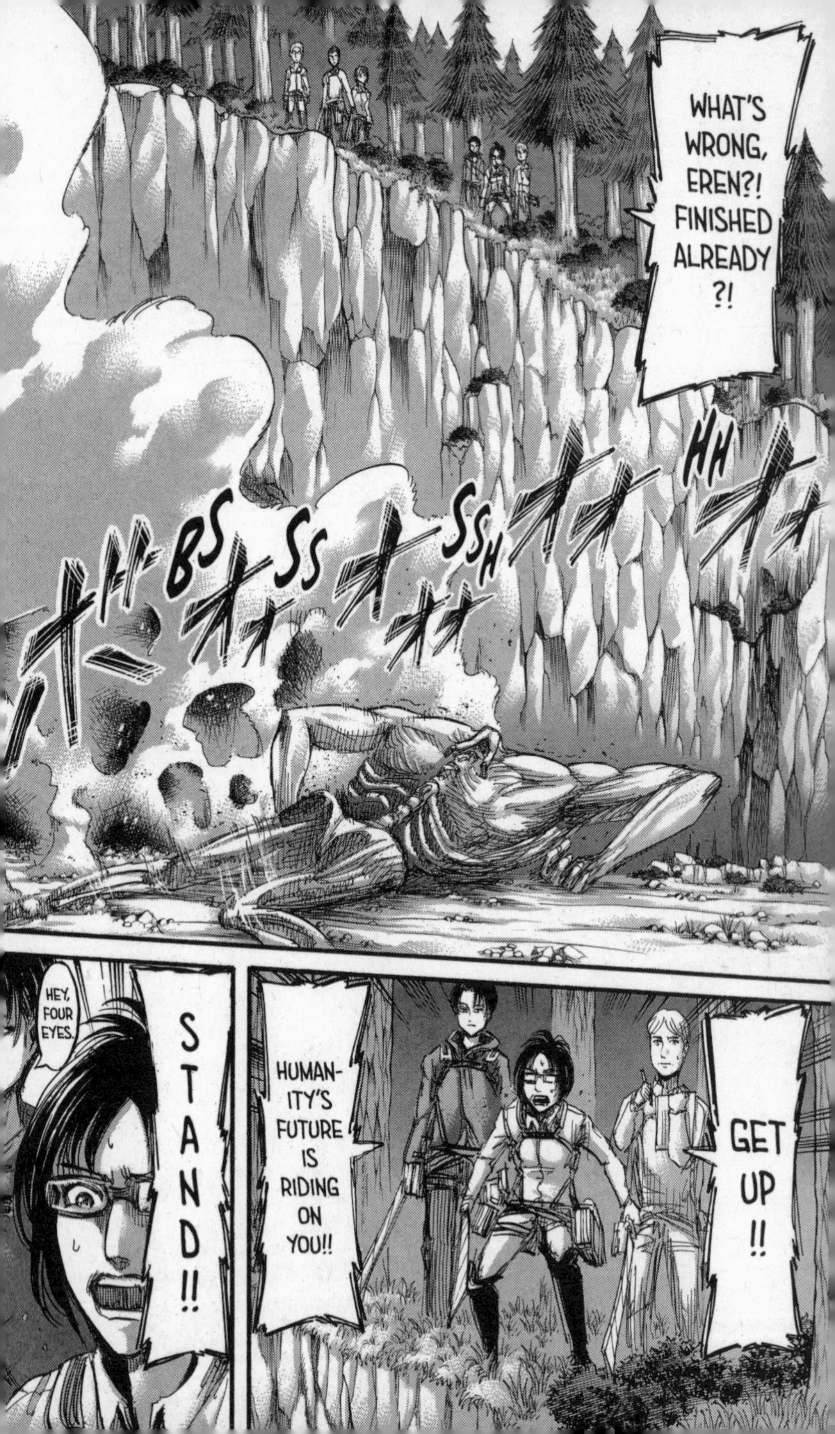

WHAT'S WRONG, EREN?! FINISHED ALREADY ?!
HH
SSH
SS
BS
GET UP !!
HUMAN-ITY'S FUTURE IS RIDING ON YOU!!
STAND!!
HEY, FOUR EYES.

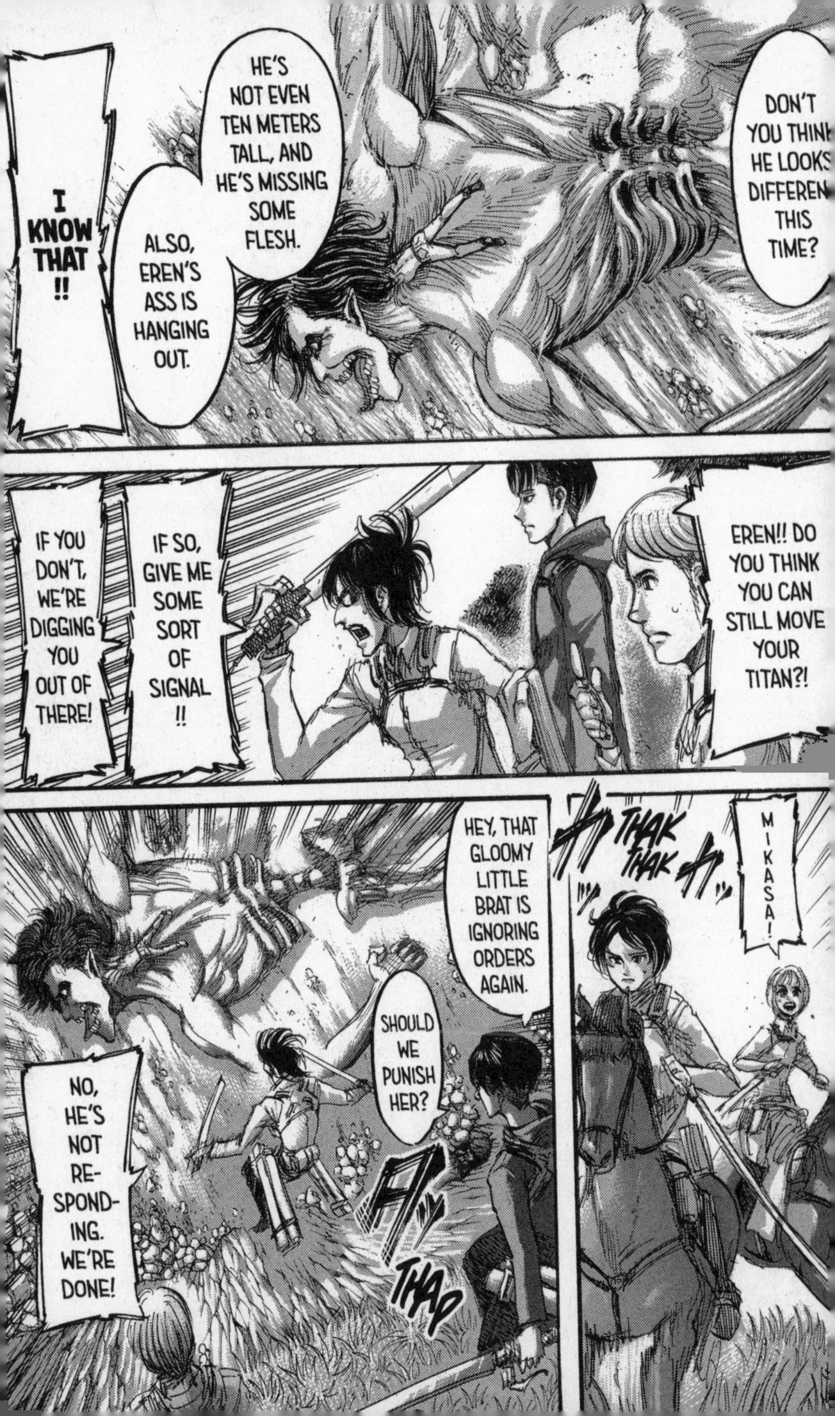
DON'T YOU THINK HE LOOKS DIFFERENT THIS TIME?
HE'S NOT EVEN TEN METERS TALL, AND HE'S MISSING SOME FLESH.
ALSO, EREN'S ASS IS HANGING OUT.
I KNOW THAT!!
EREN!! DO YOU THINK YOU CAN STILL MOVE YOUR TITAN?!
IF SO, GIVE ME SOME SORT OF SIGNAL!!
IF YOU DON'T, WE'RE DIGGING YOU OUT OF THERE!
MIKASA!
THAK THAK
HEY, THAT GLOOMY LITTLE BRAT IS IGNORING ORDERS AGAIN.
SHOULD WE PUNISH HER?
THAP
NO, HE'S NOT RE-SPOND-ING. WE'RE DONE!

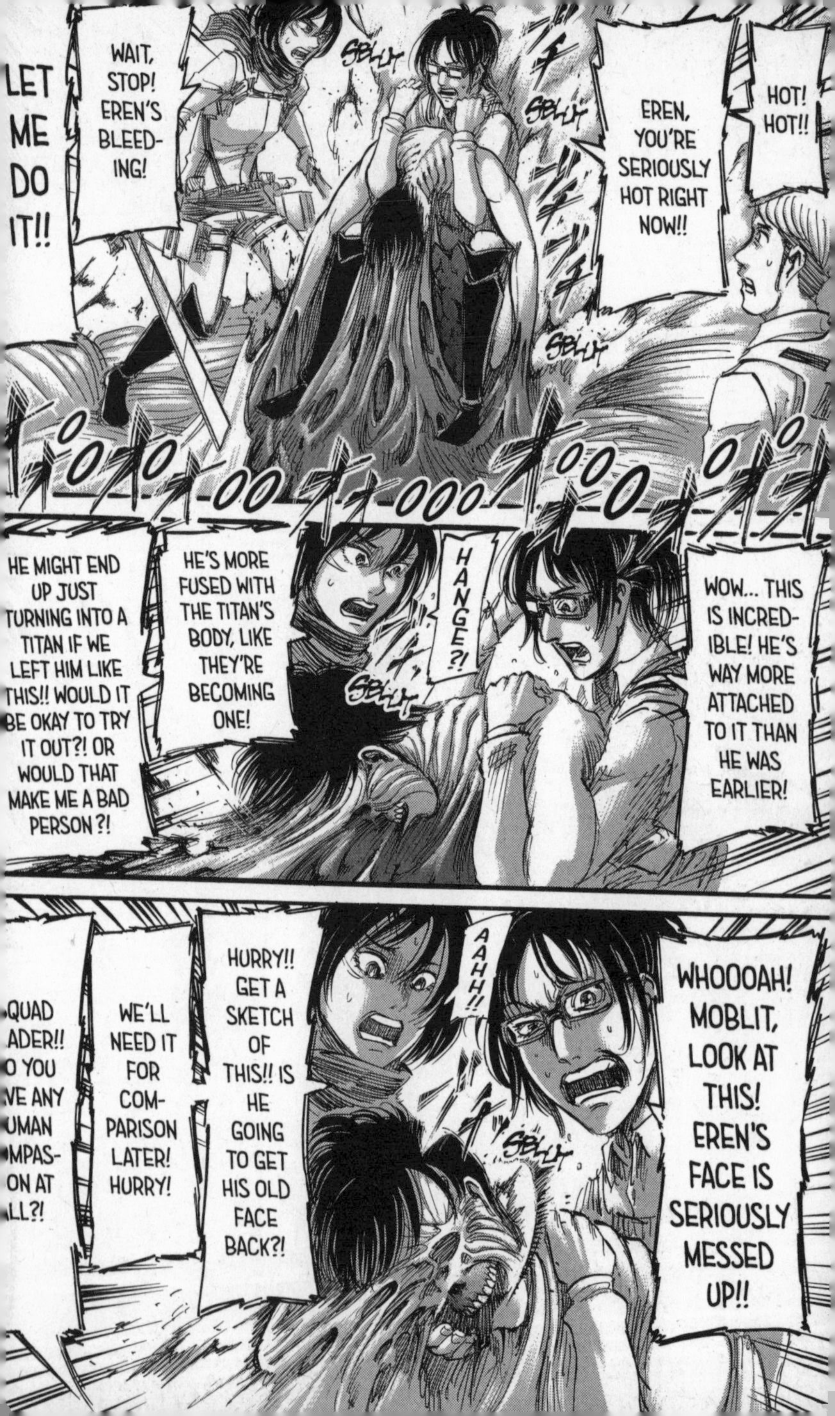
HOT! HOT!!
EREN, YOU'RE SERIOUSLY HOT RIGHT NOW!!
WAIT, STOP! EREN'S BLEED-ING!
LET ME DO IT!!
WOW... THIS IS INCRED-IBLE! HE'S WAY MORE ATTACHED TO IT THAN HE WAS EARLIER!
HANGE?!
HE'S MORE FUSED WITH THE TITAN'S BODY, LIKE THEY'RE BECOMING ONE!
HE MIGHT END UP JUST TURNING INTO A TITAN IF WE LEFT HIM LIKE THIS!! WOULD IT BE OKAY TO TRY IT OUT?! OR WOULD THAT MAKE ME A BAD PERSON?!
WHOOOAH! MOBLIT, LOOK AT THIS! EREN'S FACE IS SERIOUSLY MESSED UP!!
AAHH!!
HURRY!! GET A SKETCH OF THIS!! IS HE GOING TO GET HIS OLD FACE BACK?!
WE'LL NEED IT FOR COM-PARISON LATER! HURRY!
QUAD ADER!! O YOU VE ANY UMAN MPAS-ON AT LL?!

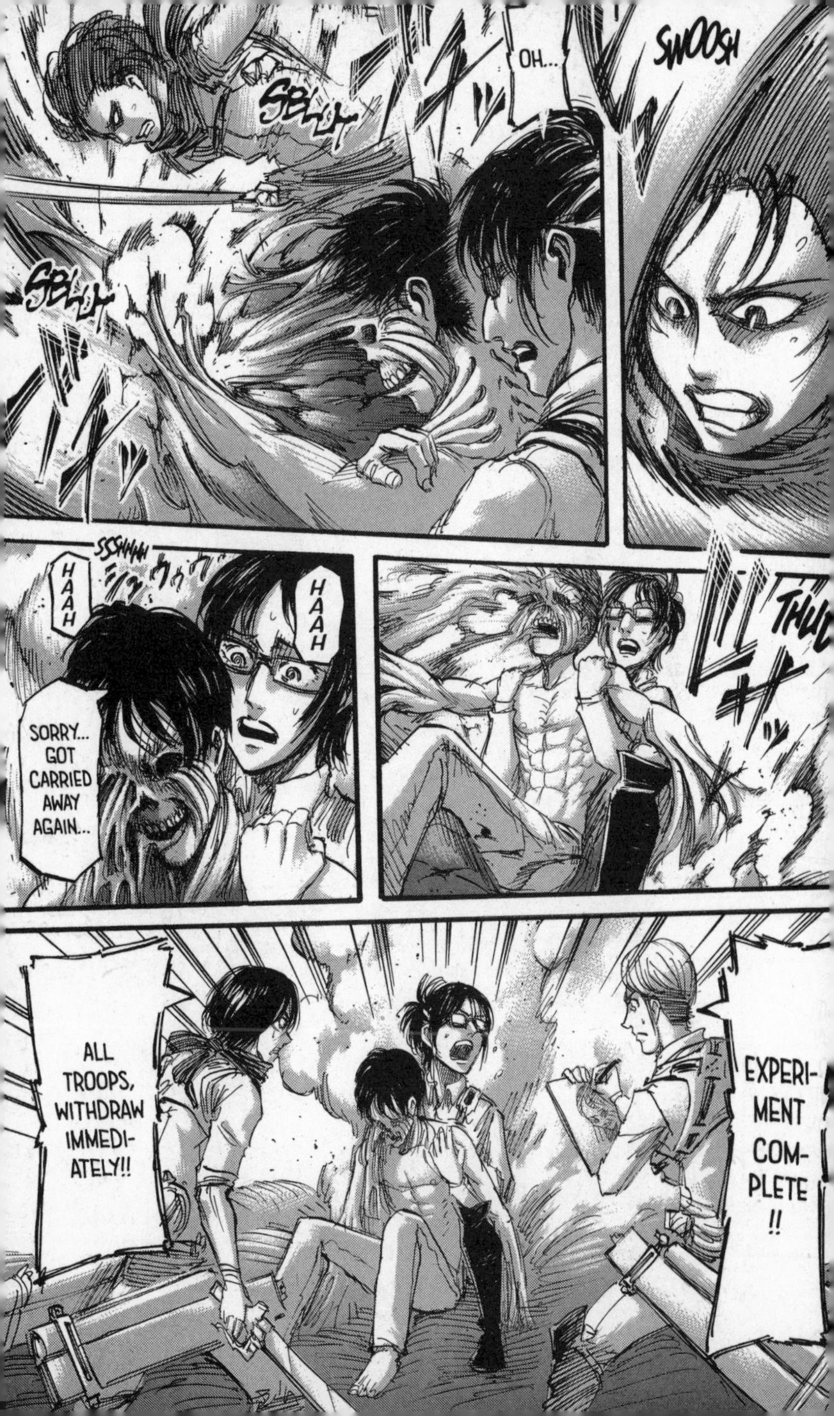
SWOOSH
OH...
SBLUT
SBLUT
THUD
HAAH
HAAH
SSSHHHH
SORRY... GOT CARRIED AWAY AGAIN...
EXPERIMENT COMPLETE!!
ALL TROOPS, WITHDRAW IMMEDIATELY!!

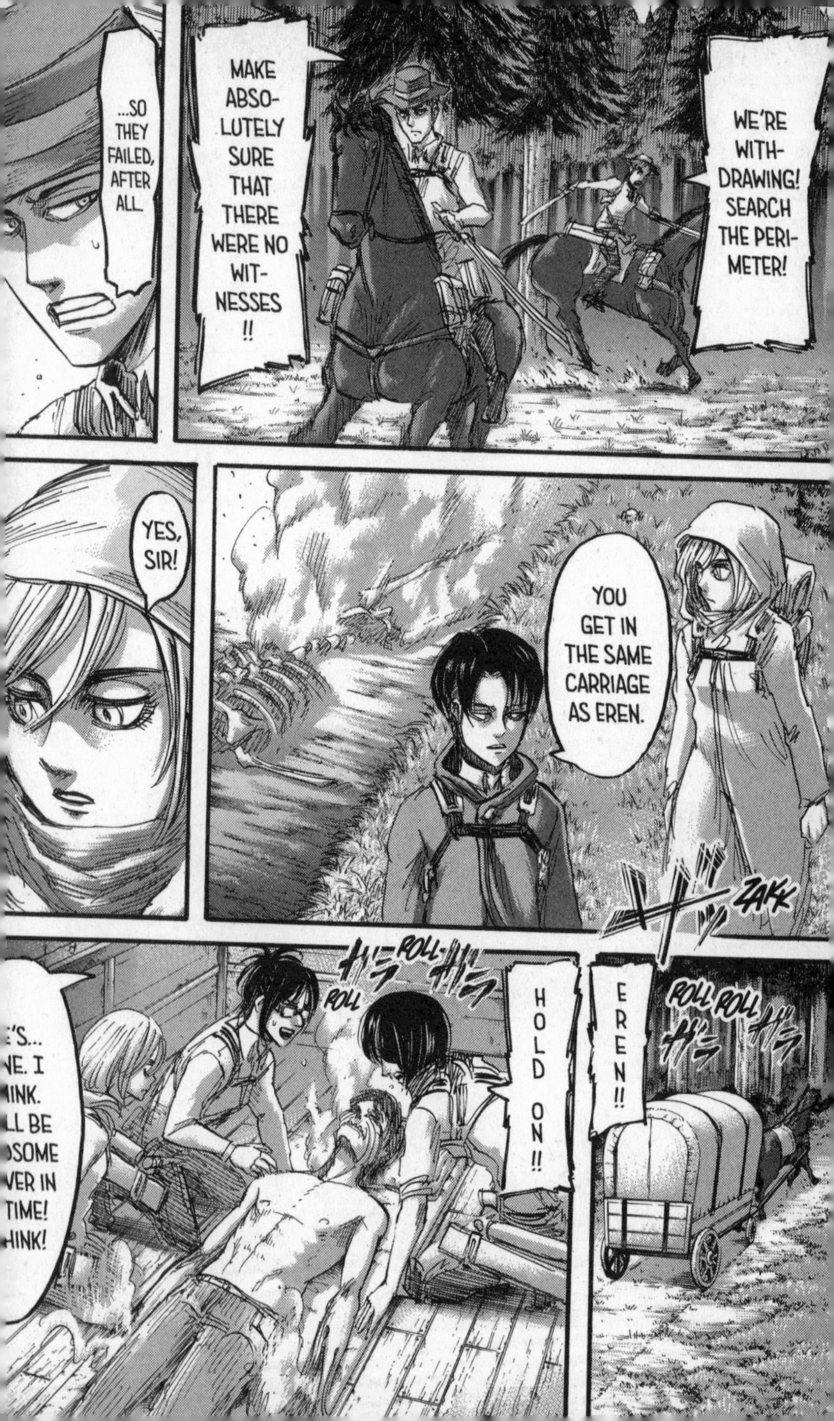
WE'RE WITHDRAWING! SEARCH THE PERIMETER!
MAKE ABSOLUTELY SURE THAT THERE WERE NO WITNESSES!!
...SO THEY FAILED, AFTER ALL.
YOU GET IN THE SAME CARRIAGE AS EREN.
ZAKK
YES, SIR!
ROLL ROLL
EREN!!
ROLL ROLL
HOLD ON!!
E'S... NE. I INK. LL BE SOME VER IN TIME! HINK!

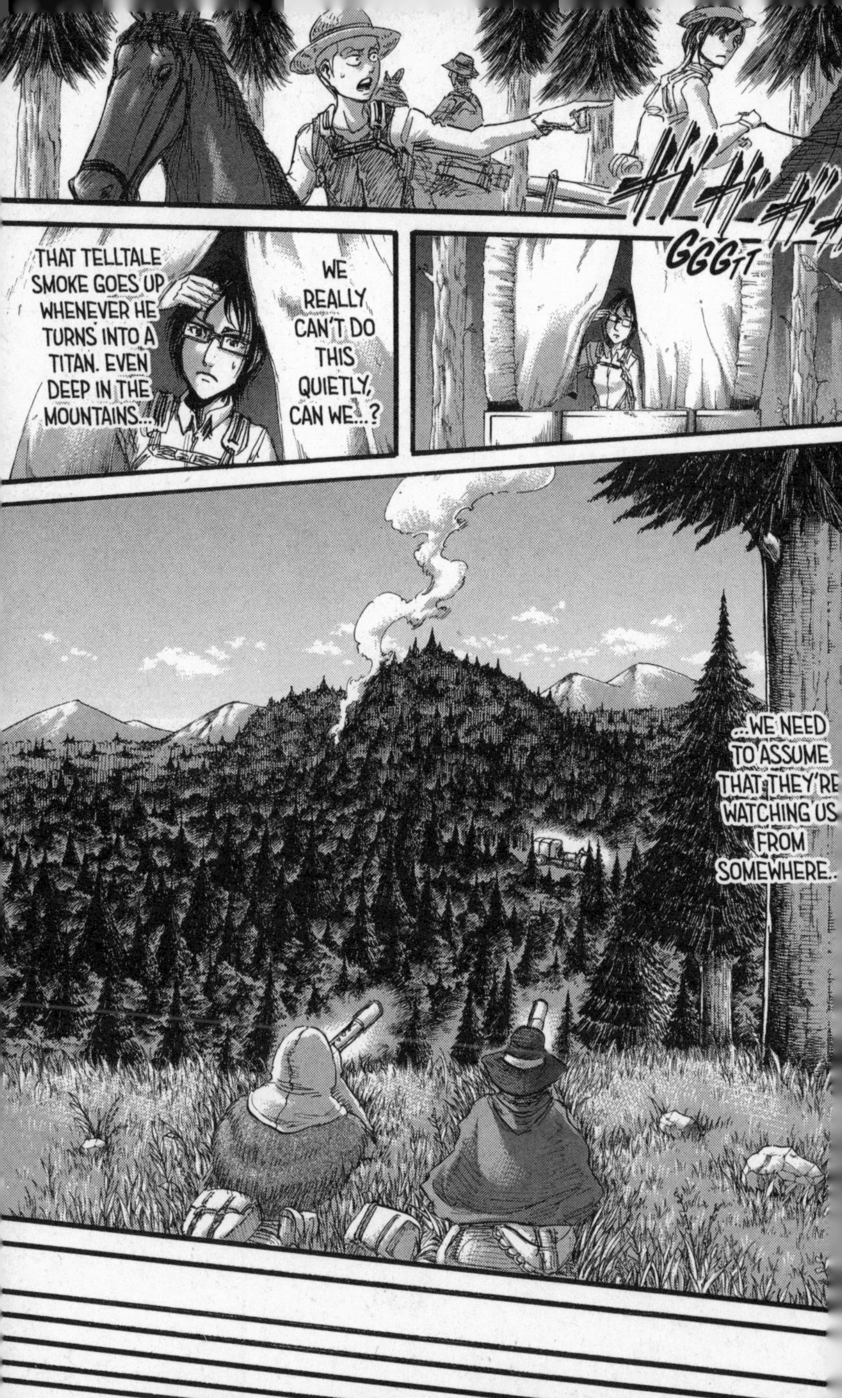
GGGTT
WE REALLY CAN'T DO THIS QUIETLY, CAN WE...?
THAT TELLTALE SMOKE GOES UP WHENEVER HE TURNS INTO A TITAN. EVEN DEEP IN THE MOUNTAINS...
...WE NEED TO ASSUME THAT THEY'RE WATCHING US FROM SOMEWHERE...

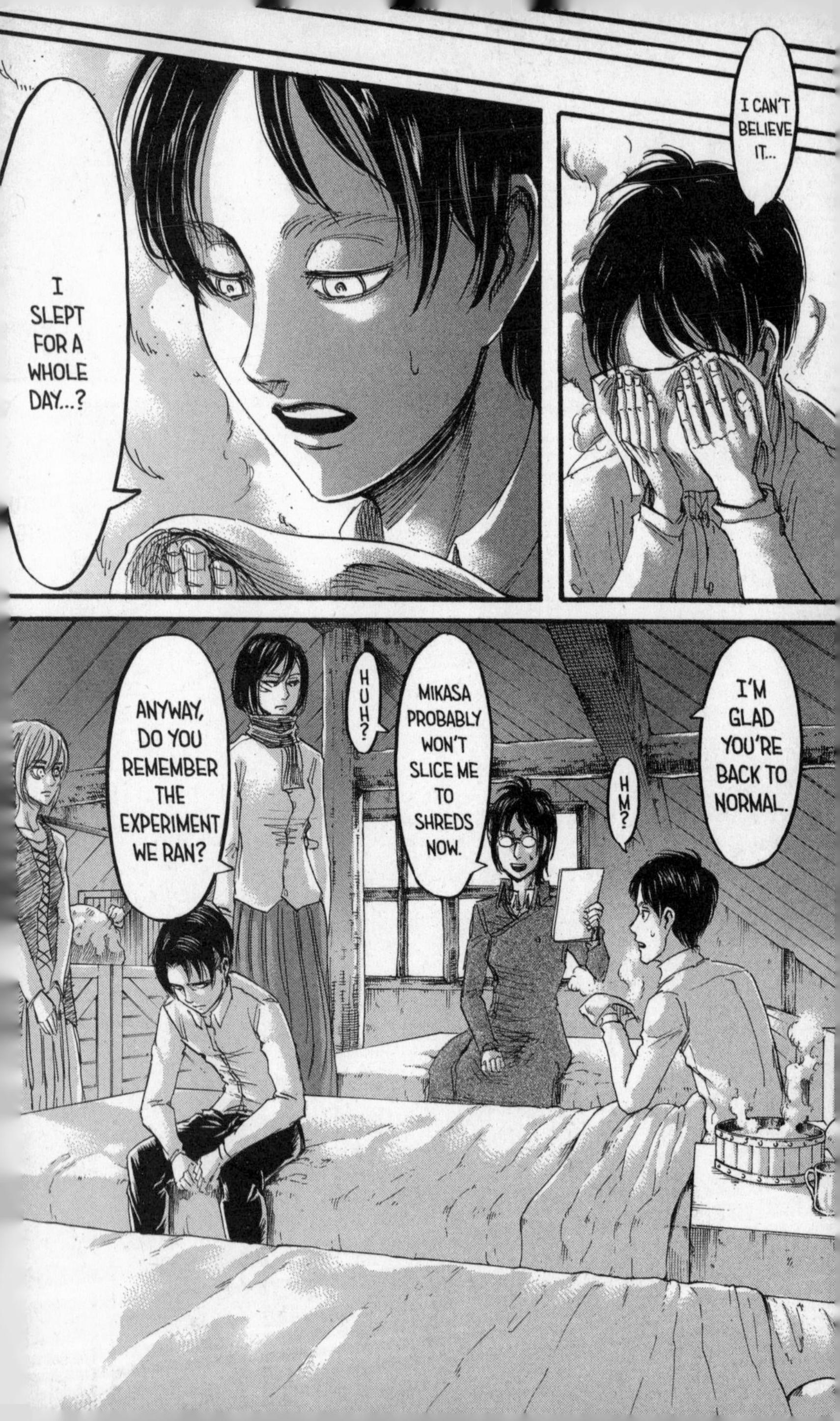
I CAN'T BELIEVE IT...
I SLEPT FOR A WHOLE DAY...?
I'M GLAD YOU'RE BACK TO NORMAL.
HM?
MIKASA PROBABLY WON'T SLICE ME TO SHREDS NOW.
HUH?
ANYWAY, DO YOU REMEMBER THE EXPERIMENT WE RAN?

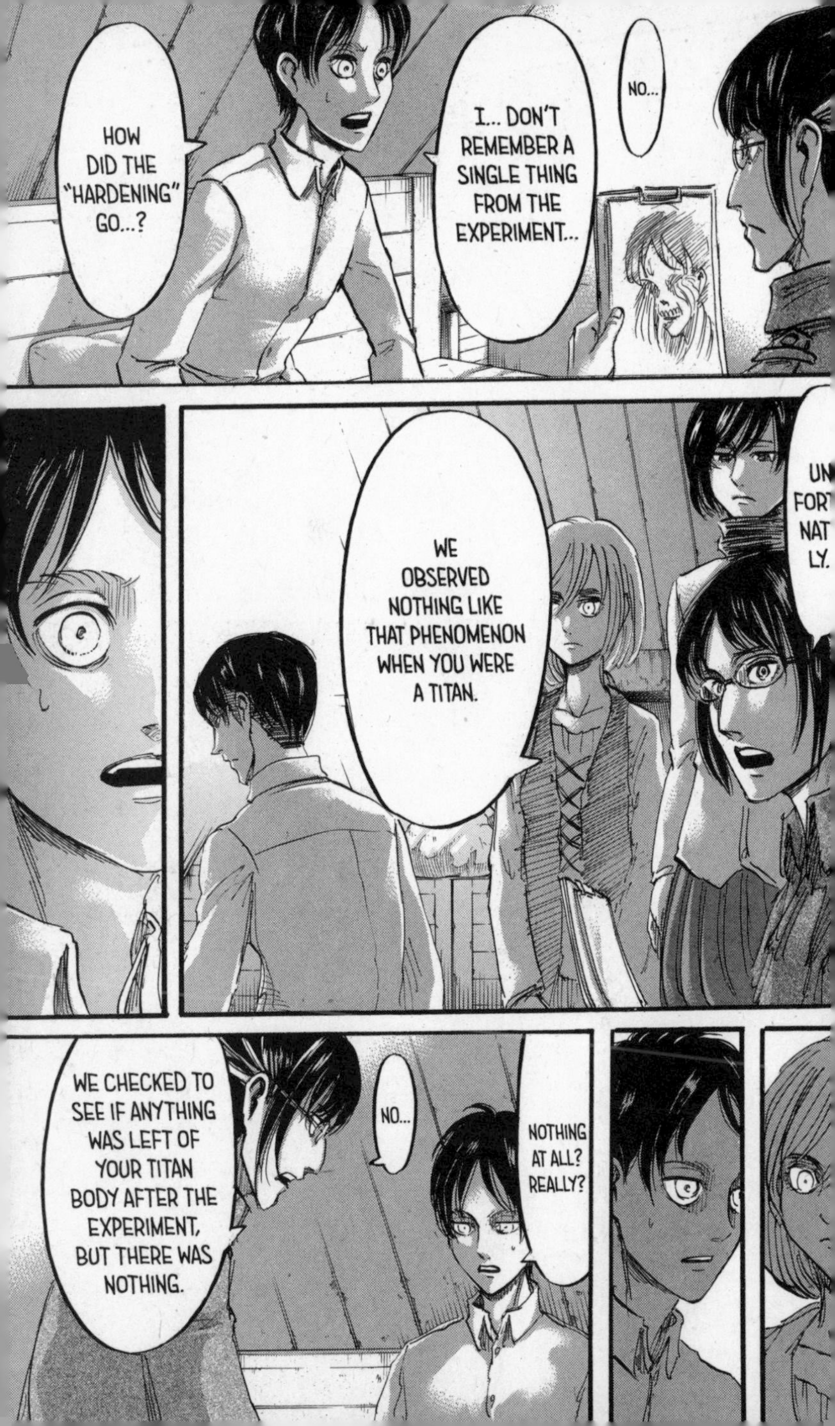
NO...
I... DON'T REMEMBER A SINGLE THING FROM THE EXPERIMENT...
HOW DID THE "HARDENING" GO...?
UN FORT NAT LY.
WE OBSERVED NOTHING LIKE THAT PHENOMENON WHEN YOU WERE A TITAN.
NOTHING AT ALL? REALLY?
NO...
WE CHECKED TO SEE IF ANYTHING WAS LEFT OF YOUR TITAN BODY AFTER THE EXPERIMENT, BUT THERE WAS NOTHING.

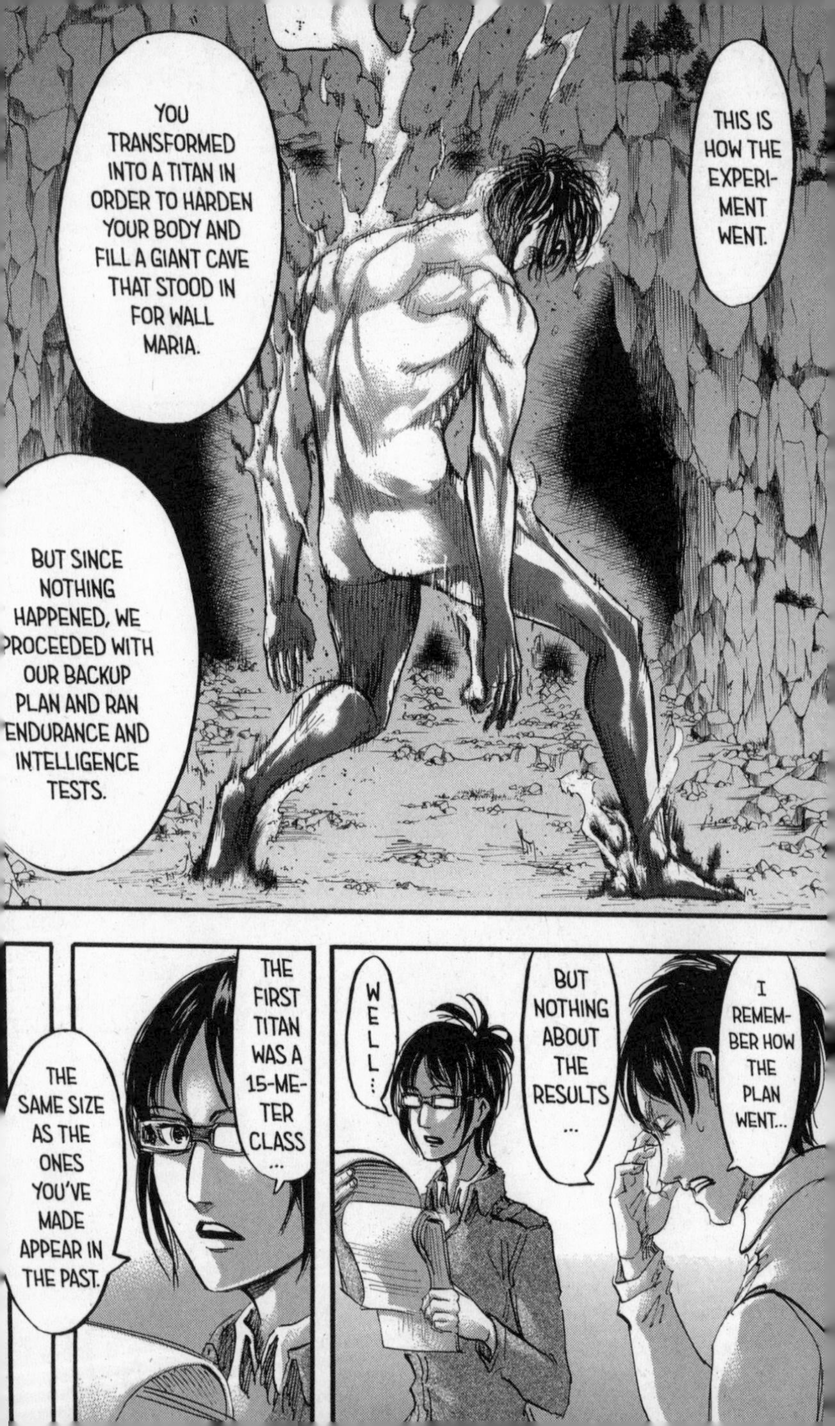
THIS IS HOW THE EXPERIMENT WENT.
YOU TRANSFORMED INTO A TITAN IN ORDER TO HARDEN YOUR BODY AND FILL A GIANT CAVE THAT STOOD IN FOR WALL MARIA.
BUT SINCE NOTHING HAPPENED, WE PROCEEDED WITH OUR BACKUP PLAN AND RAN ENDURANCE AND INTELLIGENCE TESTS.
I REMEMBER HOW THE PLAN WENT...
BUT NOTHING ABOUT THE RESULTS...
WELL...
THE FIRST TITAN WAS A 15-METER CLASS...
THE SAME SIZE AS THE ONES YOU'VE MADE APPEAR IN THE PAST.

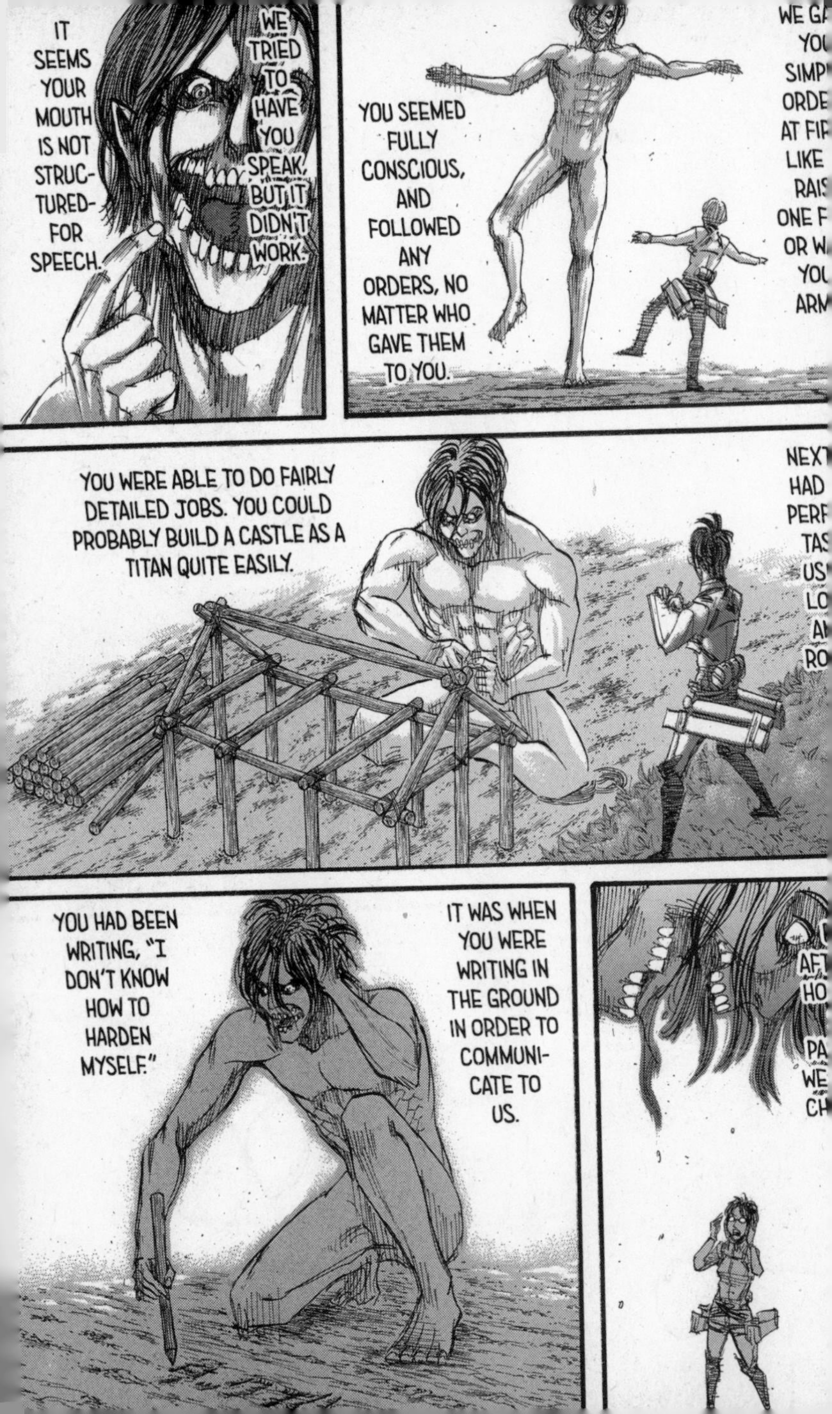
YOU SEEMED FULLY CONSCIOUS, AND FOLLOWED ANY ORDERS, NO MATTER WHO GAVE THEM TO YOU.
WE TRIED TO HAVE YOU SPEAK, BUT IT DIDN'T WORK.
IT SEEMS YOUR MOUTH IS NOT STRUC-TURED- FOR SPEECH.
YOU WERE ABLE TO DO FAIRLY DETAILED JOBS. YOU COULD PROBABLY BUILD A CASTLE AS A TITAN QUITE EASILY.
IT WAS WHEN YOU WERE WRITING IN THE GROUND IN ORDER TO COMMUNI-CATE TO US.
YOU HAD BEEN WRITING, "I DON'T KNOW HOW TO HARDEN MYSELF."

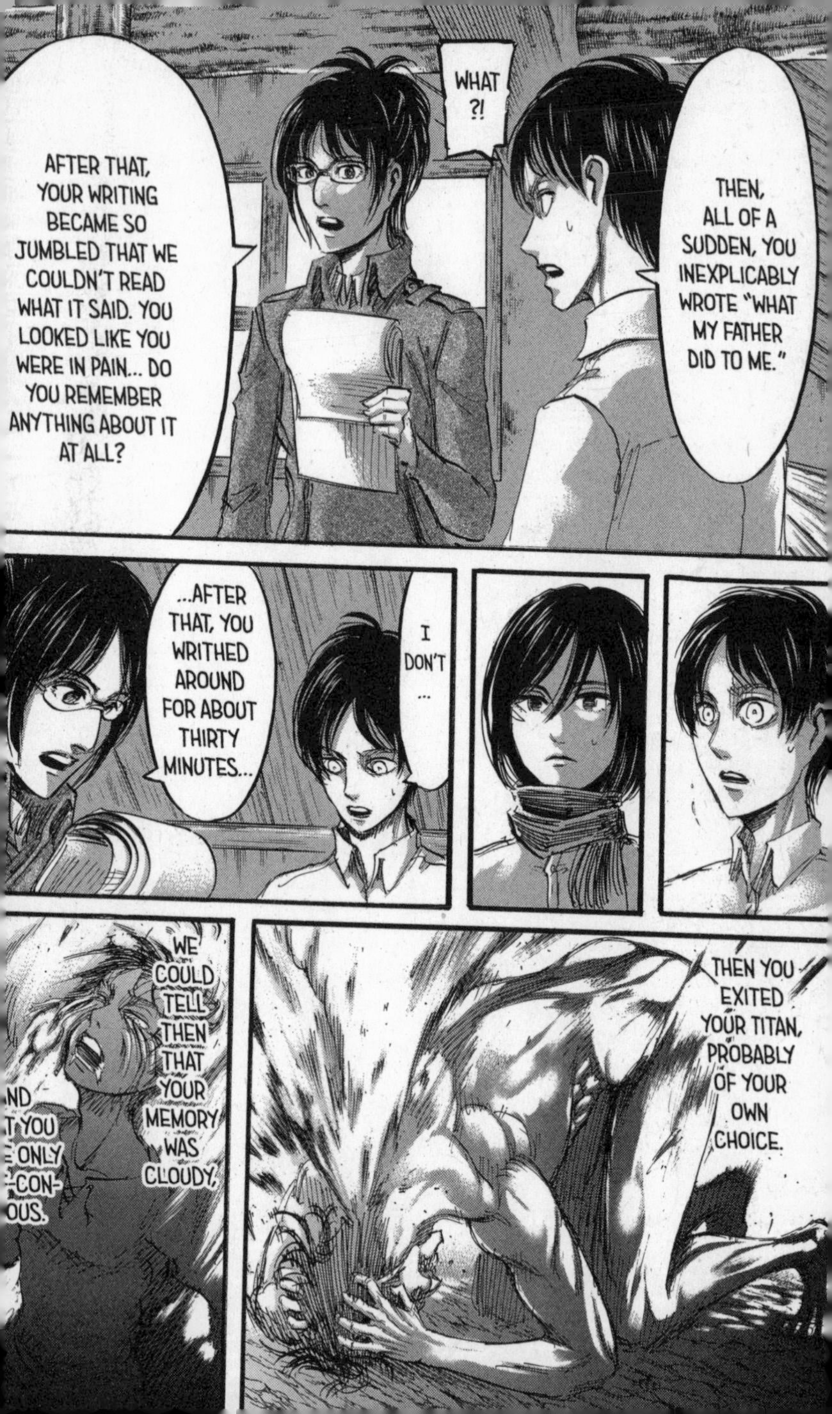
THEN, ALL OF A SUDDEN, YOU INEXPLICABLY WROTE "WHAT MY FATHER DID TO ME."
WHAT ?!
AFTER THAT, YOUR WRITING BECAME SO JUMBLED THAT WE COULDN'T READ WHAT IT SAID. YOU LOOKED LIKE YOU WERE IN PAIN... DO YOU REMEMBER ANYTHING ABOUT IT AT ALL?
I DON'T ...
...AFTER THAT, YOU WRITHED AROUND FOR ABOUT THIRTY MINUTES...
THEN YOU EXITED YOUR TITAN, PROBABLY OF YOUR OWN CHOICE.
WE COULD TELL THEN THAT YOUR MEMORY WAS CLOUDY,
ND T YOU E ONLY -CON- OUS.

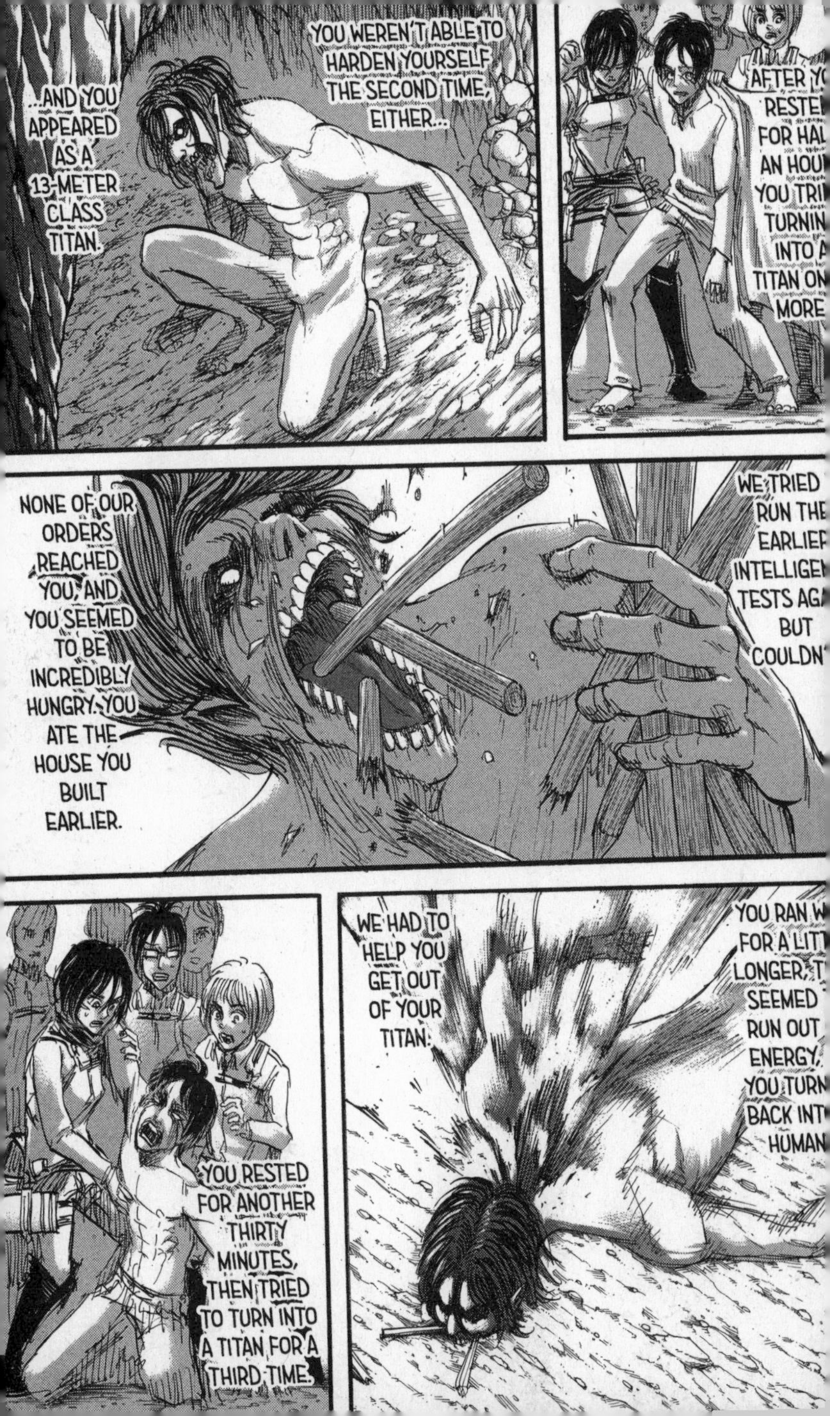
AFTER YO RESTE FOR HAL AN HOU YOU TRI TURNIN INTO A TITAN ON MORE
YOU WEREN'T ABLE TO HARDEN YOURSELF THE SECOND TIME, EITHER...
...AND YOU APPEARED AS A 13-METER CLASS TITAN.
WE TRIED RUN THE EARLIEF INTELLIGEN TESTS AGA BUT COULDN'
NONE OF OUR ORDERS REACHED YOU, AND YOU SEEMED TO BE INCREDIBLY HUNGRY. YOU ATE THE HOUSE YOU BUILT EARLIER.
YOU RAN W FOR A LITT LONGER, T SEEMED RUN OUT ENERGY. YOU TURN BACK INT HUMAN
WE HAD TO HELP YOU GET OUT OF YOUR TITAN.
YOU RESTED FOR ANOTHER THIRTY MINUTES, THEN TRIED TO TURN INTO A TITAN FOR A THIRD TIME.

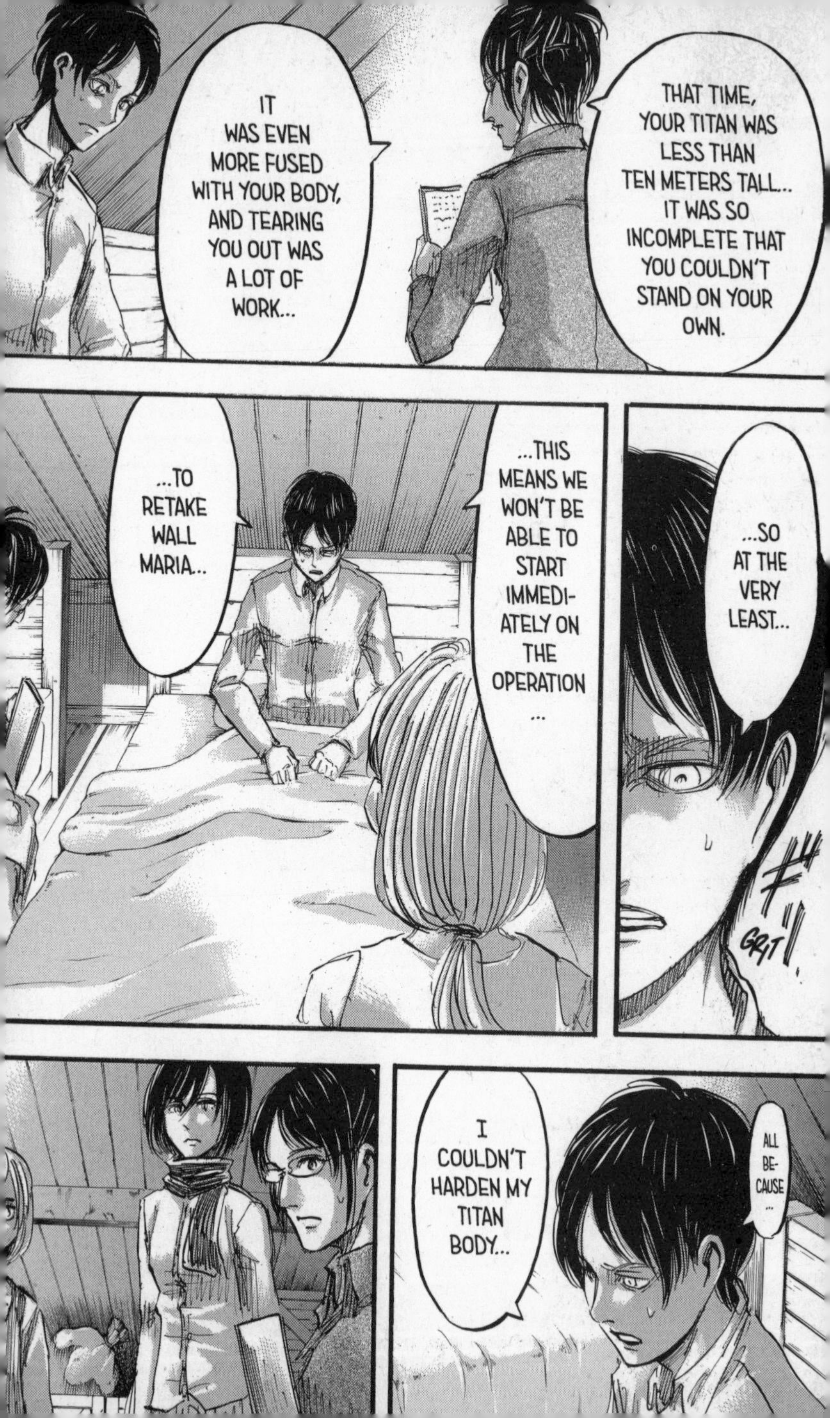
THAT TIME, YOUR TITAN WAS LESS THAN TEN METERS TALL... IT WAS SO INCOMPLETE THAT YOU COULDN'T STAND ON YOUR OWN.
IT WAS EVEN MORE FUSED WITH YOUR BODY, AND TEARING YOU OUT WAS A LOT OF WORK...
...SO AT THE VERY LEAST...
GRIT
...THIS MEANS WE WON'T BE ABLE TO START IMMEDI-ATELY ON THE OPERATION ...
...TO RETAKE WALL MARIA...
ALL BE-CAUSE ...
I COULDN'T HARDEN MY TITAN BODY...

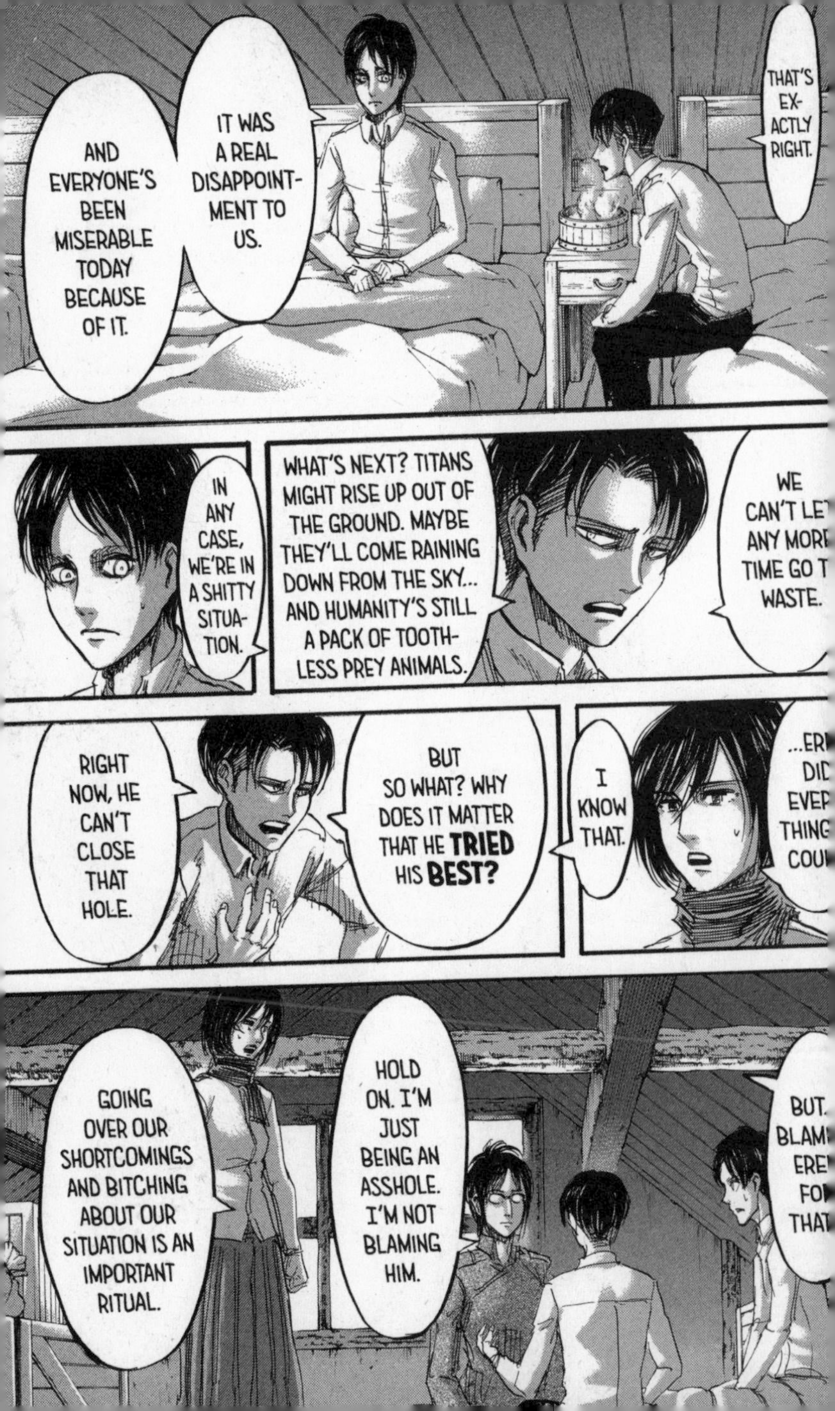
THAT'S EX-ACTLY RIGHT.
IT WAS A REAL DISAPPOINT-MENT TO US.
AND EVERYONE'S BEEN MISERABLE TODAY BECAUSE OF IT.
WE CAN'T LET ANY MORE TIME GO T WASTE.
WHAT'S NEXT? TITANS MIGHT RISE UP OUT OF THE GROUND. MAYBE THEY'LL COME RAINING DOWN FROM THE SKY... AND HUMANITY'S STILL A PACK OF TOOTH-LESS PREY ANIMALS.
IN ANY CASE, WE'RE IN A SHITTY SITUA-TION.
...ER DID EVE THING COU
I KNOW THAT.
BUT SO WHAT? WHY DOES IT MATTER THAT HE **TRIED** HIS **BEST?**
RIGHT NOW, HE CAN'T CLOSE THAT HOLE.
BUT. BLAM ERE FO THAT
HOLD ON. I'M JUST BEING AN ASSHOLE. I'M NOT BLAMING HIM.
GOING OVER OUR SHORTCOMINGS AND BITCHING ABOUT OUR SITUATION IS AN IMPORTANT RITUAL.

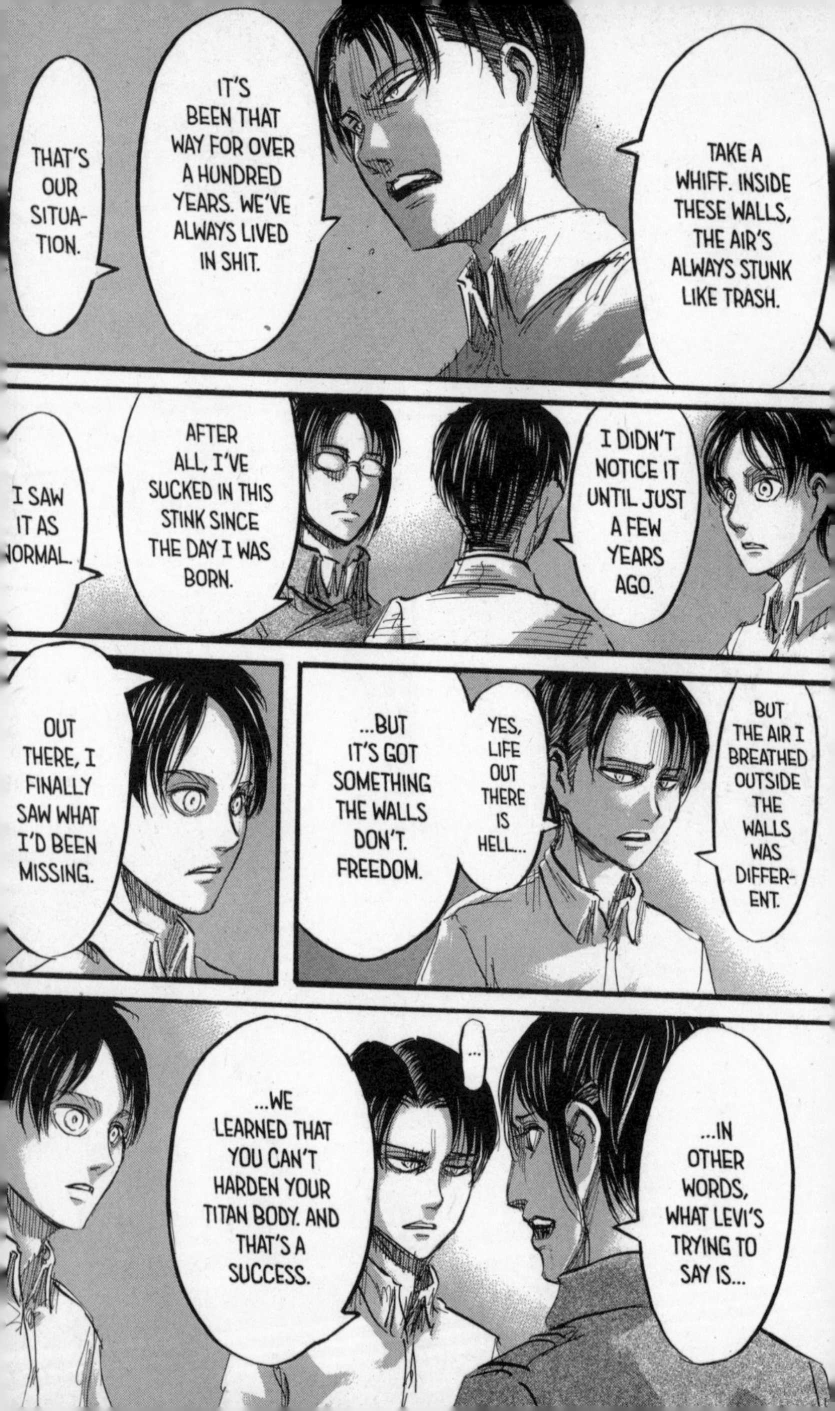
TAKE A WHIFF. INSIDE THESE WALLS, THE AIR'S ALWAYS STUNK LIKE TRASH.
IT'S BEEN THAT WAY FOR OVER A HUNDRED YEARS. WE'VE ALWAYS LIVED IN SHIT.
THAT'S OUR SITUA-TION.
I DIDN'T NOTICE IT UNTIL JUST A FEW YEARS AGO.
AFTER ALL, I'VE SUCKED IN THIS STINK SINCE THE DAY I WAS BORN.
I SAW IT AS NORMAL.
BUT THE AIR I BREATHED OUTSIDE THE WALLS WAS DIFFER-ENT.
YES, LIFE OUT THERE IS HELL...
...BUT IT'S GOT SOMETHING THE WALLS DON'T. FREEDOM.
OUT THERE, I FINALLY SAW WHAT I'D BEEN MISSING.
...IN OTHER WORDS, WHAT LEVI'S TRYING TO SAY IS...
...
...WE LEARNED THAT YOU CAN'T HARDEN YOUR TITAN BODY. AND THAT'S A SUCCESS.

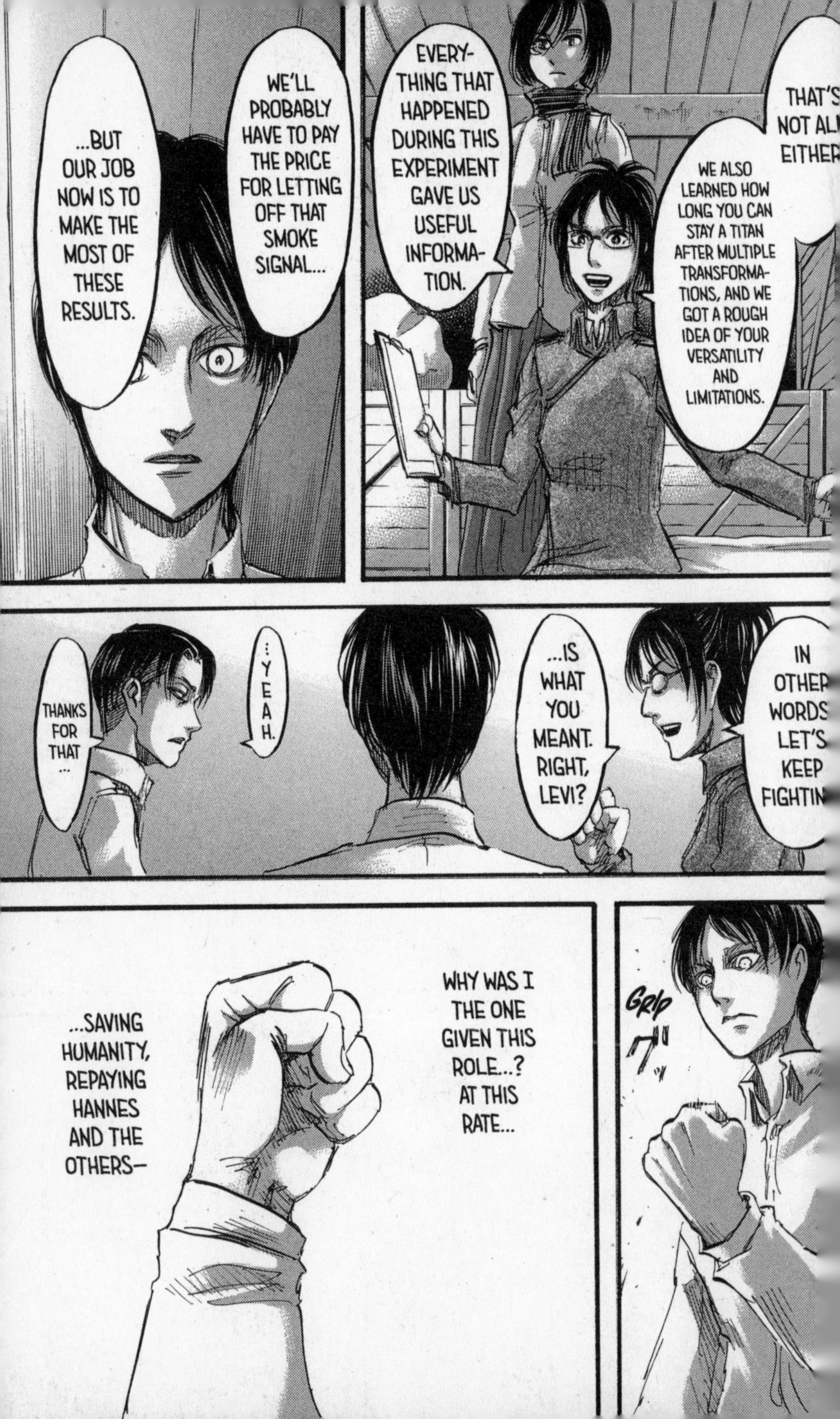
EVERY-THING THAT HAPPENED DURING THIS EXPERIMENT GAVE US USEFUL INFORMA-TION.
THAT'S NOT ALL EITHER
WE ALSO LEARNED HOW LONG YOU CAN STAY A TITAN AFTER MULTIPLE TRANSFORMA-TIONS, AND WE GOT A ROUGH IDEA OF YOUR VERSATILITY AND LIMITATIONS.
WE'LL PROBABLY HAVE TO PAY THE PRICE FOR LETTING OFF THAT SMOKE SIGNAL...
...BUT OUR JOB NOW IS TO MAKE THE MOST OF THESE RESULTS.
IN OTHER WORDS LET'S KEEP FIGHTIN
...IS WHAT YOU MEANT. RIGHT, LEVI?
...YEAH.
THANKS FOR THAT...
GRIP
WHY WAS I THE ONE GIVEN THIS ROLE...? AT THIS RATE...
...SAVING HUMANITY, REPAYING HANNES AND THE OTHERS—

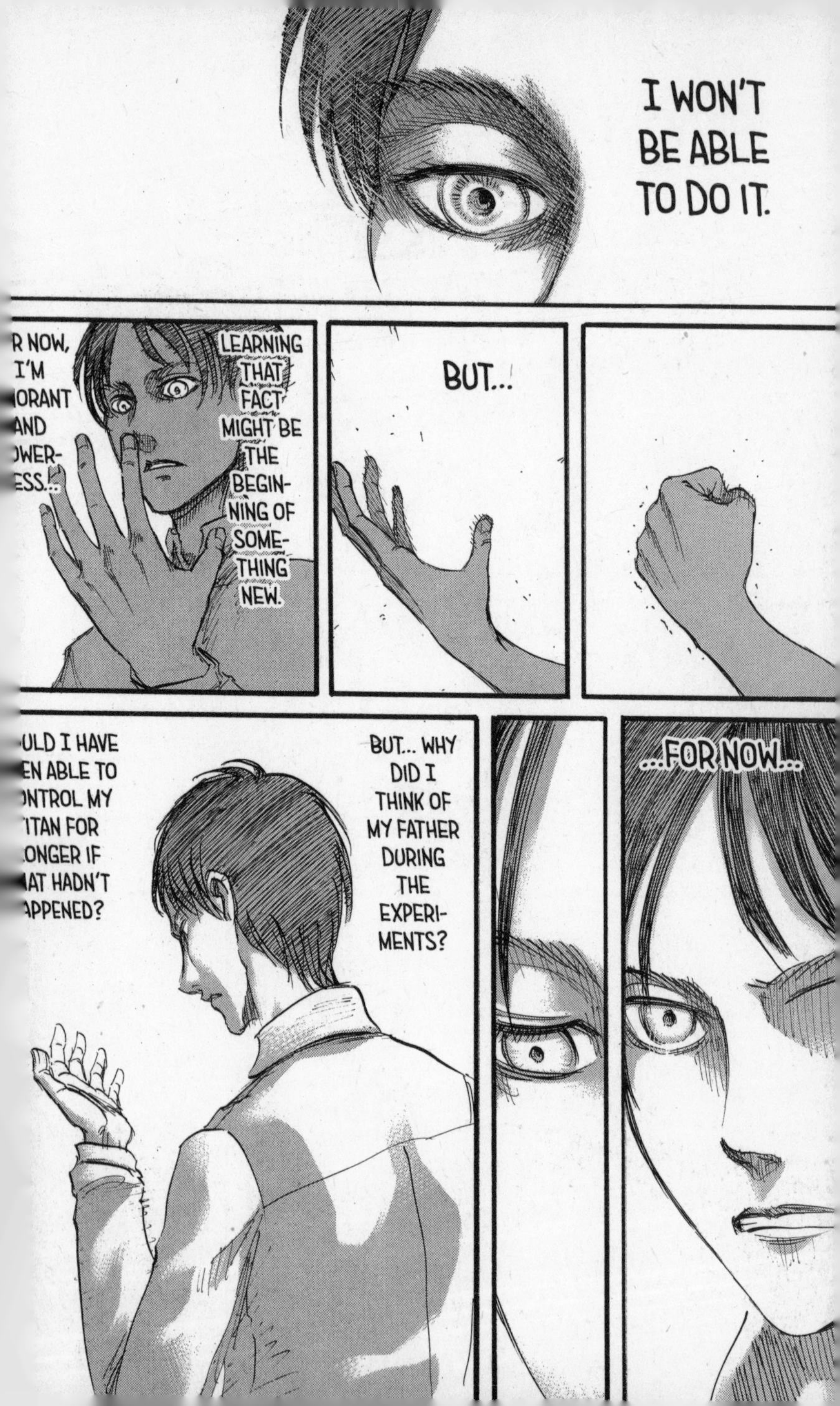
I WON'T BE ABLE TO DO IT.
BUT...
R NOW, I'M ORANT AND WER- ESS...
LEARNING THAT FACT MIGHT BE THE BEGIN- NING OF SOME- THING NEW.
...FOR NOW...
BUT... WHY DID I THINK OF MY FATHER DURING THE EXPERI- MENTS?
ULD I HAVE EN ABLE TO NTROL MY ITAN FOR ONGER IF AT HADN'T APPENED?

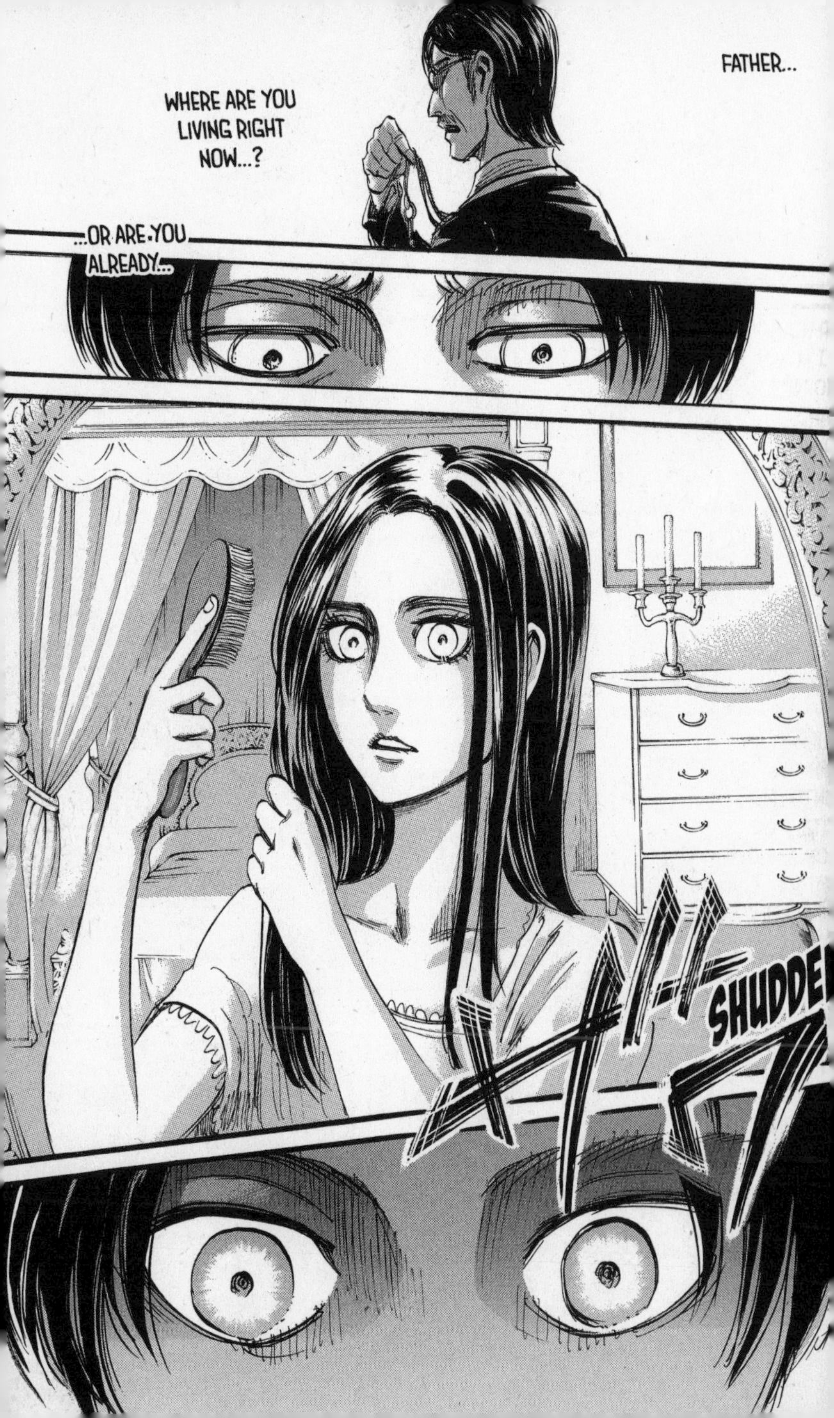
FATHER...
WHERE ARE YOU LIVING RIGHT NOW...?
...OR ARE YOU ALREADY...
SHUDDE

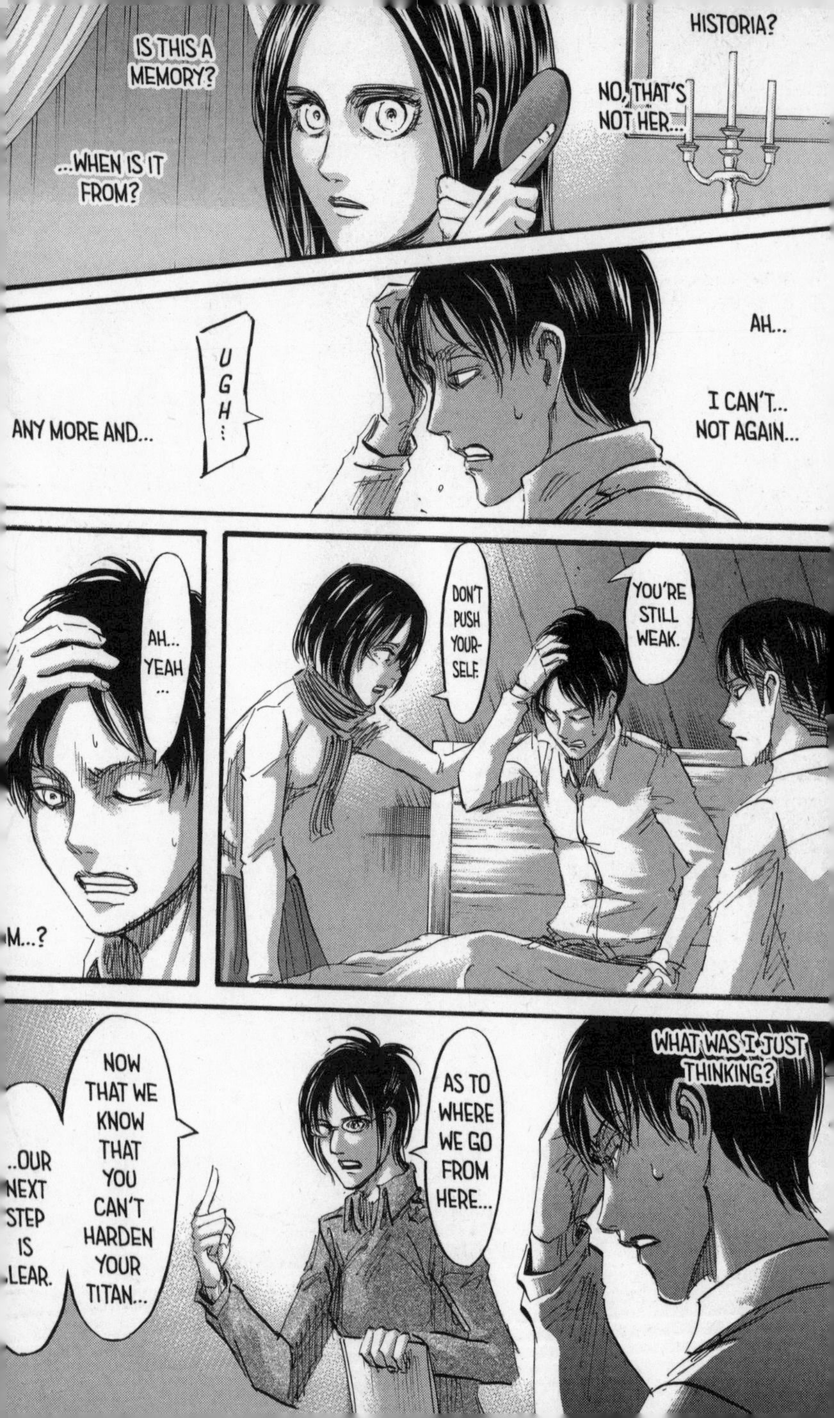
HISTORIA?
NO, THAT'S NOT HER...
IS THIS A MEMORY?
...WHEN IS IT FROM?
AH...
I CAN'T... NOT AGAIN...
UGH...
ANY MORE AND...
YOU'RE STILL WEAK.
DON'T PUSH YOUR-SELF.
AH... YEAH...
M...?
WHAT WAS I JUST THINKING?
AS TO WHERE WE GO FROM HERE...
NOW THAT WE KNOW THAT YOU CAN'T HARDEN YOUR TITAN...
..OUR NEXT STEP IS .LEAR.

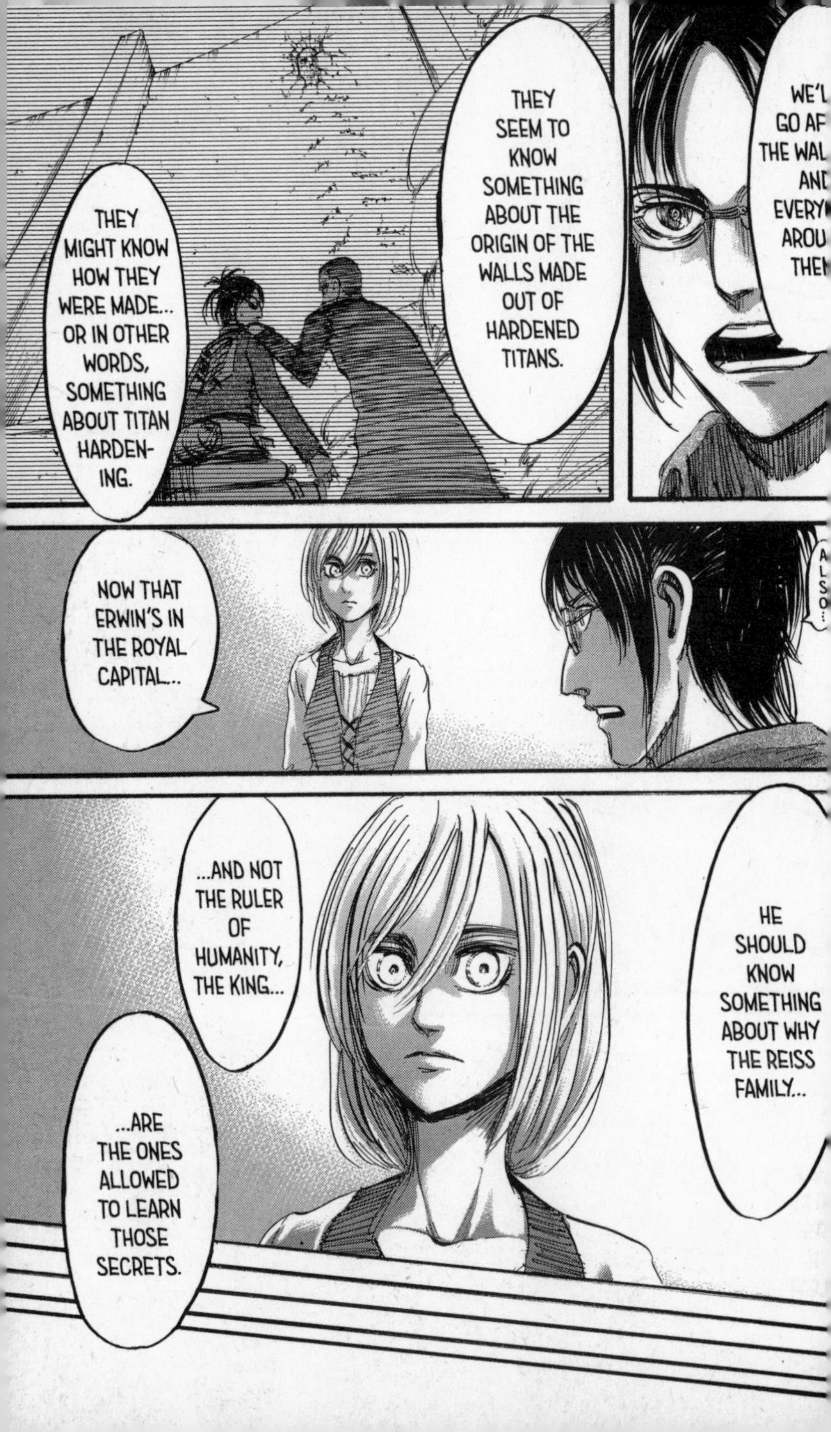
WE'L GO AF THE WAL AND EVERY AROU THEM
THEY SEEM TO KNOW SOMETHING ABOUT THE ORIGIN OF THE WALLS MADE OUT OF HARDENED TITANS.
THEY MIGHT KNOW HOW THEY WERE MADE... OR IN OTHER WORDS, SOMETHING ABOUT TITAN HARDEN-ING.
ALSO...
NOW THAT ERWIN'S IN THE ROYAL CAPITAL...
HE SHOULD KNOW SOMETHING ABOUT WHY THE REISS FAMILY...
...AND NOT THE RULER OF HUMANITY, THE KING...
...ARE THE ONES ALLOWED TO LEARN THOSE SECRETS.

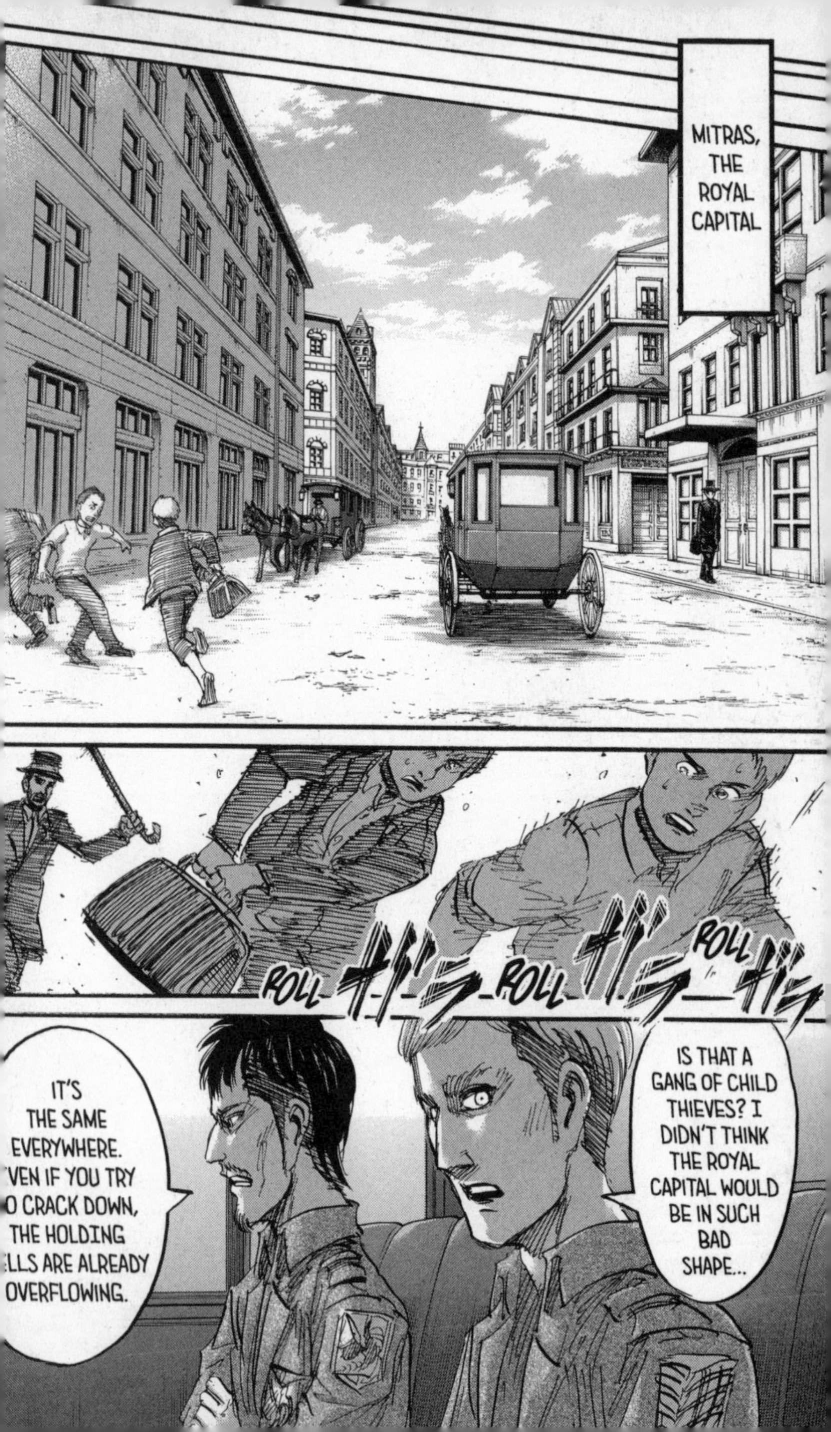
MITRAS, THE ROYAL CAPITAL
ROLL ROLL ROLL
IS THAT A GANG OF CHILD THIEVES? I DIDN'T THINK THE ROYAL CAPITAL WOULD BE IN SUCH BAD SHAPE...
IT'S THE SAME EVERYWHERE. VEN IF YOU TRY O CRACK DOWN, THE HOLDING ELLS ARE ALREADY OVERFLOWING.

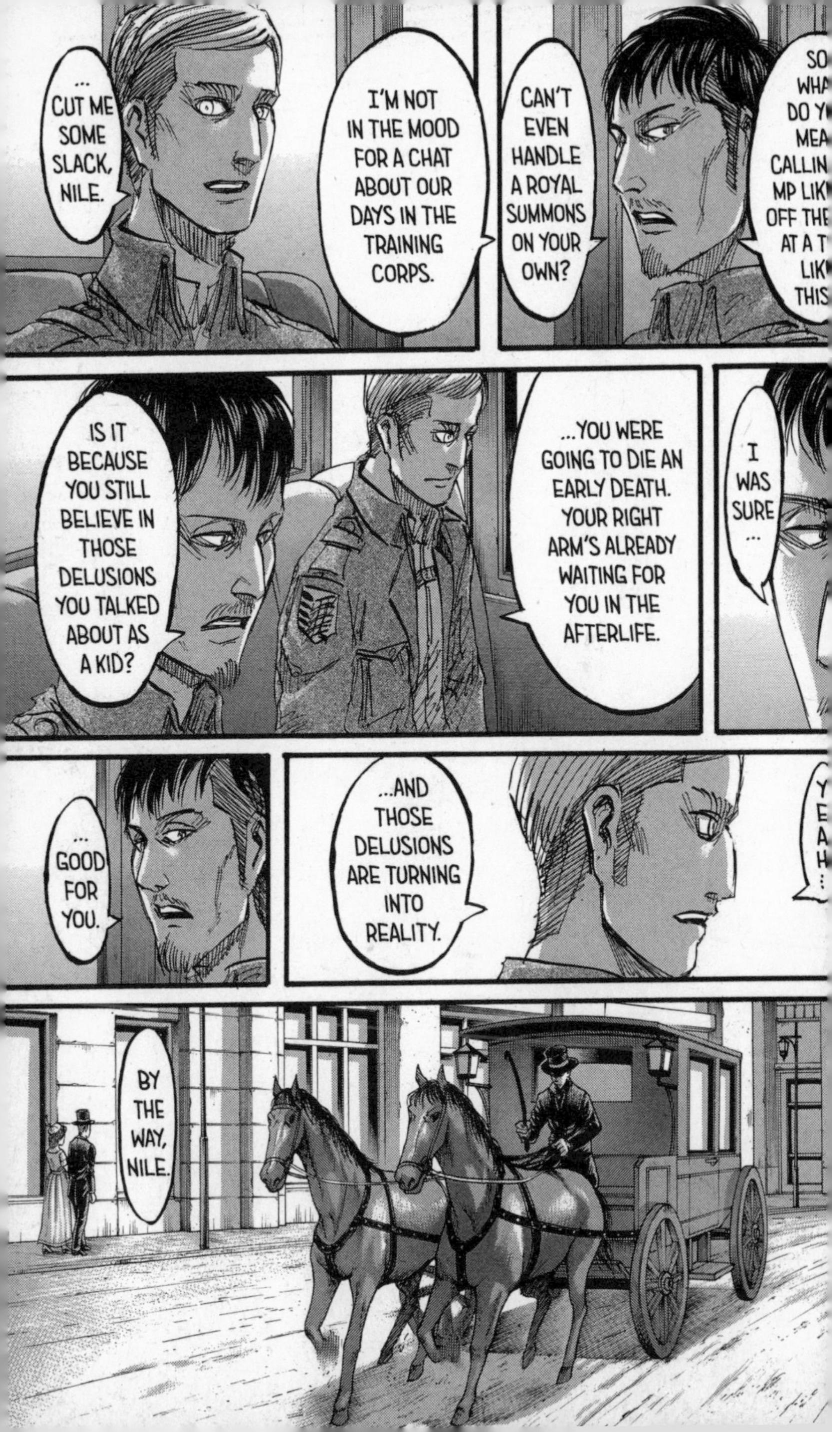
SO WHA DO Y MEA CALLIN MP LIK OFF THE AT A T LIK THIS
CAN'T EVEN HANDLE A ROYAL SUMMONS ON YOUR OWN?
I'M NOT IN THE MOOD FOR A CHAT ABOUT OUR DAYS IN THE TRAINING CORPS.
... CUT ME SOME SLACK, NILE.
I WAS SURE ...
...YOU WERE GOING TO DIE AN EARLY DEATH. YOUR RIGHT ARM'S ALREADY WAITING FOR YOU IN THE AFTERLIFE.
IS IT BECAUSE YOU STILL BELIEVE IN THOSE DELUSIONS YOU TALKED ABOUT AS A KID?
YEAH...
...AND THOSE DELUSIONS ARE TURNING INTO REALITY.
... GOOD FOR YOU.
BY THE WAY, NILE.

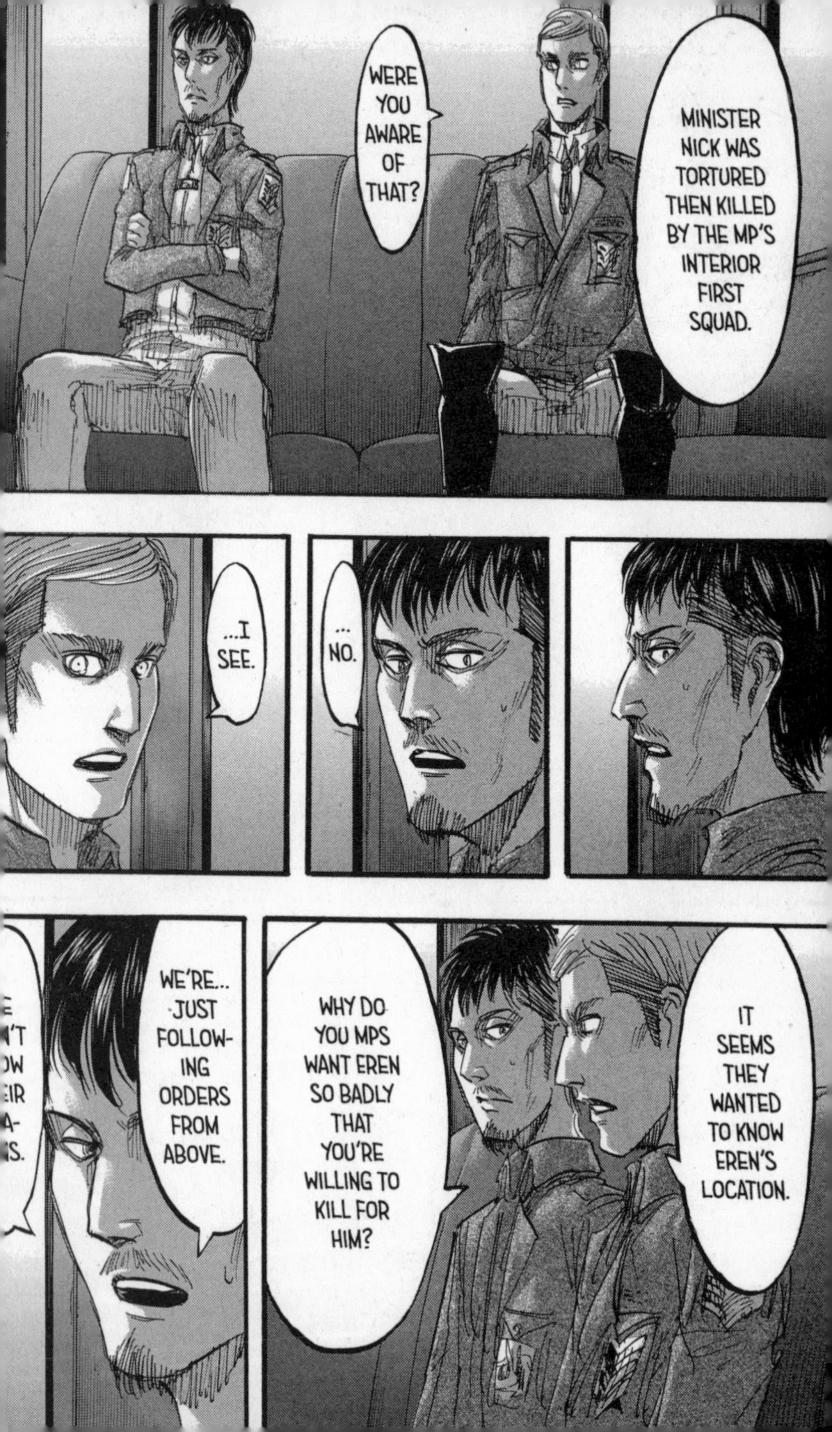
MINISTER NICK WAS TORTURED THEN KILLED BY THE MP'S INTERIOR FIRST SQUAD.
WERE YOU AWARE OF THAT?
... NO.
...I SEE.
IT SEEMS THEY WANTED TO KNOW EREN'S LOCATION.
WHY DO YOU MPS WANT EREN SO BADLY THAT YOU'RE WILLING TO KILL FOR HIM?
WE'RE... JUST FOLLOWING ORDERS FROM ABOVE.

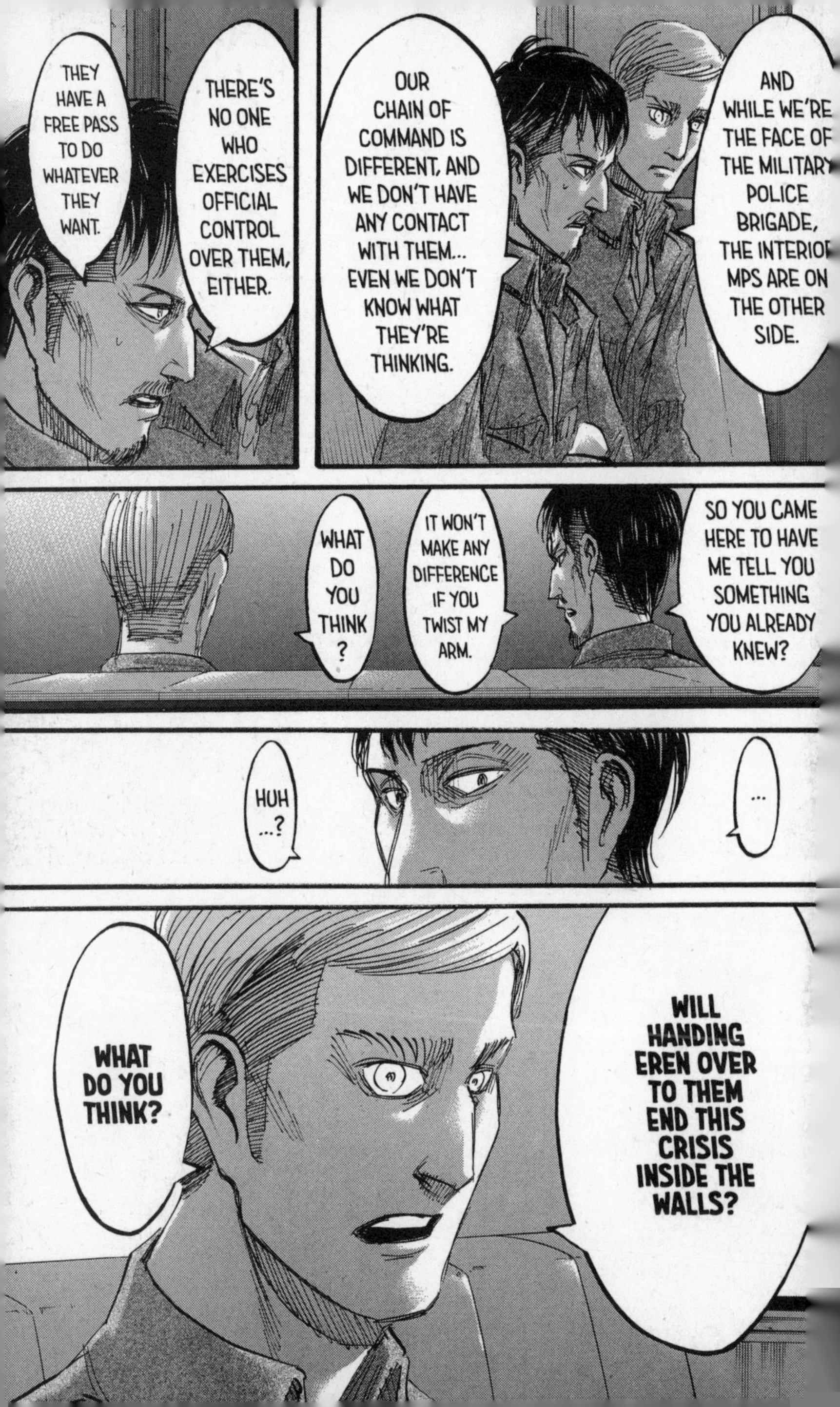
AND WHILE WE'RE THE FACE OF THE MILITARY POLICE BRIGADE, THE INTERIOR MPS ARE ON THE OTHER SIDE.
OUR CHAIN OF COMMAND IS DIFFERENT, AND WE DON'T HAVE ANY CONTACT WITH THEM... EVEN WE DON'T KNOW WHAT THEY'RE THINKING.
THERE'S NO ONE WHO EXERCISES OFFICIAL CONTROL OVER THEM, EITHER.
THEY HAVE A FREE PASS TO DO WHATEVER THEY WANT.
SO YOU CAME HERE TO HAVE ME TELL YOU SOMETHING YOU ALREADY KNEW?
IT WON'T MAKE ANY DIFFERENCE IF YOU TWIST MY ARM.
WHAT DO YOU THINK?
...
HUH ...?
WILL HANDING EREN OVER TO THEM END THIS CRISIS INSIDE THE WALLS?
WHAT DO YOU THINK?

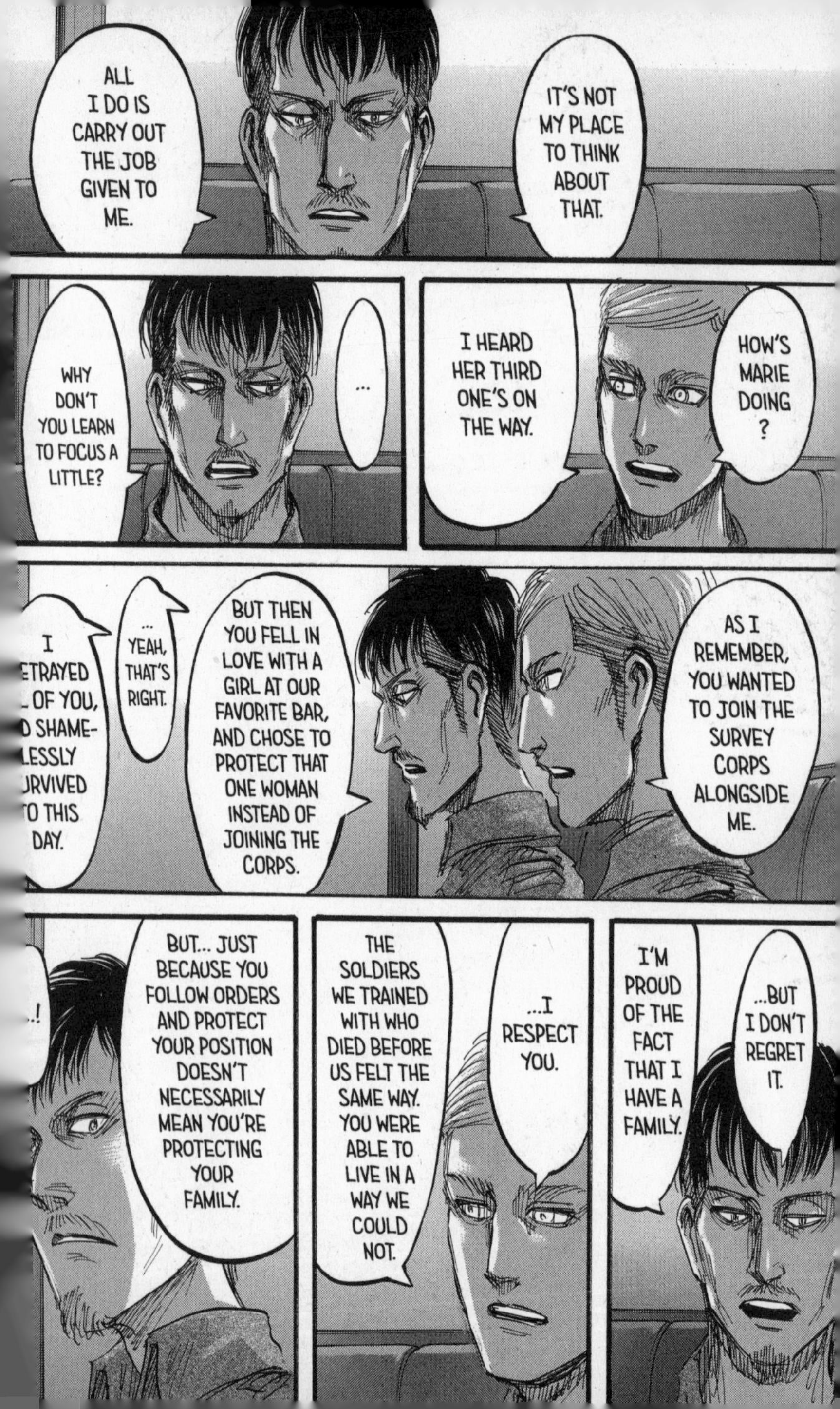
IT'S NOT MY PLACE TO THINK ABOUT THAT.
ALL I DO IS CARRY OUT THE JOB GIVEN TO ME.
HOW'S MARIE DOING?
I HEARD HER THIRD ONE'S ON THE WAY.
...
WHY DON'T YOU LEARN TO FOCUS A LITTLE?
AS I REMEMBER, YOU WANTED TO JOIN THE SURVEY CORPS ALONGSIDE ME.
BUT THEN YOU FELL IN LOVE WITH A GIRL AT OUR FAVORITE BAR, AND CHOSE TO PROTECT THAT ONE WOMAN INSTEAD OF JOINING THE CORPS.
... YEAH, THAT'S RIGHT.
I ETRAYED L OF YOU, D SHAME-LESSLY URVIVED O THIS DAY.
...BUT I DON'T REGRET IT.
I'M PROUD OF THE FACT THAT I HAVE A FAMILY.
...I RESPECT YOU.
THE SOLDIERS WE TRAINED WITH WHO DIED BEFORE US FELT THE SAME WAY. YOU WERE ABLE TO LIVE IN A WAY WE COULD NOT.
BUT... JUST BECAUSE YOU FOLLOW ORDERS AND PROTECT YOUR POSITION DOESN'T NECESSARILY MEAN YOU'RE PROTECTING YOUR FAMILY.
..!

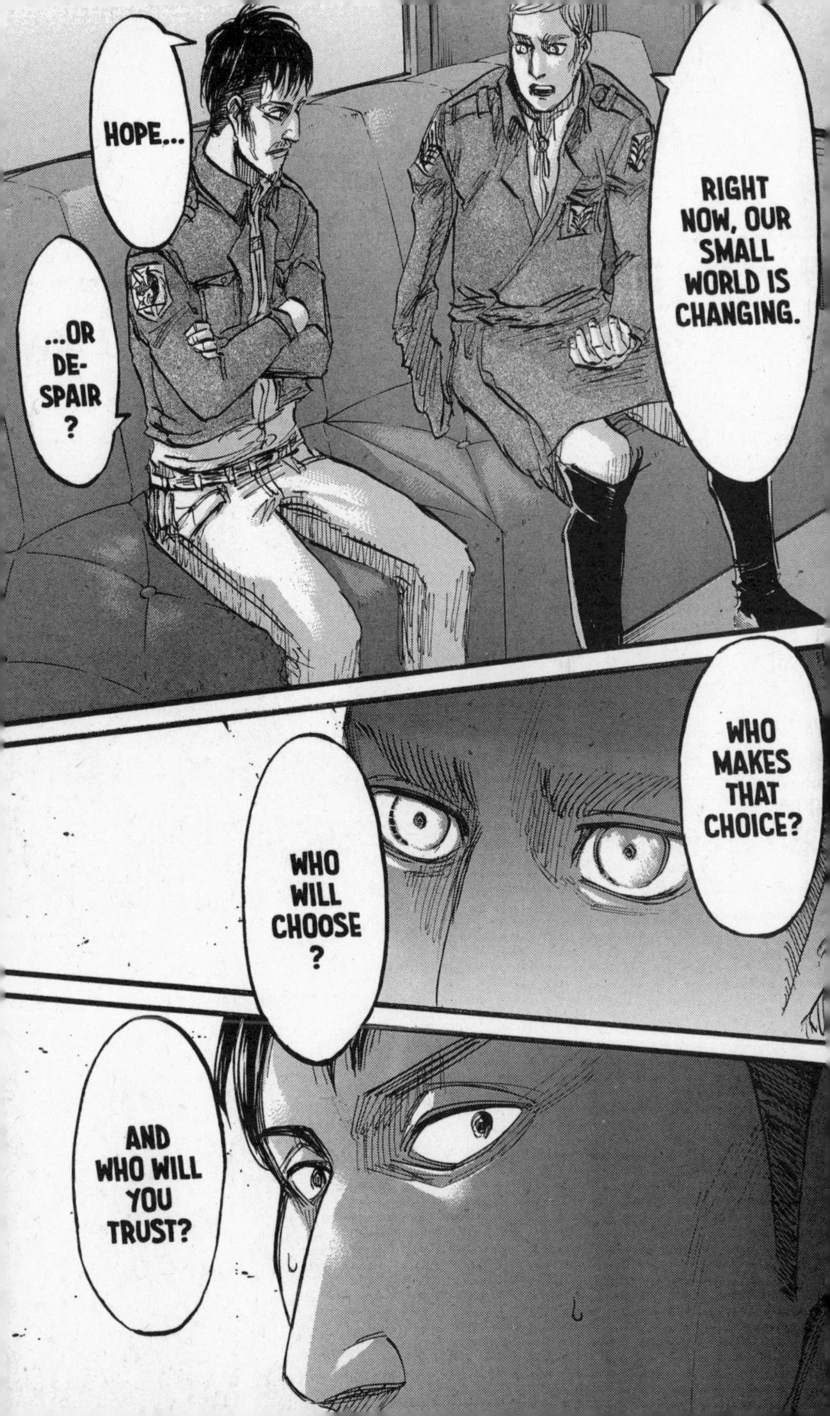
RIGHT NOW, OUR SMALL WORLD IS CHANGING.
HOPE...
...OR DE-SPAIR?
WHO MAKES THAT CHOICE?
WHO WILL CHOOSE?
AND WHO WILL YOU TRUST?

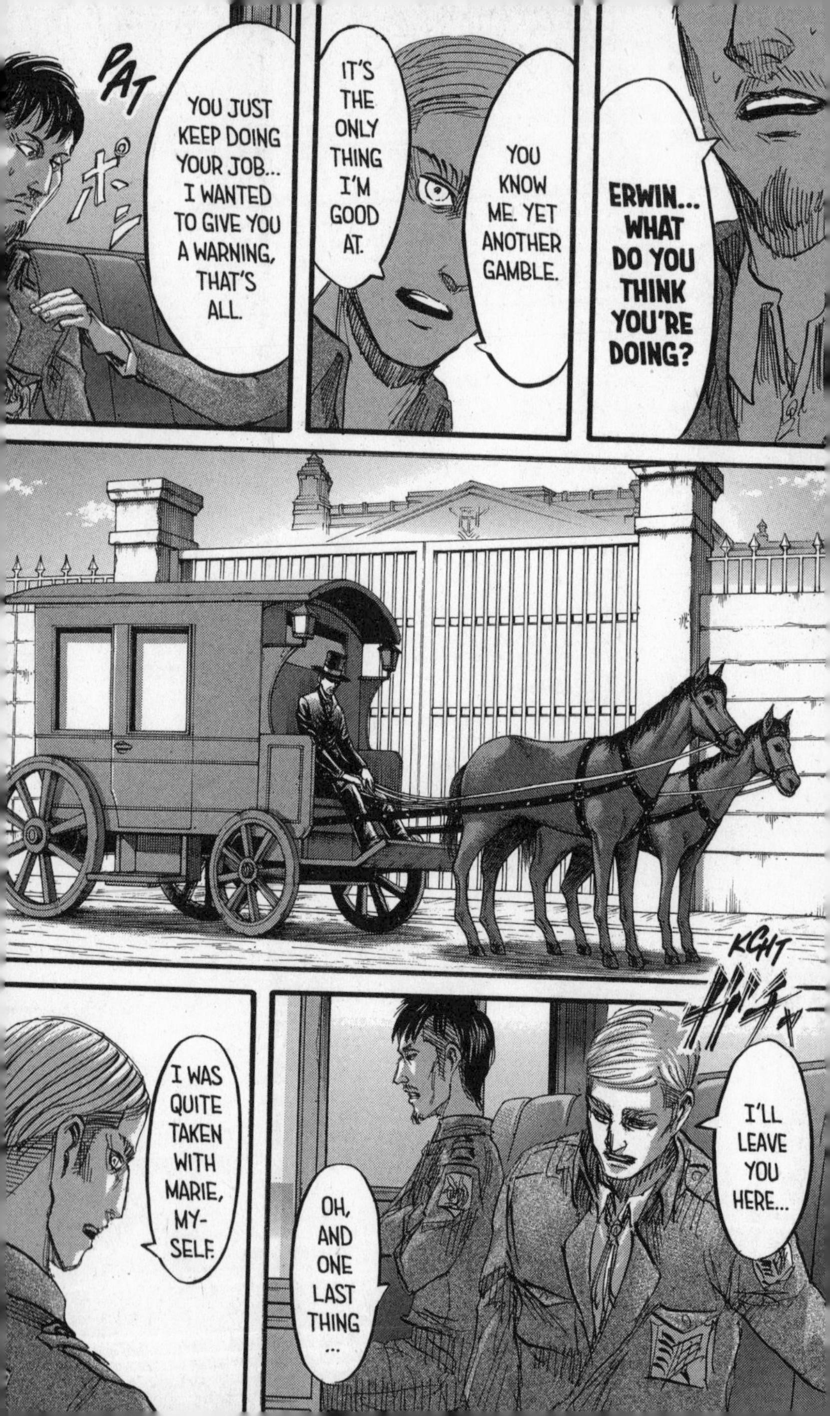
ERWIN... WHAT DO YOU THINK YOU'RE DOING?
YOU KNOW ME. YET ANOTHER GAMBLE.
IT'S THE ONLY THING I'M GOOD AT.
PAT
YOU JUST KEEP DOING YOUR JOB... I WANTED TO GIVE YOU A WARNING, THAT'S ALL.
KCHT
I'LL LEAVE YOU HERE...
OH, AND ONE LAST THING...
I WAS QUITE TAKEN WITH MARIE, MYSELF.

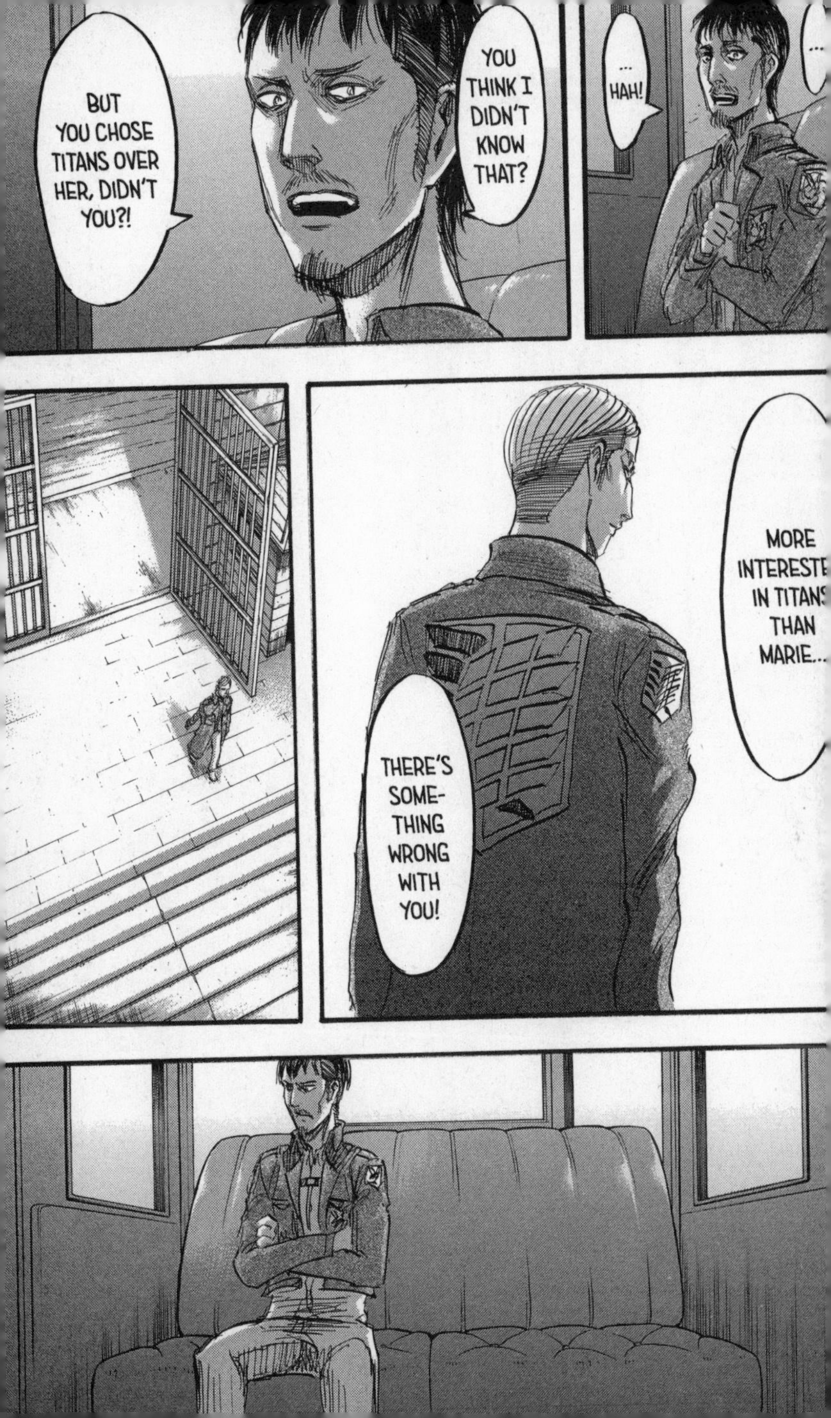

...
... HAH!
YOU THINK I DIDN'T KNOW THAT?
BUT YOU CHOSE TITANS OVER HER, DIDN'T YOU?!
MORE INTERESTE IN TITANS THAN MARIE...
THERE'S SOME-THING WRONG WITH YOU!

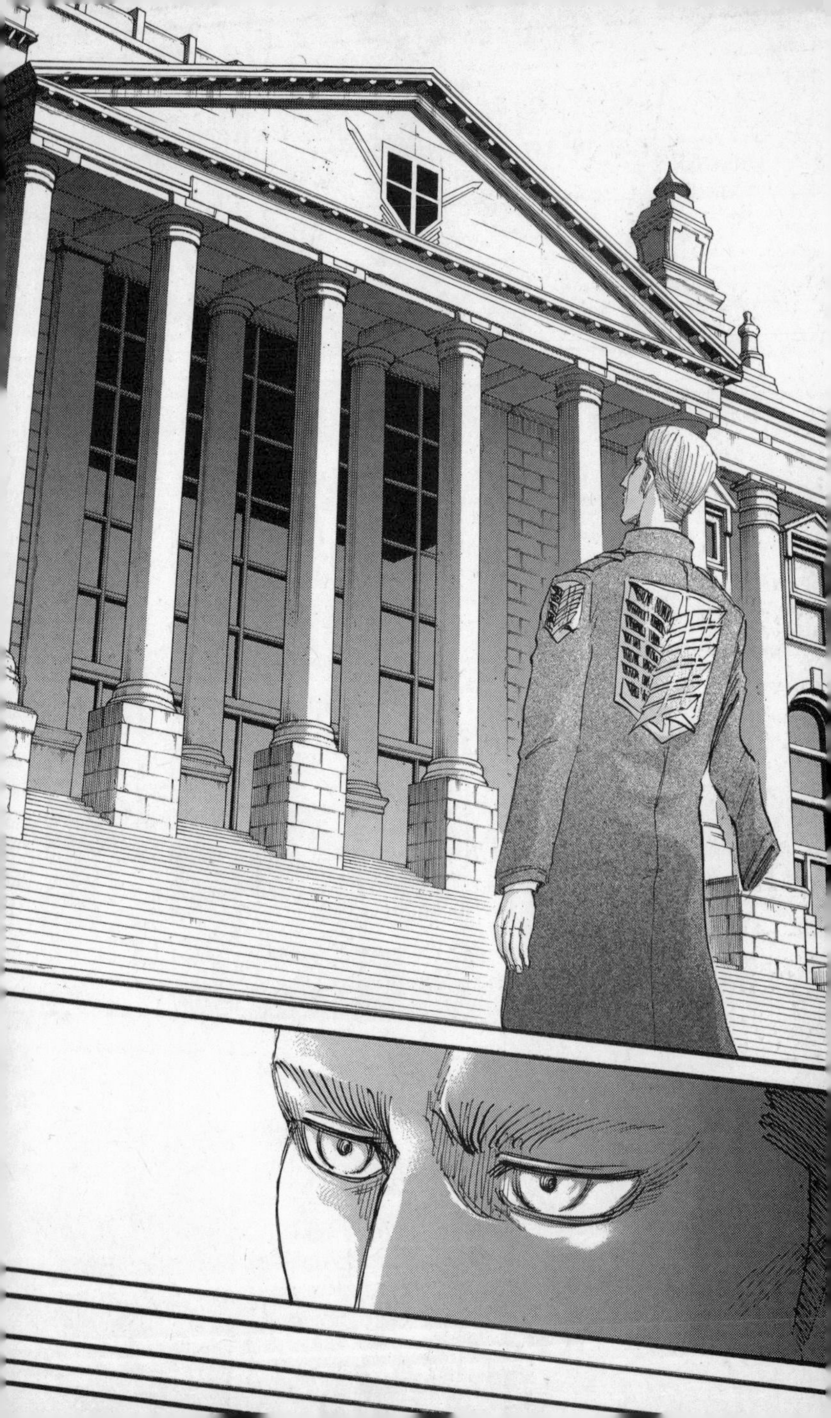

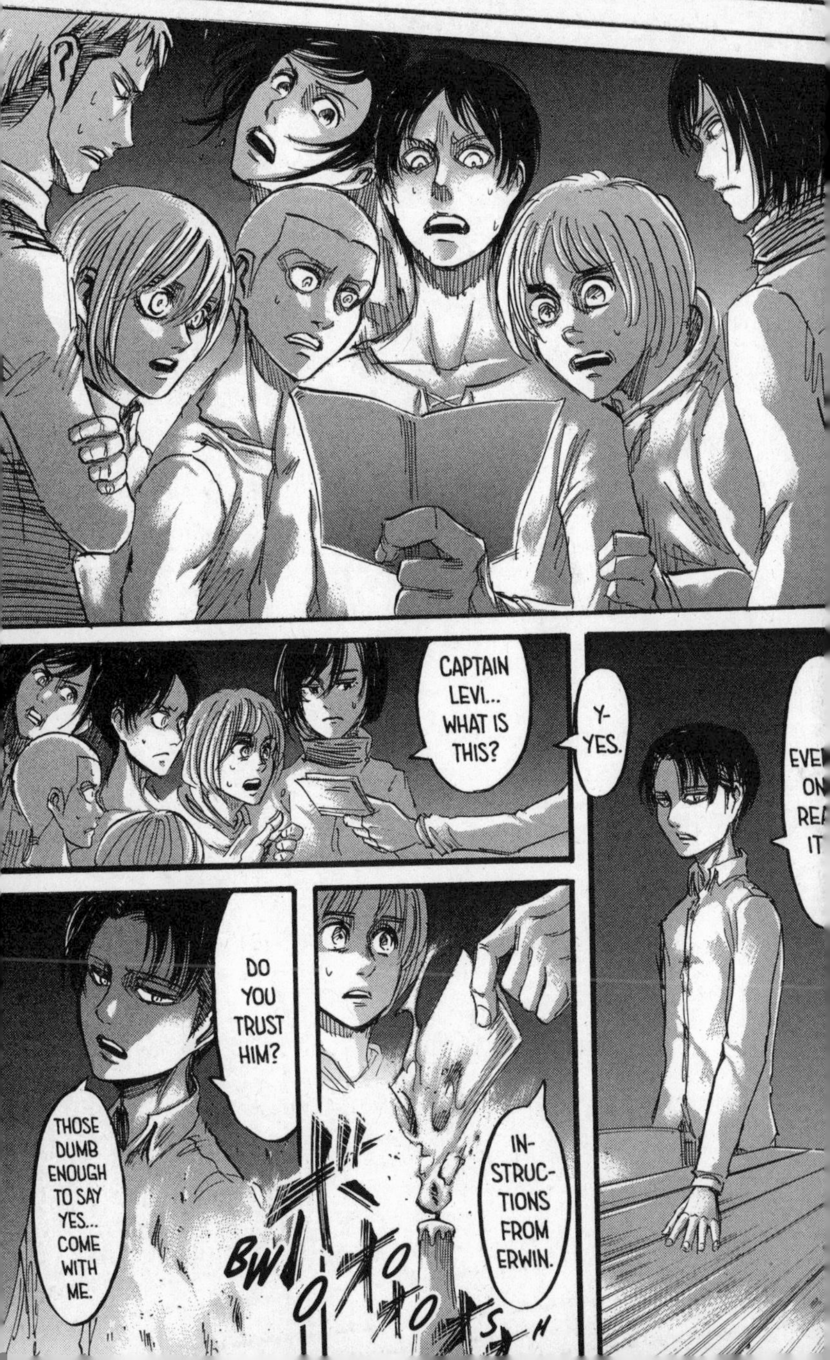

EVE ON REA IT
CAPTAIN LEVI... WHAT IS THIS?
Y- YES.
IN-STRUC-TIONS FROM ERWIN.
BWOOOOSH
DO YOU TRUST HIM?
THOSE DUMB ENOUGH TO SAY YES... COME WITH ME.

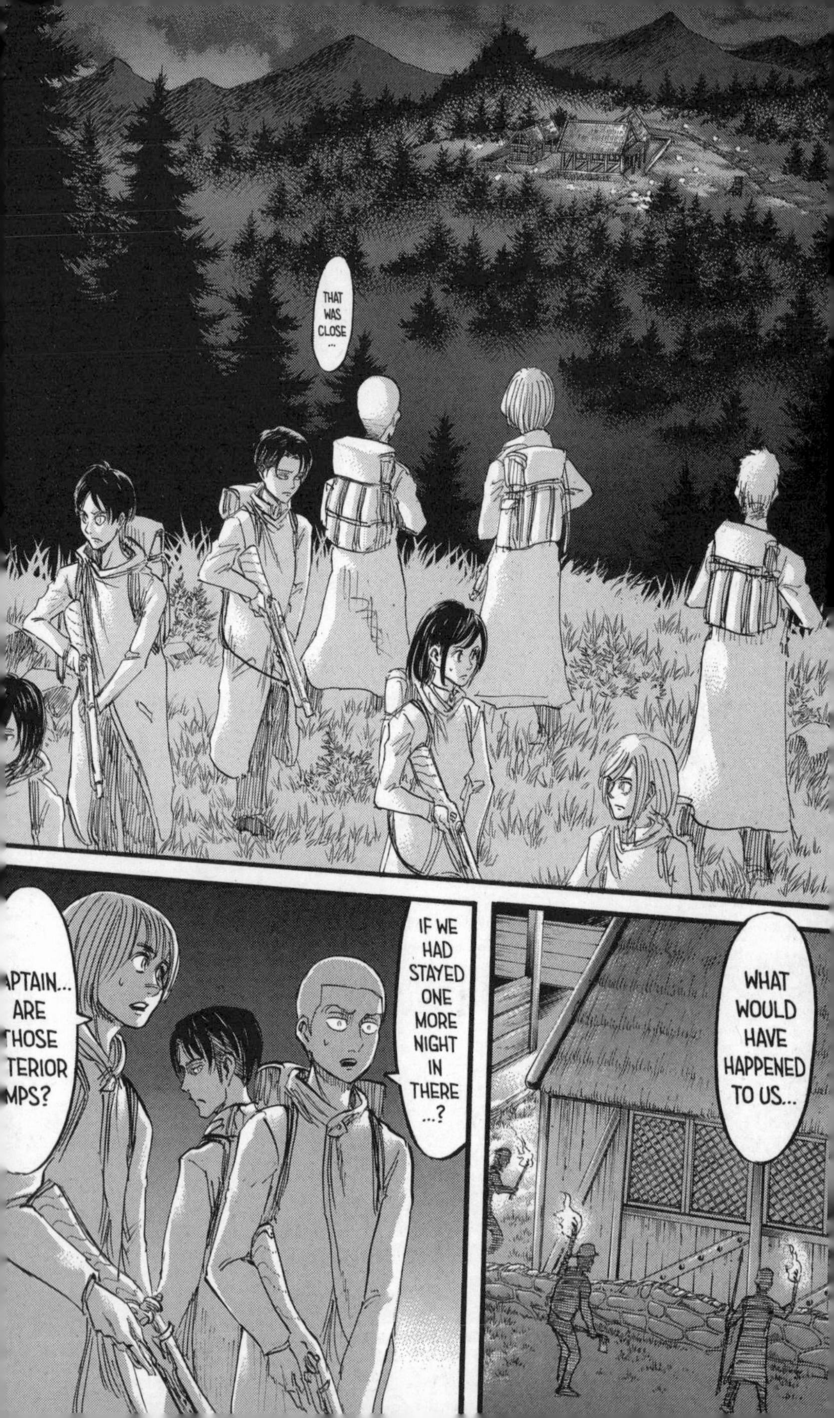
THAT WAS CLOSE ...
WHAT WOULD HAVE HAPPENED TO US...
IF WE HAD STAYED ONE MORE NIGHT IN THERE ...?
APTAIN... ARE THOSE TERIOR MPS?

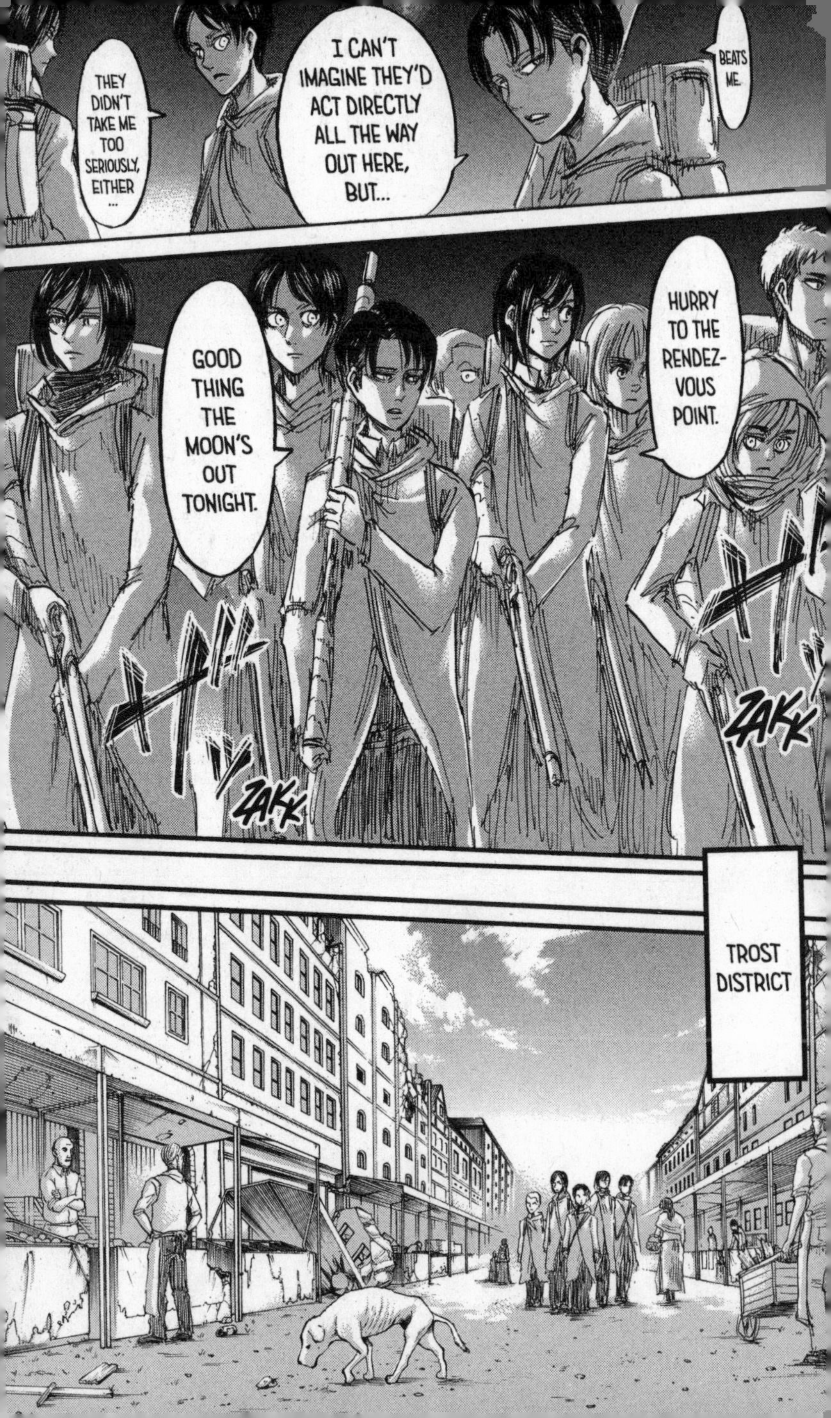
BEATS ME.
I CAN'T IMAGINE THEY'D ACT DIRECTLY ALL THE WAY OUT HERE, BUT...
THEY DIDN'T TAKE ME TOO SERIOUSLY, EITHER ...
HURRY TO THE RENDEZ-VOUS POINT.
GOOD THING THE MOON'S OUT TONIGHT.
ZAKK
ZAKK
TROST DISTRICT

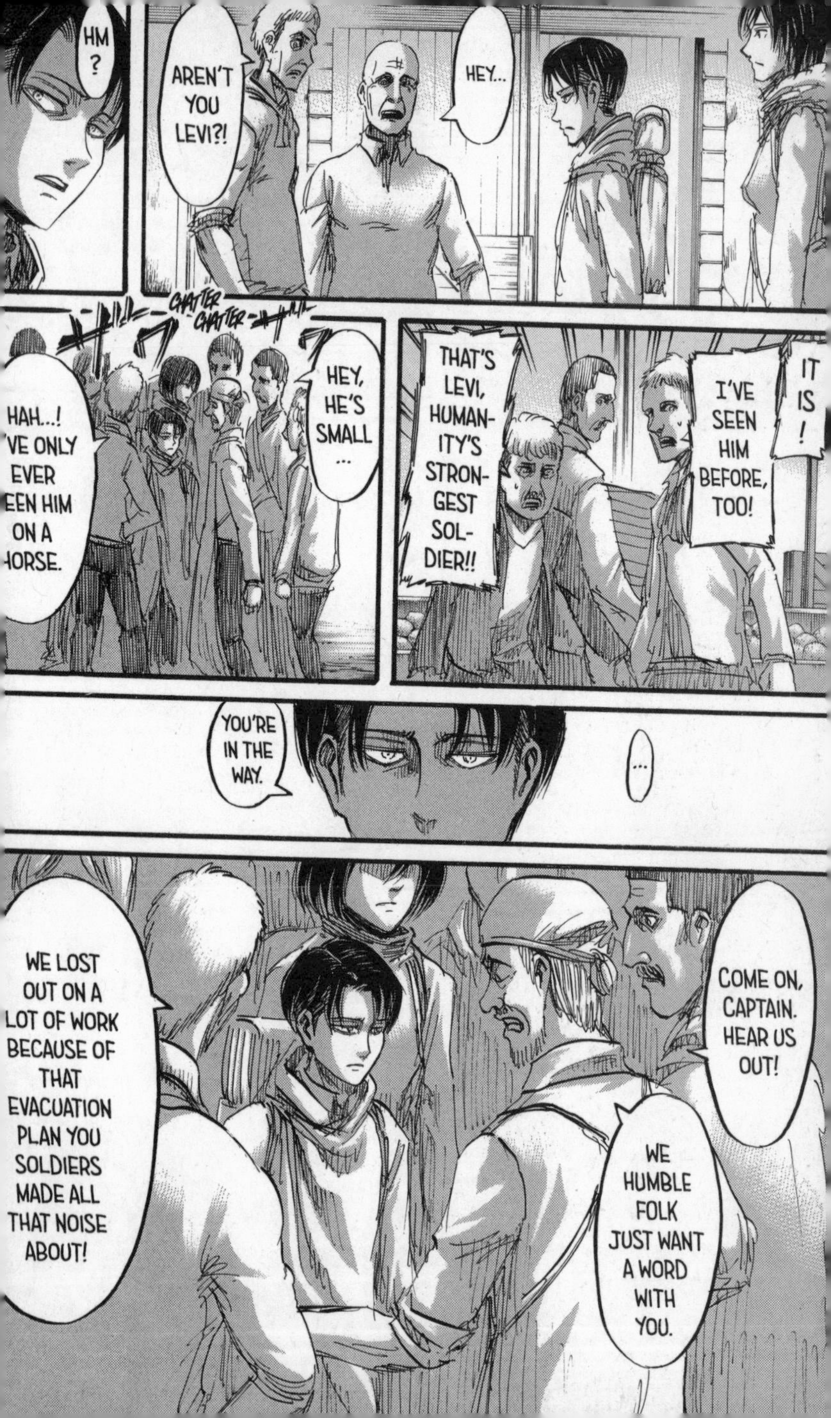
HEY...
AREN'T YOU LEVI?!
HM?
IT IS!
I'VE SEEN HIM BEFORE, TOO!
THAT'S LEVI, HUMAN-ITY'S STRON-GEST SOL-DIER!!
CHATTER CHATTER
HEY, HE'S SMALL...
HAH...! 'VE ONLY EVER EEN HIM ON A ORSE.
...
YOU'RE IN THE WAY.
COME ON, CAPTAIN. HEAR US OUT!
WE HUMBLE FOLK JUST WANT A WORD WITH YOU.
WE LOST OUT ON A LOT OF WORK BECAUSE OF THAT EVACUATION PLAN YOU SOLDIERS MADE ALL THAT NOISE ABOUT!

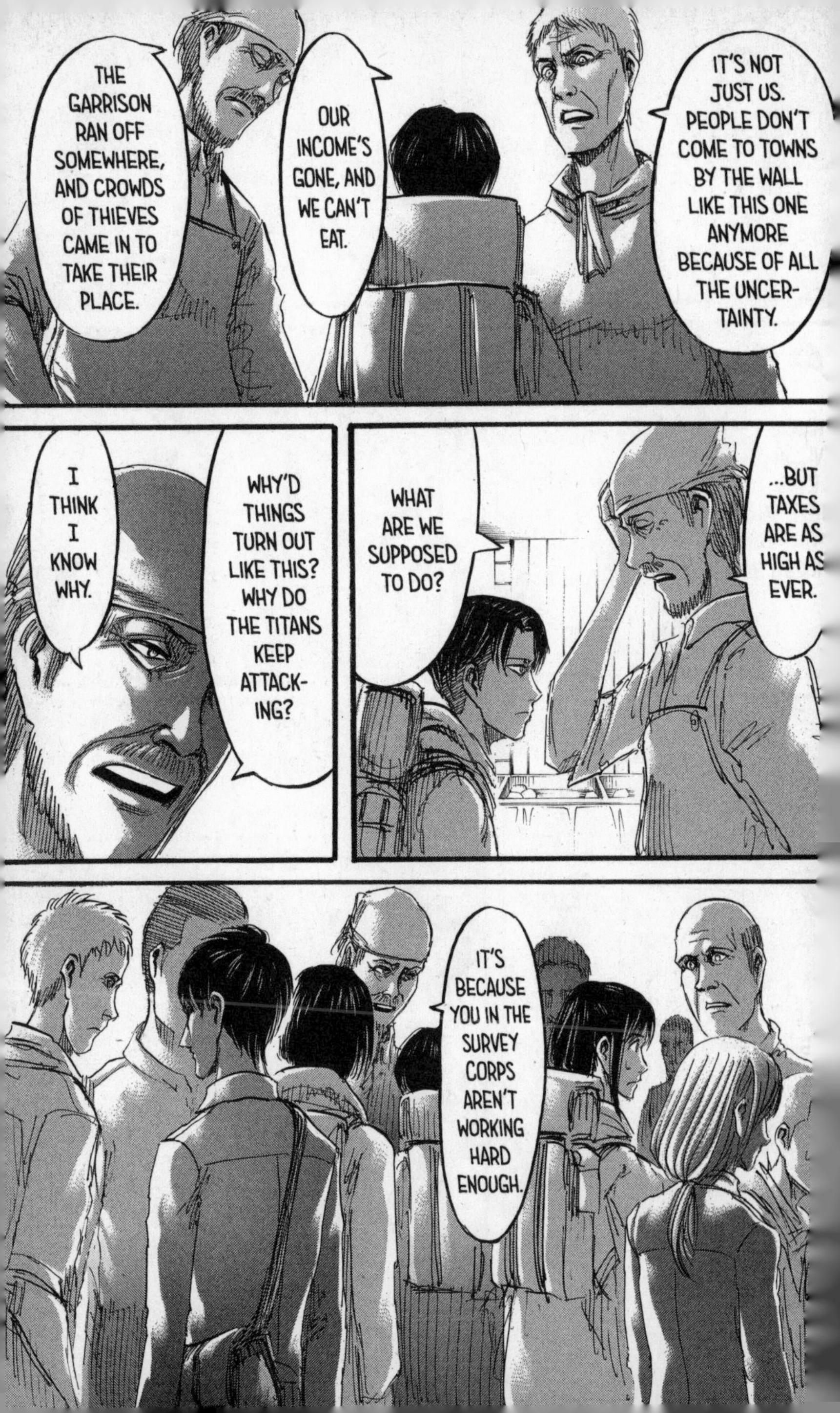
IT'S NOT JUST US. PEOPLE DON'T COME TO TOWNS BY THE WALL LIKE THIS ONE ANYMORE BECAUSE OF ALL THE UNCER-TAINTY.
OUR INCOME'S GONE, AND WE CAN'T EAT.
THE GARRISON RAN OFF SOMEWHERE, AND CROWDS OF THIEVES CAME IN TO TAKE THEIR PLACE.
...BUT TAXES ARE AS HIGH AS EVER.
WHAT ARE WE SUPPOSED TO DO?
WHY'D THINGS TURN OUT LIKE THIS? WHY DO THE TITANS KEEP ATTACK-ING?
I THINK I KNOW WHY.
IT'S BECAUSE YOU IN THE SURVEY CORPS AREN'T WORKING HARD ENOUGH.

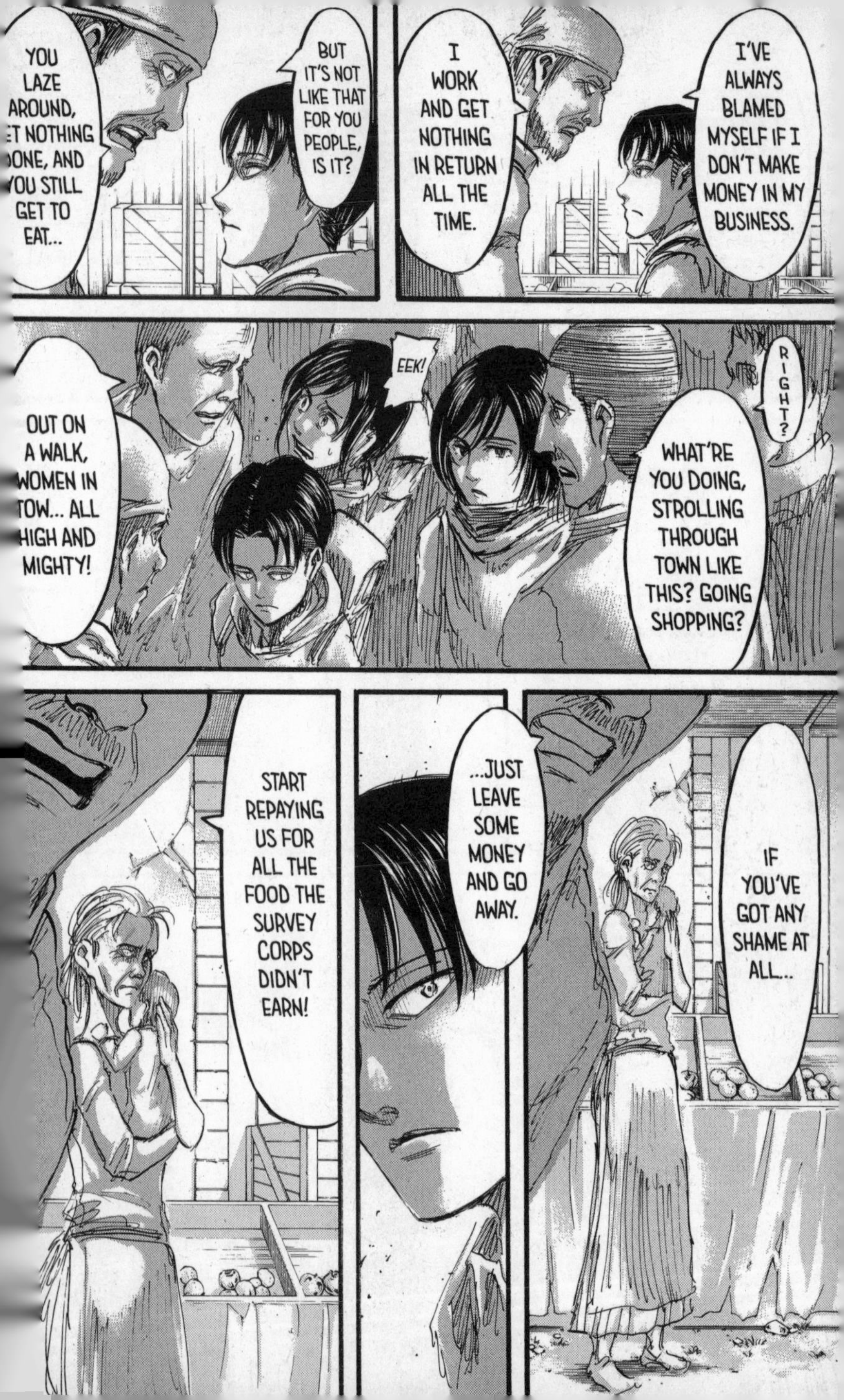
I'VE ALWAYS BLAMED MYSELF IF I DON'T MAKE MONEY IN MY BUSINESS.
I WORK AND GET NOTHING IN RETURN ALL THE TIME.
BUT IT'S NOT LIKE THAT FOR YOU PEOPLE, IS IT?
YOU LAZE AROUND, ET NOTHING DONE, AND YOU STILL GET TO EAT...
RIGHT?
WHAT'RE YOU DOING, STROLLING THROUGH TOWN LIKE THIS? GOING SHOPPING?
EEK!
OUT ON A WALK, WOMEN IN TOW... ALL HIGH AND MIGHTY!
IF YOU'VE GOT ANY SHAME AT ALL...
...JUST LEAVE SOME MONEY AND GO AWAY.
START REPAYING US FOR ALL THE FOOD THE SURVEY CORPS DIDN'T EARN!

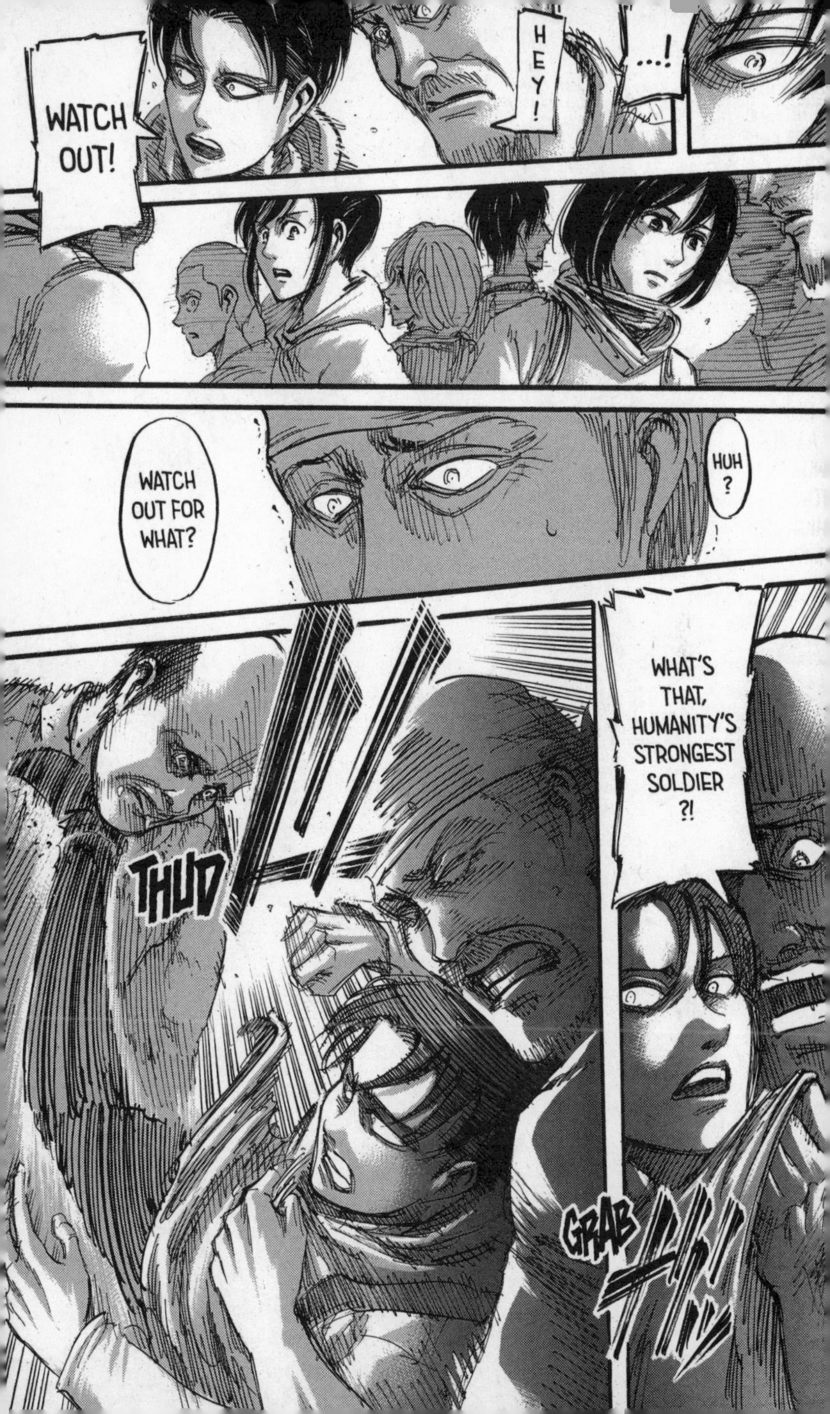
...!
HEY!
WATCH OUT!
HUH?
WATCH OUT FOR WHAT?
WHAT'S THAT, HUMANITY'S STRONGEST SOLDIER?!
GRAB
THUD

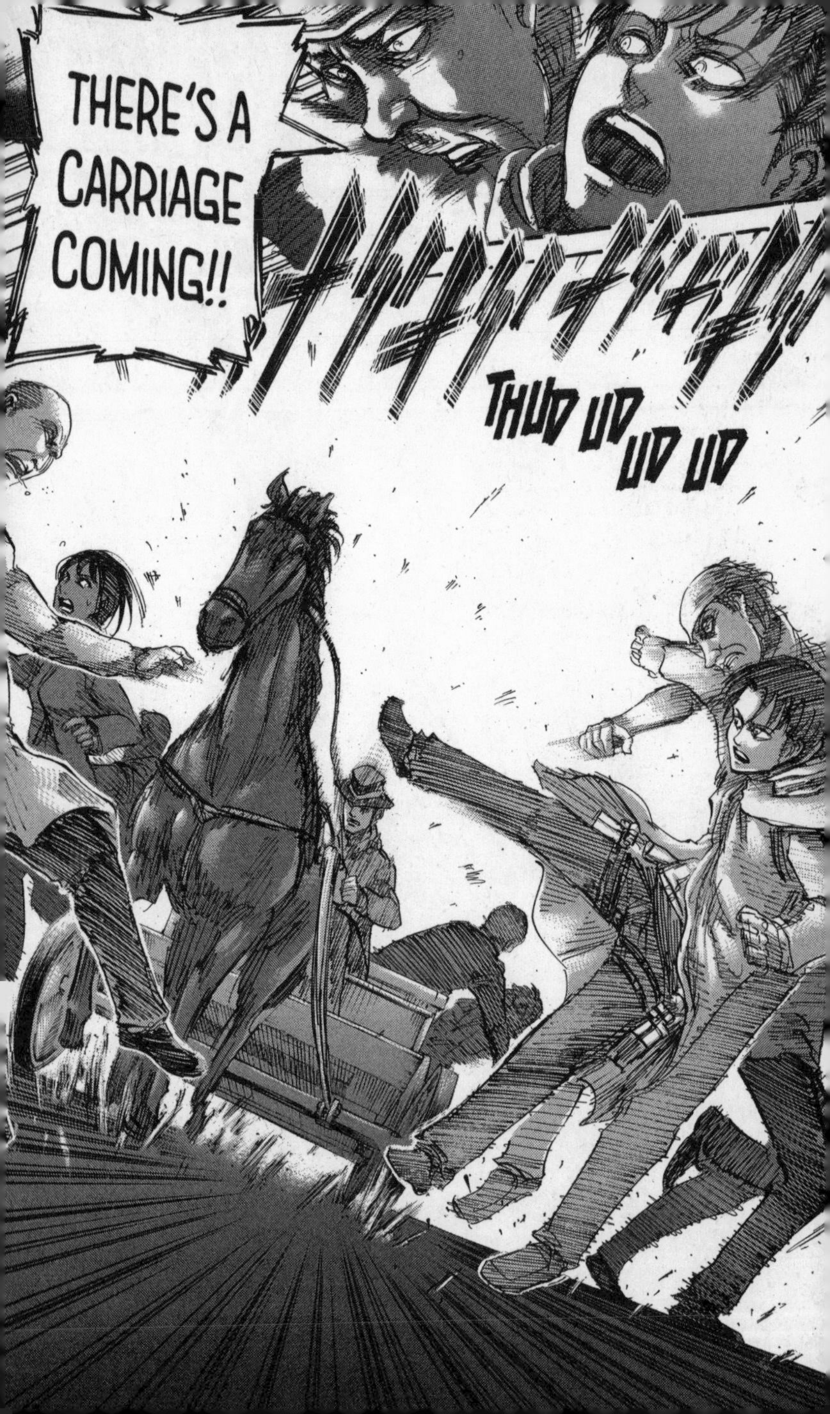
THERE'S A CARRIAGE COMING!!
THUD UD UD UD

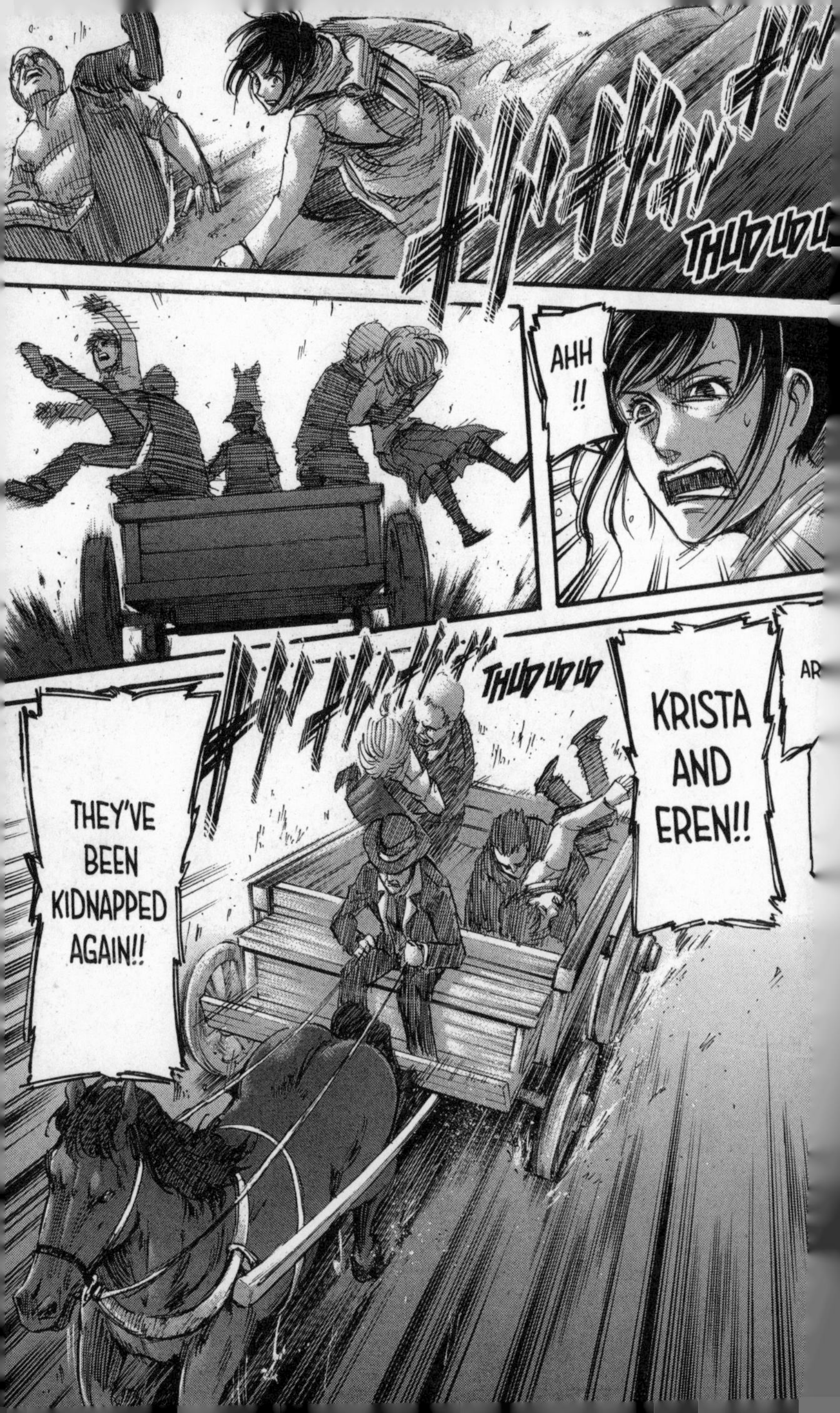
THUD UD U
AHH !!
KRISTA AND EREN!!
THUD UD UD
THEY'VE BEEN KIDNAPPED AGAIN!!

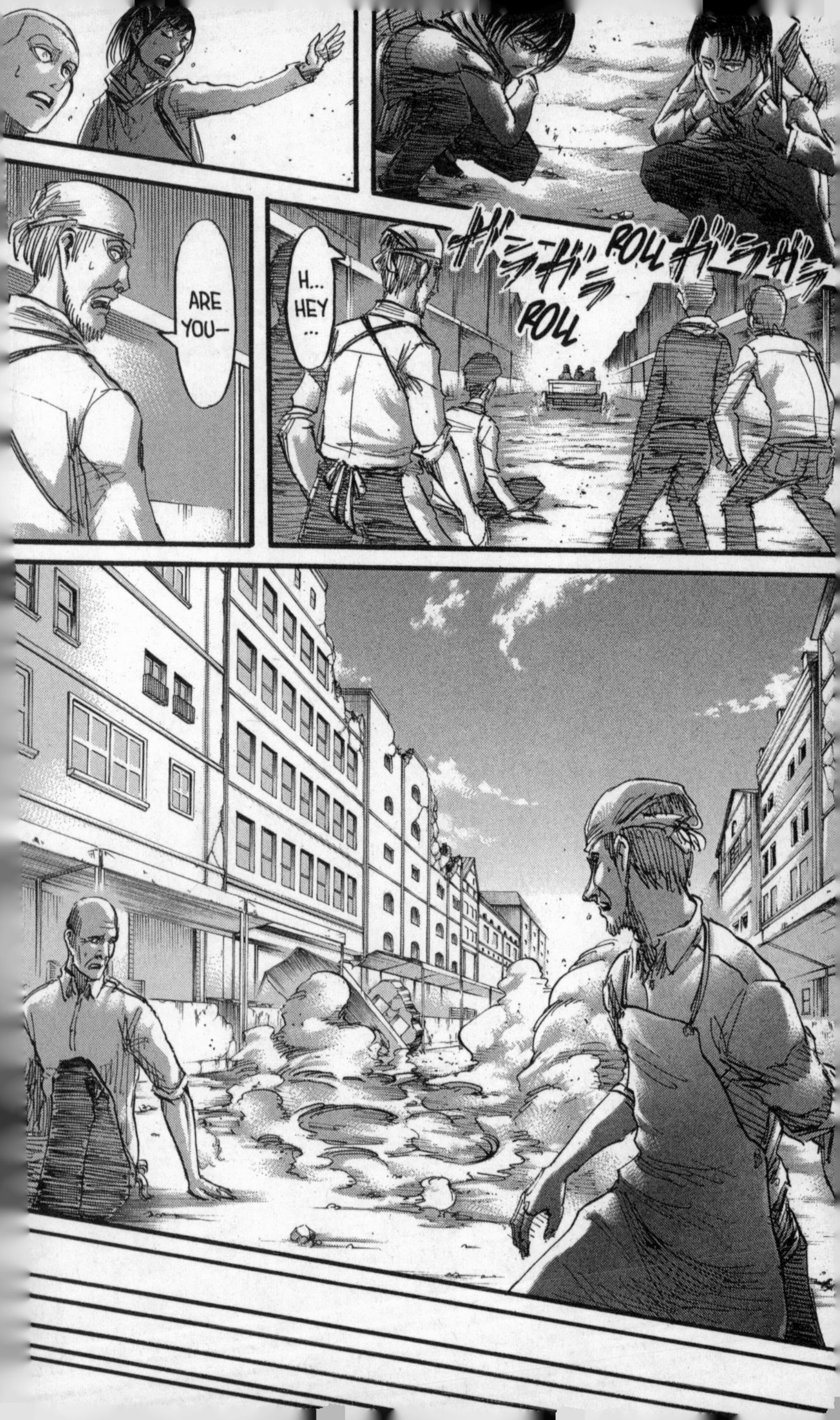
ROLL
ROLL
H... HEY ...
ARE YOU—

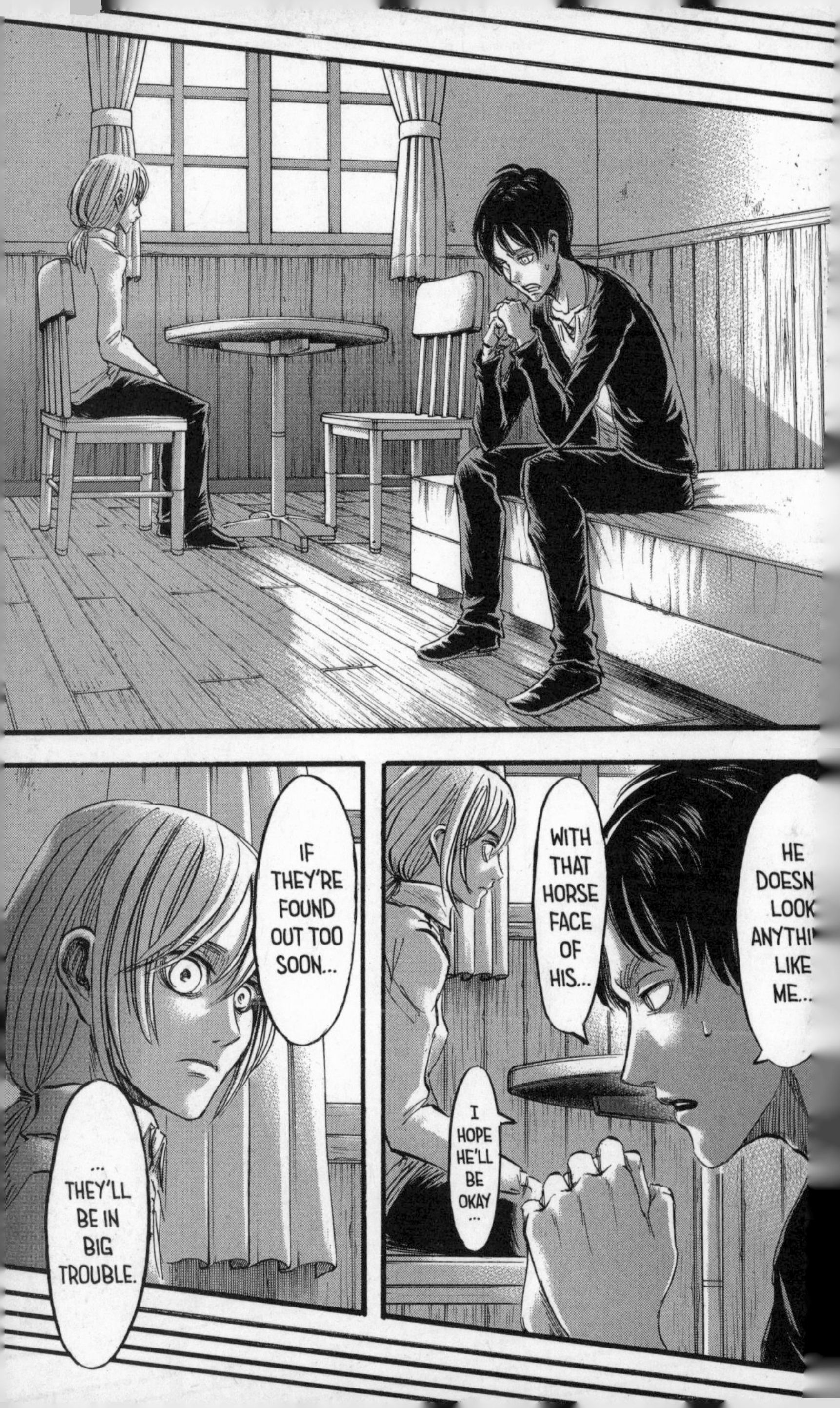

HE DOESN LOOK ANYTHI LIKE ME...
WITH THAT HORSE FACE OF HIS...
I HOPE HE'LL BE OKAY ...
IF THEY'RE FOUND OUT TOO SOON...
... THEY'LL BE IN BIG TROUBLE.

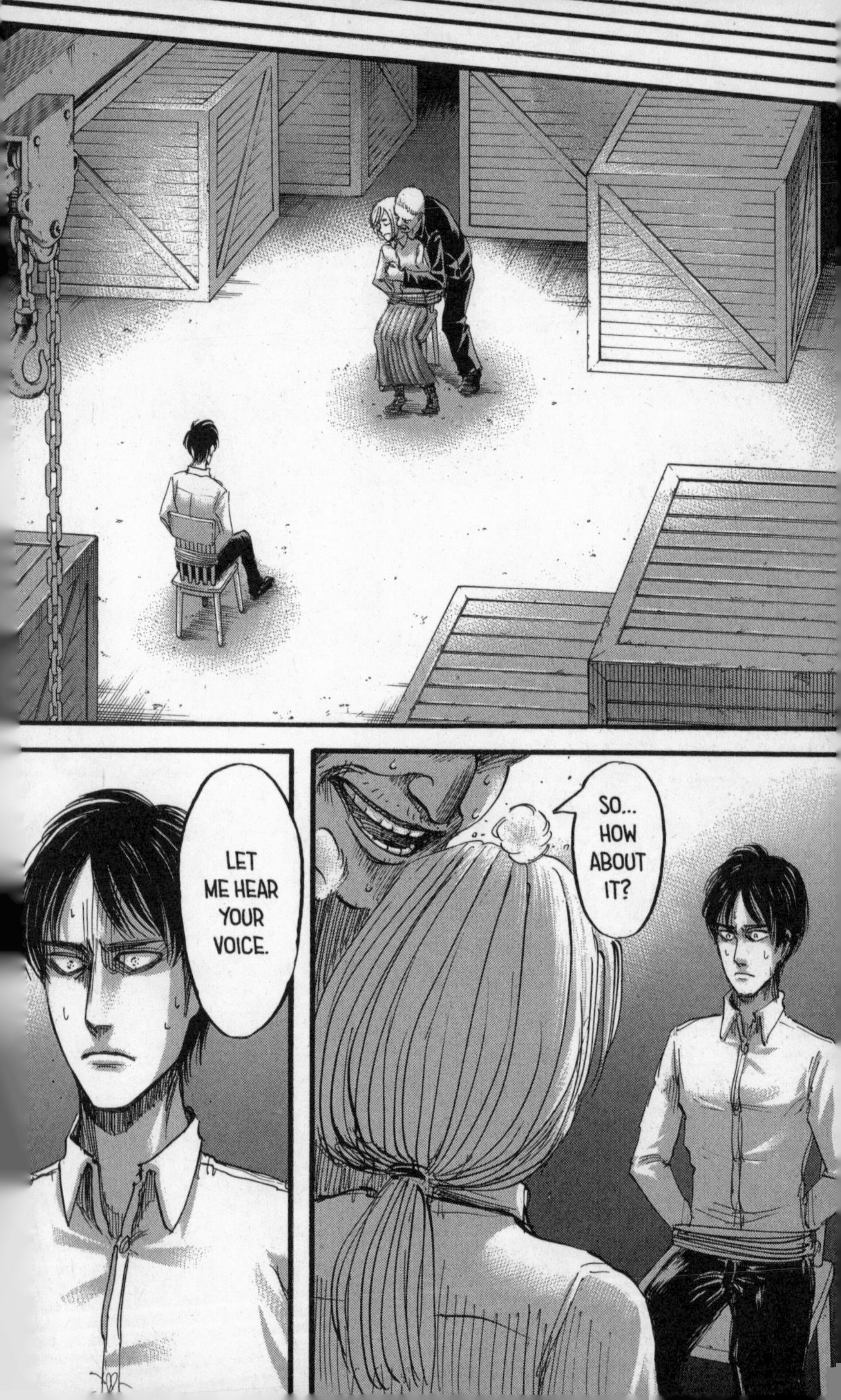
SO... HOW ABOUT IT?
LET ME HEAR YOUR VOICE.

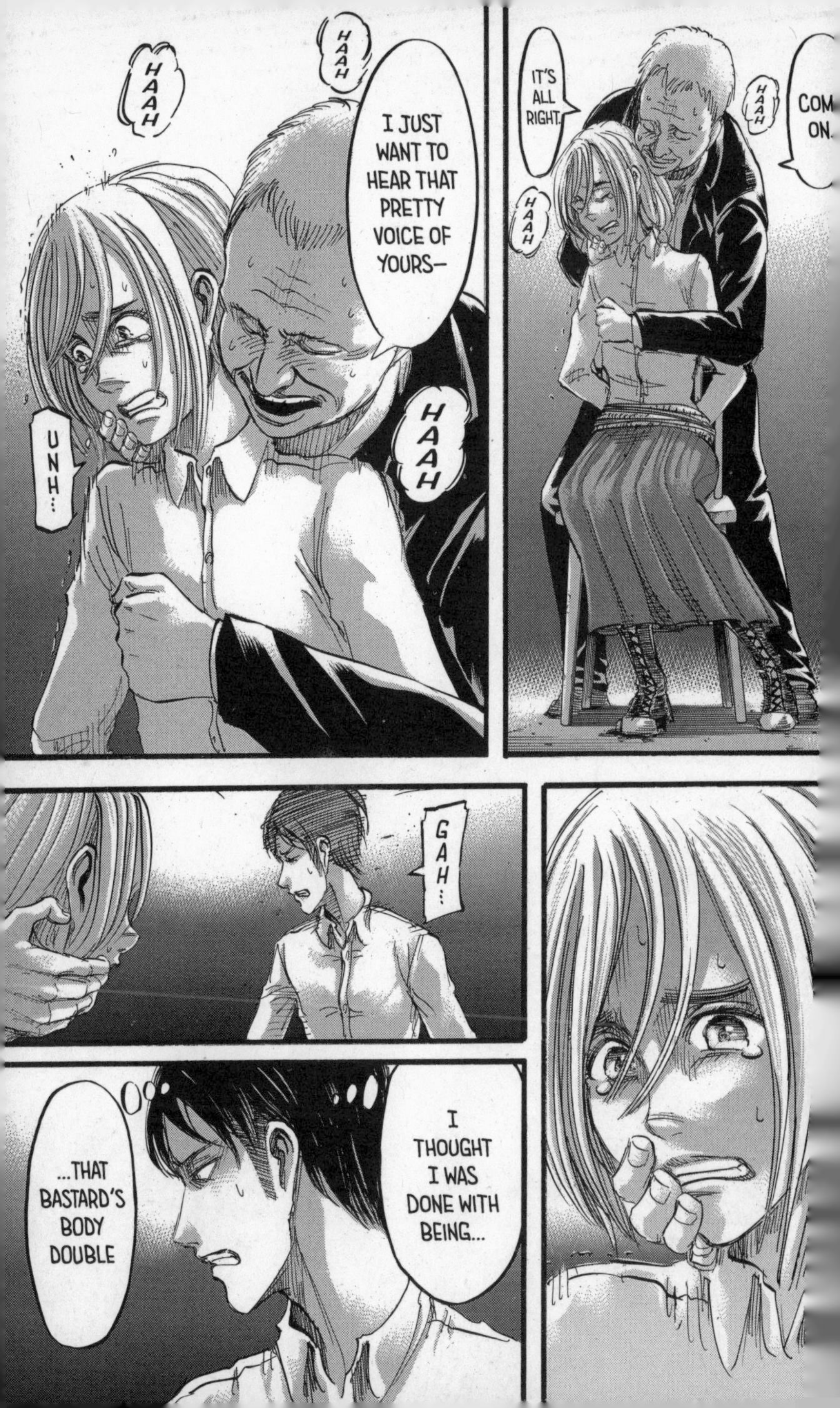
COM ON.
HAAH
IT'S ALL RIGHT.
HAAH
HAAH
HAAH
I JUST WANT TO HEAR THAT PRETTY VOICE OF YOURS—
HAAH
UNH...
GAH...
I THOUGHT I WAS DONE WITH BEING...
...THAT BASTARD'S BODY DOUBLE

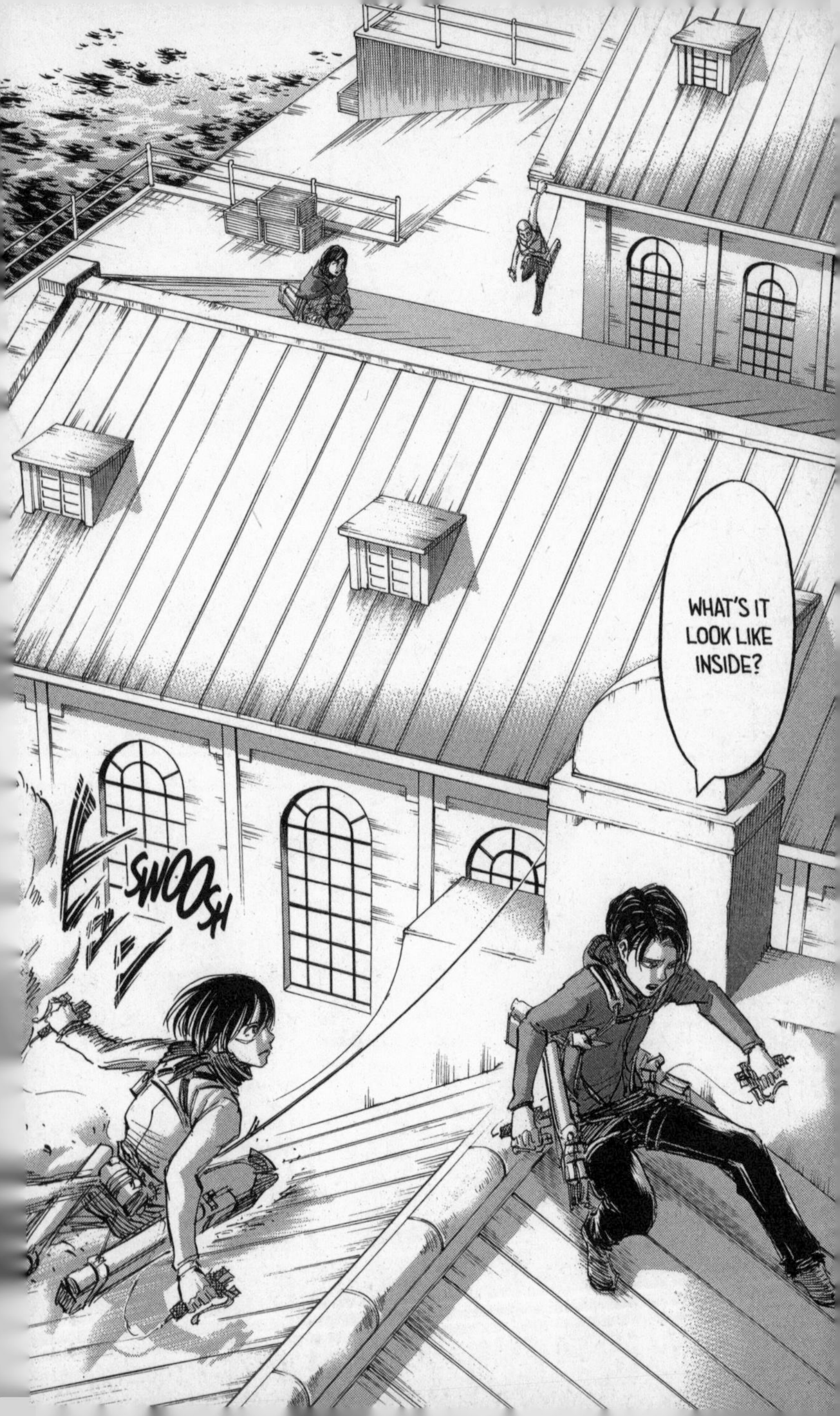
WHAT'S IT LOOK LIKE INSIDE?
SWOOSH

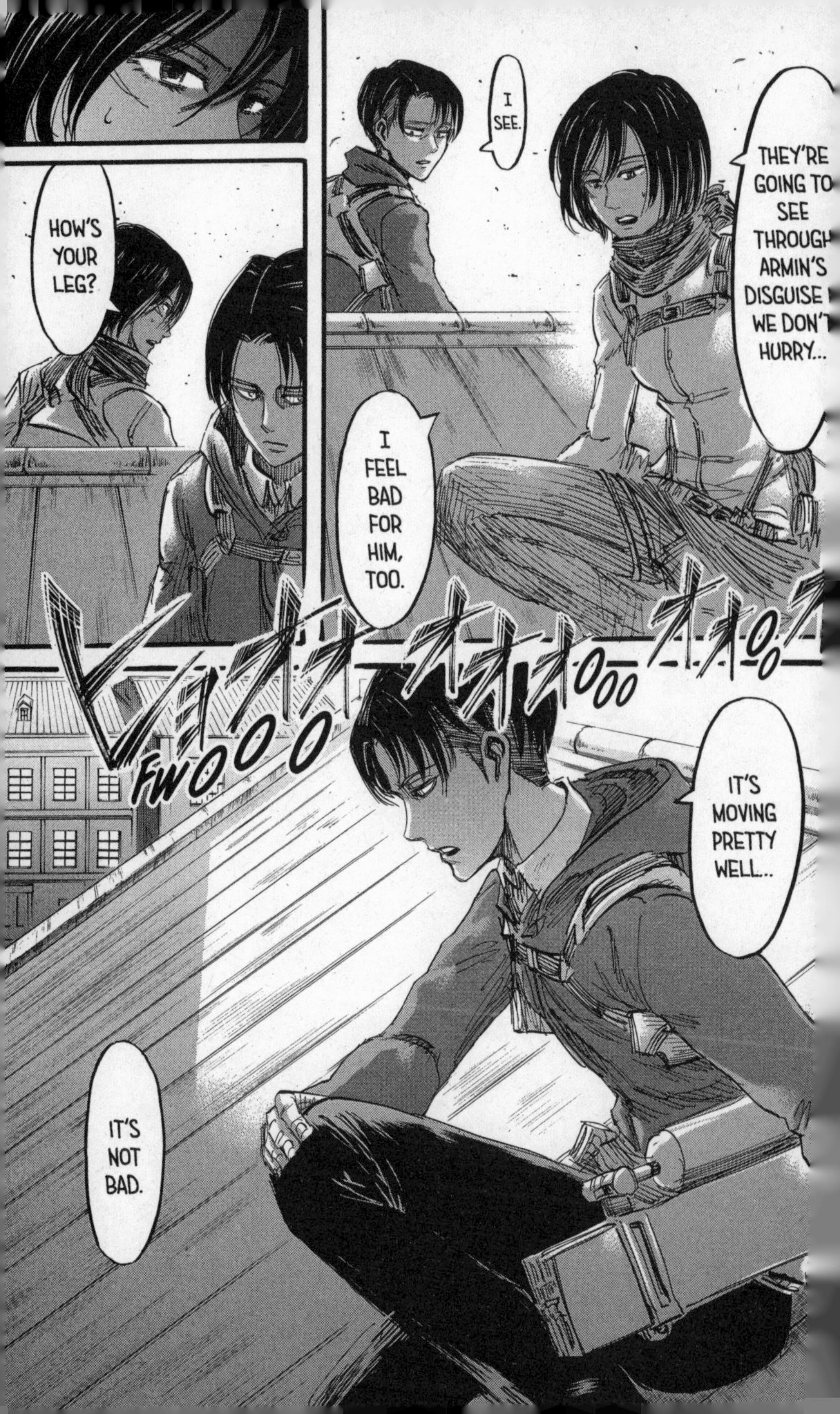
THEY'RE GOING TO SEE THROUGH ARMIN'S DISGUISE IF WE DON'T HURRY...
I SEE.
I FEEL BAD FOR HIM, TOO.
HOW'S YOUR LEG?
FWOOOO
IT'S MOVING PRETTY WELL...
IT'S NOT BAD.

ATTACK
on TITAN

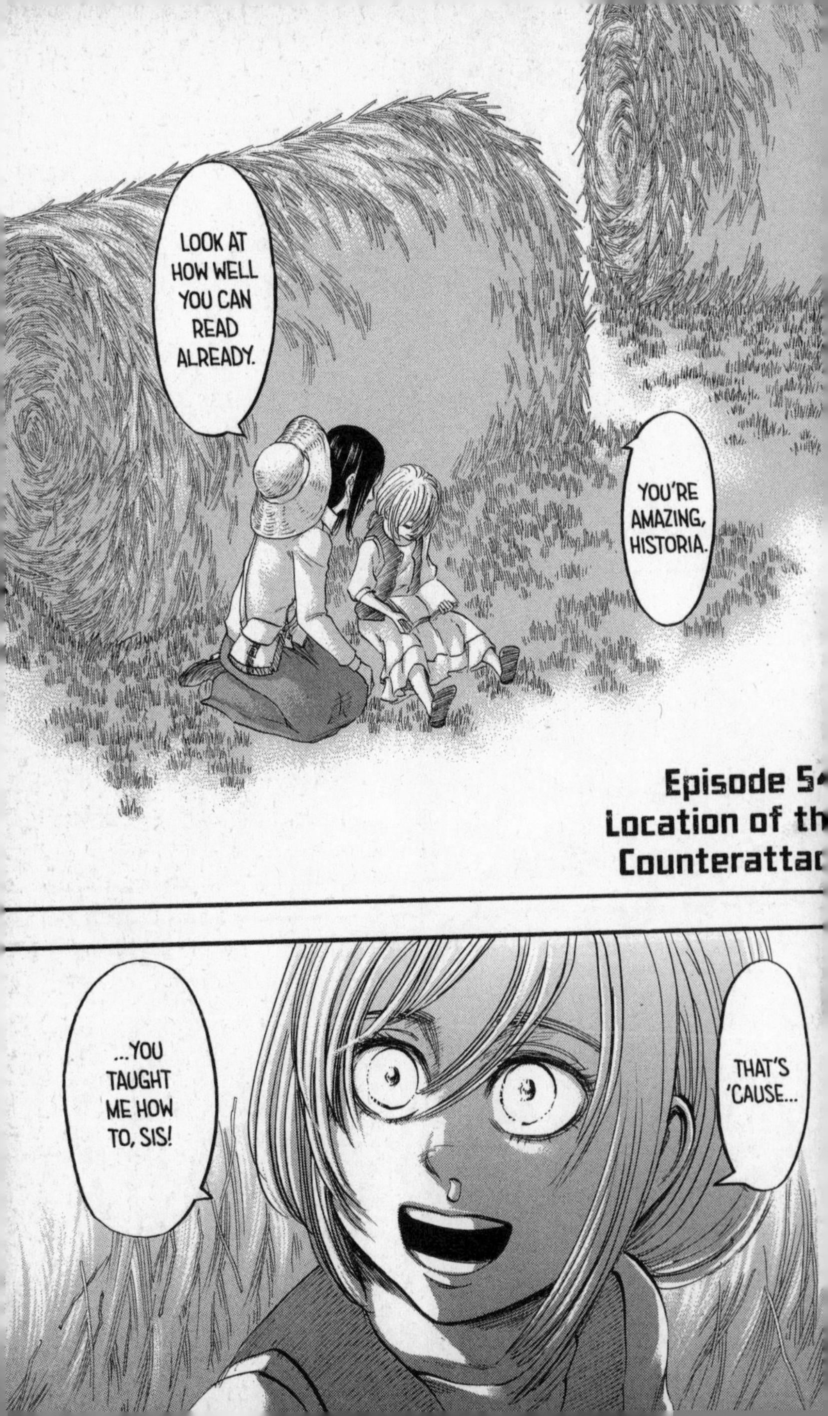
LOOK AT HOW WELL YOU CAN READ ALREADY.
YOU'RE AMAZING, HISTORIA.
Episode 5
Location of th
Counteratta
THAT'S 'CAUSE...
...YOU TAUGHT ME HOW TO, SIS!

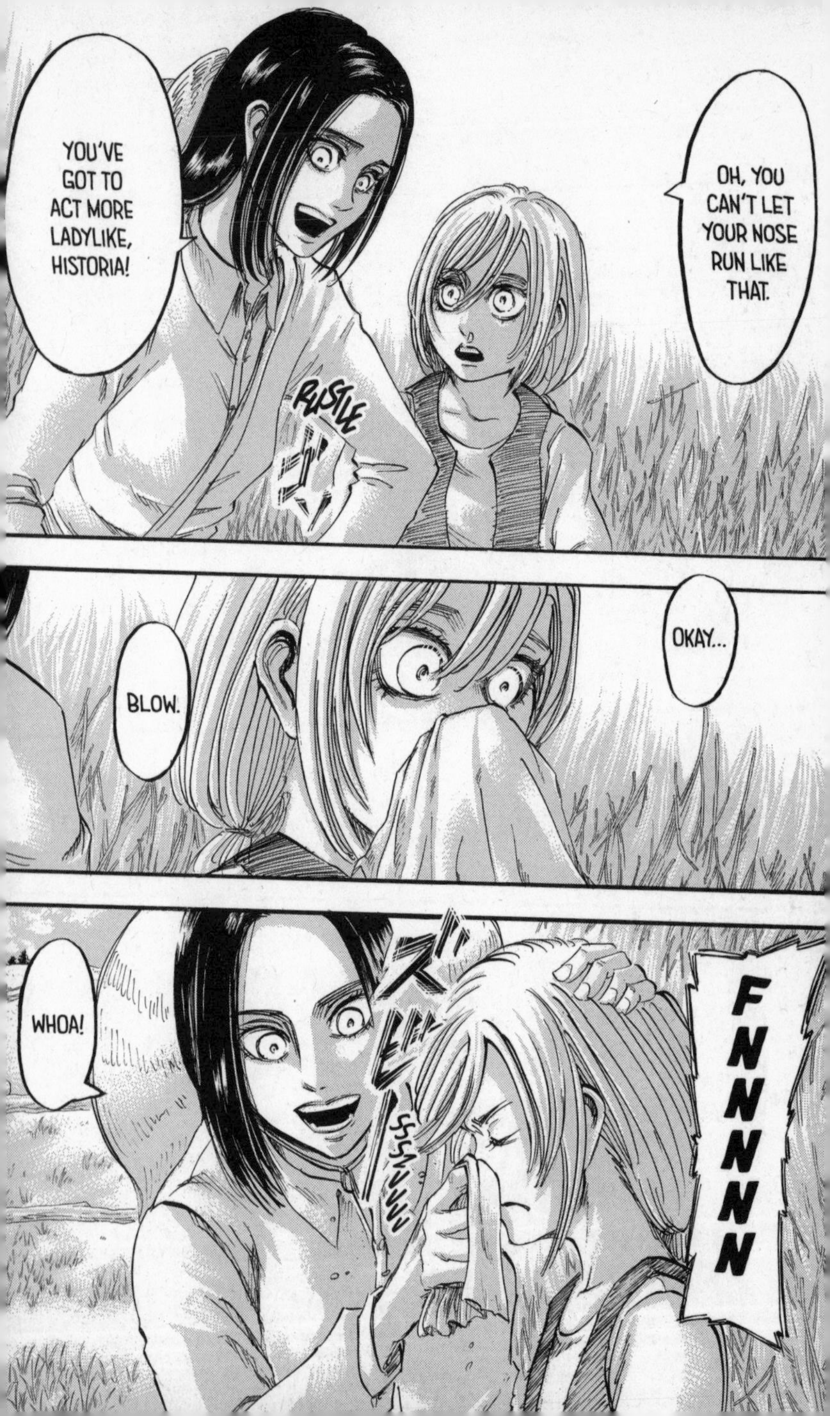
OH, YOU CAN'T LET YOUR NOSE RUN LIKE THAT.
YOU'VE GOT TO ACT MORE LADYLIKE, HISTORIA!
RUSTLE
OKAY...
BLOW.
FNNNNN
WHOA!

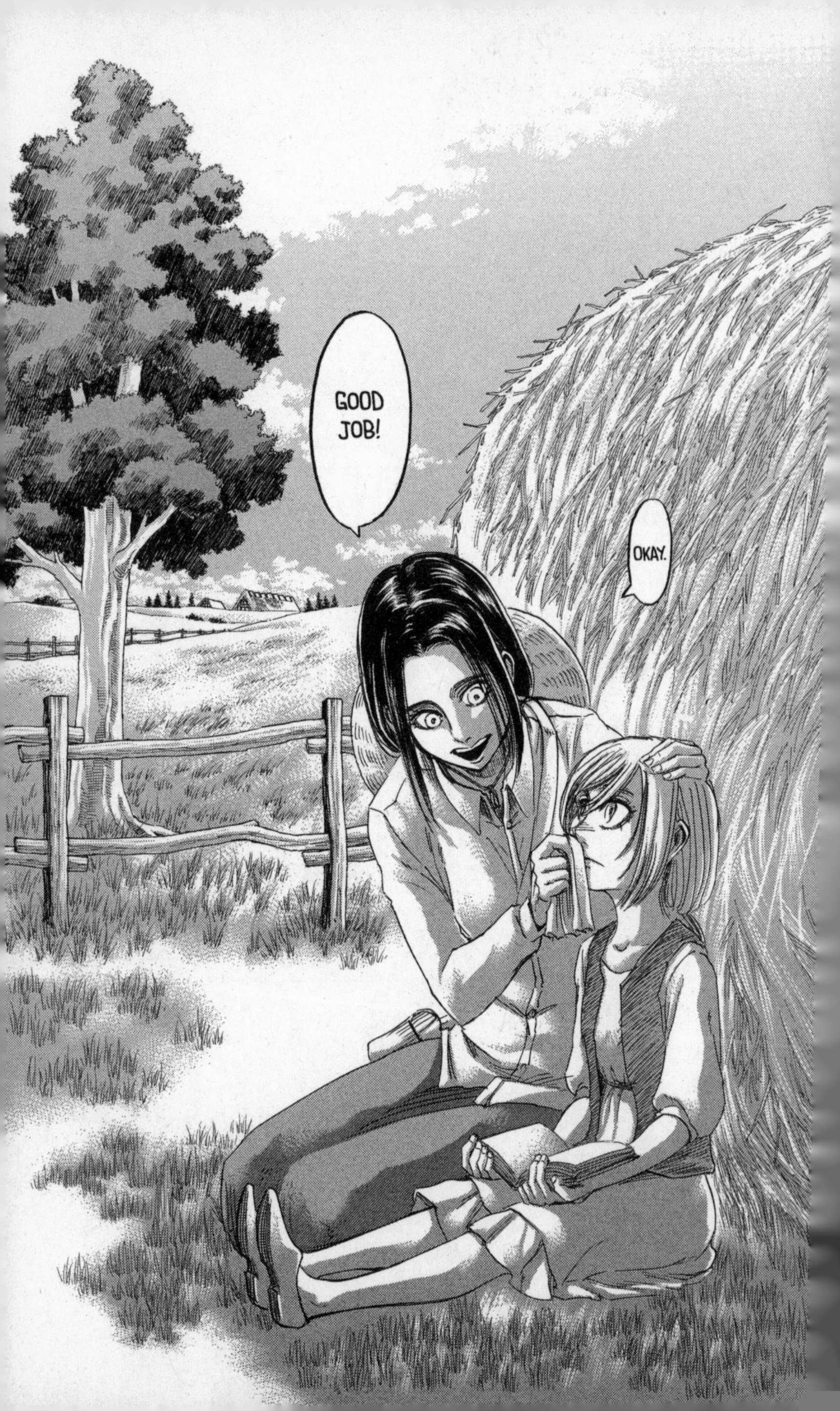
OKAY.
GOOD JOB!

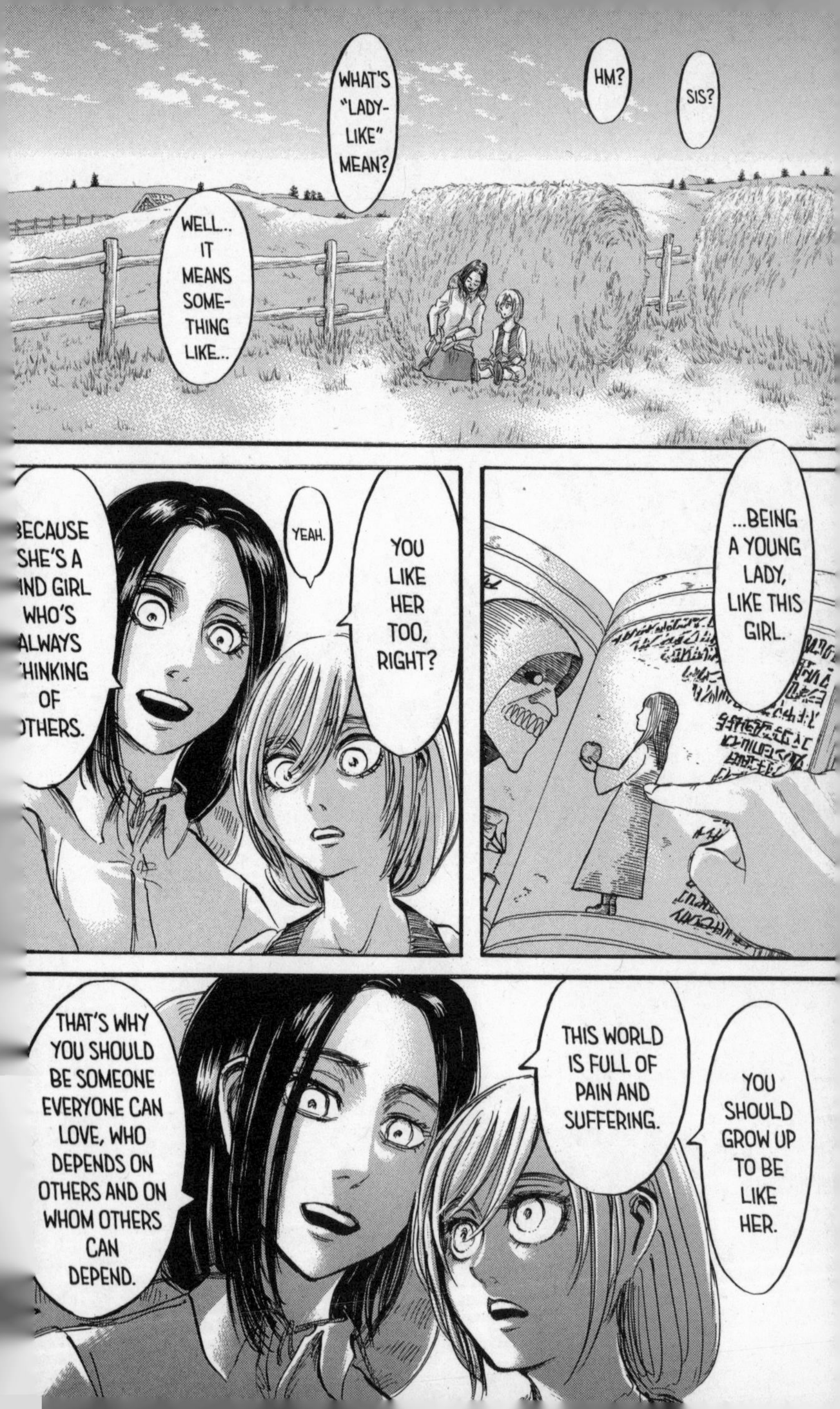
SIS?
HM?
WHAT'S "LADY-LIKE" MEAN?
WELL.. IT MEANS SOMETHING LIKE...
...BEING A YOUNG LADY, LIKE THIS GIRL.
YOU LIKE HER TOO, RIGHT?
YEAH.
BECAUSE SHE'S A KIND GIRL WHO'S ALWAYS THINKING OF OTHERS.
YOU SHOULD GROW UP TO BE LIKE HER.
THIS WORLD IS FULL OF PAIN AND SUFFERING.
THAT'S WHY YOU SHOULD BE SOMEONE EVERYONE CAN LOVE, WHO DEPENDS ON OTHERS AND ON WHOM OTHERS CAN DEPEND.

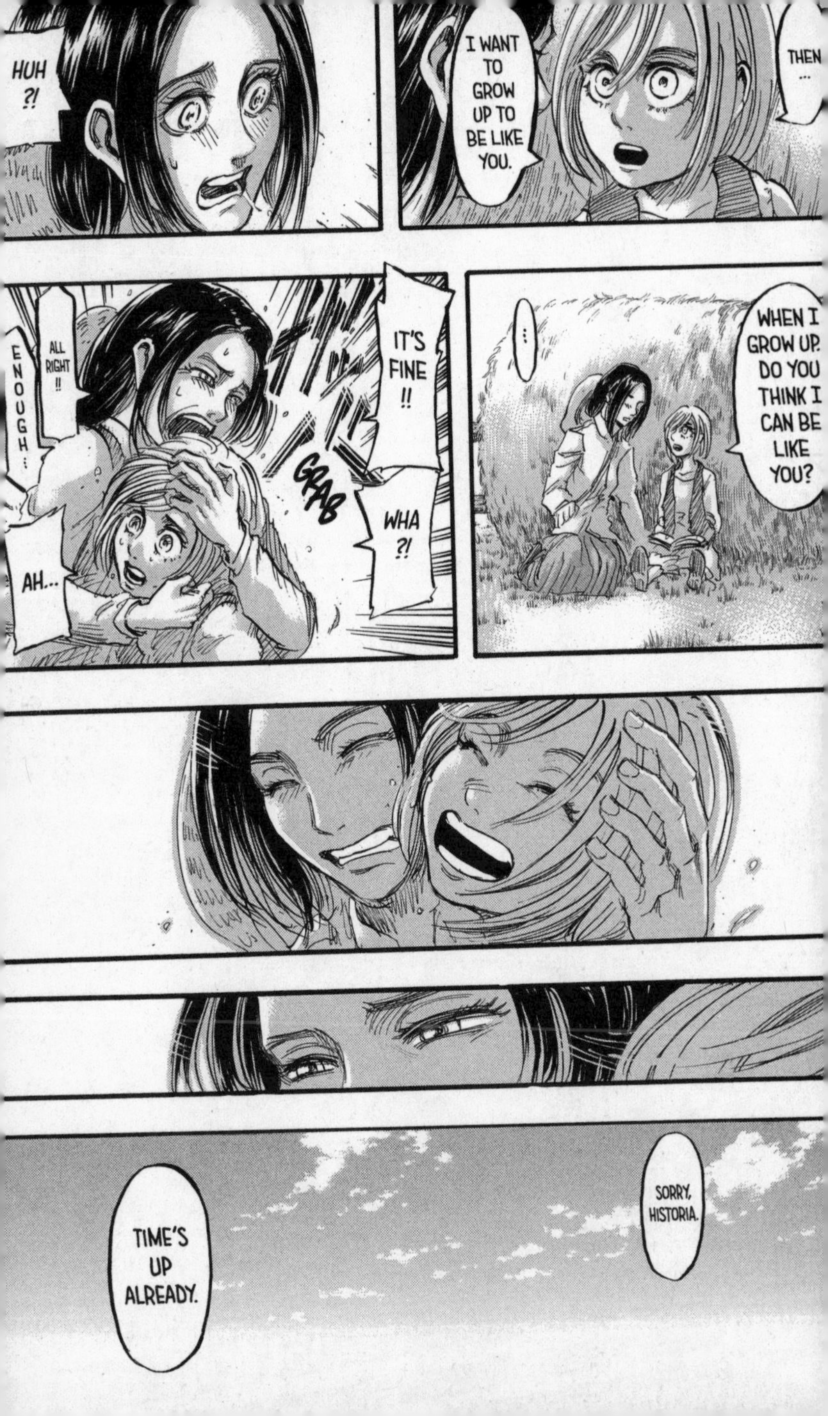
THEN ...
I WANT TO GROW UP TO BE LIKE YOU.
HUH ?!
WHEN I GROW UP. DO YOU THINK I CAN BE LIKE YOU?
...
IT'S FINE !!
WHA ?!
GRAB
ALL RIGHT !!
ENOUGH...
AH...
SORRY, HISTORIA.
TIME'S UP ALREADY.

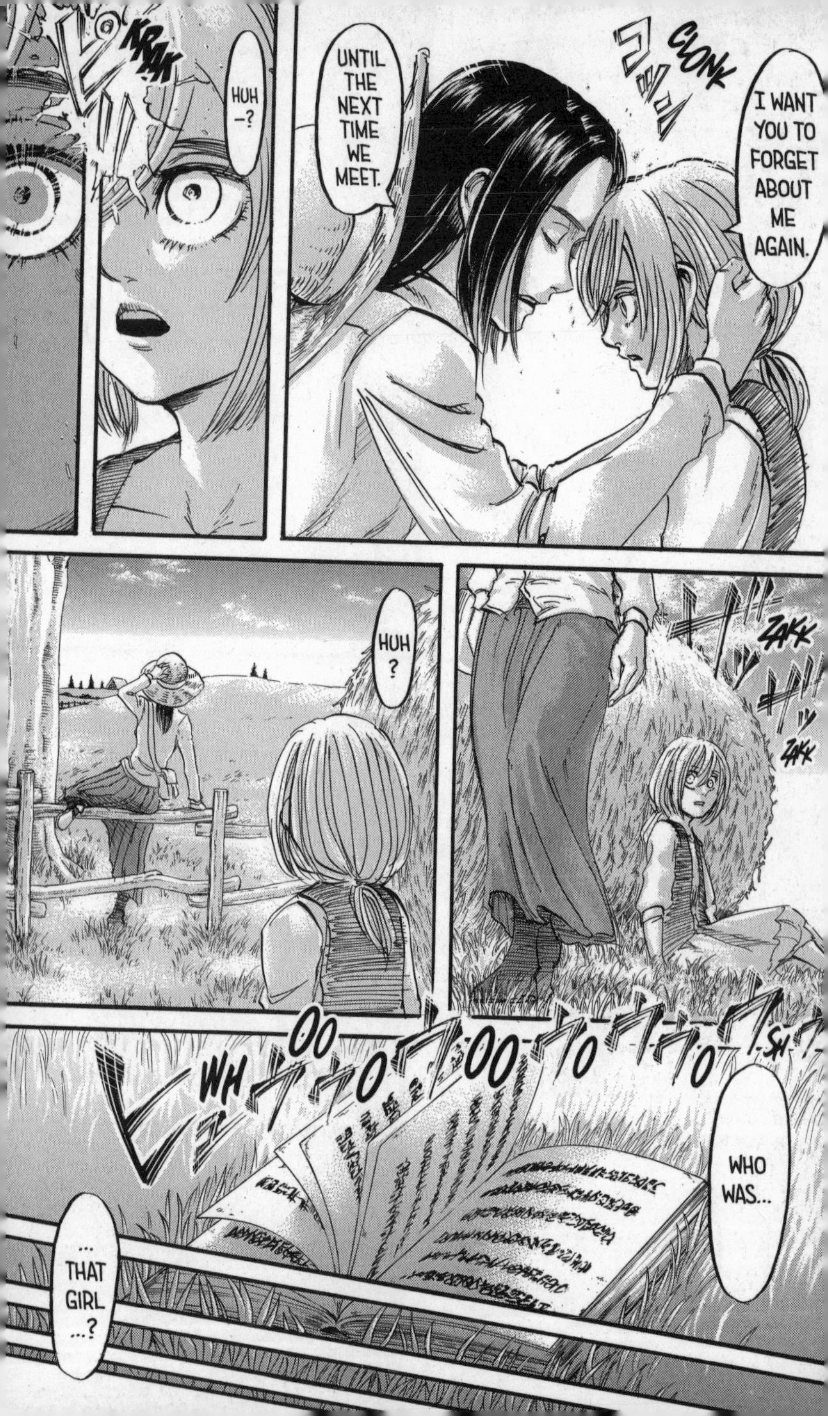
CLONK
I WANT YOU TO FORGET ABOUT ME AGAIN.
UNTIL THE NEXT TIME WE MEET.
KRAK
HUH —?
ZAKK
ZAKK
HUH ?
WHOOOOOOOOSH
WHO WAS...
... THAT GIRL ...?

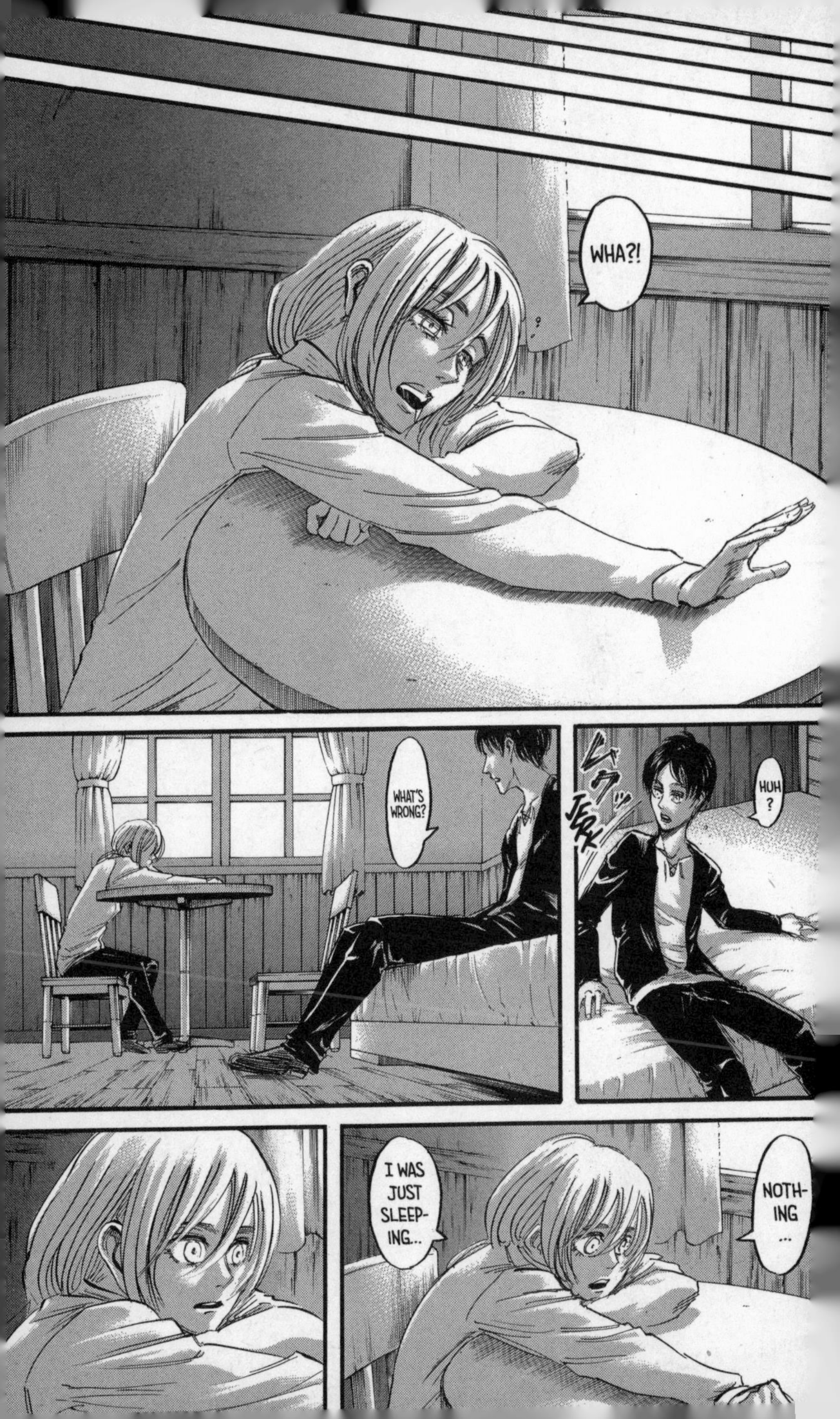
WHA?!
HUH ?
JERK
WHAT'S WRONG?
NOTH-ING ...
I WAS JUST SLEEP-ING...

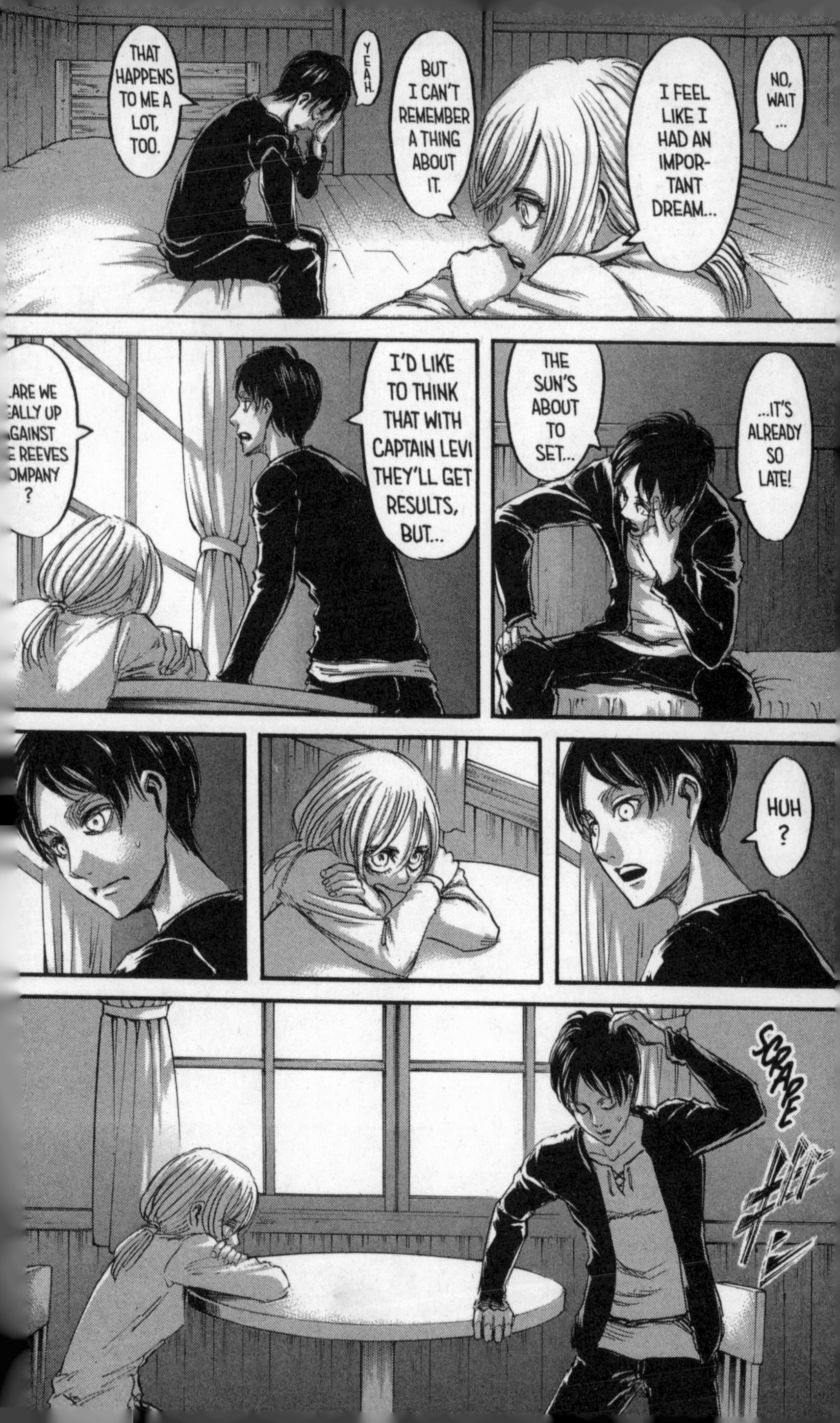
NO, WAIT ...
I FEEL LIKE I HAD AN IMPORTANT DREAM...
BUT I CAN'T REMEMBER A THING ABOUT IT.
YEAH.
THAT HAPPENS TO ME A LOT, TOO.
...IT'S ALREADY SO LATE!
THE SUN'S ABOUT TO SET...
I'D LIKE TO THINK THAT WITH CAPTAIN LEVI THEY'LL GET RESULTS, BUT...
..ARE WE EALLY UP AGAINST E REEVES OMPANY ?
HUH ?
SCRAPE

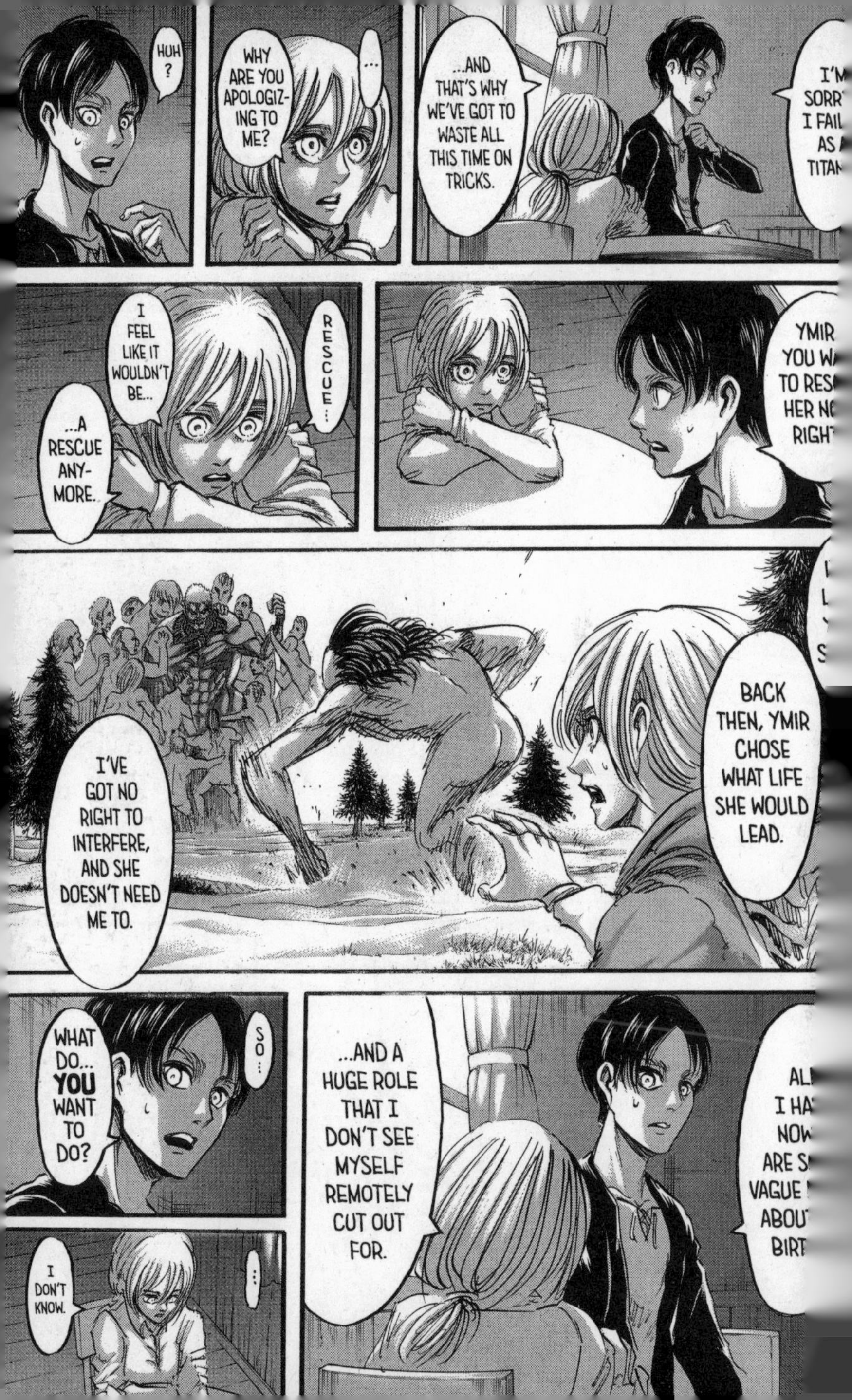
I'M SORR I FAIL AS A TITAN
...AND THAT'S WHY WE'VE GOT TO WASTE ALL THIS TIME ON TRICKS.
...
WHY ARE YOU APOLOGIZING TO ME?
HUH?
YMIR YOU WA TO RES HER N RIGHT
RESCUE...
I FEEL LIKE IT WOULDN'T BE...
...A RESCUE ANYMORE.
BACK THEN, YMIR CHOSE WHAT LIFE SHE WOULD LEAD.
I'VE GOT NO RIGHT TO INTERFERE, AND SHE DOESN'T NEED ME TO.
AL I HA NOW ARE S VAGUE ABOUT BIRT
...AND A HUGE ROLE THAT I DON'T SEE MYSELF REMOTELY CUT OUT FOR.
SO...
WHAT DO... **YOU** WANT TO DO?
...
I DON'T KNOW.

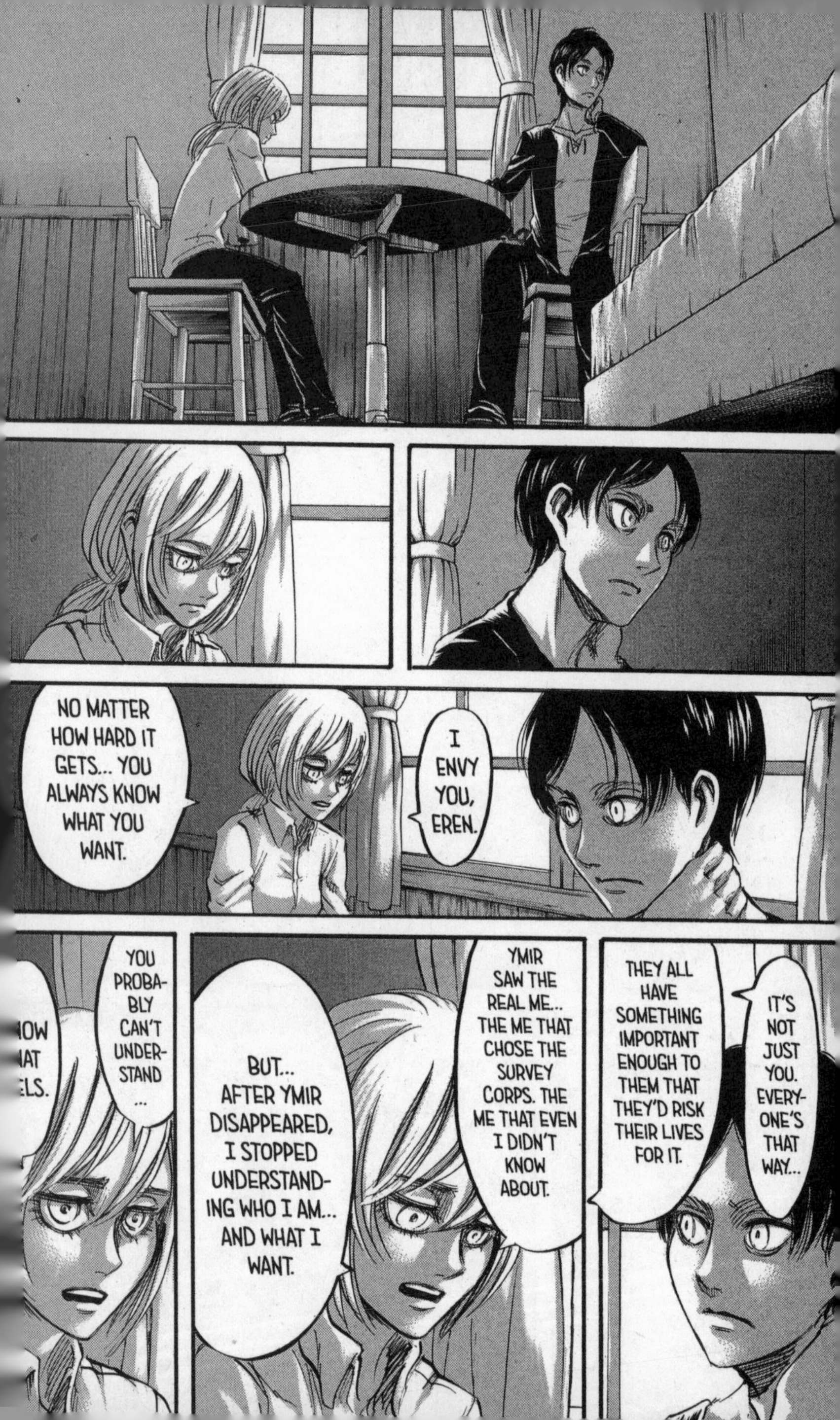
I ENVY YOU, EREN.
NO MATTER HOW HARD IT GETS... YOU ALWAYS KNOW WHAT YOU WANT.
IT'S NOT JUST YOU. EVERYONE'S THAT WAY...
THEY ALL HAVE SOMETHING IMPORTANT ENOUGH TO THEM THAT THEY'D RISK THEIR LIVES FOR IT.
YMIR SAW THE REAL ME... THE ME THAT CHOSE THE SURVEY CORPS. THE ME THAT EVEN I DIDN'T KNOW ABOUT.
BUT... AFTER YMIR DISAPPEARED, I STOPPED UNDERSTANDING WHO I AM... AND WHAT I WANT.
YOU PROBABLY CAN'T UNDERSTAND...

WE DON'T HAVE TIME TO FEEL CONFLICTED.

...WHERE IF WE DON'T DO SOMETHING, WE'LL LOSE EVERYTHING!

WE BOTH LIVE IN THIS ABSURD WORLD!

I TOTALLY UNDERSTAND.

N

BUT TO BE HONEST, I DON'T SEE WHY.

...

SORRY.

SHOULDN'T YOU BE MORE WORRIED ABOUT HIM?

RIGHT ARMIN TAKING DANGER MISSIO YOUR DOUB

KRISTA LENZ WAS A GOOD GIRL.

KRISTA PROBABLY WOULD'VE BEEN WORRIED FOR EVERYONE.

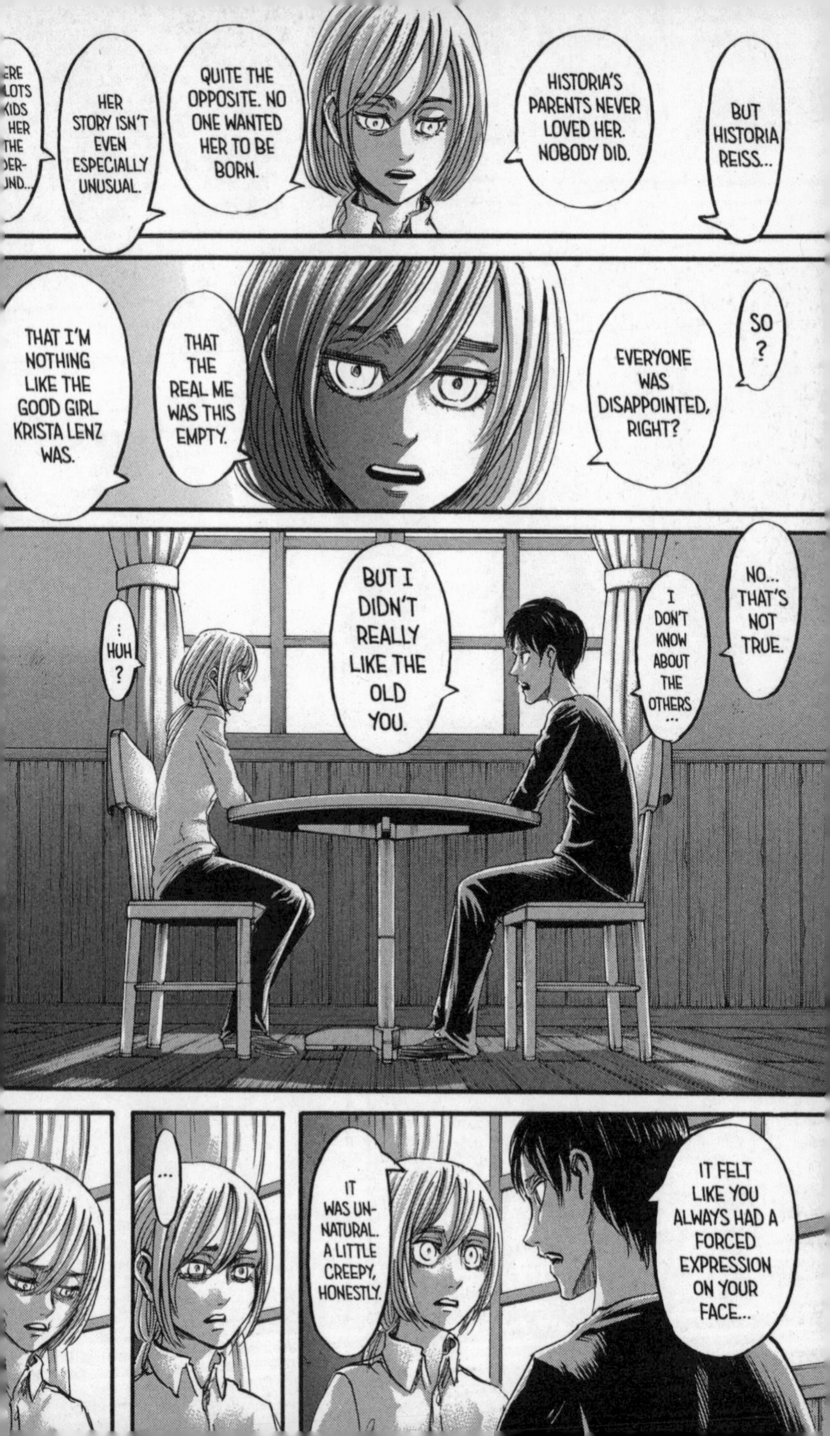
BUT HISTORIA REISS...
HISTORIA'S PARENTS NEVER LOVED HER. NOBODY DID.
QUITE THE OPPOSITE. NO ONE WANTED HER TO BE BORN.
HER STORY ISN'T EVEN ESPECIALLY UNUSUAL.
SO?
EVERYONE WAS DISAPPOINTED, RIGHT?
THAT THE REAL ME WAS THIS EMPTY.
THAT I'M NOTHING LIKE THE GOOD GIRL KRISTA LENZ WAS.
NO... THAT'S NOT TRUE.
I DON'T KNOW ABOUT THE OTHERS...
BUT I DIDN'T REALLY LIKE THE OLD YOU.
...HUH?
IT FELT LIKE YOU ALWAYS HAD A FORCED EXPRESSION ON YOUR FACE...
IT WAS UN-NATURAL. A LITTLE CREEPY, HONESTLY.
...

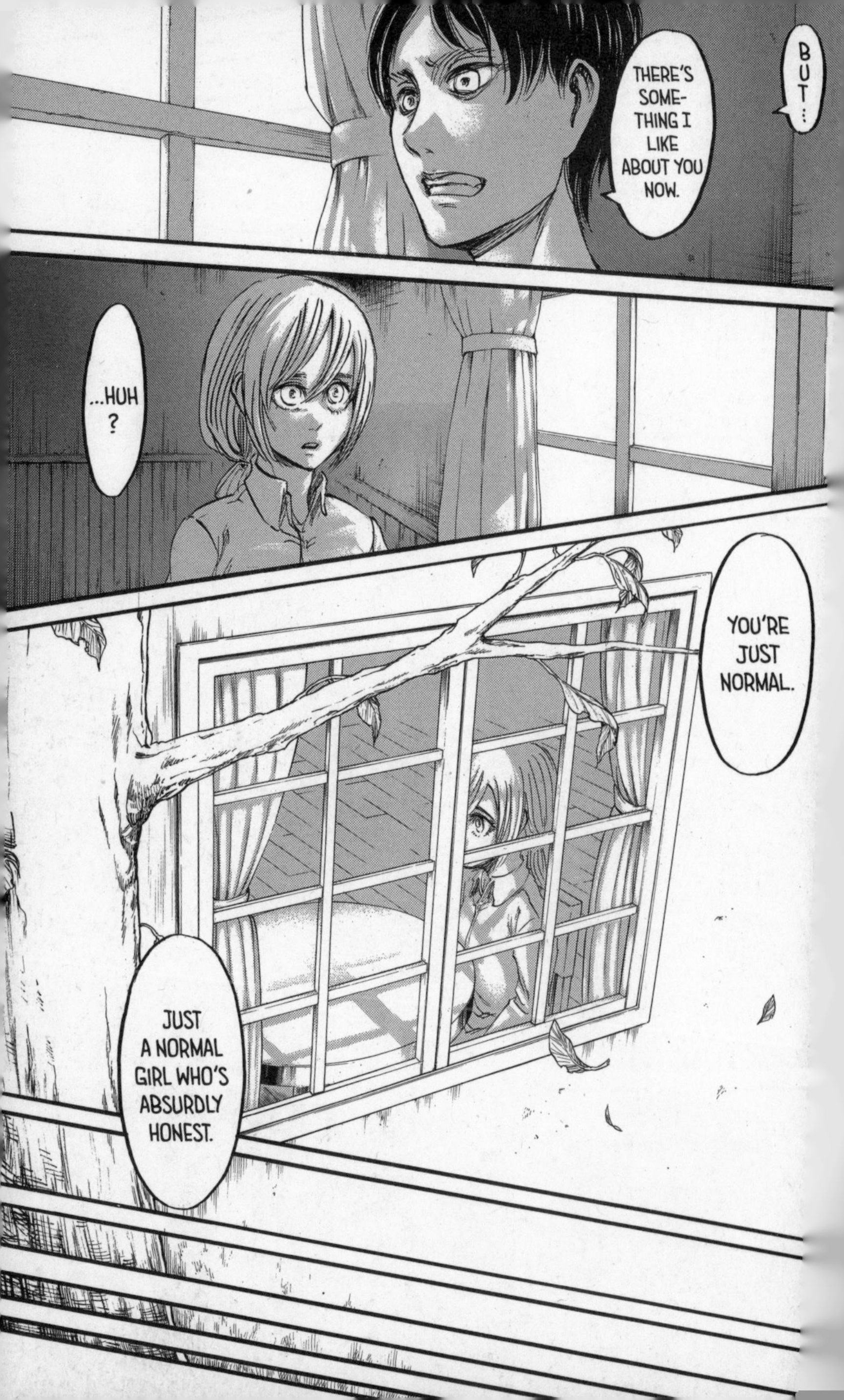
BUT...
THERE'S SOME-THING I LIKE ABOUT YOU NOW.
...HUH?
YOU'RE JUST NORMAL.
JUST A NORMAL GIRL WHO'S ABSURDLY HONEST.

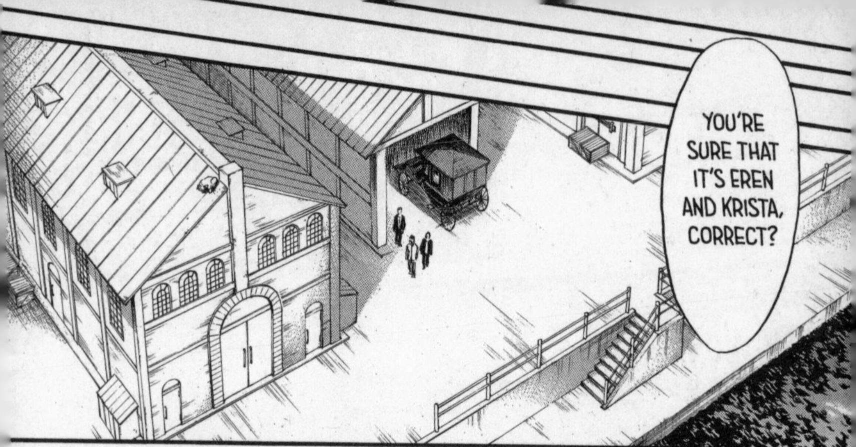
YOU'RE SURE THAT IT'S EREN AND KRISTA, CORRECT?

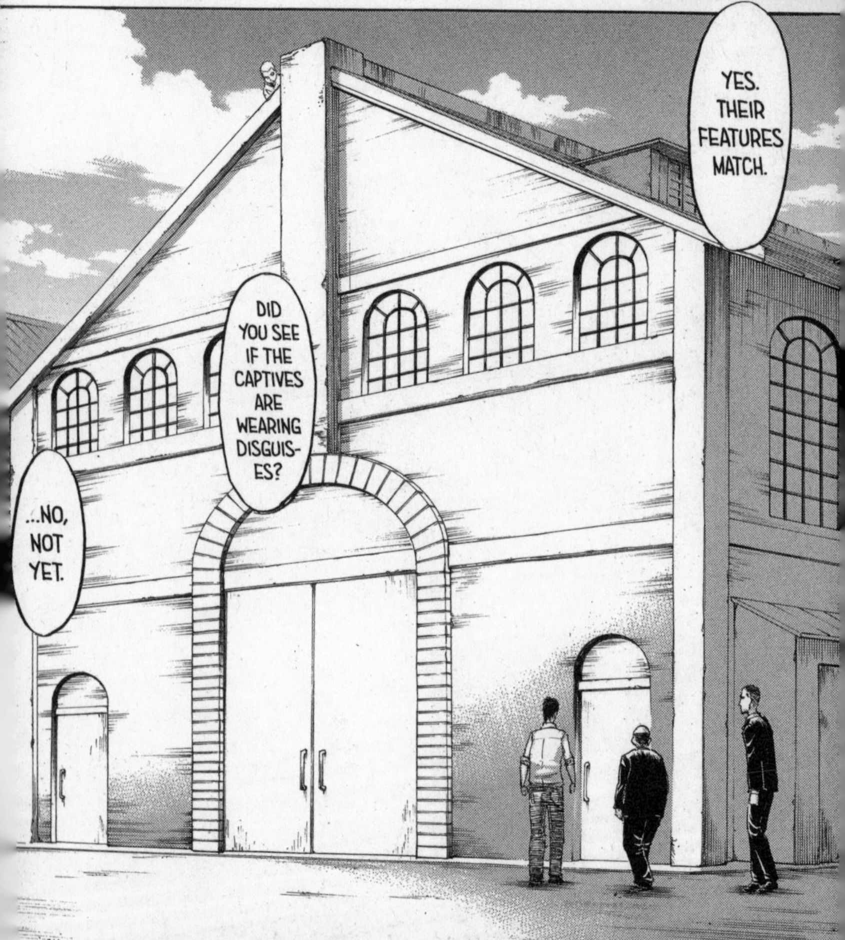
YES. THEIR FEATURES MATCH.
DID YOU SEE IF THE CAPTIVES ARE WEARING DISGUIS-ES?
...NO, NOT YET.

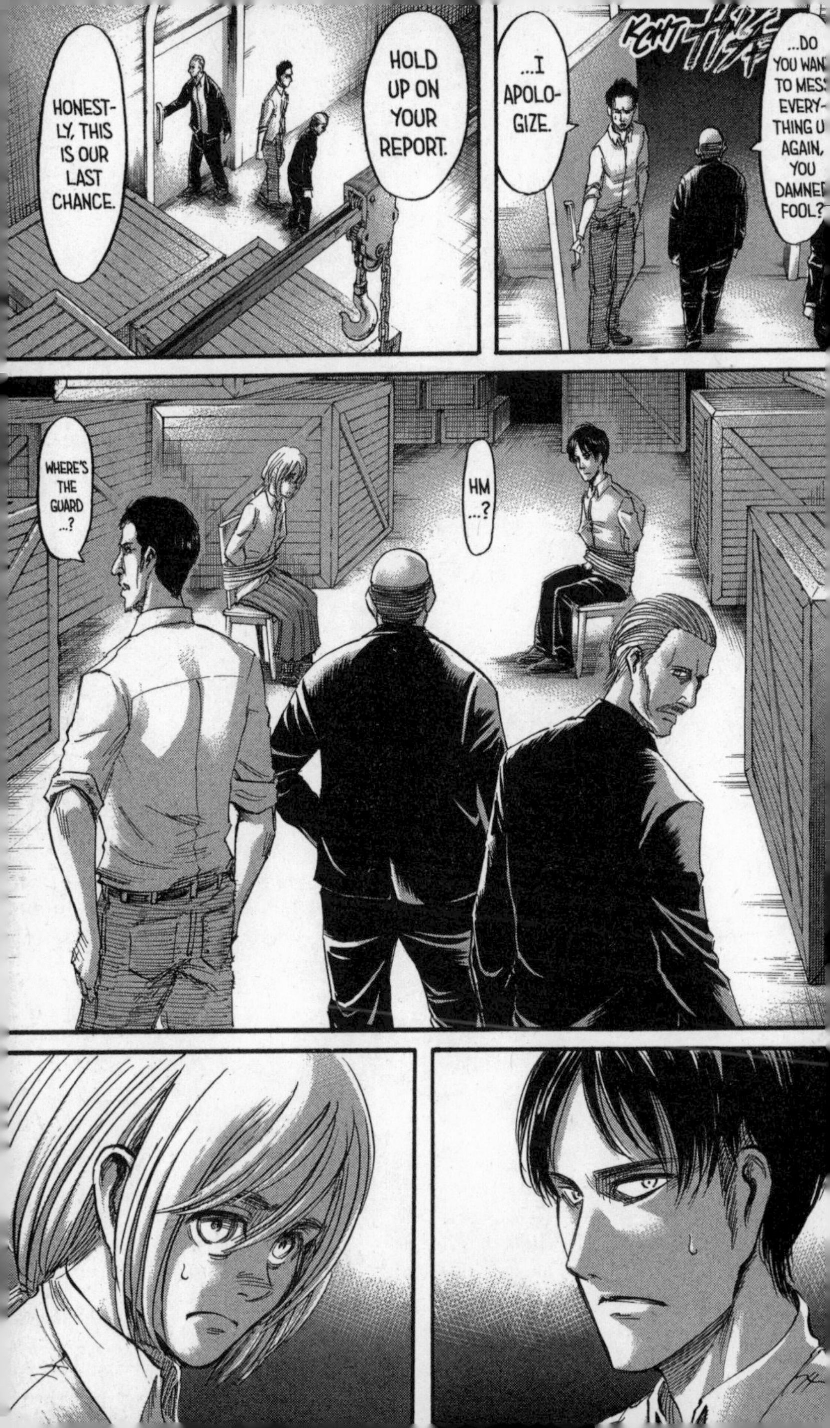
...DO YOU WAN TO MES EVERY-THING U AGAIN, YOU DAMNED FOOL?
...I APOLO-GIZE.
HOLD UP ON YOUR REPORT.
HONEST-LY, THIS IS OUR LAST CHANCE.
HM ...?
WHERE'S THE GUARD ...?

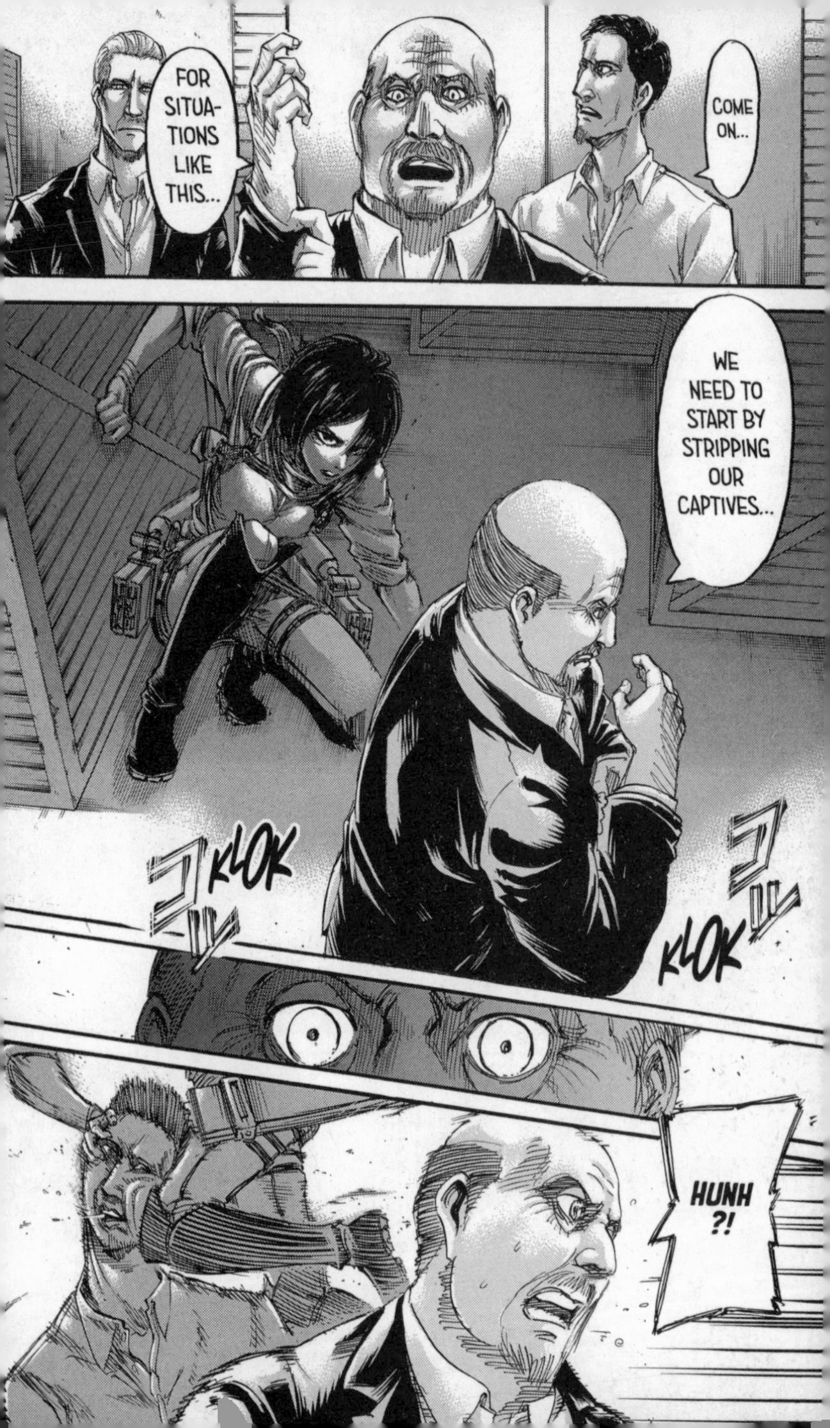
COME ON...
FOR SITUATIONS LIKE THIS...
WE NEED TO START BY STRIPPING OUR CAPTIVES...
KLOK
KLOK
HUNH ?!

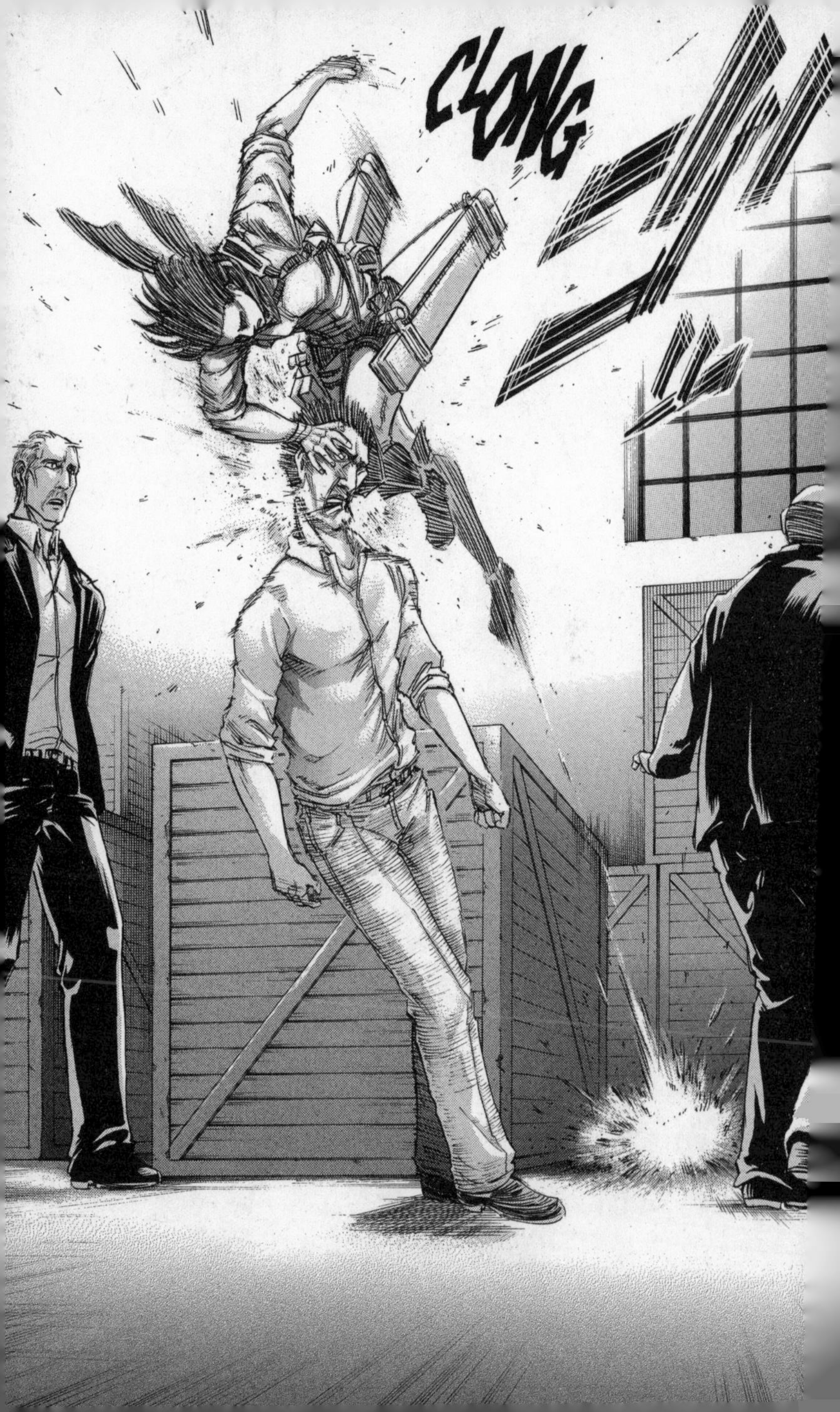
CLONG

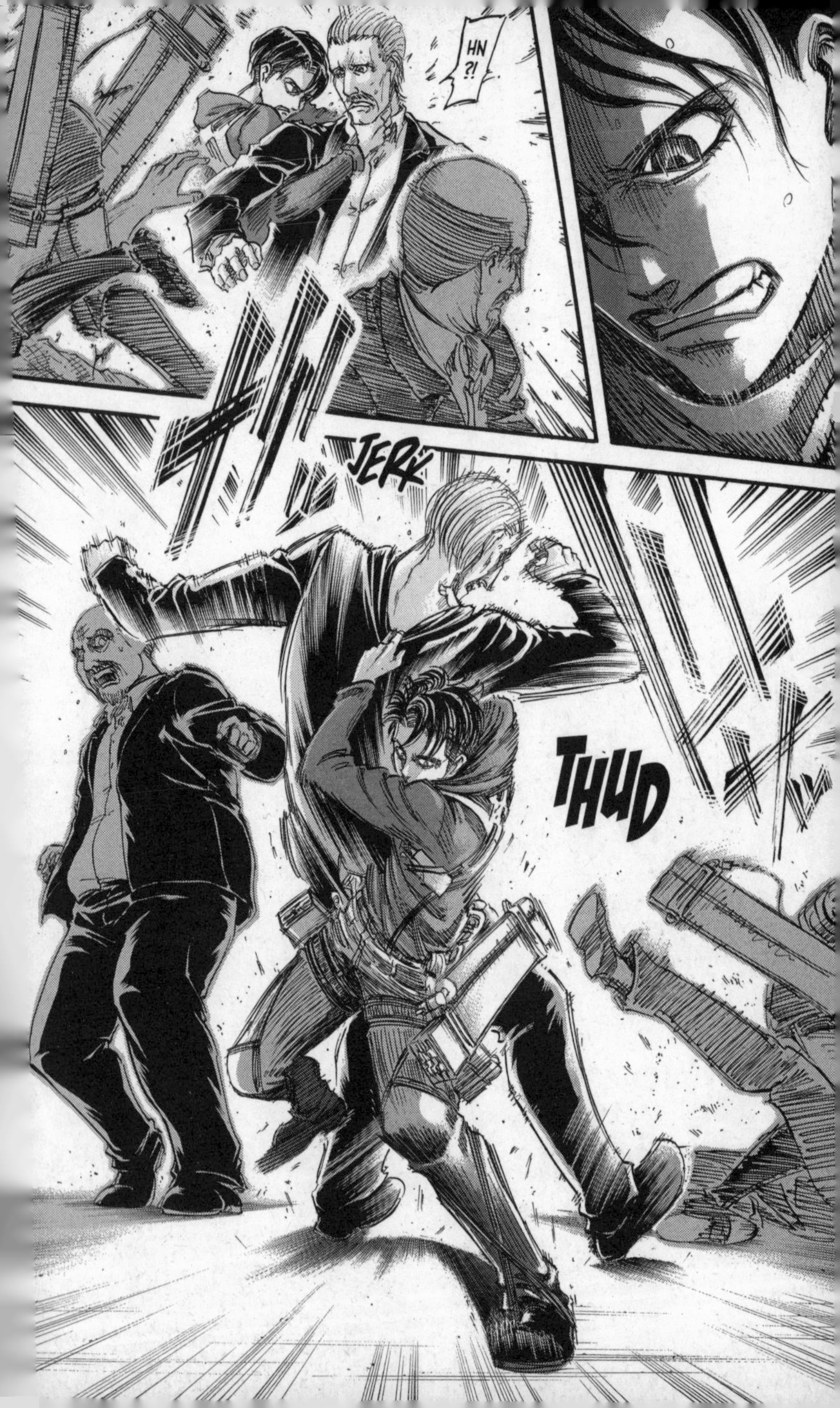
HN ?!
JERK
THUD

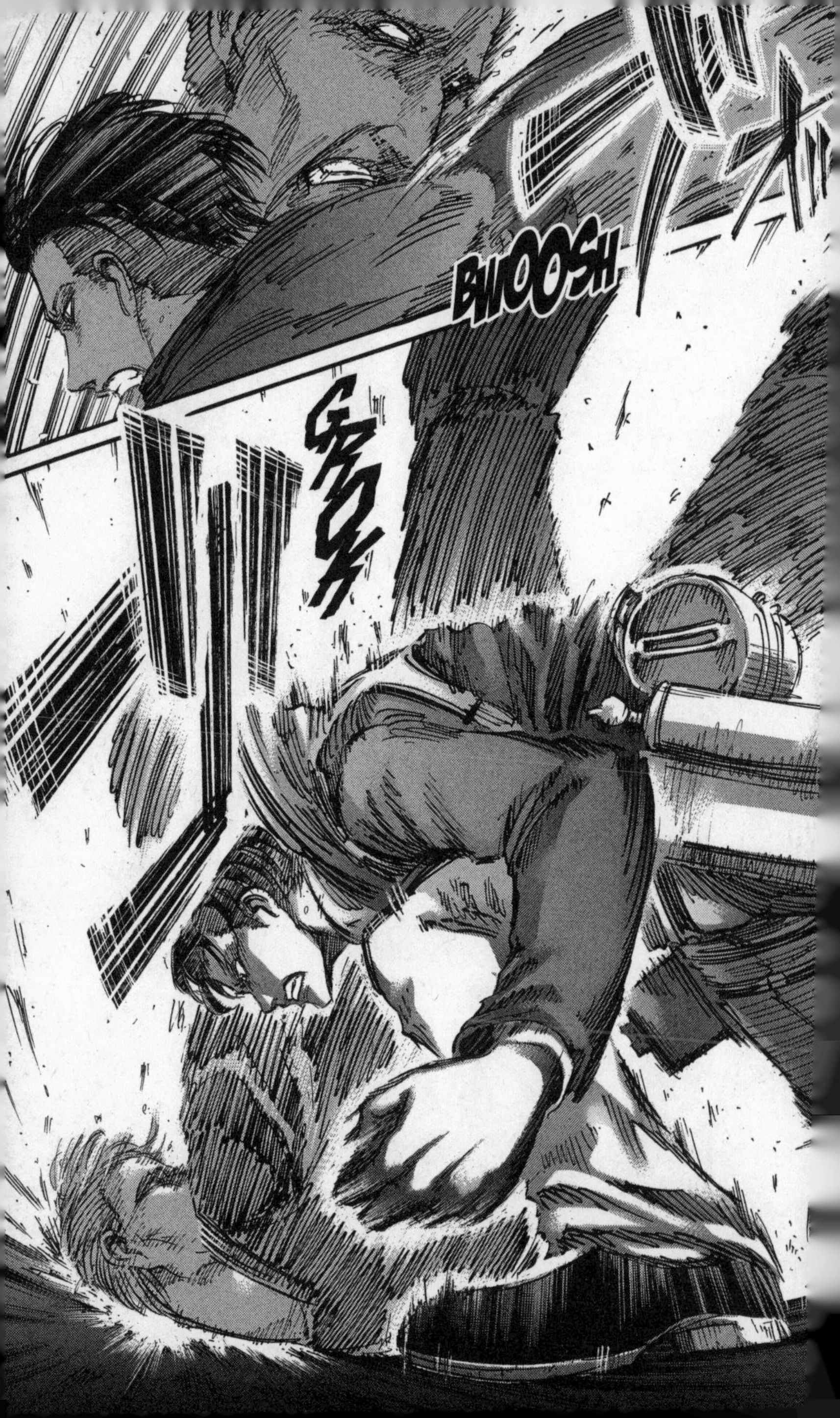
BWOOSH

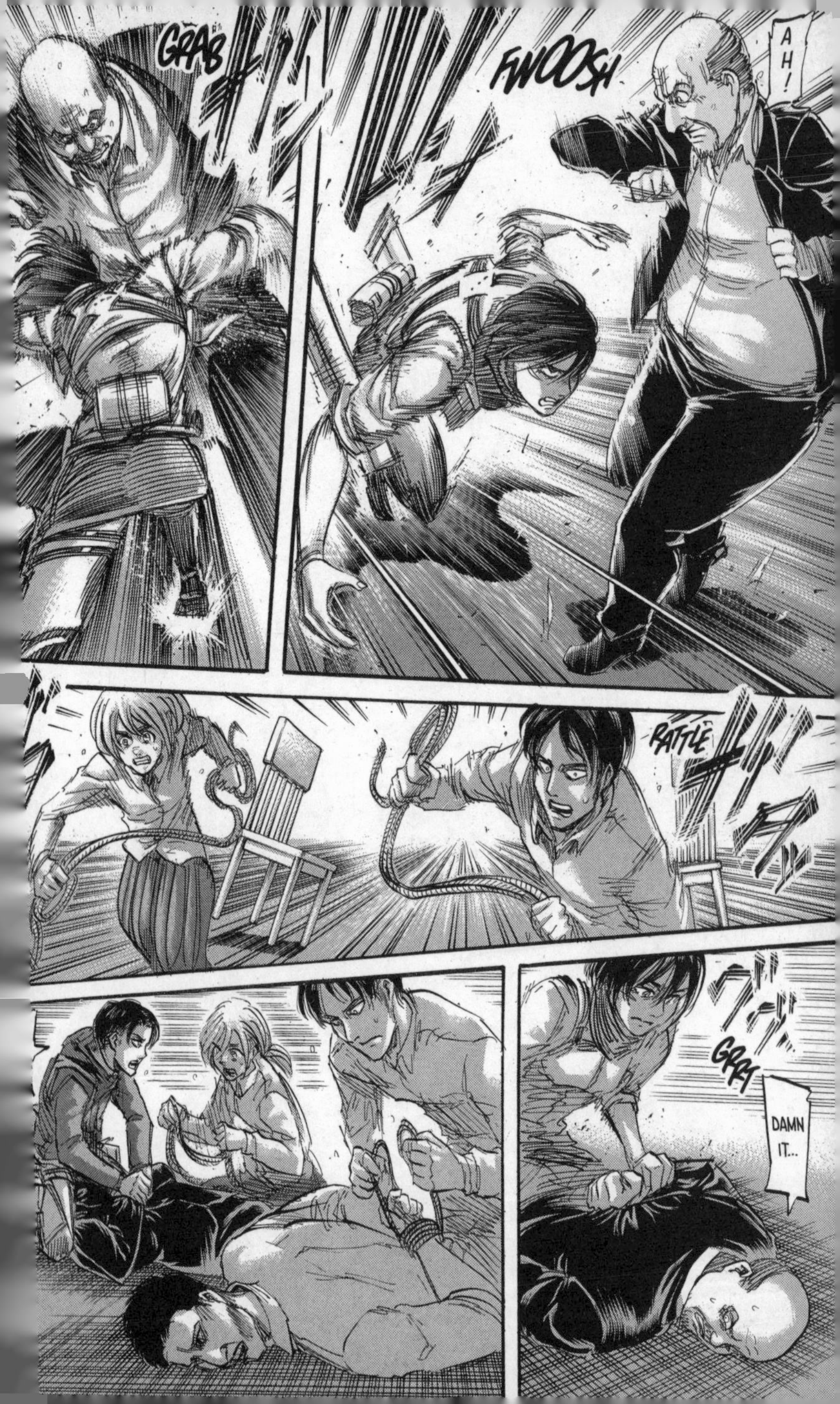
AH!
FWOOSH
GRAB
RATTLE
GRRT
DAMN IT...

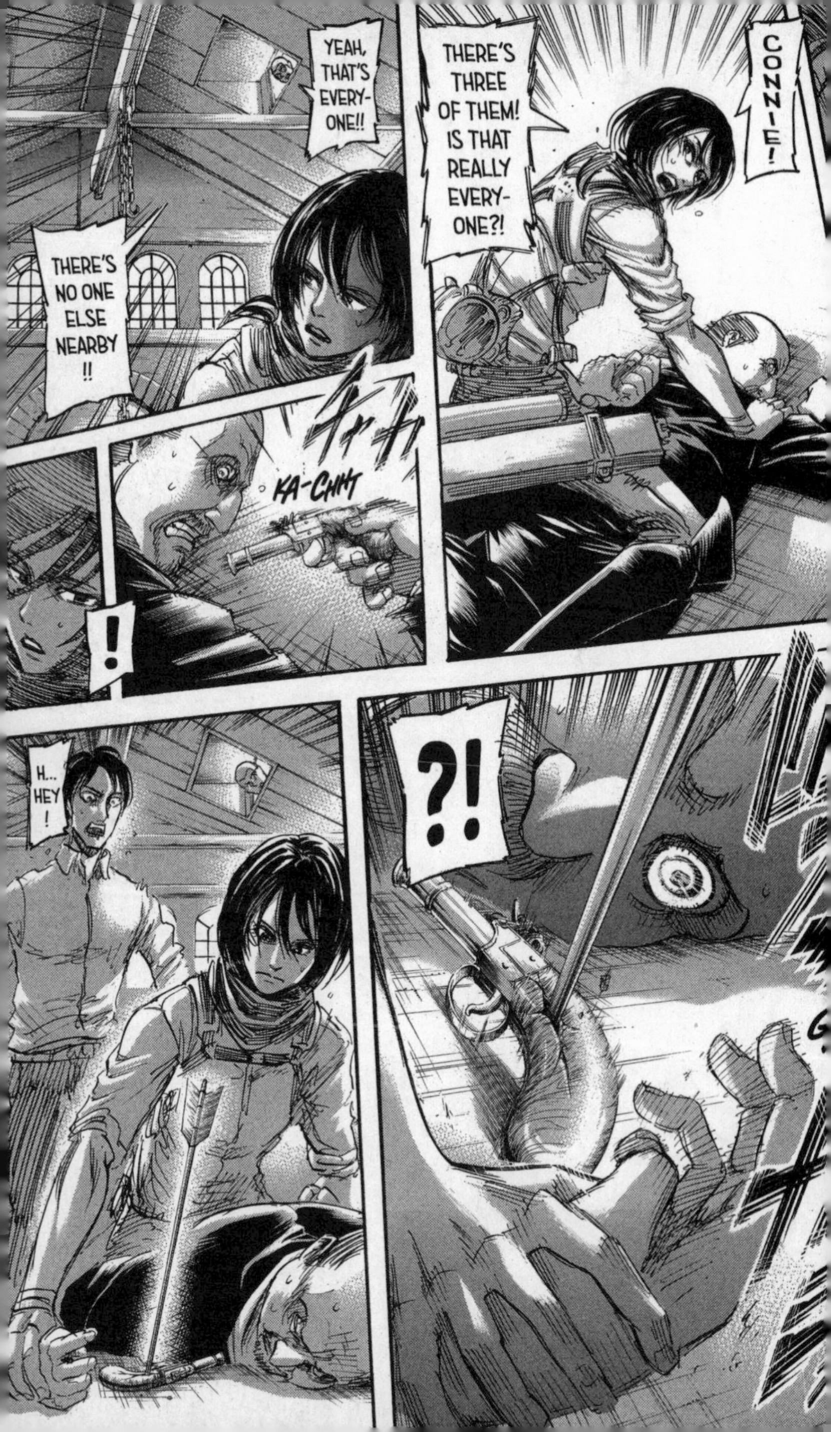
CONNIE!
THERE'S THREE OF THEM! IS THAT REALLY EVERYONE?!
YEAH, THAT'S EVERYONE!!
THERE'S NO ONE ELSE NEARBY!!
KA-CHNK
!
?!
H... HEY!

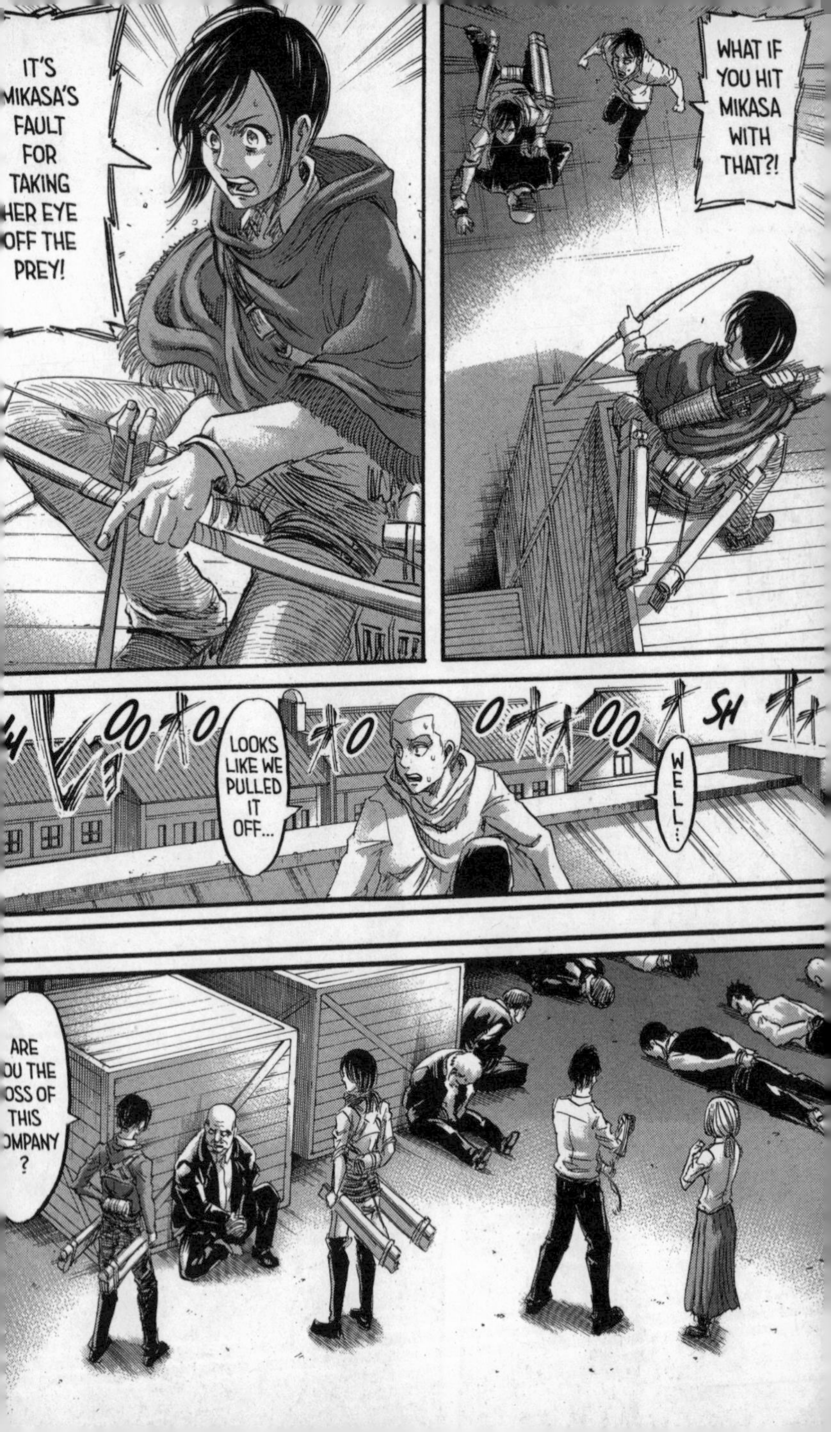

WHAT IF YOU HIT MIKASA WITH THAT?!
IT'S MIKASA'S FAULT FOR TAKING HER EYE OFF THE PREY!
SH
WELL...
LOOKS LIKE WE PULLED IT OFF...
ARE OU THE OSS OF THIS OMPANY ?

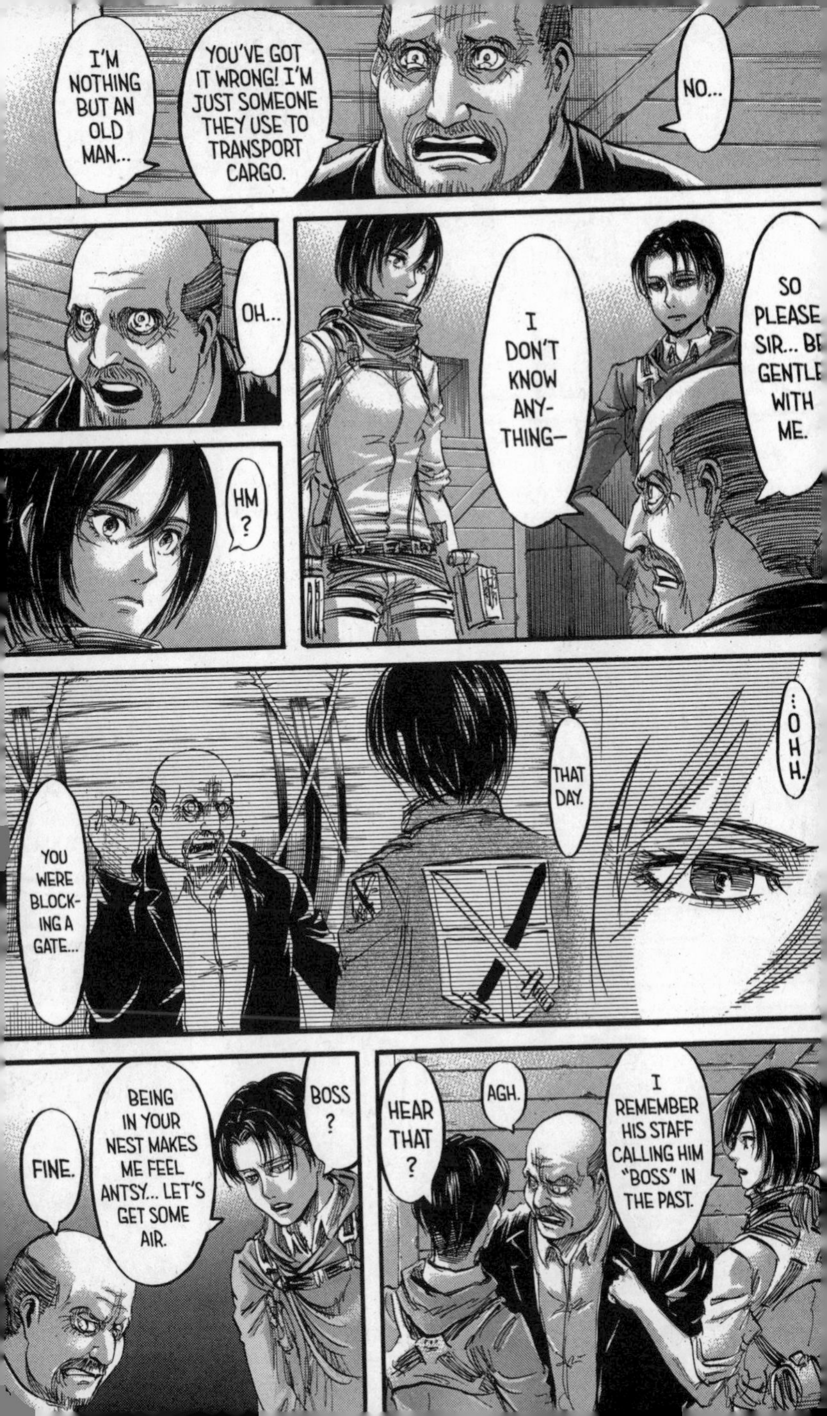
NO...
YOU'VE GOT IT WRONG! I'M JUST SOMEONE THEY USE TO TRANSPORT CARGO.
I'M NOTHING BUT AN OLD MAN...
SO PLEASE SIR... BE GENTLE WITH ME.
I DON'T KNOW ANY-THING—
OH...
HM?
...OHH.
THAT DAY.
YOU WERE BLOCK-ING A GATE...
I REMEMBER HIS STAFF CALLING HIM "BOSS" IN THE PAST.
AGH.
HEAR THAT?
BOSS?
BEING IN YOUR NEST MAKES ME FEEL ANTSY... LET'S GET SOME AIR.
FINE.

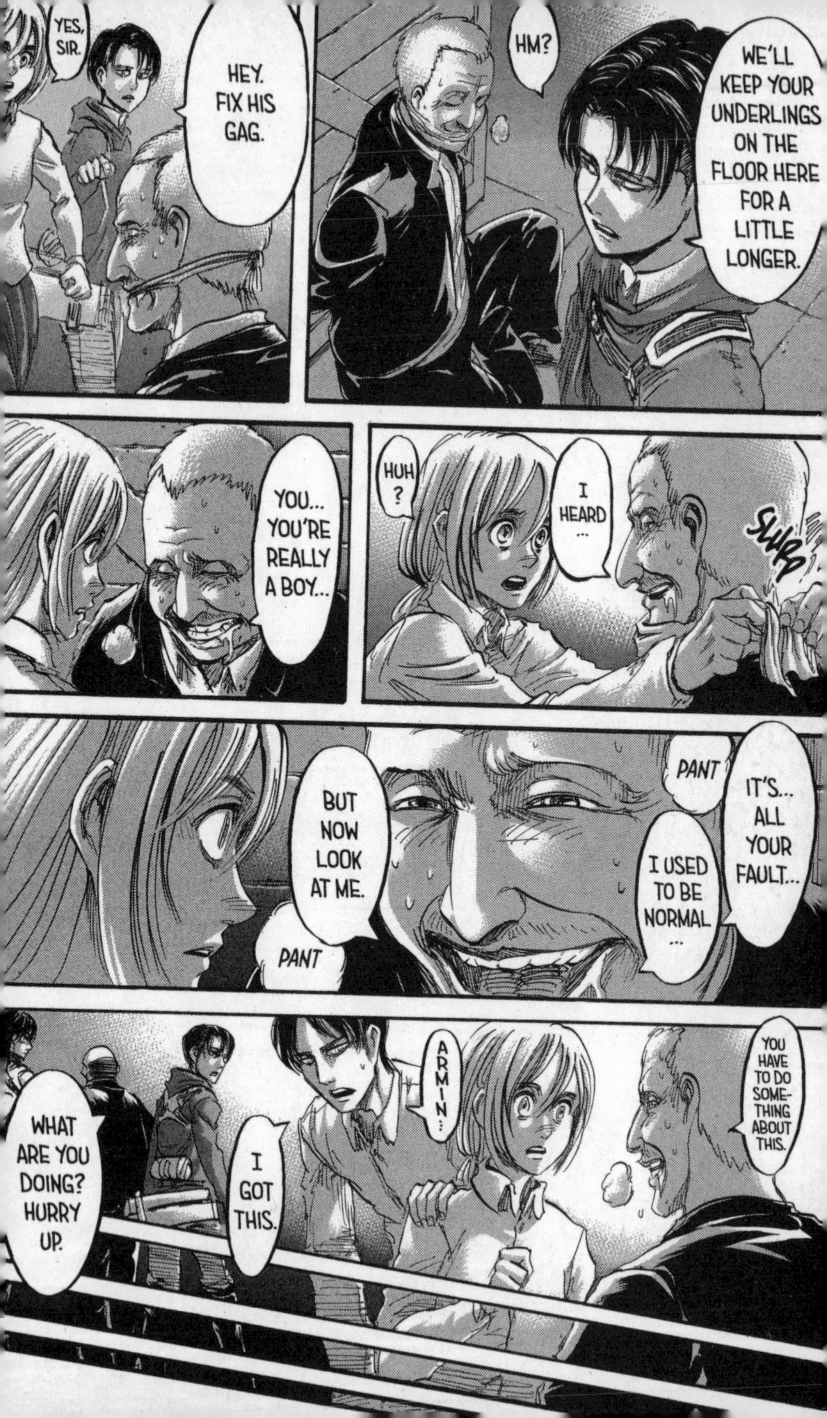
WE'LL KEEP YOUR UNDERLINGS ON THE FLOOR HERE FOR A LITTLE LONGER.
HM?
HEY. FIX HIS GAG.
YES, SIR.
I HEARD...
HUH?
YOU... YOU'RE REALLY A BOY...
IT'S... ALL YOUR FAULT...
PANT
I USED TO BE NORMAL...
BUT NOW LOOK AT ME.
PANT
YOU HAVE TO DO SOMETHING ABOUT THIS.
ARMIN...
I GOT THIS.
WHAT ARE YOU DOING? HURRY UP.

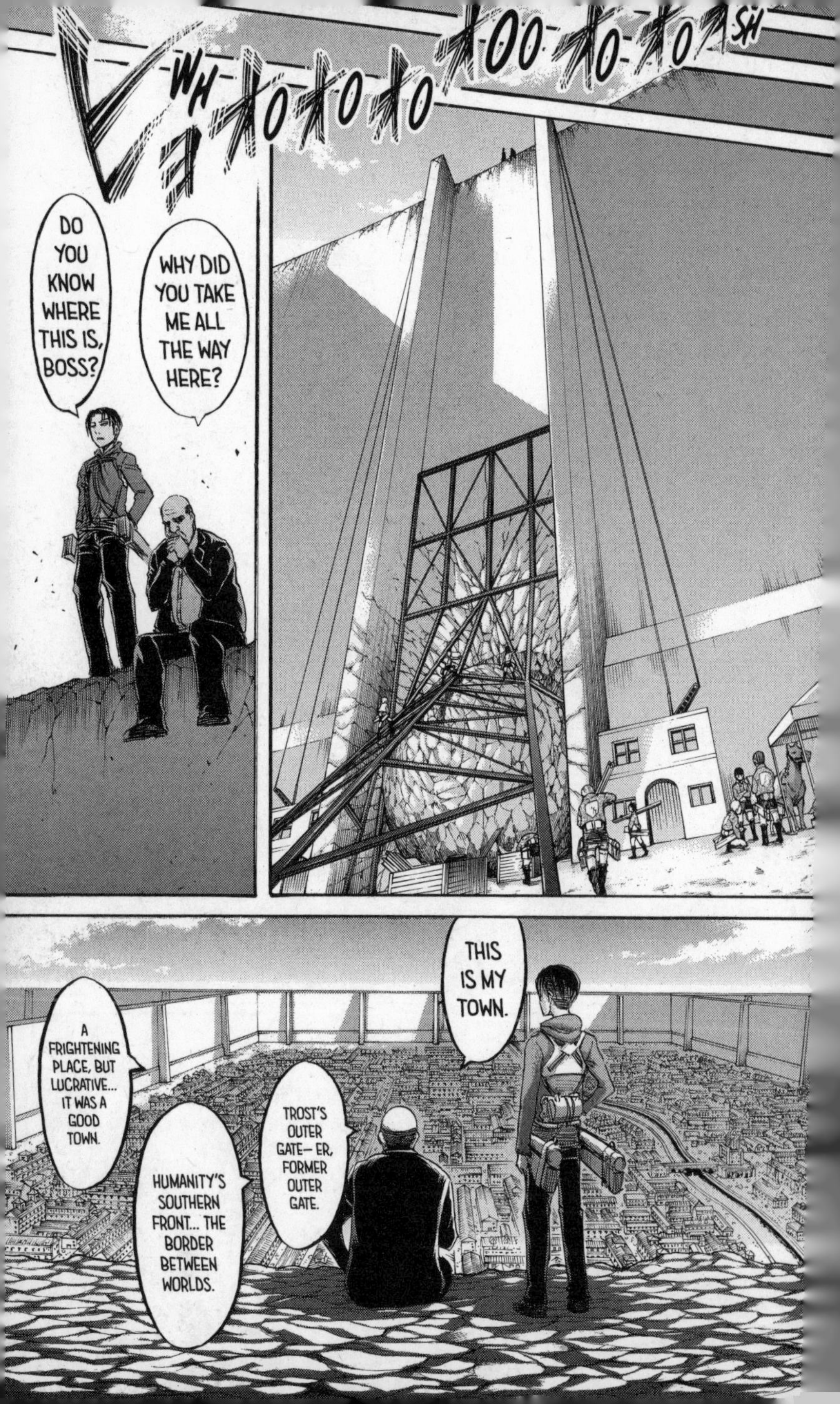

WHOOOOSH
WHY DID YOU TAKE ME ALL THE WAY HERE?
DO YOU KNOW WHERE THIS IS, BOSS?
THIS IS MY TOWN.
TROST'S OUTER GATE— ER, FORMER OUTER GATE.
HUMANITY'S SOUTHERN FRONT... THE BORDER BETWEEN WORLDS.
A FRIGHTENING PLACE, BUT LUCRATIVE... IT WAS A GOOD TOWN.

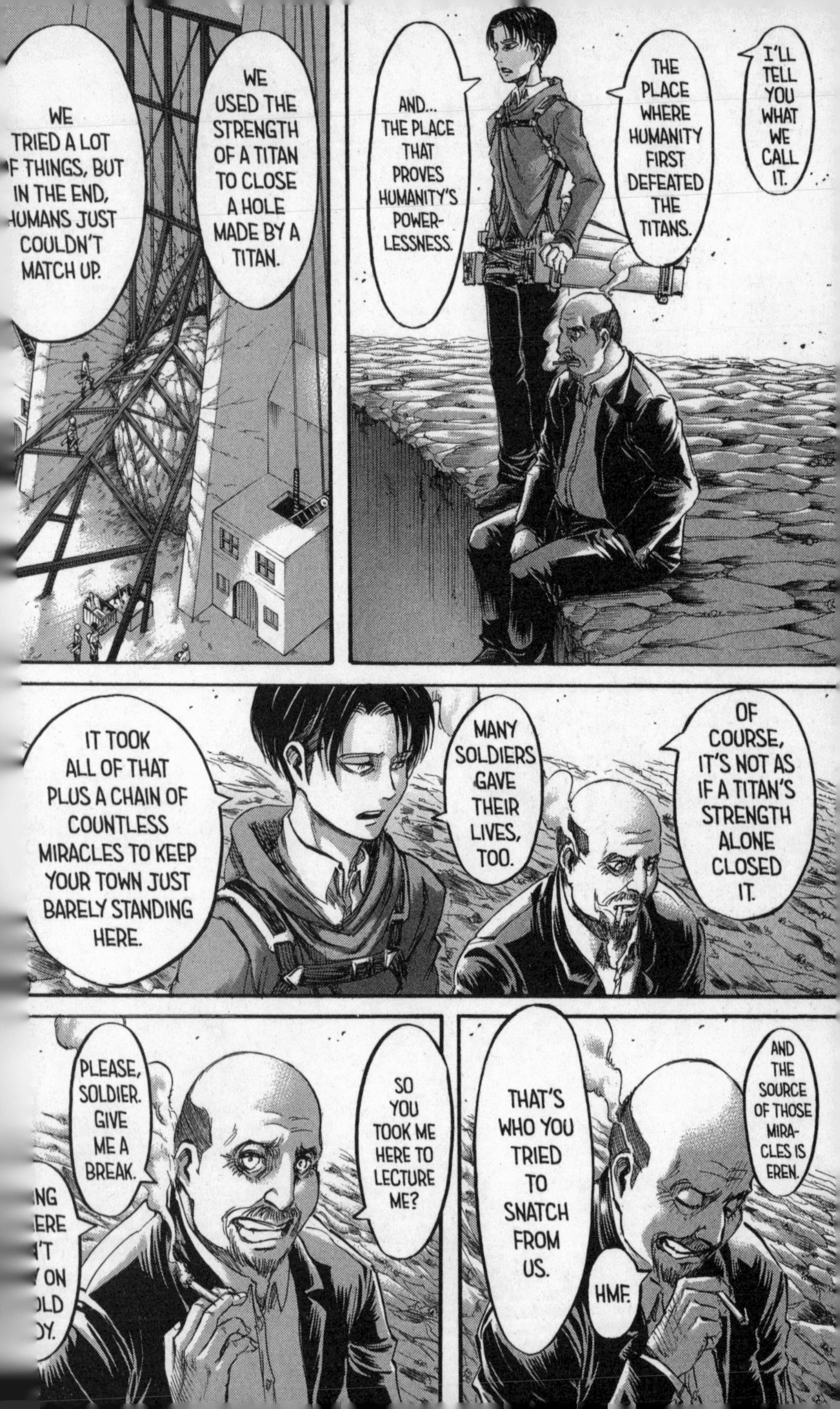

I'LL TELL YOU WHAT WE CALL IT.
THE PLACE WHERE HUMANITY FIRST DEFEATED THE TITANS.
AND... THE PLACE THAT PROVES HUMANITY'S POWERLESSNESS.
WE USED THE STRENGTH OF A TITAN TO CLOSE A HOLE MADE BY A TITAN.
WE TRIED A LOT F THINGS, BUT IN THE END, HUMANS JUST COULDN'T MATCH UP.
OF COURSE, IT'S NOT AS IF A TITAN'S STRENGTH ALONE CLOSED IT.
MANY SOLDIERS GAVE THEIR LIVES, TOO.
IT TOOK ALL OF THAT PLUS A CHAIN OF COUNTLESS MIRACLES TO KEEP YOUR TOWN JUST BARELY STANDING HERE.
AND THE SOURCE OF THOSE MIRACLES IS EREN.
THAT'S WHO YOU TRIED TO SNATCH FROM US.
HMF.
SO YOU TOOK ME HERE TO LECTURE ME?
PLEASE, SOLDIER. GIVE ME A BREAK.

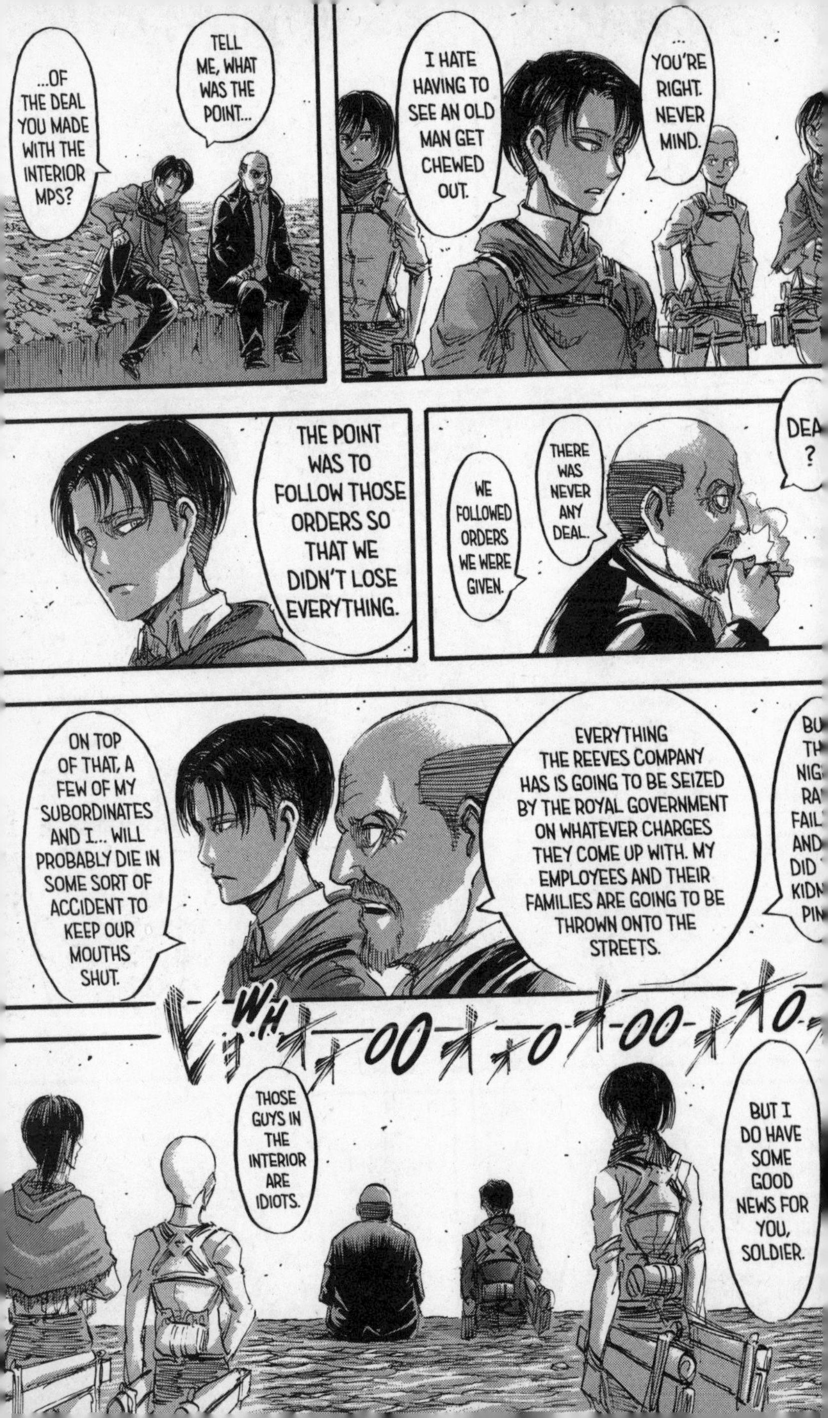
... YOU'RE RIGHT. NEVER MIND.
I HATE HAVING TO SEE AN OLD MAN GET CHEWED OUT.
TELL ME, WHAT WAS THE POINT...
...OF THE DEAL YOU MADE WITH THE INTERIOR MPS?
DEA ?
THERE WAS NEVER ANY DEAL.
WE FOLLOWED ORDERS WE WERE GIVEN.
THE POINT WAS TO FOLLOW THOSE ORDERS SO THAT WE DIDN'T LOSE EVERYTHING.
EVERYTHING THE REEVES COMPANY HAS IS GOING TO BE SEIZED BY THE ROYAL GOVERNMENT ON WHATEVER CHARGES THEY COME UP WITH. MY EMPLOYEES AND THEIR FAMILIES ARE GOING TO BE THROWN ONTO THE STREETS.
ON TOP OF THAT, A FEW OF MY SUBORDINATES AND I... WILL PROBABLY DIE IN SOME SORT OF ACCIDENT TO KEEP OUR MOUTHS SHUT.
WHOOOOOOOO
BUT I DO HAVE SOME GOOD NEWS FOR YOU, SOLDIER.
THOSE GUYS IN THE INTERIOR ARE IDIOTS.

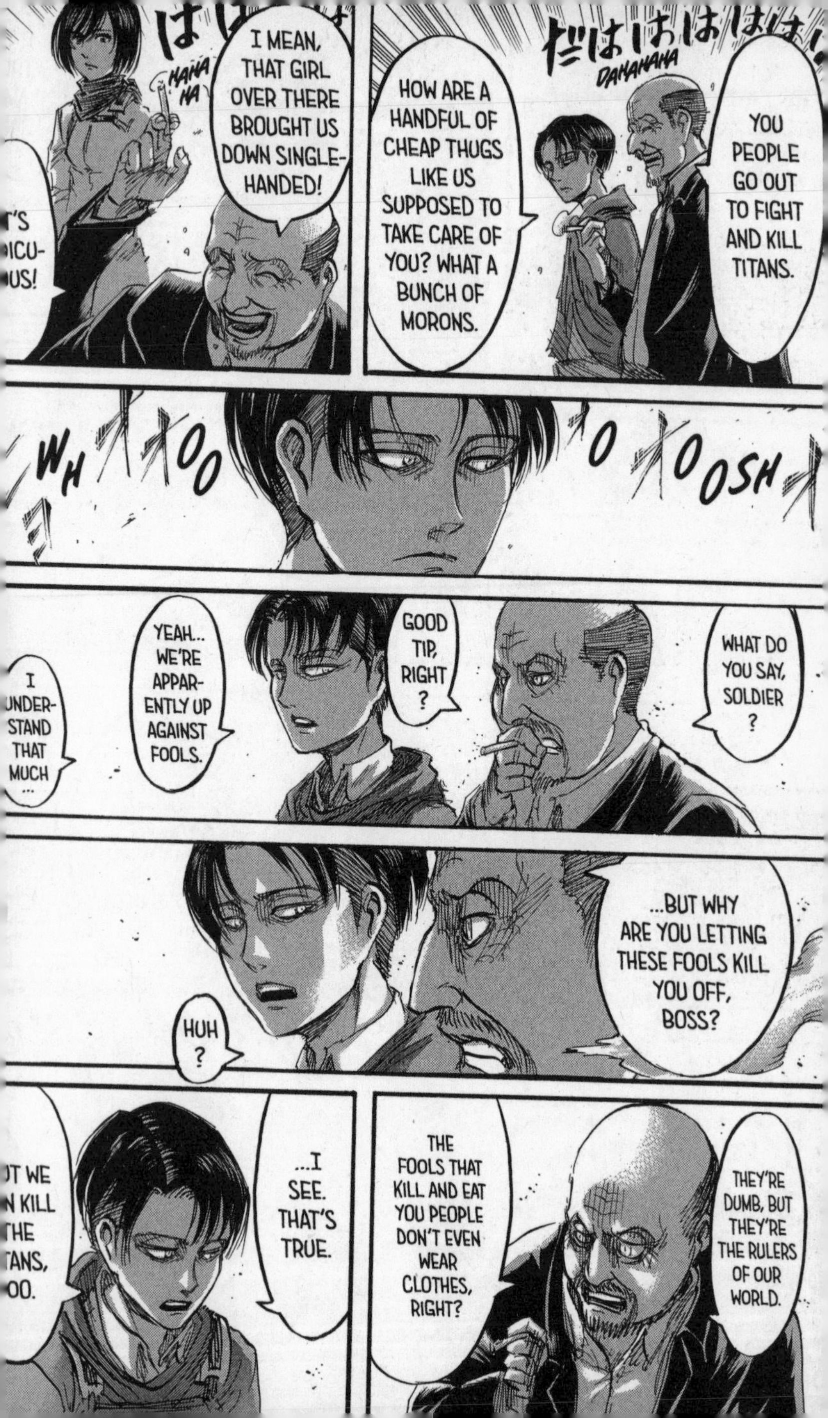
だはははははは
DAHAHAHA
YOU PEOPLE GO OUT TO FIGHT AND KILL TITANS.
HOW ARE A HANDFUL OF CHEAP THUGS LIKE US SUPPOSED TO TAKE CARE OF YOU? WHAT A BUNCH OF MORONS.
HAHA HA
I MEAN, THAT GIRL OVER THERE BROUGHT US DOWN SINGLE-HANDED!
T'S ICU- US!
WH OO O OOSH
WHAT DO YOU SAY, SOLDIER?
GOOD TIP, RIGHT?
YEAH... WE'RE APPARENTLY UP AGAINST FOOLS.
I UNDERSTAND THAT MUCH...
...BUT WHY ARE YOU LETTING THESE FOOLS KILL YOU OFF, BOSS?
HUH?
THEY'RE DUMB, BUT THEY'RE THE RULERS OF OUR WORLD.
THE FOOLS THAT KILL AND EAT YOU PEOPLE DON'T EVEN WEAR CLOTHES, RIGHT?
...I SEE. THAT'S TRUE.
T WE N KILL THE ANS, OO.

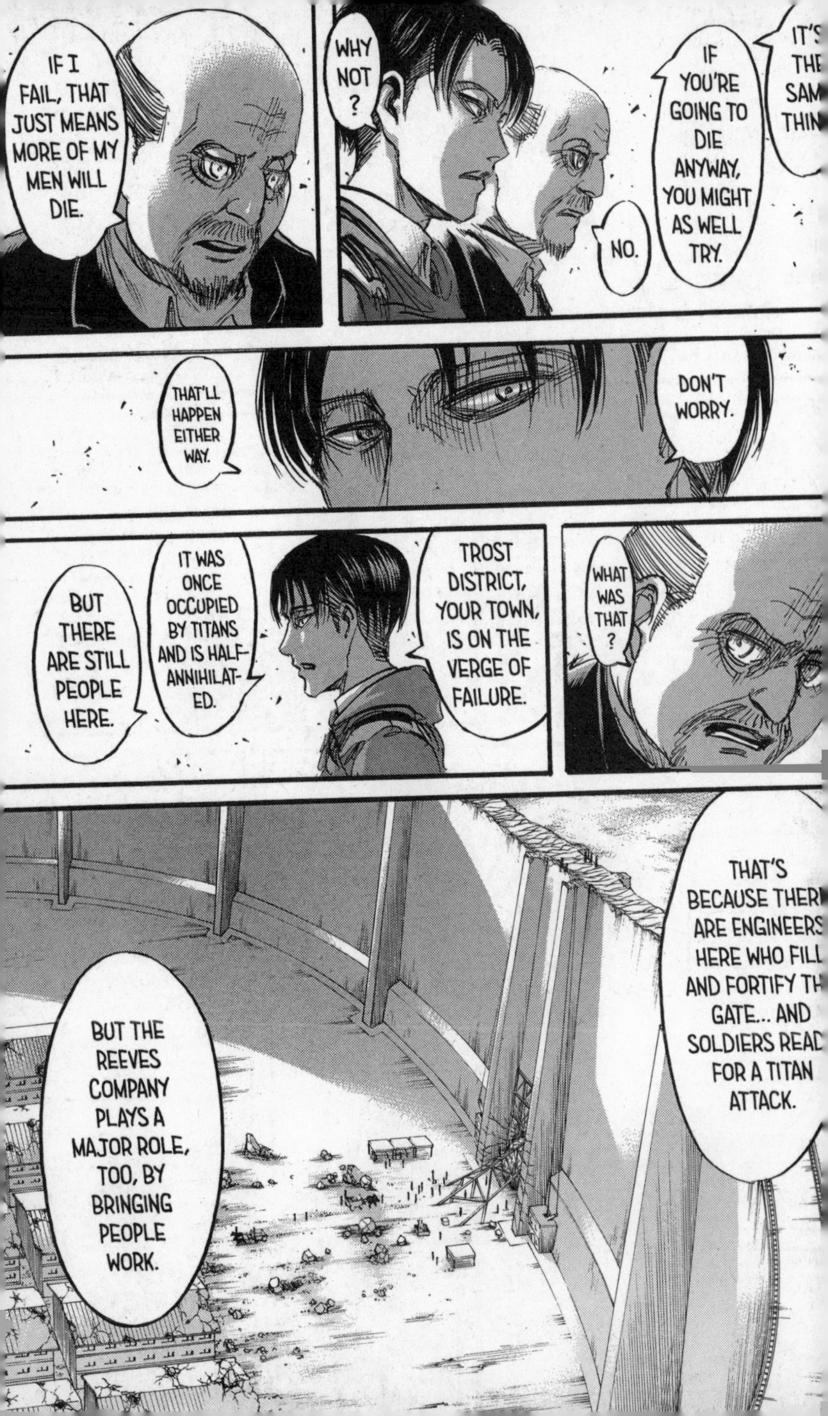

IT'S THE SAM THIN
IF YOU'RE GOING TO DIE ANYWAY, YOU MIGHT AS WELL TRY.
WHY NOT?
NO.
IF I FAIL, THAT JUST MEANS MORE OF MY MEN WILL DIE.
DON'T WORRY.
THAT'LL HAPPEN EITHER WAY.
WHAT WAS THAT?
TROST DISTRICT, YOUR TOWN, IS ON THE VERGE OF FAILURE.
IT WAS ONCE OCCUPIED BY TITANS AND IS HALF-ANNIHILATED.
BUT THERE ARE STILL PEOPLE HERE.
THAT'S BECAUSE THER ARE ENGINEERS HERE WHO FILL AND FORTIFY TH GATE... AND SOLDIERS READ FOR A TITAN ATTACK.
BUT THE REEVES COMPANY PLAYS A MAJOR ROLE, TOO, BY BRINGING PEOPLE WORK.

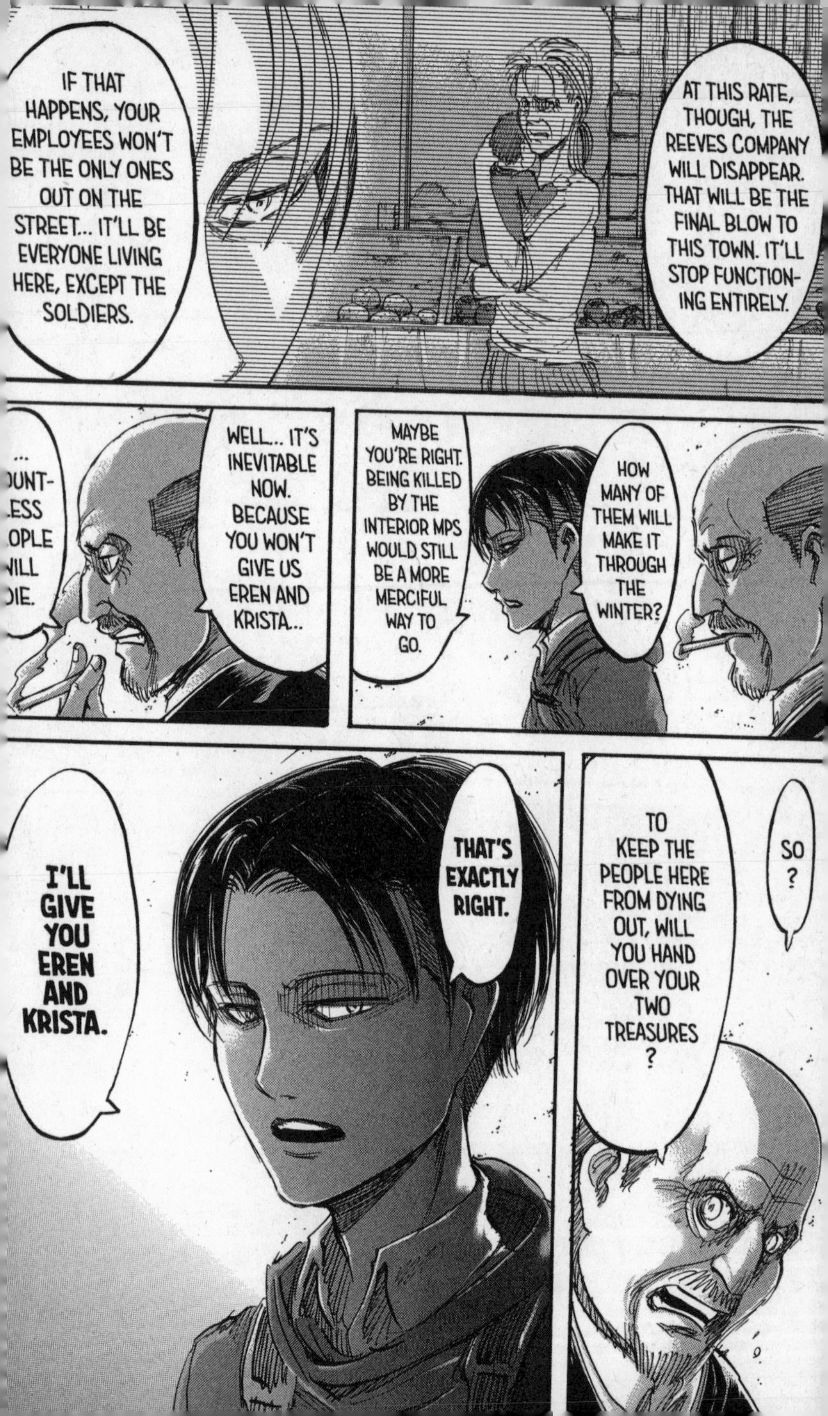
AT THIS RATE, THOUGH, THE REEVES COMPANY WILL DISAPPEAR. THAT WILL BE THE FINAL BLOW TO THIS TOWN. IT'LL STOP FUNCTIONING ENTIRELY.
IF THAT HAPPENS, YOUR EMPLOYEES WON'T BE THE ONLY ONES OUT ON THE STREET... IT'LL BE EVERYONE LIVING HERE, EXCEPT THE SOLDIERS.
HOW MANY OF THEM WILL MAKE IT THROUGH THE WINTER?
MAYBE YOU'RE RIGHT. BEING KILLED BY THE INTERIOR MPS WOULD STILL BE A MORE MERCIFUL WAY TO GO.
WELL... IT'S INEVITABLE NOW. BECAUSE YOU WON'T GIVE US EREN AND KRISTA...
... OUNT- ESS OPLE ILL IE.
SO?
TO KEEP THE PEOPLE HERE FROM DYING OUT, WILL YOU HAND OVER YOUR TWO TREASURES?
THAT'S EXACTLY RIGHT.
I'LL GIVE YOU EREN AND KRISTA.

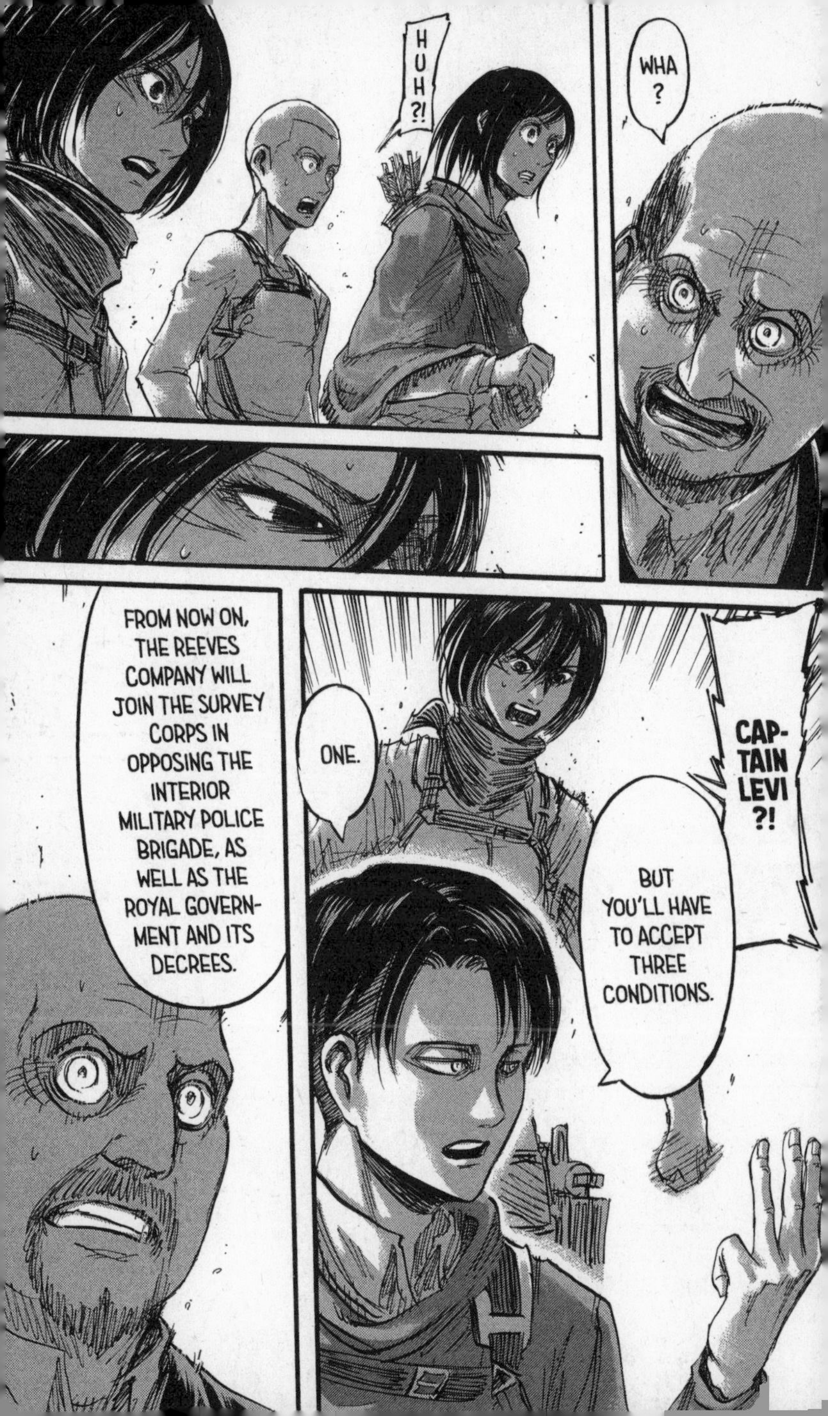
WHA ?
HUH ?!
CAP-TAIN LEVI ?!
BUT YOU'LL HAVE TO ACCEPT THREE CONDITIONS.
ONE.
FROM NOW ON, THE REEVES COMPANY WILL JOIN THE SURVEY CORPS IN OPPOSING THE INTERIOR MILITARY POLICE BRIGADE, AS WELL AS THE ROYAL GOVERN-MENT AND ITS DECREES.

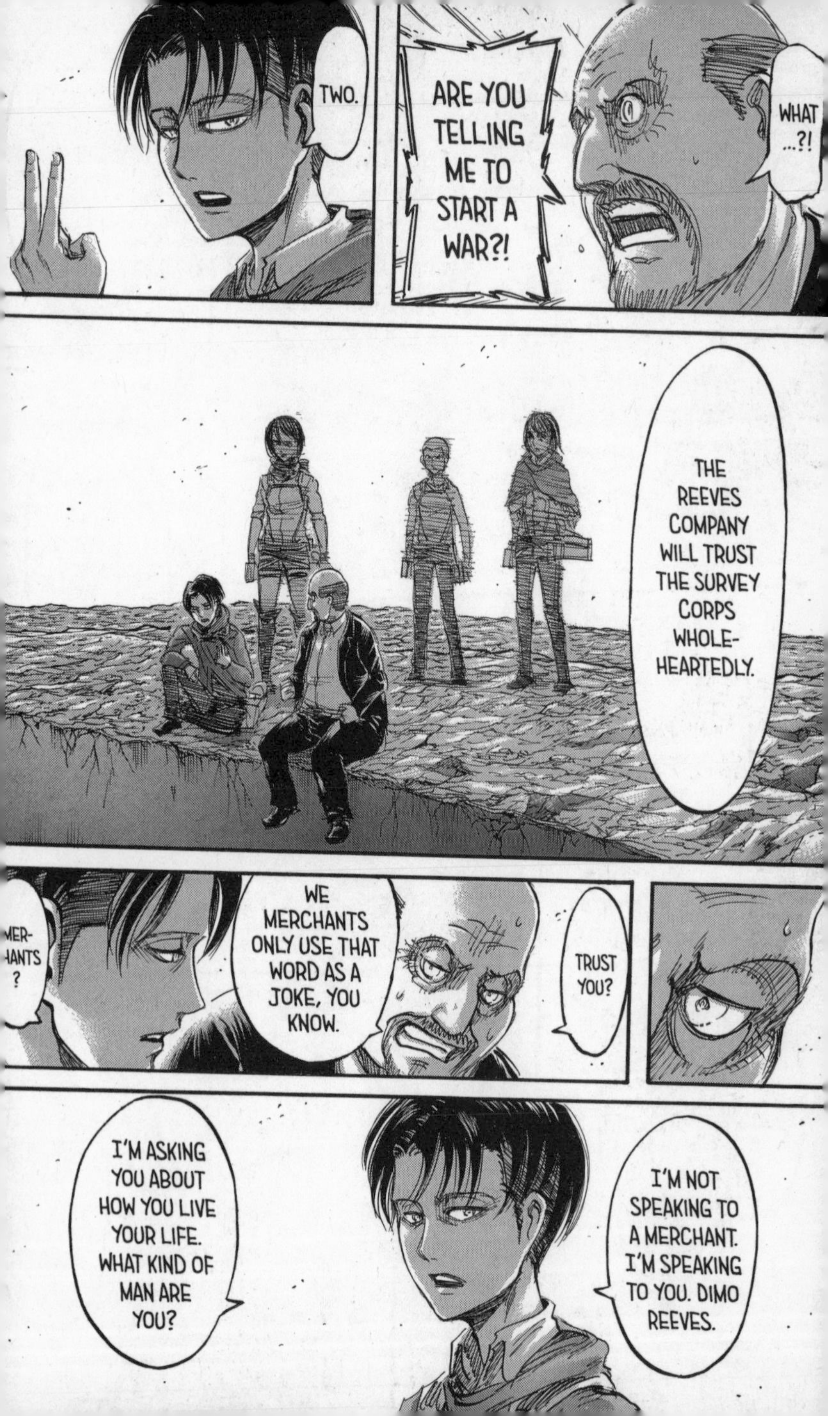
WHAT ...?!
ARE YOU TELLING ME TO START A WAR?!
TWO.
THE REEVES COMPANY WILL TRUST THE SURVEY CORPS WHOLEHEARTEDLY.
TRUST YOU?
WE MERCHANTS ONLY USE THAT WORD AS A JOKE, YOU KNOW.
MER-HANTS?
I'M NOT SPEAKING TO A MERCHANT. I'M SPEAKING TO YOU. DIMO REEVES.
I'M ASKING YOU ABOUT HOW YOU LIVE YOUR LIFE. WHAT KIND OF MAN ARE YOU?

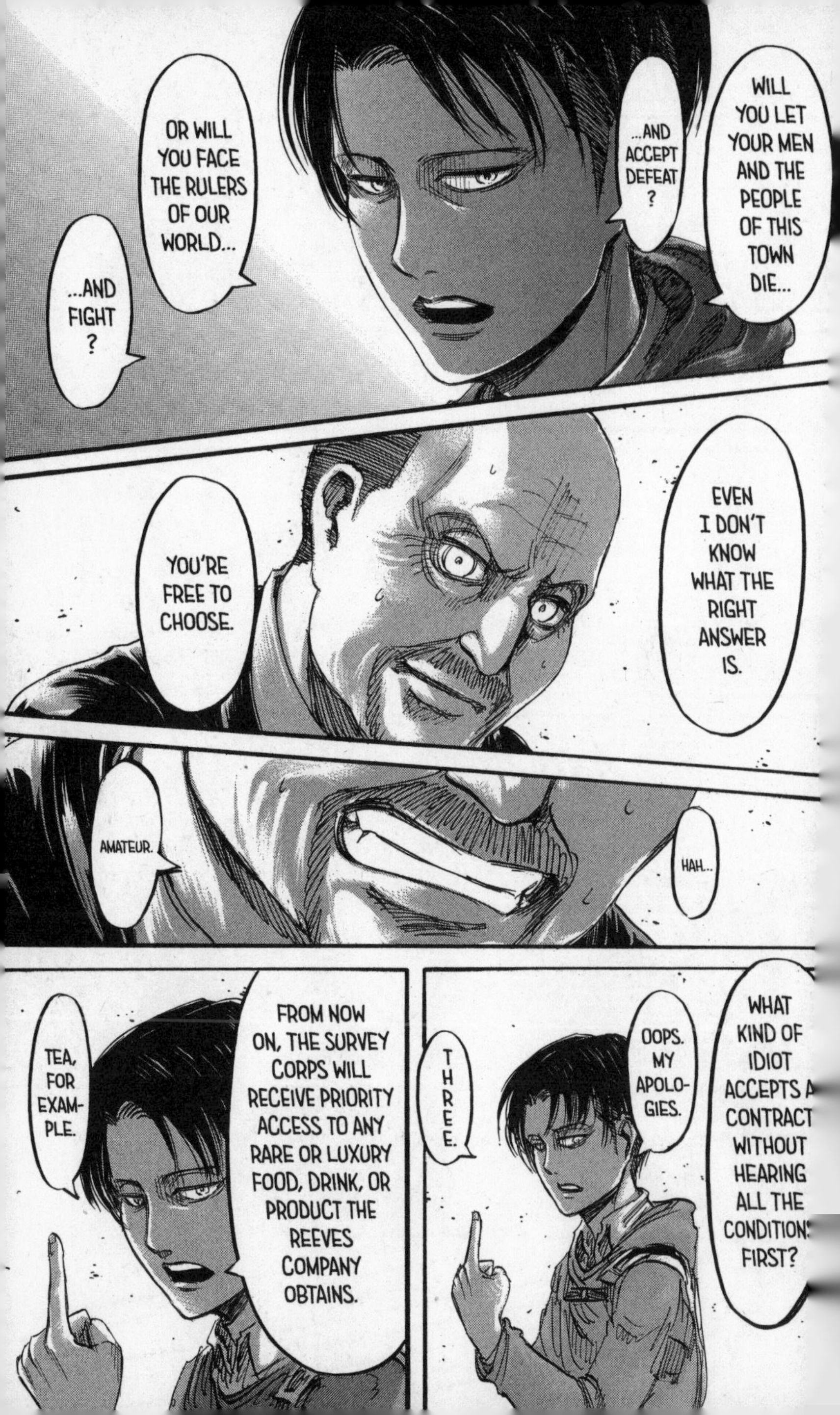
WILL YOU LET YOUR MEN AND THE PEOPLE OF THIS TOWN DIE...
...AND ACCEPT DEFEAT ?
OR WILL YOU FACE THE RULERS OF OUR WORLD...
...AND FIGHT ?
EVEN I DON'T KNOW WHAT THE RIGHT ANSWER IS.
YOU'RE FREE TO CHOOSE.
HAH...
AMATEUR.
WHAT KIND OF IDIOT ACCEPTS A CONTRACT WITHOUT HEARING ALL THE CONDITIONS FIRST?
OOPS. MY APOLO-GIES.
THREE.
FROM NOW ON, THE SURVEY CORPS WILL RECEIVE PRIORITY ACCESS TO ANY RARE OR LUXURY FOOD, DRINK, OR PRODUCT THE REEVES COMPANY OBTAINS.
TEA, FOR EXAM-PLE.

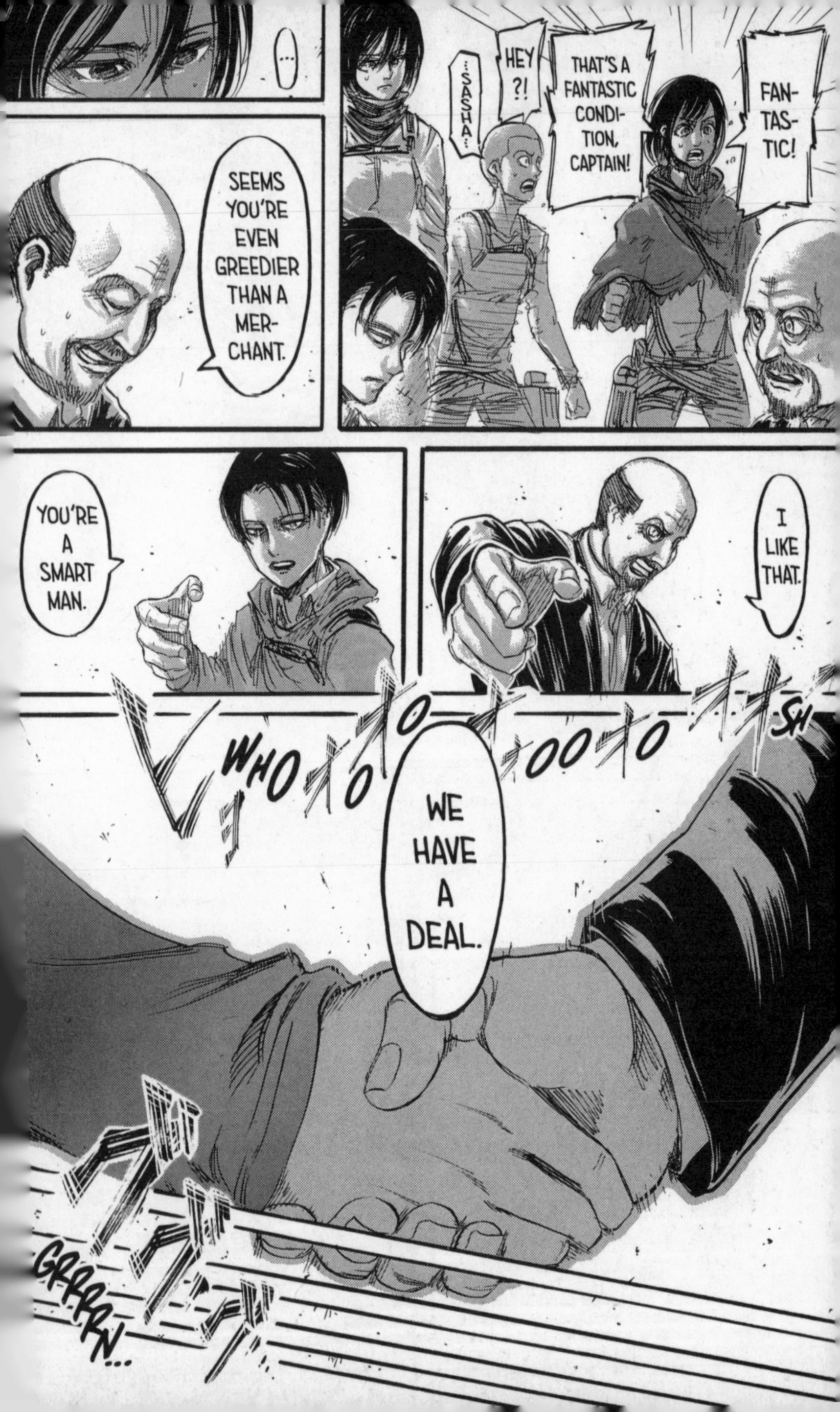
FAN-TAS-TIC!
THAT'S A FANTASTIC CONDI-TION, CAPTAIN!
HEY ?!
...SASHA...
...
SEEMS YOU'RE EVEN GREEDIER THAN A MER-CHANT.
I LIKE THAT.
YOU'RE A SMART MAN.
WHOOOOOOSH
WE HAVE A DEAL.
GRRRRN...

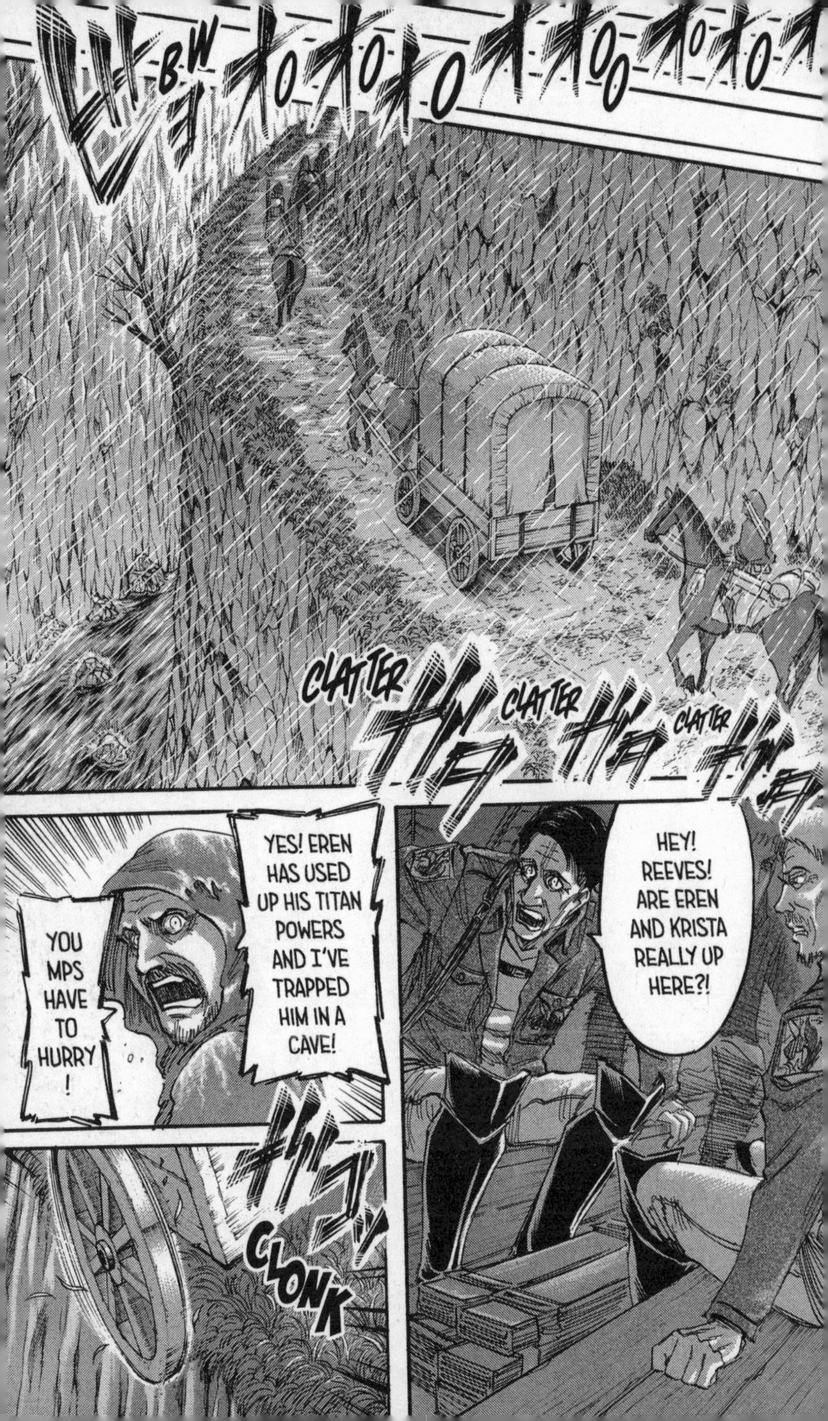
BW
CLATTER
CLATTER
CLATTER
HEY! REEVES! ARE EREN AND KRISTA REALLY UP HERE?!
YES! EREN HAS USED UP HIS TITAN POWERS AND I'VE TRAPPED HIM IN A CAVE!
YOU MPS HAVE TO HURRY!
CLONK

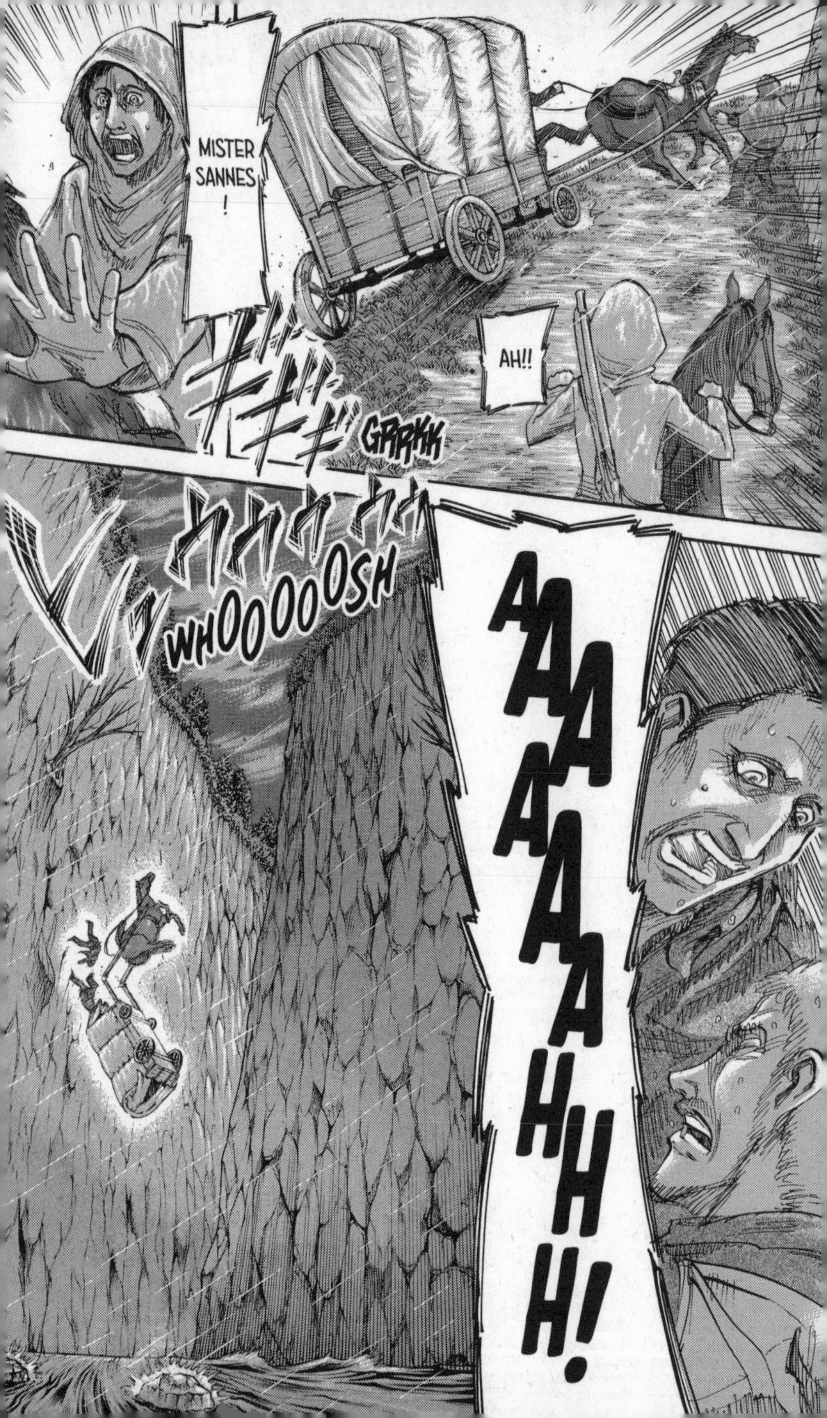
MISTER SANNES!
AH!!
GRRKK
AAAAAAHHH!
WHOOOOOSH

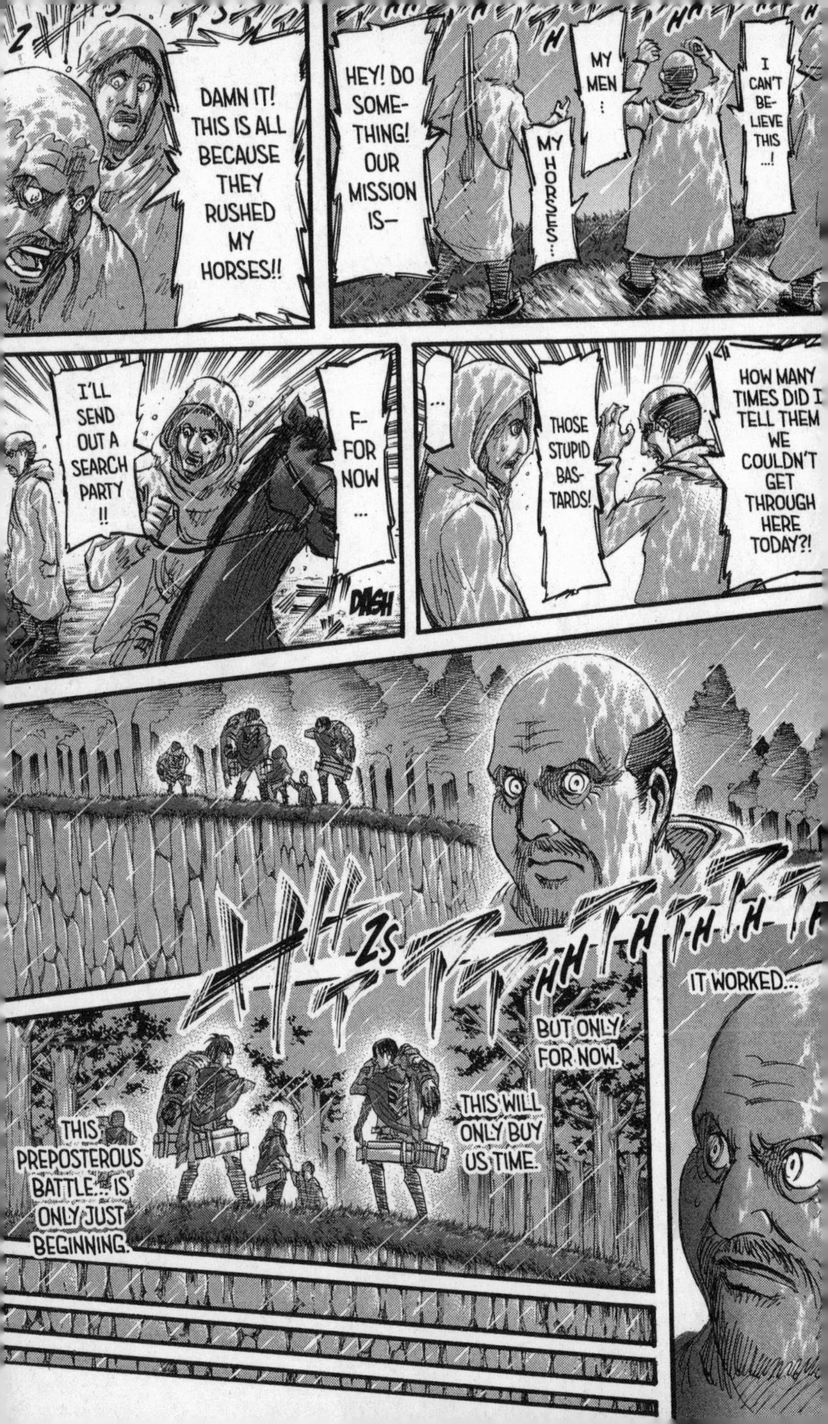
I CAN'T BE-LIEVE THIS ...!
MY MEN ...
MY HORSES...
HEY! DO SOME-THING! OUR MISSION IS—
DAMN IT! THIS IS ALL BECAUSE THEY RUSHED MY HORSES!!
HOW MANY TIMES DID I TELL THEM WE COULDN'T GET THROUGH HERE TODAY?!
THOSE STUPID BAS-TARDS!
...
F-FOR NOW ...
I'LL SEND OUT A SEARCH PARTY !!
DASH
IT WORKED...
BUT ONLY FOR NOW.
THIS WILL ONLY BUY US TIME.
THIS PREPOSTEROUS BATTLE... IS ONLY JUST BEGINNING.

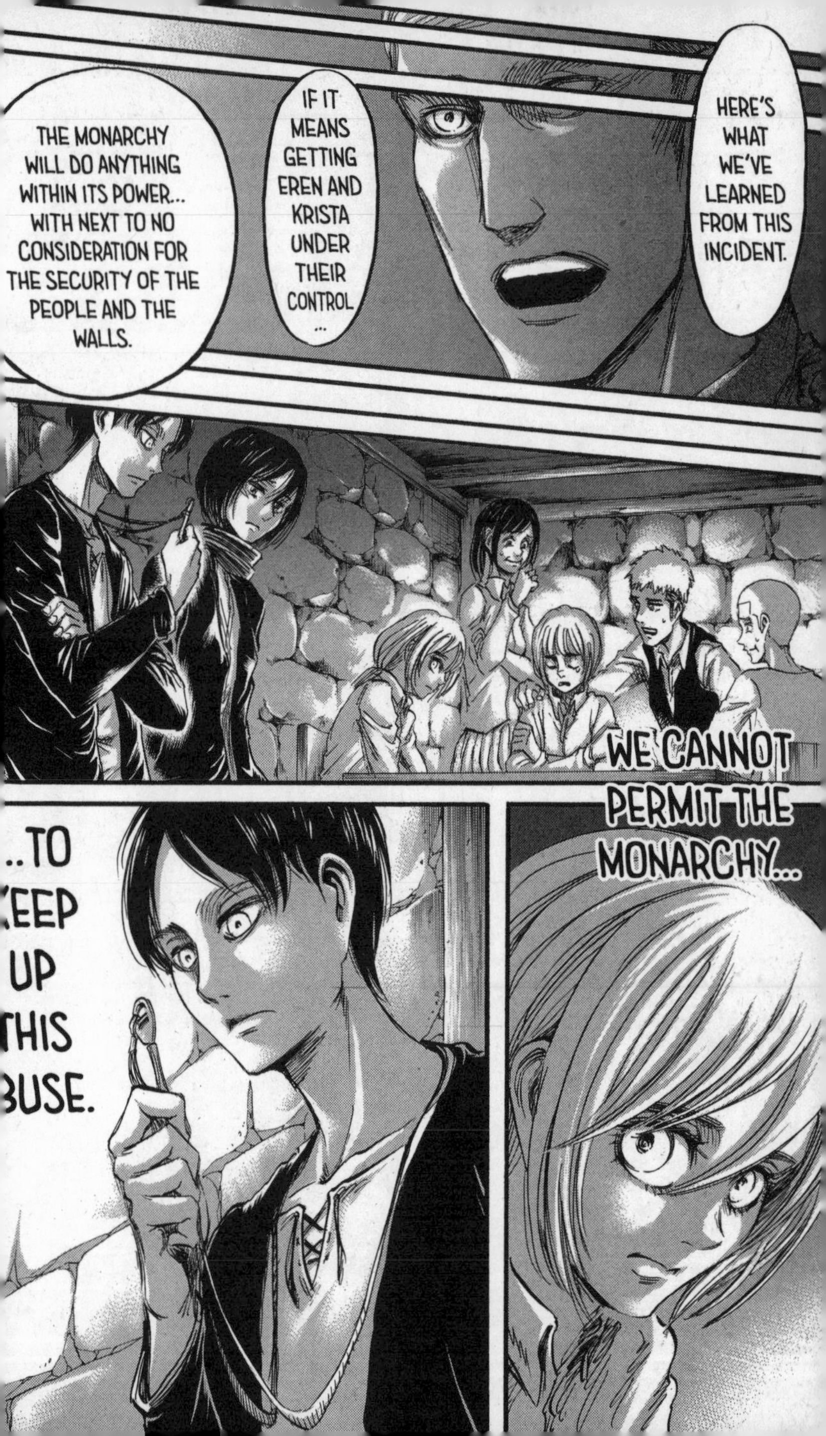
HERE'S WHAT WE'VE LEARNED FROM THIS INCIDENT.
IF IT MEANS GETTING EREN AND KRISTA UNDER THEIR CONTROL ...
THE MONARCHY WILL DO ANYTHING WITHIN ITS POWER... WITH NEXT TO NO CONSIDERATION FOR THE SECURITY OF THE PEOPLE AND THE WALLS.
WE CANNOT PERMIT THE MONARCHY...
..TO EEP UP THIS BUSE.

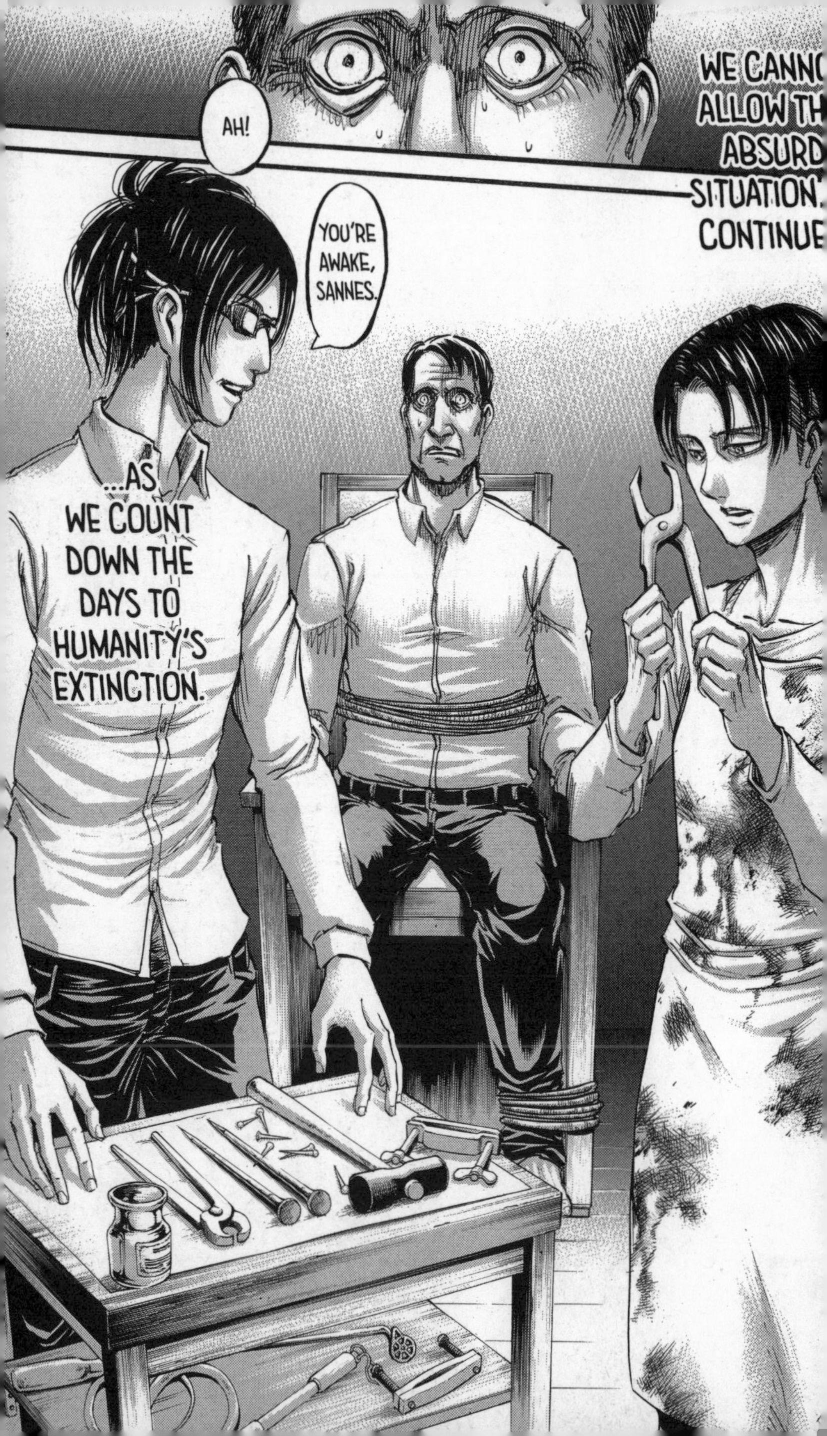
WE CANNO ALLOW TH ABSURD SITUATION CONTINUE
AH!
YOU'RE AWAKE, SANNES.
...AS WE COUNT DOWN THE DAYS TO HUMANITY'S EXTINCTION.

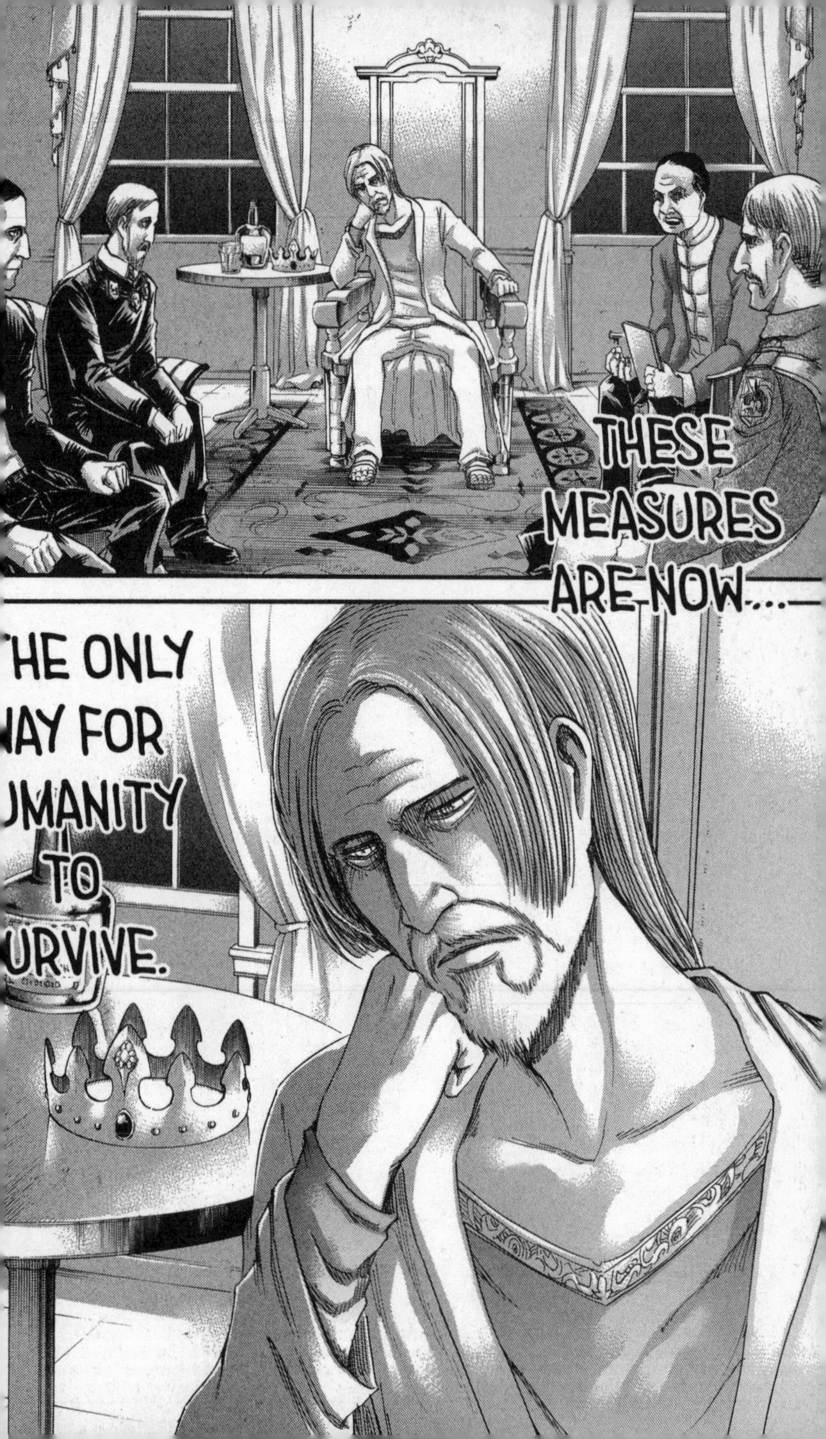
THESE MEASURES ARE NOW...
HE ONLY AY FOR UMANITY TO URVIVE.

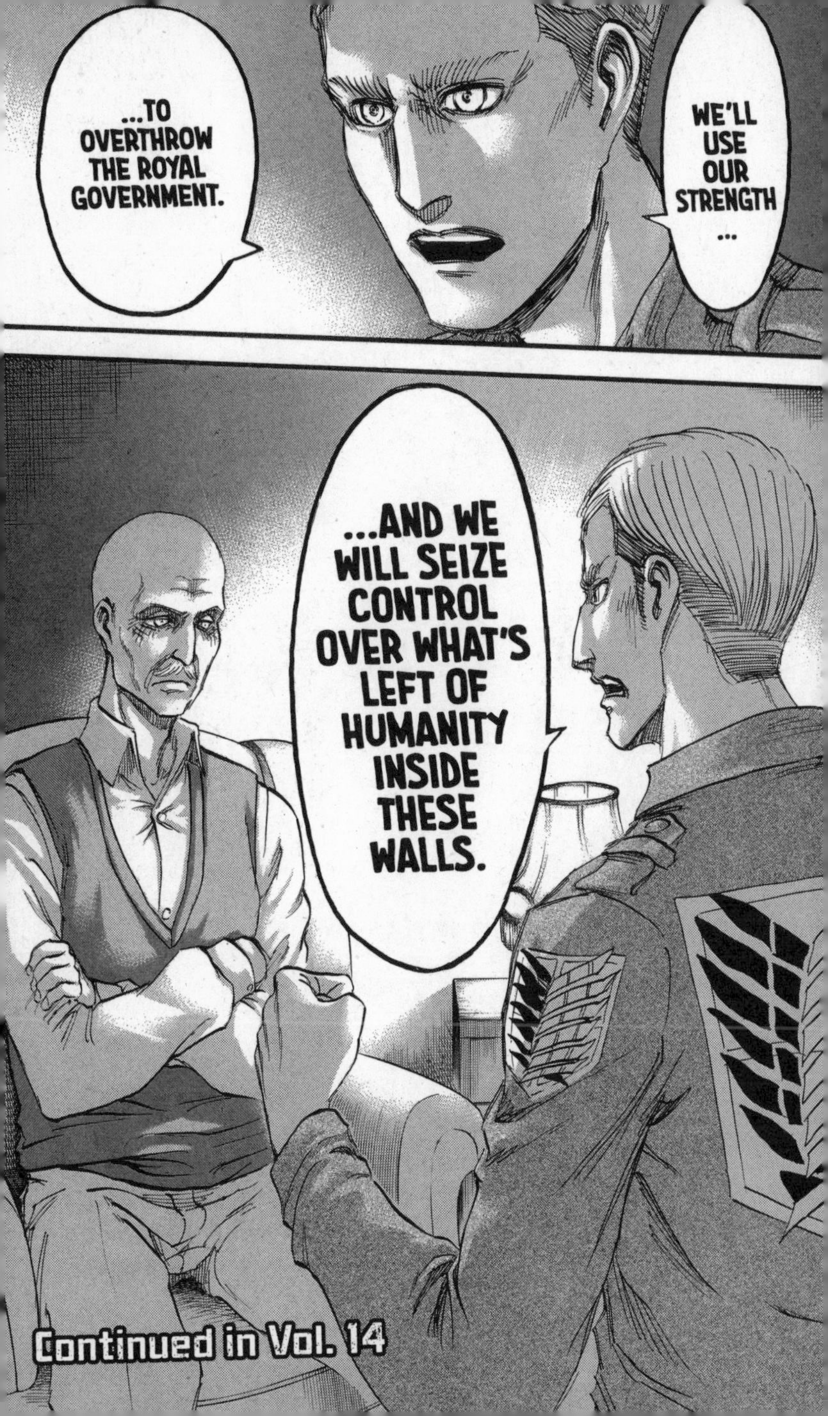
WE'LL USE OUR STRENGTH ...
...TO OVERTHROW THE ROYAL GOVERNMENT.
...AND WE WILL SEIZE CONTROL OVER WHAT'S LEFT OF HUMANITY INSIDE THESE WALLS.
Continued in Vol. 14

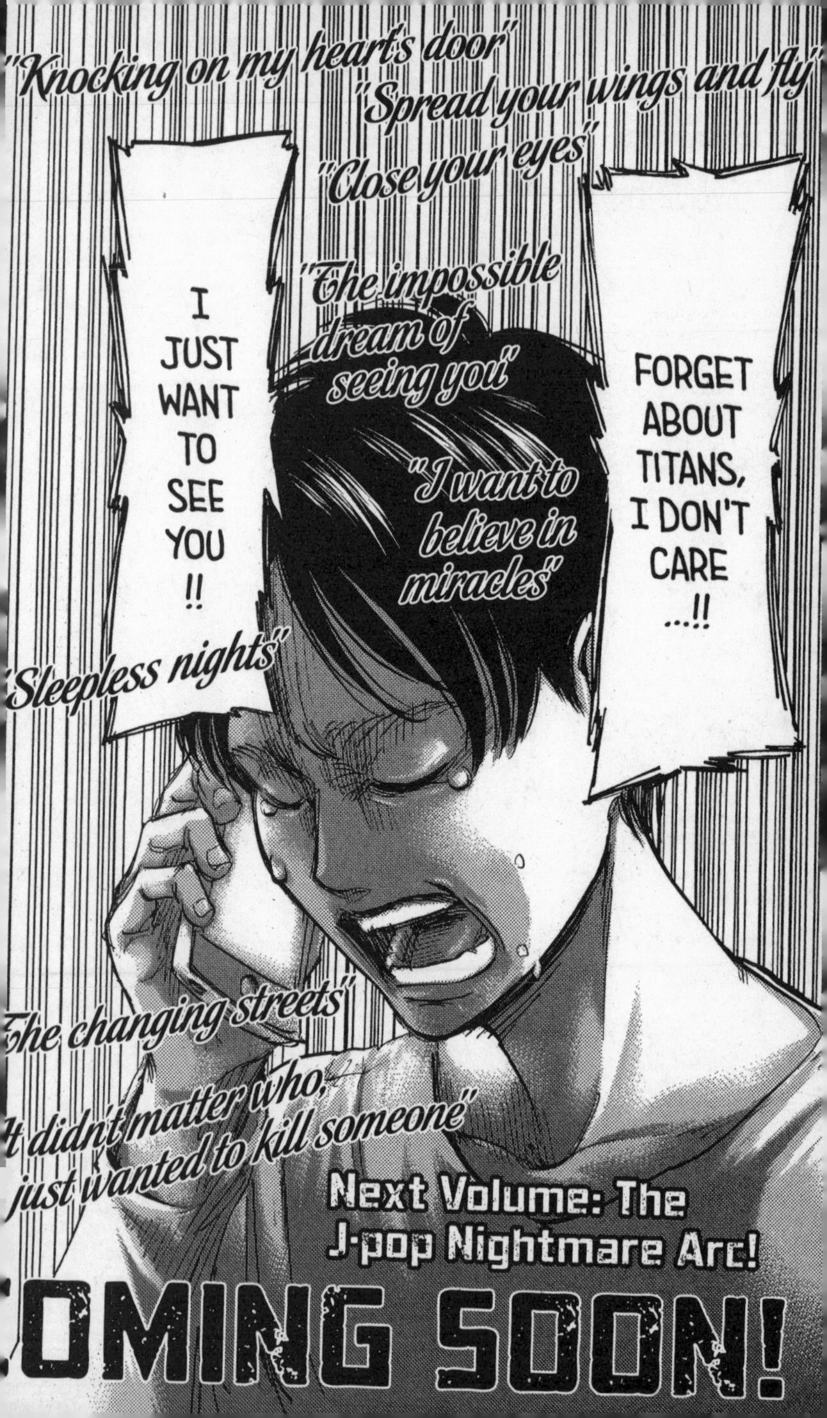
"Knocking on my heart's door"
"Spread your wings and fly"
"Close your eyes"
FORGET ABOUT TITANS, I DON'T CARE ...!!
"The impossible dream of seeing you"
I JUST WANT TO SEE YOU !!
"I want to believe in miracles"
"Sleepless nights"
"The changing streets"
t didn't matter who, just wanted to kill someone"
Next Volume: The J-pop Nightmare Arc!
OMING SOON!

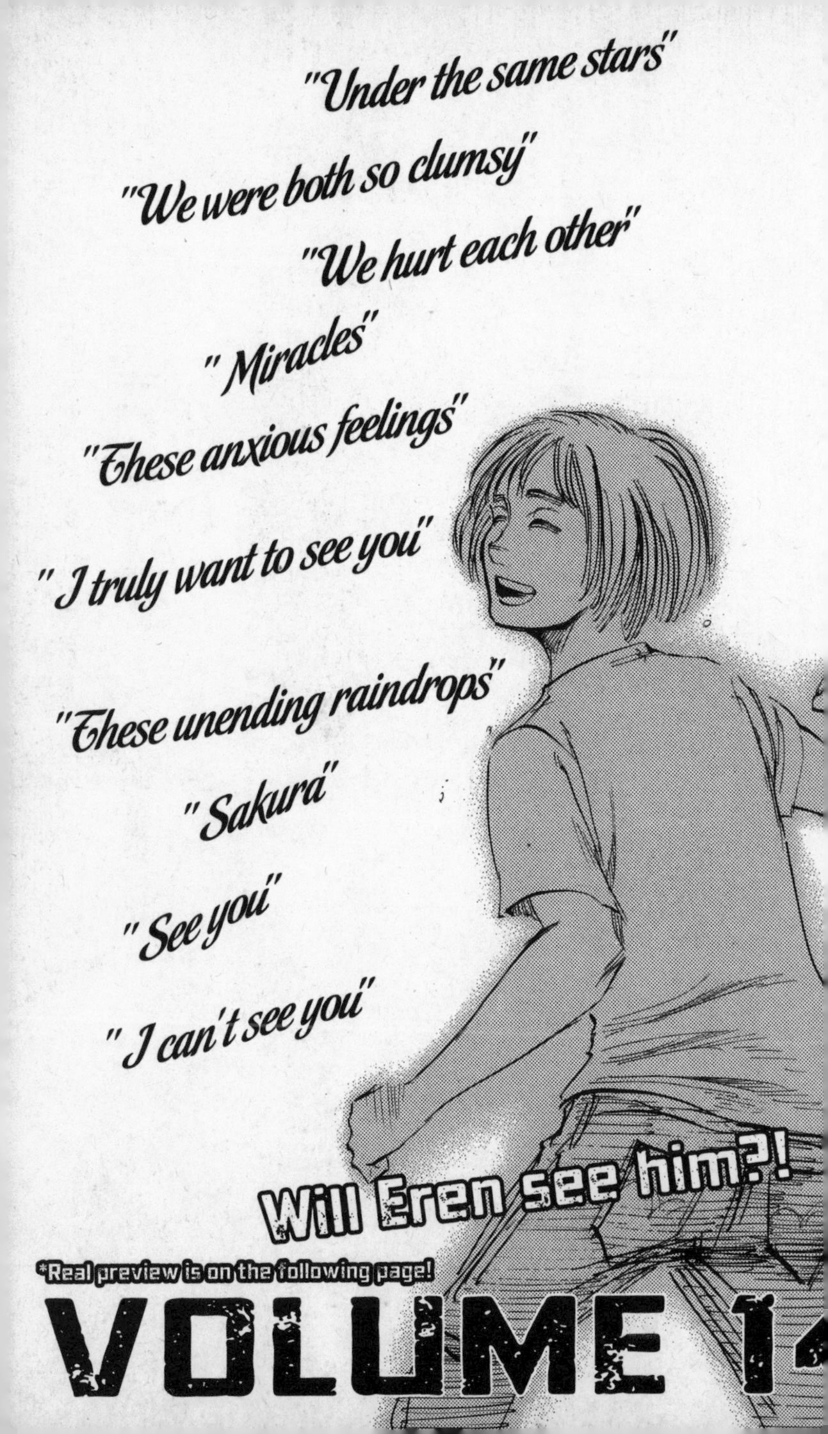
"Under the same stars"
"We were both so clumsy"
"We hurt each other"
"Miracles"
"These anxious feelings"
"I truly want to see you"
"These unending raindrops"
"Sakura"
"See you"
"I can't see you"
Will Eren see him?!
*Real preview is on the following page!
VOLUME 14

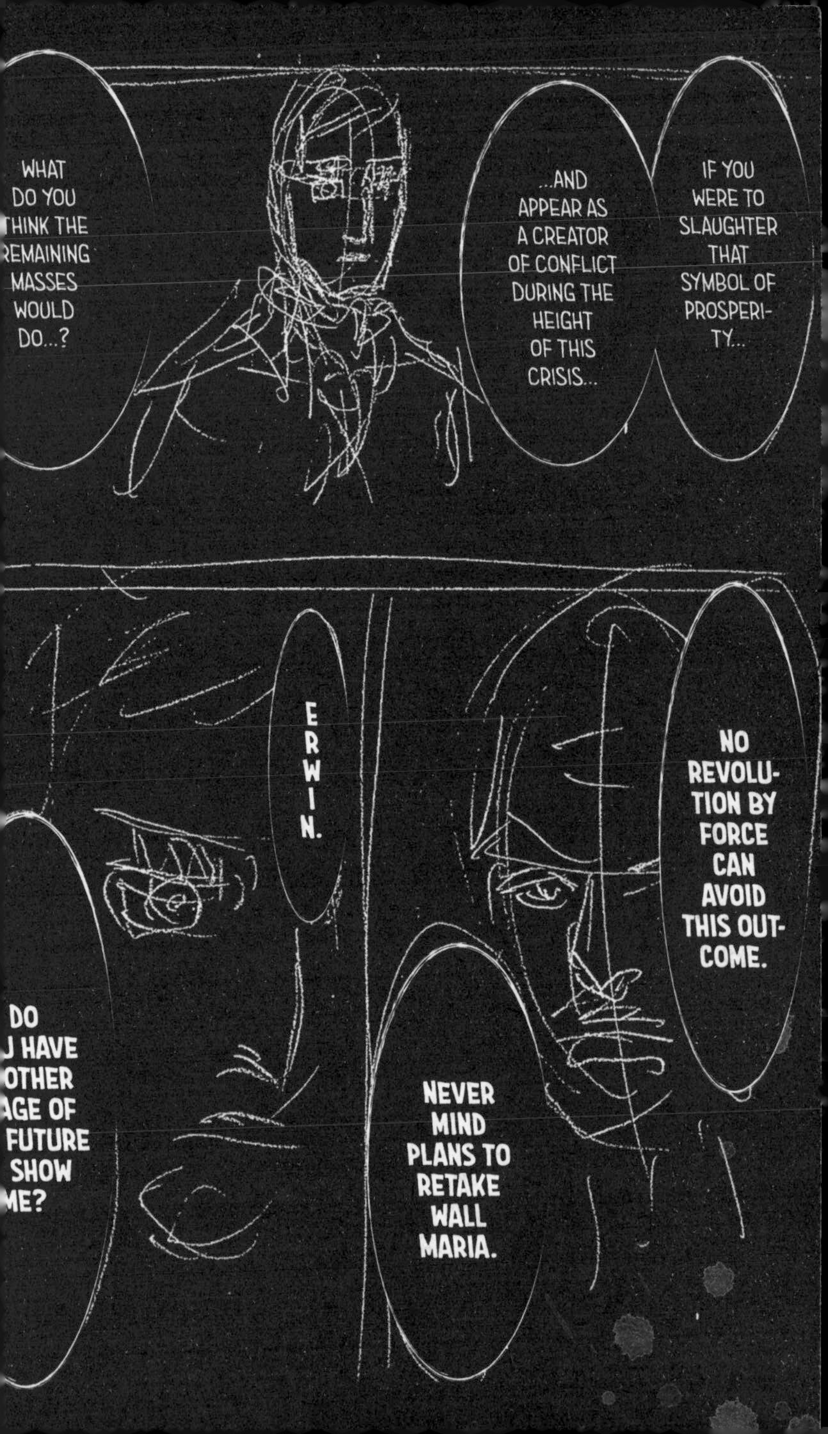
IF YOU WERE TO SLAUGHTER THAT SYMBOL OF PROSPERITY...
...AND APPEAR AS A CREATOR OF CONFLICT DURING THE HEIGHT OF THIS CRISIS...
WHAT DO YOU THINK THE REMAINING MASSES WOULD DO...?
NO REVOLUTION BY FORCE CAN AVOID THIS OUTCOME.
NEVER MIND PLANS TO RETAKE WALL MARIA.
ERWIN.
DO J HAVE OTHER AGE OF FUTURE SHOW ME?

VOLUME 14 COMING SOON!

A wall must be overcome before the monarchy can be overthrown. Its height, nearly insurmountable...

Attack on Titan volume 13 is a work of fiction. Names, characters, places, and incidents are the products of the author's imagination or are used fictitiously. Any resemblance to actual events, locales, or persons, living or dead, is entirely coincidental.

A Kodansha Comics Trade Paperback Original

Published in the United States by Kodansha Comics, an imprint of Kodansha USA Publishing, LLC, New York.

Publication rights for this English edition arranged through Kodansha Ltd, Tokyo.

First published in Japan in 2014 by Kodansha Ltd., Tokyo as *Shingeki no Kyojin*, volume 13.

ISBN 978-1-61262-679-6

Original cover design by Takashi Shimoyama (Red Rooster)

Printed in the United States of America.

www.kodanshacomics.com

9 8 7 6 5 4 3 2 1
Translation: Ko Ransom
Lettering: Steve Wands
Editing: Ben Applegate
Kodansha Comics edition cover design by Phil Balsman